THE BOOK OF AMERICAN DIARIES

D0104563

THE
BOOK
OF
AMERICAN
DIARIES

Edited by

RANDALL M. MILLER
and
LINDA PATTERSON MILLER

AVON BOOKS ◆ NEW YORK

Permissions and credits are listed on pages 502-522, which constitute a continuation of the copyright page.

THE BOOK OF AMERICAN DIARIES is an original publication of Avon Books. This work has never before appeared in book form.

AVON BOOKS
A division of
The Hearst Corporation
1350 Avenue of the Americas
New York, New York 10019

Copyright © 1995 by Avon Books
Published by arrangement with the editors
Library of Congress Catalog Card Number: 94-17807
ISBN: 0-380-76583-7

All rights reserved, which includes the right to reproduce this book or portions thereof in any form whatsoever except as provided by the U.S. Copyright Law. For information address Avon Books.

Library of Congress Cataloging in Publication Data:
The Book of American diaries / edited by Randall M. Miller and Linda Patterson Miller.
    p.   cm.
1. American diaries. 2. United States—Social life and customs—Sources. I. Miller, Randall M.   II. Miller, Linda Patterson, 1946–   .
CT211.B66   1995   94-17807
973'.099—dc20   CIP

First Avon Books Trade Printing: January 1995

AVON TRADEMARK REG. U.S. PAT. OFF. AND IN OTHER COUNTRIES, MARCA REGISTRADA, HECHO EN U.S.A.

Printed in the U.S.A.

OPM   10 9 8 7 6 5 4 3 2 1

For Nathaniel

⌒ACKNOWLEDGMENTS⌒

This book of many voices took many hands to create. Our editors at Avon Books—April Mason, who suggested the book several years ago, David Highfill who nudged the book along for two years, and Lisa Considine who saw the book to its completion—won our confidence and earned our thanks many times for their uncommon patience and encouragement and, most of all, for their vision and courage in allowing us so much freedom to define the book as we thought best.

For reading the introduction and commenting on the conception of the book, we thank Paula Benkart, Stephen Whitfield, and Michael Zuckerman. So, too, appreciative nods go to those students and colleagues at Saint Joseph's University, especially David Burton and Owen Gilman, who bounced around ideas about diaries and autobiographies in discussions on American images, myths, and realities. We owe Donald Vining, a close student of American diaries, a debt both for graciously granting permission to use material from his collections and for identifying other sources. Finally, we thank David Allmendinger, Janet Golden, Kenneth Kusmer, Nelson Lankford, Emma Jones Lapsansky, John M. Mulder, George Pozzetta, Marion Roydhouse, and Morris Vogel for suggesting materials and sharing ideas on American character.

During the several years we "lived" with our subjects, reading their diaries and poking into their biographies, we received the assistance of many archivists, librarians, and other professionals who supported our work by their own expertise and interest. The staffs at the following archives and libraries provided research assistance, ready access to sources, and, when necessary, permission to publish from their collections: the American Antiquarian Society, Worcester; Balch Institute for Ethnic Studies, Philadelphia; Canaday Library of Bryn Mawr College; Bertrand Library of Bucknell University; Bancroft Library of the University of California at Berkeley; Camden County (New Jersey) Historical Society; Chicago Historical Society; Civil War Library and Museum, Philadelphia; Connecticut Historical Society; Western History Department of the Denver Public Library; Perkins Library of Duke University; Hagley Museum and Library, Wilmington; Houghton Library of Harvard University; Magill Library of Haverford College; Moorland-Spingarn Research Center of Howard University; Huntington Library, San Marino; University Libraries of the University of Iowa; Library Company of Philadelphia; Library of Congress; Maine State Library; Massachusetts Historical Society; Minnesota Historical Society Research Center, St. Paul; New York Public Library; Southern Historical Collection of the University of North Carolina at Chapel Hill; Theodore Hesburgh Library of the University of Notre Dame; Oregon Historical Society; Enoch Pratt Free Library, Baltimore; Presbyterian Historical Society, Philadelphia; Historical Society of Pennsylvania; Van Pelt Library of the University of Pennsylvania; Free Library of Philadelphia; Speer Library of Princeton Theological Seminary; Seeley G. Mudd Manuscript Library of Princeton University; Drexel Library of Saint Joseph's University; University Archives of Santa Clara University; South Caroliniana Library of the University of South Carolina, Columbia; Paley Library of Temple University; Howard-Tilton Memorial Library of Tulane University; Virginia Historical Society; Alderman Library of the University of Virginia; and the Penrose Memorial Library of Whitman College. To all, we again extend our thanks.

Support for research and publication of this book was provided by Saint Joseph's University and the Pennsylvania State University.

ᵍCONTENTSᵍ

CONTENTS

ℰINTRODUCTIONℰ

Americans were diarists before they were Americans. The first American diaries were kept by English Puritans embarked on an "errand into the wilderness." Amid tempests, shipboard diseases, and murmurings against their captains while crossing the Atlantic, the Puritans comforted themselves in their journals with the assurance, as Richard Mather wrote in April 1635, that the fears and travails of the New World would be lessened by the "clearness of my calling from God this way." Over the next 350 some years thousands of other Americans took up the journal habit. Not all shared Mather's conviction about God's special purpose for them, but many still recorded their hopes and fears and also the rhythms of their daily lives with the conviction that America held a unique place in Providence's design. From such daily musings, we have selected for our composite "American diary" passages written by roughly two hundred different diarists spanning three centuries—diary writing that, we believe, reveals America's collective soul.

Americans generally are not known by their diaries. Many scholars insist that autobiography rather than diary is *the* American form. Benjamin Franklin, Frederick Douglass, Henry Adams, Booker T. Washington, Jane Addams, Malcolm X, Richard Nixon, and so many others chose autobiography to present their lives. In doing so, they sought to monopolize the definition of their own lives and to force all who would try to know them to look first through the lenses they themselves had shaped for posterity. Autobiography suits the American character. In a mobile, immigrant nation one can be whatever he or she chooses to be—or so the story goes. Autobiography has allowed an invented people to reinvent themselves on paper, a mobile people to fix their place in history.

Yet, Americans also have been a diary-keeping people, almost religiously so. In their diaries many Americans talked to themselves about who they were and what they wanted—or thought God wanted them—to become. And some, like the autobiographers, wrote with posterity in mind. More so, though, in their diaries they simply revealed the regular rhythms of life and habits of mind that gave America its peculiar imprint in the world. Diarists are observers of people and events rather than "masters" of them, as are autobiographers. For such reasons, we offer our American diary believing that through diaries readers can appreciate the contingency of national character and experience America's past. Readers especially can appreciate, as Walt Whitman said of himself, Americans' ongoing "song of ourselves."

"Why some of us write diaries," Harry Miller observed in 1930, "is no more easily explained than why some collect stamps or snuff-boxes or watches." The need to write was compelling, even addictive, to many diarists. No diarist anywhere beat Arthur Crew Inman (1895–1963) for compulsion. Spending much of a forty-year period holed up in his Boston apartment, Inman daily typed the news and stories of "his times" into his journal. Before he shot himself to death in 1963, he made microfilm copies of his life's work, totalling more than ten million words, and provided in his will that whoever edited his diary could not delete one word. All or nothing, the American way. (Inman's diary remains unpublished in full form, but Daniel Aaron brought out a two-volume condensation in 1985.) Though not so obsessive as Inman, settlers trudging west, soldiers marching to battle, and prisoners of war going nowhere often found keeping a journal the only way of relieving the monotony and brutality of daily life and preserving their sanity. Such individuals went to extraordinary lengths and even risked their lives to record their daily activities and thoughts. One prisoner of war in Germany during World War II, for example, made a diary by folding down the metal sides from powdered milk containers and then scratching out entries listing the books he read, the names and addresses of fellow prisoners, and the calendar of his captivity—all to keep from going crazy.

Others wrote because the diary made them writers. Bronson Alcott never regretted "being shown, when a boy, in the old oaken cabinet, my mother's little journal, that set me out in this chase of myself, continued and now fixed by habit as a part of the day," for the daily discipline taught him everything about writing. He wrote in his journal believing that should he "succeed in sketching to the life a single day's doings," he would "esteem" himself "as having accomplished the chiefest feat in literature." Keeping a diary forced Theodore Dreiser to observe life around him and then say something about it on paper. He fought writer's block in doing so. The diary might be therapy, as it was in a way for Sylvia Plath, among others. Whatever it was, it imposed a regular regimen of grappling with words. Forgetting his notebook one day in August 1858, Henry David Thoreau stripped bark from a birch tree to use as paper and then wrote: "The writer who postpones the recording of his thoughts uses an iron which has cooled to burn a hole with." The diary provided a hot iron for writing every day.

Some American artists dismissed the diary as dull and dulling in its very dailiness, even as they kept journals themselves. In *The Innocents Abroad* (1869), Mark Twain related that when he was a boy and "a confiding and a willing prey to those impossible schemes of reform which well-meaning old maids and grandmothers set for the feet of unwary youths" each new year, he had begun a journal. He offered the following extracts: "*Monday*—Got up, washed, went to bed. / *Tuesday*—Got up, washed, went to bed." And so on for a week. He gave up on the project after a month because "Startling events appeared to be too rare, in my career, to render a diary necessary," though he reflected "with pride" that "even at that early age I washed when I got up." The journal "finished" him so that Twain "never had the nerve to keep one since." Although Twain did forego further daily jottings about his personal hygiene, for over forty years he carried with him pocket-sized buff-leather or morocco notebooks in which he regularly recorded his travels west and abroad, his diet, and, most of all, his impressions of the land and people he saw and the stories he heard.

For Twain and other artists, their notebooks provided the "stuff" of their own stories. Henry David Thoreau needed only pencil and notebook to be alive as he wandered by Walden Pond, or anywhere. So, too, Ralph Waldo Emerson, Louisa

May Alcott, Theodore Dreiser, Sherwood Anderson, Clifford Odets, May Sarton, and many other authors incorporated into their published works insights gleaned by recording mundane observations.

Most diarists, however, wrote to tell about themselves. The thrust of American diaries changed over time from the early Puritans' search for their sins and recognition of God's power and providence to the modernists' search for self and lament of America's lost soul. Yet, the need to tell one's own story persisted. Regardless of its content, a diary is a way to assert individuality. Sydney George Fisher spoke for many when he wondered in May 1859 why he bothered to fill numerous volumes with observations on his world and himself. It was, he concluded, partly a proof of his "idle life, I suppose, for if I were busy in external things I should not write so much in my diary," but it was also "partly habit, partly the pleasure of writing, partly for the sake of future satisfaction in reading the history of my daily life, which, however uneventful and obscure, is *my* life, that is, all I have as a position in this great, busy world, which knows and cares nothing about me." Poet Gamaliel Bradford confessed in 1921 to the "morbid charm" of coming to his journal to make, and to read, "daily, even trivial records." It was a fixed habit impossible to give up. Self-communion is not only good for the soul, but for the psyche and sense of self-worth. Without a diary, writes Ronald Blythe, "almost everything we do or say or think or feel slips very quickly into oblivion." A strong claim, perhaps too strong, but one with truth in it. Because many diarists believed in that truth, they wrote, as May Sarton once said, in "an effort against loss," cheating death itself by leaving a record.

Keeping a diary also is a way of beginning a new life. Hooked on drugs and run away from home, the fifteen-year-old "Alice" of *Go Ask Alice* (1971) bought a new diary and then closed her old one by writing, "You dear Diary, will be my past. The one I buy when we get home will be my future." Alice's new diary did not save her, and, indeed, she died three weeks after deciding to give up her diary habit, but other troubled Americans have found new life in journals that allowed them to fight physical and psychological torments and to believe in the future. Similarly, by tearing out the pages of the old, the diarist can symbolically erase the past. Thomas Merton confessed to such an act, when upon entering his contemplative life in the abbey in 1941, he wrote in his journal: "I should tear out all the other pages of this book, and all the other pages of anything else I have ever written and begin here." In that statement Merton spoke volumes on the Americans' peculiar habit of renewal and reinvention. Like the confessional diaries of the Puritans, the religious and secular journals of latter-day Americans recorded new birth, but most Americans still carried a profound sense of history with them, especially as they contemplated national holidays and visited graveyards and memorials. They sought not so much to escape or deny their past as to control it by capturing it in words that conveyed their particular perspectives. For many American diarists, new life came from facing the old. Their diaries let them do so.

In many ways, it is the very ordinariness and dailiness of the diary that gives it appeal and power. Most American diaries followed a natural pattern. First came the weather, then health and family followed by the trivia of daily chores, routines, and pastimes. Such daily rhythms were punctuated periodically by a few words on the visit of some person or unusual event or by a reflective moment on life's meaning, but the ordinary more than the extraordinary ruled the lives of the "common folk" keeping diaries. Much can be learned from such repetition and attention to the mundane.

Take food, for example. American diarists wrote much about food—growing it, finding it, consuming it, and complaining about it. For explorers and pioneers, such as Lewis and Clark and the emigrants on the Overland Trail, eating on the American plan meant a diet of venison, buffalo, rabbit, dog, and anything else that might be caught or bought along the way, all swished down with water from the streams and rivers that led west. Soldiers from the Revolutionary War through World War II often groused about subsisting on embalmed beef, hardtack, and other "rations," when they were fed at all. Schemes to steal a chicken or some other "supplement" from a hapless farmer filled pages of soldiers' diaries, especially during the Civil War. Just as often soldiers confessed to gulping down rum or whiskey to keep from gagging on the government issue. Travelers and "gentlemen" epicurians carped about eating coarse fare and sharing common bowls at roadside inns or public gatherings. Pretensions of class and "breeding" led some diarists to sniff at what was served in a democratic society, but most American writers were content as long as the food was abundant, edible, and cheap. Americans were what they ate. To follow the diarists' tastes in food, and their eating habits, is to see American diversity and realize the abundance of the land.

The diarists also told about America itself. Especially they wrote about the land—its newness and its power. One of the major themes in American historical experience has been the movement across the land in search of a new life. The journals and maps of such explorers as Lewis and Clark made the West comprehensible and accessible, if also awesome, to Americans looking westward. Of the quarter million or so emigrants who braved the Overland Trail and other routes to the Pacific during the nineteenth century, many hundreds kept diaries of their journey both for reasons of sentiment and subsequent settlement. The information collected in their journals might encourage and guide family and friends to follow safely in the diarists' tracks. Knowing about the land meant survival.

Moving across so vast and varied a terrain became a transforming process for those on the trails, symbolized by the excess baggage the emigrants discarded along the way. They could hardly keep from writing about so monumental and so wondrous an experience, or about so inscrutable a land of plains, deserts, and mountains unlike anything they had seen before. Typical of such journals is a combination of the prosaic and the poetic. Amid the emigrants' preoccupations with practical matters of food, family, comfort, safety, and other concerns of everyday life—women more with matters of home and health and men more with hunting and horses— are notations on virtually every page of their diaries describing a natural curiosity or admiring a natural wonder. The land humbled the people, even as it promised new life. Likewise, amid the rush to California in 1849 and after, many prospective golddiggers kept diaries that showed how much their experiences in getting there, more than any minerals dug out of the ground, made them into new men. Even east of the Mississippi travelers bowed before the majesty of hardwood forests in upstate New York or the might of muddy rivers flowing inexorably through cotton fields to the sea. And so it continued in this century as Americans in touring cars discovered the purple mountains and fruited plains anew.

Perhaps the most revealing diaries are those kept during war. America was born in war, not peace, and born again during the Civil War. Under fire, then, Americans thought about their national character as never before. In speeches and policy statements public figures rallied support for the cause by reminding the people what they were fighting to preserve. In private the people weighed the costs of war and its significance in shaping their own individual identities. American wars generated a huge surge of diary writing, even though military policy from World War II on has discouraged diary keeping in favor of letter writing and telephoning loved ones. During the Civil War especially the diary rivaled the Bible as the book a soldier likely would stuff in his haversack or backpack. Young men and women facing death began to think about life. In war their lives suddenly assumed meaning as part of history in the making, just as the imminence of death demanded that some record of their individual lives be left behind. The diary was a way of staying alive. It might even save its author's life, as in the case of at least one Civil War soldier whose diary, which now is on permanent display at the National Museum of Health and Medicine in Washington, stopped a bullet from piercing his chest.

Diarists who survived war rarely kept up the journal habit once they left the battlefields and campfires for home. The war had been their moment of decision when they discovered the truth about their character and felt the need to get their stories down. The diary, more than letters or autobiography, became the one place where one might tell all the horrors one saw and terrors one felt, where one might confess to fear and to sins committed away from home. The intensity of wartime conditions often magnified American prejudices and beliefs—the basic contempt for arbitrary authority and display, especially for the puffed-up posing of generals who would not fight, and even for government itself. The same intensity also heightened the Americans' love of humor and irony, their respect for straight talk and direct action, and, it must be said, their savagery. Most of all, in wartime diaries Americans collectively bespoke their faith in democratic principles. They came to believe in themselves. Their diaries tell us so.

Diary writing in America is a democratic form. Nowhere else in the world has diary writing been so widespread among the "common folk" as in the United States. Increasing literacy in the nineteenth century allowed many different classes of Americans to write—and to read—journals so that diaries became a popular literary form. Indeed, many journals of the period were written for mass consumption in an affected literary style that would appeal to middle-class readers. But most diarists, then as now, wrote for themselves or their families alone. They also wrote in the way they ordinarily spoke about their daily activities and concerns. Diary writing, with its immediacy, recalls more fully than any other written form the way people speak and think. American diaries give us real American voices.

The selection of diarists and diary entries in this book is both personal and purposeful. We had no absolute standards, save only that the authors be American and the accounts genuine. We sought journals that had American stories to tell. We used both self-described "diaries" and "journals," for the terms are almost interchangeable, both deriving from a Latin root meaning "daily." The dailiness of the diary/journal and the authenticity of the writer rather than the length of the account or the fame of the author determined which works were selected. With only a few exceptions, we excluded ships' logs, business daybooks, newspaper dispatches, travel accounts, and "political" diaries intended to place the writers in a favorable light in history. We also excluded diaries that lacked dated entries—a decision dictated by the structure of our American diary, which moves from day to day to provide a full year of entries. Many insightful, readable diaries were lost by such a strategy. Withal, we found many others rich in story and real in character.

One of the delights of our reading was the discovery of so many crisp *American* voices among the common folk who kept diaries. There was more salty wisdom in the words of midwestern-born, college-educated Dorothea Moulton Balano, who married and went to sea with a Maine fisherman, than in the prose of many self-proclaimed writers, who sat on the rocks, sketchbooks and journals in hand, and saw and smelled nothing even as the Atlantic waters splashed against them and the ships came in. And what novelist has yet told the story of the American Civil War so truly as the many hundreds of diarists who lived through it? *E pluribus unum.* If America is one made out of many, we have sought the many to find the one.

Some readers will be disappointed to find their favorite "hero" missing from our American diary. Many famous people are not present in this volume. While we looked for writers who "represented" America and seemed true to themselves, we also sought out interesting passages on key moments in American life and history. For the same reason, just as it does not always include the "usual suspects" among prominent diarists, our American diary offers slices of lives rather than a sociological cross-section of the country. Diary keeping was not, and is not, a universal habit. Minority groups and immigrants are underrepresented in this book, for they kept few diaries, and fewer still were kept for them by historical societies and manuscript collections. Women and men, however, appear in roughly equal numbers, a fact resulting entirely from the nature of the sources themselves.

It is not true, as Tallulah Bankhead once asserted, that "only good girls keep diaries" because "bad girls don't have the time." Plenty of good and bad girls and boys took the time. Neither sex can claim dominion over the genre by force of numbers alone. Chapbook diaries sold steadily to men and women on the go during the nineteenth century. Only over time did diary-keeping come to be seen as a "feminine" habit. Beginning in the late nineteenth century young girls received embroidered, lockable diaries as Christmas gifts, almost as a rite of passage into literate girlhood and a private life. Boys growing out of their knee britches rarely got such presents. Even today, pocket diaries designed for girls are ready fare at stationery stores, and girls remain the single largest market for the five million plus blank diaries sold each year in America. Yet, men who would get ahead in the world were expected to develop a different version of the journal habit, as the proliferation of stationers' shelves of daybooks for personal accounts, appointments, and notes attests. Thus men and women had their respective pocket notebooks, as today they both have the same Filofaxes.

Interestingly, neither women nor men were expected to reveal too much of themselves in their store-bought diaries. The few lines allotted to each day in the neatly ruled journals sold to the masses demanded brevity. Diaries for both sexes were for business—recording recipes, rules, and appointments—more than pleasure. If you loved someone, you could only count the ways. The page left no room for reflection or introspection. Many people obeyed the prescriptions. Many others let their words and feelings spill over the lines and into the margins, crowding out the next day's space to tell of this day's doings and feelings. Or, they bought and filled bigger diaries.

Students of diaries disagree about the extent to which American diarists honestly revealed and confronted themselves. Our reading suggests that many diarists wanted to tell about themselves through their diaries and that many others, who did not want to do so, did anyway. Even when self-consciously posing for the public and posterity and writing more to be interesting than truthful, these diarists reveal much about themselves—and about American values and identities—by their style and the subjects they chose to present.

In arranging the diary entries we selected for this book, we developed parallel as well as intersecting lines. Some diarists appear regularly throughout the book, a constant and familiar presence amid the many and varied American voices. Other diarists show up only when they have something revealing and interesting to say about an American experience, event, or individual. We included many long passages to catch the personality of individual diaries and the flavor of American dialect. Observation and experience counted more than aphorism when we decided which excerpts to use, though admittedly we have included the ever aphoristic and self-consciously American Ralph Waldo Emerson and Henry David Thoreau to round out the American voices.

We arranged the material by the days of the year, with several entries from different years for each day, so that the different voices maintain their individual identity. Moving back and forth in time this way as the book progresses through the year not only shows how American identity transcends any strict chronology, but it also creates a final portrait of America that is a modernist montage rather than a linear historical narrative. The truth about the American character revealed by the collected diaries of so many Americans is that the past is never past.

Thus, although the reader can profitably look at and isolate individual entries and diarists, this book is best read whole. Its narrative truth lies less with any chronology than it does with its expressionistic portrait of America. In the same way that an array of images, with their seeming discontinuities of time and place, achieves coherence and integrity as a collage, a joining together and layering of diverse and often clashing elements, the narrative moves back and forth, up and down, and even sideways. The truth emerges as all the American diarists continually check and balance one other. Events repeat themselves then move beyond and, finally, into themselves so that the reader comes to understand Robert Penn Warren's idea that the true American moves "out of history into history and the awful responsibility of Time."

By reading the stories many different Americans told and retold to themselves in their diaries, it is possible to see an American past that is ever evolving and reinventing itself. The Civil War never ends, just as Abraham Lincoln never dies. Near the conclusion of our American diary the reader may be surprised to encounter William Bradford, newly arrived in America in November 1620. Barricading himself against the harsh physical elements offshore and the corruptions of the Old World left behind, Bradford simultaneously contemplates the prospects and dangers of a New World yet to be hewn from the forests. Meeting Bradford in November reminds the reader of the recycling of American experience and memory, of the telling and retelling of stories that mark the American character that stands at the center of our American diary's purpose.

Historian Laurel Thatcher Ulrich recently observed that, "Opening a diary for the first time is like walking into a room full of strangers. The reader is advised to enjoy the company without trying to remember every name." So it is with this book. If nothing else, we hope readers will enjoy the company they meet here, and we have tried not to disrupt the flow of the daily entries with editorial notes and asides. Rather, we let each entry stand on its own account and each day, or sequence of days, to develop its own identity based on the juxtaposition of entries. We have supplied brief headnotes to establish place and brief emendations set off by brackets to identify people mentioned only when such information is essential. Otherwise, we trust that the meaning and flavor of each entry will be evident from a simple reading of it. A *dramatis personae* at the end of the book gives thumbnail sketches of the diarists and any unusual circumstances regarding their respective diaries.

Regarding the texts, we have silently corrected typographical errors and, for reasons of clarity, modernized spelling in a few diaries from the seventeenth and eighteenth centuries. For economy, we have run together lines rather than maintain the often capricious paragraphing of the different diarists. Principally, though, we have preserved the peculiar spelling, grammar, and phrasing of each diary so that the individual character of the various diarists might come through the words. This, after all, is their book, with their voices giving us individually and collectively an American diary, an American "song of ourselves."

Stefan Kanfer, a student of the diary as a genre, once wrote that a diary is "a kind of looking-glass" that at first reflects the diarist but in the end also reveals the reader. By presenting this "American diary" free of editorial clutter, we hope that readers might see American identity and interests and, at the same time, see their American selves.

⇒ JANUARY ⇒

JANUARY 1

*B*esides my making my preparations for the approaching Sabbath, I have little to remark concerning this Day, as it looks as if very many kindred and most of my Dayes have rolled away without anything worth noting upon them. Some are left Blank because of the Confusion I am put into by *Diem perdidi;* or because with all my Desire to Improve my time, I prove but of little importance either to Myself, or anyone else. I had through the whole of this Day crowds of imperfect Reflections upon the Consumption of Time.

—EBENEZER PARKMAN (1726)

[At Fort Clatsop] *T*his morning I was awakened at an early hour by the discharge of a volley of small arms, which was fired by our party in front of our quarters to usher in the New Year. This was the only mark of respect which we had it in our power to pay this celebrated day. Our repast of this day . . . consisted primarily in the anticipation of [next year]. . . . At present we were content with eating our boiled elk and wappato, and solacing our thirst with our only beverage, *pure water.*

—MERIWETHER LEWIS (1806)

1

[On the South Carolina Sea Islands] *A*bout ten o'clock the people began to collect by land, and also by water. . . . The multitude were chiefly colored women, with gay handkerchiefs on their heads, and a sprinkling of men, with that peculiarly respectable look which these people always have on Sundays and holidays. There were many white visitors also. . . . Our companies [of one black and several white Union regiments] were marched to the neighborhood of the platform and allowed to sit or stand, as at the Sunday services. . . . The services began at half past eleven o'clock, with prayer by our chaplain. . . . Then the colors were presented to us by the Rev. Mr. French, a chaplain who brought them from the donors in New York. All this was according to the programme. . . . The very moment the speaker had ceased, and just as I took and waved the flag, which now for the first time meant anything to these poor people, there suddenly arose, close beside the platform, a strong male voice (but rather cracked and elderly), into which two women's voices instantly blended, singing, as if by an impulse that could no more be repressed than the morning note of the song-sparrow.—"My Country, 'tis of thee,/ Sweet land of liberty,/ Of thee I sing!" People looked at each other, and then at us on the platform, to see whence came this interruption, not set down in the bills. Firmly and irrepressibly the quavering voices sang on, verse after verse; others of the colored people joined in; some whites on the platform began, but I motioned them to silence. I never saw anything so electric; it made all other words cheap; it seemed the choked voice of a race at last unloosed.

—THOMAS WENTWORTH HIGGINSON (1863)

*U*gly night. Doped myself to sleep. Dreamed that Malcolm Cowley was leading troops into battle.

—SHERWOOD ANDERSON (1936)

I begin this 36th year of my life on the way to invade the island of Luzon in the Lingayen Gulf. This month will mark

2

the 12th month of the 1st cruise of the Epping Forest and my 14th month aboard. 40,000 miles and six major invasions has been our lot to date. . . . Observed holiday routine yesterday with the usual abandon ship drill. Dear Hank, the moron from Sapulpa, must have his fun. Day headlined by 6 or 7 sub contacts with several good attacks, results possible. Found the crew had drained the alcohol from the magnetic compasses for Christmas celebration, replacing it with water.

—WALTER L. RHINEHART (1945)

The only holiday that is at all distinctly holy, to my mind: the day sacred to Time. Such other gods as I care for—Memory, Sex, Language—have no particular season or fixed feast.

—GLENWAY WESCOTT (1952)

JANUARY 2

My birthday. I am 8 years old. For my birthday present Father and Mother gave me "The Children's Garland" and some paper. Father prayed for us this morning in the Nursery. We had a show this morning. The log cabin with a garden around it, soldiers frightening a poor old woman nearly out of her wits, and several other things. Father told me about the Heathen gods today.

—M. CAREY THOMAS (1865)

Love-making with gusto just before taking train—she took a douche with Angostura bitters by mistake—in lower berth together sat up till late talking and laughing—conversation punctuated by stopper blowing out of gin bottle to our great hilarity (stopper blew out of other gin bottle in suitcase and

3

saturated clothes with gin, violet border to colorless stain). . .
I loved looking out at the Connecticut country covered with
snow—dark towns with snow-paved streets, with big squarish
houses and here and there a light.

—EDMUND WILSON (1931)

JANUARY 3

*O*ne party, from necessity having been obliged to subsist
some length of time on dogs, have now become extremely
fond of their flesh. It is worthy of remark that while we lived
principally on the flesh of this animal, we were much more
healthy, strong, and more fleshy than we had been since we
left the buffalo country. For my own part, I have become so
perfectly reconciled to the dog that I think it an agreeable
food and would prefer it vastly to lean venison or elk.

—MERIWETHER LEWIS (1806)

I can imagine nothing more happy in life than an evening
spent in my cosy little sitting room, before a bright fire of soft
coal, my books all around me, and playing backgammon with
my own dainty mistress.

—THEODORE ROOSEVELT (1883)

I am sitting in the upper room of our cheerless [Italian]
villa at the table that has the pink lace skirt-thing on it, a
table at which the lady of the house once sat to do up her
hair—now, alas, fallen & stained with tea and ink and candle-
grease. . . . All day long we sit about and drink tea with figs
in it, glancing out now and then at the dreary winter of the
Venetian Plain . . . where Italian soldiers tramp meaning-

4

lessly back & forth through the cold. . . . There are airraids at night, and in the day the sun shines and we walk through the mud and go to look at the campaniles of Venice across the lagoons. . . . Barbed wire stretches in long blue strips across the wheatfields and vineyards looking like some obscure crop sprung up in a nights growth. . . . I suppose that if the Germans break through at Asiago—the Italians will thus fall back . . . abandoning Venice & this entire strip of land. Lets hope they retreat before we leave.

—JOHN DOS PASSOS (1918)

[Pacifist A. J.] *M*uste had been delayed by having to speak at a meeting of garment workers—he ought to have remembered, he said, that New York time is not God's time and that when you spoke to a garment workers' meeting you would have to answer questions afterwards about how they were to get rid of their officers. He looked worn, tense, and hardworked, one lock of hair down over his forehead, his eyes getting round under his pained and dismayed eyebrows . . . like those of an amazed old hick, his cheeks fevered at the cheekbones and showing hollows below, his mouth dingy darkened by the traces of his beard . . . his shoulders hunched up and sitting on his hands or afterwards during the discussion with one leg twisted around the other and his hands clasped in front of him—when somebody asked him a question which perhaps embarrassed him a little, he would knock the cigarette ashes off his clothes with little pats of his rather fine thin fingers or take a nervous pull on the cigarette.

—EDMUND WILSON (1934)

JANUARY 4

*T*his evening I went to lyceum with Charles Emery. We deliberated and agreed to admit none to our slip . . . except

5

handsome girls. Shortly entered the fay I fell in love with a week ago and with her two others. Before long they were seated in ours, Miss Pierce next to me. In a few moments Miss Pierce was beckoned away and left me beside Miss [Margaret] Spring. . . . She held a muff in her lap and I commenced my overtures with unconsciously passing my fingers through the fur. Next, in a few minutes, my hand dropped down near the entrance to it, and soon my forefinger came thrillingly in contact with her wrist. She then removed her hand and I did the same. Soon her hand returned. Mine ditto, and my fingers resumed their place. The next time she attempted to withdraw her hand I gently retained it and she then suffered it to abide. Then my hand crept stealthily over the No. 5½ kid glove fitting so closely on her beautifully delicate, little hand, and in fifteen minutes she had pushed her muff toward me and under it lay concealed both our hands, nestling and playing. I felt and pressed her fingers, her whole little tremulous palm. I glowed, my eyes swam, my face burned (so did hers). I was in a delicious ecstasy, and the unwelcome rising at the conclusion of the lecture sounded like a death knell. The lecture was by Professor Hitchcock of Amherst, and his subject, "Fossil Footmarks."

—Benjamin Browne Foster (1850)

[At Union Hotel Hospital, Georgetown D. C.] *U*p at six, dress by gaslight, run through my ward & fling up the windows though the men grumble & shiver. . . . Poke up the fire, add blankets, joke, coax, & command, but continue to open doors & windows as if life depended on it; mine does, & doubtless many another, for a more perfect pestilence-box than this house I never saw—cold, damp, dirty, full of vile odors from wounds, kitchens, wash rooms, & stables. . . . Till noon I trot, trot, giving out rations, cutting up food for helpless "boys," washing faces, teaching my attendants how beds are made or floors swept, dressing wounds, taking Dr. Fitz Patrick's orders, (privately wishing all the time that he would be more gentle with my big babies,) dusting tables, sewing bandages, keeping my tray tidy, rushing up & down after pillows, bed linen, sponges, books & directions. . . . When dinner is over some sleep, many read, & others want letters

6

written. . . . Night nurses go on duty, & sleep & death have the house to themselves. . . . It leaves me time for a morning run. . . . up & down the streets in all directions, some times to the Heights, then half way to Washington, again to the hill over which the long trains of army wagons are constantly vanishing & ambulances appearing. That way the fighting lies, & I long to follow.

—Louisa May Alcott (1863)

*B*reakfasted this morning off huova all'burro at the little trattoria—Sat watching the grey warmish half light of the dark wooden tables coming out from the two walls, regularly, like pews, and the brilliant white light on the walk across the street against which anyone coming in was silhouetted, as he opened the glass door—All the time a string of soldiers marched down the road outside—helmets and guns and blanketrolls showing out strangely against the brilliant light. . . . [Later that night] two big snorting explosions shook the windows and the glasses on the table—air bombs. Then the electric light snapped off and the fun commenced. I stood on the balcony . . . & watched the searchlights ineffectual in the glare of the moon & the red flashes of guns & the spit of machineguns as everything let loose at the sky. Once I imagined I saw a shadow like a plane across the beam of the searchlight—but it is unlikely—The main effect of the roughhouse was the whimpering sound and the menacing rattle as they hit, of pieces of shrapnel falling.

—John Dos Passos (1918)

*D*ecide to drive on to Miami. The moving developments here. A new Venice! Sea land lots $12,000 each. And thousands of houses representing 50 to $100,000 invested. The giant excavating cranes. Digging canals. For the first time in America I see cities being built to a plan! . . . To Miami City. A wretched road of shacks & gas stations & camps & junk & garages—with millions being spent on the seaside everywhere. . . . Then to Miami Beach. . . . More city planning. The paradise of the western world. The contrast with California. Here wealth builds. Out there is the world of moderate means.

—THEODORE DREISER (1925)

JANUARY 5

I rose about 7 o'clock and read nothing because Tom Turpin was here. He came with 30 hogs from the Falls. He told me all was well above. I said my prayers and ate boiled milk for breakfast. I danced my dance. About 9 o'clock came Major Harrison and the captain of the "Pelican." I gave them a bottle of sack. Then we played at billiards and I won 7 shillings, and sixpence. About one o'clock we went to dinner and I ate some boiled beef. In the afternoon we were merry and made the Quaker captain drink the Queen's health on his knees. About 2 o'clock came my brother and sister Custis and sat down to dinner. They brought no news. My sister was much tired. In the evening the captain and Major Harrison went away to Mrs. Harrison's where I understood that Mr. Clayton was come. We drank a bottle of wine at night. This day a negro of mine at Falling Creek had a tree fall on his head and had his brains beat out. I neglected to say my prayers and had good health, good thoughts, and good humor, thank God Almighty.

—WILLIAM BYRD (1712)

I care but little whether I have any [salt] with my meat or not, provided the meat is fat, having from habit become entirely careless about my diet; and I have learned to think that if the cord be sufficiently strong which binds the soul and body together, it does not so much matter about the materials which compose it.

—WILLIAM CLARK (1806)

8

$\mathscr{I}$ decided to learn a profession; that is, to learn either to make cigars or to sew on Singer's machine. I decided for the latter and began to learn in earnest. Tuition $3. I will probably have to learn for five or six weeks. However, I can make a living. It is hard work, to be sure, but I am now in America; that means working.

—JACOB SAUL LANZIT (1859)

"$\mathscr{M}$r. Wescott, did you read where tears cured human cancer in a mouse?"

"No, Anna. In what paper was it?"

"That I don't know. I didn't read it myself. Our laundryman was telling me yesterday."

She took a turn around the room, then came back and stood facing me.

"Anyway, you know, Mr. Wescott, someday they will just stumble on something stupid, like that Fleming. He left his food on his plate, and it moldered, and so he just stumbled on penicillin."

—GLENWAY WESCOTT (1955)

JANUARY 6

$\mathscr{I}$ rose about 8 o'clock because my wife made me lie in bed and I rogered her. I read nothing and neglected to say my prayers but had boiled milk for breakfast. About 10 o'clock came Mr. Clayton and brought me two English letters without any news because they were of an old date. I gave him a dram and about 11 o'clock we walked to church where we heard a good sermon from Mr. Anderson. I invited Colonel Hill to dine with me and ate wild goose for dinner. In the afternoon it rained so that Colonel Hill agreed to stay all night. In the evening we drank a supper bottle and were merry with nonsense but Colonel Hill's head ached a little.

However it did not mar the supper or conversation. The Colonel is a man of good sense and good principles notwithstanding what has been said of him. I neglected to say my prayers but had good health, good thoughts, and good humor, thank God Almighty.

—William Byrd (1712)

JANUARY 7

*H*ere to-day from Philadelphia. The railroad, which was but a toy coach the other day, is now a dowdy, lumbering country wagon. . . . The Americans take to the little contrivance as if it were the cradle in which they were born.

—Ralph Waldo Emerson (1843)

*R*ainy—didn't call this morning on the ladies at Hill's as I promised on account of the weather. Went to the Capitol as usual. Heard a tedious speech on the state of the Treasury from Niles in the Senate. I thought he would never get done. The truth is, these members don't know when they are done speaking. Every idea that suggests itself, they think must be uttered of course. And after they get through with these, they go floundering on still, struggling desperately to drag up from the muddy depths of their invention other *thoughts,* if they deserve the name. They don't recollect that the great men of the first Congress rarely spoke more than ten minutes.

—James Lawson Kemper (1847)

*V*ery cold. . . . Captain John Brown, the old partisan hero of Kansas warfare, came to see me. I had a long talk with him.

10

He is a calm, temperate, and pious man, but when roused he is a dreadful foe. He appears about sixty years old.

—AMOS A. LAWRENCE (1857)

A queer day. Up early, and had my bread and milk and baked apples. Fed my doves. Made May a bonnet, and cut out a flannel wrapper for Marmee, who feels the cold in the Concord snowbanks. Did my editorial work in the P.M., and fixed my dresses for the plays. . . . To Dorchester in evening, and acted Mrs. Pontifex, in "Naval Engagements," to a good house. A gay time, had flowers, etc. Talked half the night with H. A. about the fast ways of young people nowadays, and gave the child much older-sisterly advice, as no one seems to see how much she needs help at this time of her young life. Dreamed that I was an opera dancer, and waked up prancing.

—LOUISA MAY ALCOTT (1868)

*R*eading the tayles of how C. Mackay is wood-wroth that his daughter hath wedded I. Berlin, I was minded of a night last June, when G. Seldes the journalist came to my room in the Hotel Russie in Rome, and said, Do you know who this Mackay girl is? And I said Yes. And he told me that he had a cable from his journal, to the effect that the Vatican was considering at that moment the granting of a dispensation. And at that moment the band in the courtyard began to play, "What'll I Do?" and whether the Vatican was deliberating then none of us ever found out, but as I thought of the days when I. Berlin was a singing waiter on the Bowery, I thought it was dramatick enough.

—FRANKLIN PIERCE ADAMS (1926)

*S*travinsky, in his coarse, schoolmaster manner, is conducting the Polish Symphony of Tchaikovsky. It is fine blue and brown weather; I should be taking a healthful walk. . . .

11

Instead I have been remembering Isadora Duncan as I knew her at the end of her life in the South of France. The very last time I saw her she complained bitterly of her dissatisfaction with the autobiography she had written, and she asked me to help her with it. I refused, assuring her that it did not matter, it would be all right; the less apparent literary art there was about it the better. She told me that it was the only thing she had ever done just for money, and she was ashamed, and having spent the money she could not give it up. It was worse than I knew, she said. Not only was the style poor and stilted, there was bad grammar in it. There had been many objections to her dancing, but there had been no bad grammar in that; and she wept. So I promised to come on the next Wednesday or Thursday to have a look. But when that day came she was dead, in the strangest automobile accident I ever heard of. With her friend Marie Desti and our friend Monroe Wheeler I sat up all night beside her glorious beheaded body in a kind of wake. I think Mrs. Desti was Irish. Half the night she told us tales of Isadora's great days; and sometimes she keened, like the bereaved heroines of the plays of John Millington Synge . . . There was also an American woman whose name I have forgotten, who went to the garage where the fatal automobile was and bought a bit of the fringe of the shawl Isadora was wearing, and thrust it inside her dress and hastened to Monte Carlo to gamble, thinking it would bring her luck.

—GLENWAY WESCOTT (1940)

JANUARY 8

*P*roceeded to the place the whale had perished. Found only the skeleton of this monster on the sand, between 2 of the villages of the Tillamook nation. The whale was already pillaged of every valuable part by the Tillamook Indians in the vicinity, of whose villages it lay on the strand, where the waves and tide had driven up and left it. . . . I returned to the village of 5 cabins on the creek. . . . Found the natives busily engaged boiling the blubber, which they performed in a large, square wooden trough, by means of hot stones. The oil, when extracted, was secured in bladders and the guts of the whale. . . . The Tillamooks, although they possessed large quantities of this blubber and oil, were so penurious that they disposed of it with great reluctance, and in small quantities only; insomuch that my utmost exertions, aided by the party, with the small stock of merchandise I had taken with me, were not able to procure more blubber than about 300 pounds and a few gallons of oil. Small as this stock is, I prize it highly; and thank Providence for directing the whale to us; and think Him much more kind to us than He was to Jonah, having sent this monster to be swallowed *by* us, instead of swallowing *of* us, as Jonah's did.

—WILLIAM CLARK (1806)

*O*ut, questing about here and there, and met J. Dempsey the former boxer, and he shook my hand for a short count, and seemed greatly delighted at meeting me, for he gave my hand a pressure that I can still feel, albeit I am writing this seventeen hours later.

—FRANKLIN PIERCE ADAMS (1929)

*B*eginning to recover from the flu. Pretty well. Worked just a little—sat in the sun—very lovely day. In the evening at home, playing cards—nothing important. No thoughts. No dreams.

—SHERWOOD ANDERSON (1937)

JANUARY 9

*T*he Philadelphia officers of the Regiment applied to me today, to represent to the General [Washington] the propriety of the officer of the Day, on guard, dining at his table,—but I replied that such an invitation should come from the General himself, and, if he was not courtly enough to confer that honor on the officer of the guard, he would feel it as a censure on his want of Etiquet if it was pressed upon him, and therefore advised them, in case the General admitted his compliment, to consider their own tables as pleasant and honorable as his, that true honor consisted in acts of virtue and that the merit of their patriotism would not be lessened by the General omitting the required compliment.

—CAPTAIN THOMAS RODNEY (1777)

I hear that R. M.——, a rich old farmer who lives in a large house, with a male housekeeper and no other family, gets up at three or four o'clock these winter mornings and milks seventeen cows regularly. When asked why he works so hard he answers that the poor are obliged to work hard. Only think, what a creature of fate he is, this old Jotun, milking his seventeen cows though the thermometer goes down to minus 25, and not knowing why he does it,—draining sixty-eight cows' teats in the dark of the coldest morning! Think how helpless a rich man who can only do as he has done!

—HENRY DAVID THOREAU (1860)

*G*reat storm & cold. Read.

—LOUISA MAY ALCOTT (1886)

*L*ots of skaters on the river these days. My father never allowed me to skate when a girl at home, lest I get hurt and now my husband is going to teach me.

—MARTHA FARNSWORTH (1895)

14

JANUARY 10

*A*t night I attended in the hall of the house, and heard a lecture from Ralph Waldo Emerson on the Anglo Saxon. His language was chaste, strong and vigorous—much of his thought just—his voice good—his delivery clear, distinct and deliberate—his action nothing. He limned a good picture of an Englishman, and gave us some hard raps for our apishness of English fashions & manners.

—ORVILLE BROWNING (1853)

*C*old. 14 below zero at my house. Much colder elsewhere, especially in New Hampshire and Vermont. 38 in Montpelier and in some other places. Rode over to Cambridge. Asked a boy about a poor woman who is dying of consumption. He knew her and told me she had been burnt out (of the old Porter Tavern) and was living near. He jumped on my horse and rode him up and down the road while I went in and found the poor woman. She was overjoyed at seeing me, and laughed and cried by turns.

—AMOS A. LAWRENCE (1859)

A foot sore walk over slippery kilometers—twenty three of them or twenty seven of them to Padua—there the severe coldness of one of its restaurants & a little excitement over a German plane that calmly sailed to & fro in the azure above the city. Cold.

—JOHN DOS PASSOS (1918)

*T*he day at home, packing, etc. Very little work. . . . Dreamed of Theodore Roosevelt, became a gentle retiring man with whom I walked and talked.

—SHERWOOD ANDERSON (1937)

15

JANUARY 11

People sometimes wonder that persons wholly uneducated to write, yet eminent in some other ability, should be able to use language with so much purity and force. But it is not wonderful. The manner of using language is surely the most decisive test of intellectual power, and he who has intellectual force of any kind will be sure to show it there. For that is the first and simplest vehicle of mind, is of all things next to the mind, and the vigorous Saxon that uses it well is of the same block as the vigorous Saxon that formed it, and works after the same manner.

—Ralph Waldo Emerson (1832)

News today of a fearful tragedy at Lawrence, Massachusetts, one of the wholesale murders commonly known in newspaper literature as accident or catastrophe. A huge factory, long notoriously insecure and ill-built, requiring to be patched and bandaged up with iron plates and braces to stand the introduction of its machinery, suddenly collapsed into a heap of ruins yesterday afternoon without the smallest provocation. Some five or six hundred operatives went down with it—young girls and women mostly. . . . Of course nobody will be hanged. Somebody has murdered about two hundred people, many of them with hideous torture, in order to save money, but society has no avenging gibbet for the respectable millionaire and homicide. Of course not. He did not want to or mean to do the massacre; on the whole, he would have preferred to let these people live. . . . He did not compel these poor girls and children to enter his accursed mantrap. . . . It was a matter of contract between capital and labor; they were to receive cash payments for their services. No doubt the legal representatives of those who have perished will be duly paid the fractional part of their week's wages up to the date when they became incapacitated by crushing or combustion, as the case may be, from rendering further service. Very probably the wealthy and liberal proprietor will add (in deserving cases) a gratuity to defray funeral charges. It becomes us to prate about the horrors of slavery! What Southern capitalist trifles with the lives of his operatives as do our philanthropes of the North?

—GEORGE TEMPLETON STRONG (1860)

JANUARY 12

It strikes me the residents of Washington are worse informed about public and Congressional doings than any other people in the U. S. Their minds are excited by the thousand rumors which are confined to the Metropolis, and being just in the theatre of action they are guided by feeling more, and reflection less, than persons at a distance. I overheard today a conversation between two sensible men who live here on the subject of the duel (that was to be) between Judge Baily & Garrett Davis. They really thought that Baily had procured his own arrest, and had since apologized to Davis in the House, [and] had recanted all offensive language, without anything being conceded or done by Davis! The people of Washington should go from home to learn the news of their own place.

—JAMES LAWSON KEMPER (1847)

This evening attended a lecture by Rev. Henry Ward Beecher of Brooklyn. The subject was "Patriotism." I thought the lecture extremely interesting, and many parts of it very touching and beautiful. His manner is not at all polished or elegant, but he says so many excellent things with such forcible earnestness or irresistible humor, that we quite forget it. As I had hoped he bore his testimony against the wicked and unjust laws of our land, which it is not *patriotism* to make or to obey. He also eloquently advocated the right of woman to vote; and paid a beautiful tribute to the lovely and noble-minded Lucretia Mott. In listening to Mr. Beecher one feels

17

convinced of his *sincerity;* and we would always rather know that a person *means* what he says, even if we differ from him.

—CHARLOTTE FORTEN (1856)

I went ahead, trying for the feel of the new short story. Very much colder—streets icy. Went into the Loop and sat with advertising men. In the evening a group of young Trotskyists came and there was much revolutionary talk until midnight.

—SHERWOOD ANDERSON (1938)

I woke to gray light, howling wind . . . a real blizzard. . . . It's a strange sight to look down the field now and get the illusion that it is breaking up . . . as big waves crash in white foam against the white snow. It's still snowing hard, so it will be some time before the ploughs come, and Dixon opens the frozen garage door to set me free.

—MAY SARTON (1976)

JANUARY 13

My suggestion that he feel free to associate with other women shook his Calvinistic facade of righteousness to his timbers. He has been moaning and groaning about how bad he was to me. I can stand the Victorian self-deception, for I know about Prince Edward going from brothel to high mass within the hour, but I shall let Fred writhe a bit. It's good for his soul. Basically he's just a healthy stallion and can't get enough, but when he plays Sunday School it revolts me and 'tis hard not to show it, although I must not let him know that I see too far through him. He must feel superior. And so the "wanton wiles". . . . One moment Fred and his sea-going peers from Maine are like the Squire in Fielding's *Tom Jones*, ready to roll in the hay with anything that can accommodate their lust; the next moment they boast of the stained window they gave the chapel. Their Sunday-go-to-meeting faces are shed as quickly as their blue serge suits and become goatish leers of pure corruption. The village is loaded with Lowells, Conants, and other old Puritan names, the descendants of the boys sent downeast from Plymouth and Boston and Salem to fish for the greater glory of those Lowells and Conants who stayed home and went to Harvard. The downeast cousins don't write much poetry, but their low brows outsmart the fish and their broad bottoms, low-slung to make good ballast for the dories, are more practical than the high brows of their sou'west relatives. If east met west, they could hardly communicate unless the talk was of herring.

—DOROTHEA MOULTON BALANO (1912)

JANUARY 14

*W*e have special orders for every non commissioned officer to have chevrons on their arms and stripes on their pants. The quarter master hasn't any, we have to take old blouses and make them ourselves. It is laughable to see the boys all at work with their needles. You may depend some of the stitches are long.

—SAMUEL A. CLEAR (1865)

*C*oasting is perfect down our side hill today and every child in Oakdale is out there. Funny to see them plod up time after time and never seem to tire. But ask one of them to walk the half-mile to the village for some useful purpose and they'd look abused.

—DOROTHY ROBINSON (1935)

JANUARY 15

*W*rote all day. . . . In the evening . . . to hear Fanny Kemble read "The Merchant of Venice." She was a whole stock company in herself. Looked younger and handsomer than ever before, and happy, as she is to be with her daughters now. We went to supper afterwards at Mrs. Parkman's, and saw the lioness feed. It was a study to watch her face, so full of varying expression was it,—always strong, always sweet, then proud and fierce as she sniffed at nobodies who passed about her. Being one, I kept away, and enjoyed the great creature afar off, wondering how a short, stout, red woman *could* look so like a queen in her purple velvet and point lace. Slipped behind a door, but Dr. [Oliver Wendell] Holmes [Sr.] found me out, and affably asked, "How many of you children are there?" As I was looking down on the top of his illustrious head, the question was funny. But I answered the little man with deep respect, "Four, sir." He seemed to catch my naughty thought, and asked, with a twinkle in his eye, looking up as if I were a steeple. "And all as tall as you?" Ha! ha!

—Louisa May Alcott (1868)

[At Midnight] *R*eading Butler. Someone is playing the *Seraphina* on the phonograph—There's a festival brass in it that makes me think of health resorts—a continental watering place on a warm summer's night with lights & crowds walking about & sharing cafes and a ship—a long string of lights—coming into the harbor from the sea.

—John Dos Passos (1918)

*B*ut I cannot really love the art of Van Gogh; I am too American, that is, a believer in good fortune and good temper and good looks; a lover of the calm and definite kind of form set apart somehow in brilliant uncluttered space; a lover of the deliberate pose, the steady brush, the third (not the fourth) dimension. That, roughly speaking, always has been the style of our American painting when it has been very good: the farm pictures of Homer, before he began splashing watercolor about like Sargent; the scenes of shooting and sculling by Eakins which have a background of dewy field or geometrically rippled water. You can always tell that we are a people very empiric and sportive, not overeducated and not really religious, not maniacal, not even logical; and that our continent is not narrow, our atmosphere not opalescent or shadowy. Even our "primitives," and odds and ends not consciously artistic, have it: a certain insolent or childish simplicity, very neat, very spacious, almost vacuous; a little look of constant sensuality without much moral trend one way or the other. Even the aquatints of old Audubon, intended to be merely informative of the native birdlife, seem now emblematic of what kind of native art we are apt to have, if any.

—GLENWAY WESCOTT (1939)

A day that commences with a visit to the dentist can go nowhere but up. Dr. Magnani wants to sell me several thousand dollars' worth of false teeth. His nurse, sounding like a shoe salesman, says—I think it is supposed to be complimentary—that I have a wide arch.

—E. J. KAHN, JR. (1987)

JANUARY 16

I see that to some men their relation to mankind is all important. It is fatal in their eyes to outrage the opinions and customs of their fellow-men. Failure and success are therefore never proved by them by absolute and universal tests. . . . The Englishman and American are subject equally to many national superstitions with the Hindoos and Chinese.

—HENRY DAVID THOREAU (1852)

*V*ery cold. Got up late. Worked on the book. Took a walk up to the park and to see the skaters in Rockefeller Center. Then in the evening went off to a dinner of the Euthanasia Society. Mostly doctors. Made a short speech. They thought I was Maxwell Anderson so I let it go at that.

—SHERWOOD ANDERSON (1940)

*S*ome years ago, mailing a tax return to the IRS at Holtsville, N.Y. 00501, I got to wondering just what and where this Holtsville was, and Shawn agreed a visit might result in a "Talk" piece [for *The New Yorker*]. I have an ulterior motive: to see if I can't get somebody out there to correct their computers' spelling of my wife's name as "Eleanuor." I am hospitably enough received. The IRS woman I have lunch with is an admirable public servant; she will not let me pay for her hero and Coke and put it on my expense account. That makes me feel guilty, because she could have bought her combo more cheaply at her federal cafeteria than at the restaurant I drag her to so I can buy myself a drink. She has some complaints about her own taxes—but only the Long Island real-estate sort. . . . I am advised that there is no way anybody anywhere in Holtsville can, without recourse to mysterious forces far away and much higher up, contrive to delete that "u" from "Eleanuor."

—E. J. KAHN, JR. (1987)

JANUARY 17

*G*oing nowhere, very thoroughly. Same tack with strong headwinds. Steward made doughnuts. Like lead. Fred gobbled them. Wonderful shrimp salad for me. My [diamond] ring is a consolation. For all my spiteful remarks about Herring Gut and the degeneration of sea-going descendants of my ancestors, I know that I would never have had such a ring

22

had I stayed on my father's "intellectual farm." Maine waters
send forth men who may not read without moving their lips,
but they can hire or marry people who can. Is that so far
from the old kings and nobles who fought and hunted but
had to hire clerks to keep the records? Charlemagne could
not read, but he was no ignoramus. Oh Dora! Now you're
rationalizing. Please bring up your own children to be full
people, both strong of mind and body.

—DOROTHEA MOULTON BALANO (1912)

*H*ulbert Footner, the novelist . . . is full of amusing anec-
dotes about the yokels of Calvert county, the most remote
and backward county in the State [of Maryland]. Not long
ago, a farmer named Gantt was murdered down there. . . .
Footner knew Gantt, and often employed him at odd jobs.
Some time ago, he said, he set him to work painting a room.
It was to be done in two colors of blue, and Gantt labored at
it for weeks. He would first paint the light blue part and then
proceed to the dark blue part. Every time he made this switch
some of the dark blue paint got splashed on the light blue
part and the light blue part had to be done over again. When
this was undertaken, some of the light blue paint splashed
on the dark blue part, and so there was need for another
coat. Footner says that Gantt finally got seven coats on the
room. Footner then fired him, and Gantt left muttering. . . .
He always carried all his money in his pocket, and was fond
of exhibiting it when drunk. This habit cost him his life.

—H. L. MENCKEN (1939)

[At Parker's Ferry, Yemassee, South Carolina] *T*he very
cold night cleared away the clouds, and by evening the sunshine had warmed us up a little; so we went for a long walk.
There was an incomparable sunset, and as it happened we
saw it through the Negroes' cemetery, the voodoo cemetery,
which is a grove of the oldest, most twisted, moss-wound
oaks: lumpy molten gold, and a stream of pale bright green
running away to the south, and a bank of pale bright purple

23

which finally caught fire. Then suddenly it died away, leaving smoke, soot, silt. Then the full moon rose, just between the swamp and the marsh, and I went down on the levee alone to watch it. The tide was rushing out with a noise, and it shook the golden reflection as if it were a flag whipping in a wind. All around me there were water birds ill at ease, and I heard what William says may have been turtles, growling or barking.

—GLENWAY WESCOTT (1946)

JANUARY 18

Clear and pleasant. I was Calld from Mrs Moore to Steven Hinkleys wife at 10 hour morning. Shee was delivered at 11 of a son. I part drest the infant and was Calld to return to Mrs Moore. Find her more unwell. Shee was delivered at 4 hour 30 minutes of a son. The Children were the first Born of thier mamys. I returnd home at 8 hour Evening. Brother Ebenezer Moore sleeps here. I made Beds, washt dishes, swept house, and got supper. I feel some fatagud.

—MARTHA BALLARD (1796)

When Father Coughlin, the Detroit radio priest, appeared before one of the committees of Congress Mrs. [Alice Roosevelt] Longworth met him at the Capitol. She invited him to drop in to see her some day, and told him that she served cocktails almost every afternoon. Coughlin showed up the very next afternoon, accompanied by three other priests. He seemed somewhat stiff and suspicious, and drank only one cocktail. A few weeks later he appeared in Washington again, called up Mrs. Longworth, and told her he'd like to make her another visit. This time he appeared with two priests and drank two cocktails. A little while later he came the third time. Now he had only one priest—and drank three cocktails.

Mrs. Longworth told [Frank R.] Kent that she expected him to appear alone the next time and to drink at least a dozen cocktails.

—H. L. Mencken (1935)

JANUARY 19

I rose about 8 o'clock and read a chapter in Hebrew and three chapters in Greek. I said my prayers, and had boiled milk for breakfast. The weather was cold and cloudy, the wind northeast, and it snowed a little all the morning, which, however, did not hinder me from calling for my daughter about 12 o'clock and carrying her to Mr. Lindsay's to dinner, who was very kind to her. I ate some boiled chicken for dinner, and Mr. A-d-l-n dined there likewise. After dinner we sat and talked till 4 o'clock and then drank tea. About six Mr. Lindsay went to Sir Robert D-s-r and left me and his wife together, and I gave her a ticket for the masquerade and she told me her dress. Here I stayed till supper (only I sent away my daughter about seven) and I ate some roast lamb, and went home about eleven and said my prayers. I kissed the maid till my seed ran from me.

—William Byrd (1718)

*O*ur new TV set arrives from 47th Street Photo. The delivery man is an Orthodox Jew, in full regalia. I wonder if he will accept a tip. As he is leaving, he says to me, "*Gesund*—you know what that means?" He knows a lapsed Jew when he sees one. I know what "gesundheit" means. I have been sneezing all day. I say, tentatively proffering a tip, "Sure, and *Gesund* to you." He accepts my pourboire. Ellie says later that Orthodox Jews are not supposed to look strange women in the eye, but this one did.

—E. J. Kahn, Jr. (1987)

JANUARY 20

*D*on't trust children with edge tools. Don't trust man, great God, with more power than he has, until he has learned to use that little better. What a hell should we make of the world if we could do what we would! Put a button on the foil till the young fencers have learned not to put each other's eyes out. Is it not true that our power does increase exactly in the measure that we learn how to use it?

—RALPH WALDO EMERSON (1832)

*C*hang and Eng, the Siamese twins, died last week at their home in North Carolina, surrounded by their wives and children. One died of paralysis, it would seem, and the other, though in good health, survived but a couple of hours. Their physician, if they had any, did not venture on amputation, cutting the Mezentian bond.

—GEORGE TEMPLETON STRONG (1874)

*A*t Cambridge. Much amusement from watching the Baptist Church burn. It is curious to see such masses of men under the influence of excitement. It is always fascinating to watch fire. . . . I was much impressed also by the extraordinary quickness with which they conquered the flames. Wonderful development, indeed, are these lately added powers which so extend our control over the world! The pyramids are a monument of immense labor; but in all probability they represent rather patience than force. The marvel in our works is the speed with which we do them. Where the nineteenth century has gained is in quickness of life.

—GAMALIEL BRADFORD (1883)

26

JANUARY 21

*H*ere is a case of a soldier I found among the crowded cots in the Patent Office. He likes to have some one to talk to, and we will listen to him. He got badly hit in his leg and side at Fredericksburgh that eventful Saturday, 13th of December. He lay the succeeding two days and nights helpless on the field, between the city and those grim terraces of batteries; his company and regiment had been compell'd to leave him to his fate. . . . At the end of some fifty hours he was brought off, with other wounded, under a flag of truce. I ask him how the rebels treated him as he lay during those two days and nights within reach of them—whether they came to him— whether they abused him? He answers that several of the rebels, soldiers and others, came to him, at one time and another. A couple of them, who were together, spoke roughly and sarcastically, but nothing worse. One middle-aged man, however, who seem'd to be moving around the field, among the dead and wounded, for benevolent purposes, came to him in a way he will never forget; treated our soldier kindly, bound up his wounds, cheer'd him, gave him a couple of biscuits, and a drink of whiskey and water; ask'd him if he could eat some beef. This good Secesh, however, did not change our soldier's position, for it might have caused the blood to burst from the wounds, clotted and stagnated. Our soldier is from Pennsylvania; has had a pretty severe time; the wounds proved to be bad ones. But he retains a good heart, and is at present on the gain. (It is not uncommon for the men to remain on the field this way, one, two, or even four or five days.)

—WALT WHITMAN (1863)

*W*ent on as Section Officer of Day at 10:30. Unpacked chair. They used to kid me for toting a chair to the Great War. Could sell it to-day for any price. No substitute for chairs. Nor for fires. Tried to start one, but our only stick wouldn't burn.

—HOWARD O'BRIEN (1918)

$\mathscr{D}$r. Marjorie Nicolson, dean of Smith College, was here for lunch yesterday. . . . She has been in Washington attending a meeting of the Smith Alumnae Association. With her there was young Constance Morrow, sister to Mrs. Lindbergh. . . . Dr. William A. Neilson, president of Smith, was at Flemington, New Jersey, at the time of the opening of the Hauptmann trial and saw a great deal of the Lindberghs. He told Dr. Nicolson that Mrs. Lindbergh laughed at the newspaper accounts of her heroic bearing on the stand. She said that the kidnapping was now an old story to the Morrow family, and that they had begun to look at it objectively—in fact, they had reached such a point that they made limericks on the names of the witnesses at the trial. All of the shock and sorrow were endured and survived long ago. Lindbergh, according to Dr. Neilson, goes to the trial as to a show, and is delighted that he has so good a seat. Like his wife, he has absolutely no heat against Hauptmann. The thing, he feels, is now out of his hands, and what interests him mainly is the sheer drama of it.

—H. L. Mencken (1935)

JANUARY 22

$\mathscr{T}$o the club with Father. A good paper on the "Historical View of Jesus." Father spoke finely. It amuses me to see how people listen and applaud *now* what was hooted at twenty years ago. The talk lasted until two, and then the hungry philosophers remembered they had bodies and rushed away, still talking. . . . Got a snow-slide on my bonnet, so made another in the P.M., and in the evening to the Antislavery Festival. All the old faces and many new ones. Glad I have lived in the time of this great movement, and known its heroes so well. War times suit me, as I am a fighting *May*.

—Louisa May Alcott (1868)

$\mathcal{G}$oing through a big city newspaper my eye picked up an obscure item with a date line from my home town. I have had this happen again and again. In fact, I will pick up the name of this town, and focus on it, when it is buried in the middle of a newspaper story over which my eye is merely roaming. This suggests that getting "attention" is far more a matter of what you say than it is of the size space you say it in. In short, it is doubtful whether "attention," like the Kingdom of Heaven, can be taken by force. The reasons for using large space are of other kinds.

—JAMES WEBB YOUNG (1943)

$\mathcal{I}$t could save people like me a lot of grief if people who print up date books and calendars would just put "Super Bowl" on them along with "Yom Kippur" and "Thanksgiving."

—E. J. KAHN, JR. (1987)

JANUARY 23

$\mathcal{A}$ngels. Rainy, stormy, beans and dish-water, for break-fast at the Frenchman's; dish-water and beans for dinner, and both articles warmed over for supper.

—MARK TWAIN (1865)

$\mathcal{Y}$esterday they gave [Earl] Browder [leader of the U.S. Communist party] four years in jail for a minor offense which usually would go by unmentioned. Obviously the Roosevelt government has decided to put up Browder's head on a pike, to satisfy the clamor of reactionaries who think Fascists and Communists paddle the same canoe. Browder is out on bail and spoke last night at a Lenin memorial meeting in the Garden. I think it was mistake of taste, a real error to say, as he did, that Roosevelt is interested in war and munitions because a son of his married a Du Pont girl. They will probably find some other silly misdemeanor with which to convict another Communist leader or two and then call it quits.

—Clifford Odets (1940)

To Dr. Gorham's at dawn for my annual checkup. A pleasant surprise: on his admirable scales I weigh a pound and a half less than a year ago. . . . I reach the office at ten, having already walked the dog and had a thoroughgoing probe. It's easy to feel smug in such circumstances. Dr. Gorham pronounced me fit enough for someone my age, and he didn't seem too interested in my gout. When I see him again next year—assuming there's no need for an intervening consultation—I must remember to tell him about a really awful senescent thing that happened when I got on a bus this morning a few minutes after leaving him. A young woman offered me her seat.

—E. J. Kahn, Jr. (1987)

JANUARY 24

Friday night and Satterday were extream cold, so that the Harbour frozen up, and to the Castle. This day so cold that the Sacramental Bread is frozen pretty hard, and rattles sadly as broken into the Plates.

—Samuel Sewall (1686)

In the evening went to a party at Mrs. Moncure Robinson's, a dance with one carpet up. . . . Home at 1 o'clk in a bad humour with myself. Am spending my time foolishly and un-profitably, when I should be doing much. Yet, except study, I have nothing to do. I have the ability to work but no work before me, and this waiting thro the best years of life is a miserable affair. Must write something, no matter what. Always feel better satisfied when thus employed. It is creating something, and there is an effect produced.

—SIDNEY GEORGE FISHER (1839)

*M*y second hyacinth bloomed pale blue, like a timid hope, and I took the omen for a good one, as I *am* getting on, and have more than I can do of the work that I once went begging for. Enjoyed the little spring my little flower made for me, and Buzzy, my pet fly, moved into the sweet mansion from his hanging garden in the ivy pot.

—LOUISA MAY ALCOTT (1868)

JANUARY 25

I had dinner last night [in New York] with Theodore Dreiser. I called for him at the Ansonia Hotel, and after a drink there we started out in the snow to find a restaurant. Dreiser had in mind an Italian place in 45th street, but when we got there it couldn't be found. A taxi driver then directed us to 48th street, and after heavy struggles in the snow we finally got there. Once I lost my footing, fell into Dreiser and knocked him down. A minute later he came down on his own, and with a very heavy thump. He was, however, not injured. The dinner was the usual Italian thing, and we drank a quart and a half of bad Chianti. We sat until after 12 o'clock. During the last hour or two we were the only customers in the restaurant. Dreiser is full of a plan to go back to California, and then to make a motor trip to Alaska. It appears that a motor road clear to Sitka has been opened. . . . He proposed that I join the party.

—H. L. MENCKEN (1935)

*W*akened early by the clop-clop of a horse's hoofs coming down our city street, followed by the rattle of milk bottles. Thought for a moment I was back in my boyhood, in that automobileless world which the generation after mine cannot even picture. Later in the day I talked with a taxi driver who was bemoaning his inability to get any recreation, now that he couldn't drive for pleasure. Told him how I used to ride with my girl on a streetcar, to the city limits, and then take a walk in the country. He was appalled at the notion.

—JAMES WEBB YOUNG (1943)

JANUARY 26

*D*isappointed in D.'s [Charles Dickens] appearance. We have heard him called 'the handsomest man in London' &c. He is of the middle height, (under if anything) with a large expressive eye, regular nose, matted, curling, wet-looking black hair, a dissipated looking mouth with a vulgar draw to it, a muddy olive complexion, *stubby* fingers & a hand by no means patrician, a hearty, off-hand manner, far from well bred, & a rapid, dashing way of talking. He looks 'wide awake,' 'up to anything,' full of cleverness, with quick feelings & great ardour. You admire him, & there is a fascination about him which keeps your eyes on him, yet you cannot get over the impression that he is a low bred man. Tom Appleton says "Take the genius out of his face & there are a thousand young London shop-keepers, about the theaters & eating houses who look exactly like him." He has what I suppose to be the true Cockney cut.

—RICHARD HENRY DANA (1842)

When I took the ether [at the dentist's] my consciousness amounted to this: I put my finger on myself in order to keep the place, otherwise I should never have returned to this world.

—HENRY DAVID THOREAU (1856)

The solemn boom of cannon today announced that the convention have passed the ordinance of secession. We must take a reef in our patriotism and narrow it down to State limits. Mine still sticks out all around the borders of the State.

—ANONYMOUS (1861)

Spoke before the Legislature at Austin. But a comedian getting up before one of those bodies of men is just lost. I would be like Rudee Valee trying to sing before an audience composed of all grand opera singers. He would just be outclassed. And that's the way I was.

—WILL ROGERS (1931)

JANUARY 27

Attended the auction of Deacon Brown's effects a little while to-day,—a great proportion of old traps, rubbish, or trumpery, which began to accumulate in his father's day, and now, after lying half a century in his garret and other dust-holes, is not burned, but surviving neighbors collect and view it, and buy it, and carefully transport it to their garrets and dust-holes, to lie there till their estates are settled, when it will start again. Among his effects was a dried tapeworm and various articles too numerous and worthless to mention. A pair of old snow-shoes is almost regularly sold on these occasions, though none of this generation has seen them worn here.

—HENRY DAVID THOREAU (1854)

[On board ship from New York to Savannah] The sea, the sea, the crinkling sea. Here in my chair with a book and the sssh of the water in my ears. Dull people go by. My ears are troubled with inanities. I hear clatter concerning ghastly trivialities. But the sum of all life is not trivial or it does not appear so. . . . The clouds in the east reach out like hands. They beckon and signal, like fingers speaking of lands that never were. They talk to me of dreams that I had in my youth. "Better lands than this," they say, "await you." "Out! Come forth, Shake off the thing that holds you. Spring up into the blue. Be spirit not matter". . . . Nothing is more interesting to me than just the silent passing of moods in the mind, hour after hour, day after day, year after year though nothing is said. A man draws near—you dislike him. He goes again and is forgotten. The sun comes out. You say silently to yourself—how beautiful. Life is good. In its light colorful dreams and moods rise and fall like the waves of the sea—all in silence. The sun goes under a cloud. Life is not so pleasing any more. . . . On this boat sitting alone I have noticed this—dwelt on it. I have watched my moods shift chameleon like from grave to pleasant but with never a word to me from anyone.

—THEODORE DREISER (1916)

A few degrees warmer but still 10 below. I did some work in the morning and then went off to town with Doctor Henry, sitting in a small room, back of his office and listening in on his conversation with patients.

—SHERWOOD ANDERSON (1938)

34

JANUARY 28

*R*ain and wind all day and all night. Chili-beans and dish-water three times today as usual and some kind of "slum" which the Frenchman called "hash." Hash be damned!

—MARK TWAIN (1865)

*W*rote in a.m. Smoke all a.m. & at 1 found floor on fire under fire place. Still alarm. Men came pulled up floor & found beams burning. Put it out. Shoddy work & dangerous. Not upset. Kept cool. Long awake, silly women kept up such a fuss all night.

—LOUISA MAY ALCOTT (1888)

*S*till enroute [to Savannah]. . . . Woke to hear the first breakfast bell clanging. . . . Open my window & looked out. A soft south wind was blowing—very summery & gay. The sun was out too—lovely. All the cold and drearyness of N.Y. gone. . . . Went out . . . & stood in the very prow of the boat watching the ship's nose cut the water forty feet below, feeling the cool air blowing over me, alluring dreams of a new heaven & new earth to sway me. I thought how wonderful it would be to create a new world out of a pathless sea. The water to my right in the shade of the boat was black like coal or black glass. . . . Sea weed was about. I thought of what Columbus saw days before he discovered land. . . . We cut on, mile after mile.

—THEODORE DREISER (1916)

I read today that [United Mine Workers president] John Lewis said Roosevelt had many words, talents, and abilities, but that he is essentially superficial. . . . Brilliant, but super-ficial, like an actor of the John Barrymore sort—style, swing,

35

background, ease and facility, but superficial. And yet how the American people, myself included, yearn towards this man, as to a comforting father. . . . By virtue of its youth the American character is always yearning for a hero, someone to look up to and admire, a person to lead and express by his very being all the yearning of the boyish heart.

—CLIFFORD ODETS (1940)

JANUARY 29

The way I manage, I still save money. The Enlisch tong is becoming easier and easier for me.

—JACOB SAUL LANZIT (1859)

We had the unusual good fortune to catch our Chief Magistrate [Abraham Lincoln] disengaged, just after a Cabinet council, and enjoyed an hour's free and easy talk with him. We were not boring him, for we made several demonstrations toward our exit, which he retarded severally by a little incident he remembered or a little anecdote he had "heered" in Illinois. He is a barbarian, Scythian, yahoo, or gorilla, in respect of outside polish . . . but a most sensible, straightforward, honest old codger. . . . His evident integrity and simplicity of purpose would compensate for worse grammar than his, and for even more intense provincialism and rusticity. He told us a lot of stories. Something was said about the pressure of the extreme anti-slavery party in Congress and in the newspapers for legislation about the status of all slaves. "Wa-al," says Abe Lincoln, "that reminds me of a party of Methodist parsons that was travelling in Illinois when I was a boy thar, and had a branch to cross, ye know, because the waters was up. And they got considerin' and discussin' how they should git across it, and they talked about it for two hours, and one on 'em thought they had ought to cross one way when they got there, and another another way, and they got quarrellin' about it, till at last an old brother put in, and he says, says he, 'Brethren, this here talk ain't no use. I never cross a river until I come to it.' "

—GEORGE TEMPLETON STRONG (1862)

*T*he old, old thing. We shall *have* to stand the weather, but as J. says we *won't* stand the dish-water and beans any longer, by God.

—MARK TWAIN (1865)

I have just asked the wireless man & he tells me we should get to Savannah by eleven. A pearly mist encircles us at a distance, landwards, I think. Immediately beyond the prow of the boat, say a thousand yards, is a rainbow of mist, very pale and diaphanous but a rainbow still. I stand at the prow of the boat and note a rainbow about my head—a fact which pleases me. . . . I watch the land go by, thinking of rice & cotton fields & wild ducks. . . . Savannah in the distance—a delicate penciling of buildings and chimneys over a flat waste of brown marsh grass. . . . We make the wharf in town. No bridges. Negroes. The river front is like that of New York— lumber yards, oil yards, coal packets, ware houses. Negroes fighting for money. . . . Go ashore. Buses and small Fords. Negro town. Every house a porch or covered doorstep. . . . Old low square brick houses with fretted iron balconies and open doors & windows. Canary birds hung out in cages. Palm trees—yes real ones. All trees still green & the grass. I feel very hot & wish I had on a lighter suit & underwear.

—THEODORE DREISER (1916)

37

JANUARY 30

*L*ectured this week at Newton-Corner, W. Newton, Fitchburg & Waltham. This lecturing about at villages, gives one curious development in the differences of manners & notions among men. The Newton-corner & Jamaica Plains Committee came for me in a carriage & drove me to & from. The Committee (of one) from W. Newton walked me all the way, in the worst walking we have had this year, to the station & back, & gave me no tea, kept me waiting while others went to tea, hurried me off by the cars to avoid the trouble & expenses of driving me to my house, & entertained me all the way with a homily on philanthropy & humanity.

—RICHARD HENRY DANA (1853)

*M*oved to the new hotel, just opened—good fare and coffee that a Christian may drink without jeopardizing his eternal soul.

—MARK TWAIN (1865)

*S*avannah on Sunday. Church bells. Negroes idling. Police station just back of this house. Palms look so inviting. Can't believe they are native to this region but afterwards find them growing wild. . . . Segregation of blacks an odd but necessary custom. Character of Southerners—peaked, whiny, suspicious, jealous, touchy—an offensive company. All this is due to the perversion of naturalness following upon a promoralistic atmosphere. The result of sex suppression is jealousy, suspicion, envy, false witness, false pretense, a better than thou viewpoint. Women going about like saints craving subconsciously what they sniff at openly—sex. It is a horrible case of race or national perversion which will end in disaster. The south as it stands today will be destroyed. It will pass away.

—THEODORE DREISER (1916)

38

JANUARY 31

I rose at 5 o'clock and read two chapters in Hebrew and some Greek in Lucian. I said my prayers and ate boiled milk for breakfast. My wife quarreled with me about not sending for Mrs. Dunn when it rained to [lend her John]. She threatened to kill herself but had more discretion. I danced my dance and then read some English about [love]. It rained again all the morning. I ate some roast shoat for dinner. In the afternoon Nurse was taken sick of a [purging]. I took a walk to see the boatwright at work. My wife came into good humor again and we resolved to live for the future in love and peace. At night I ate some battered eggs with her and drank some cider. I said my prayers and had good health, good thoughts, and good humor, thank God Almighty. The wind was still northeast as it was when the moon was at full and since that a good deal of rain has fallen. The boy whose thigh was swollen grew worse.

—WILLIAM BYRD (1711)

*P*aris doesn't seem especially excited about us. Its interest exclusively in our francs. Sam Browne belts have no thrill for chambermaids, cabbies, *maquereaux,* shopkeepers, etc. *Sales cochons!* Not like down South, where a kid helped me carry bag half a mile and saluted proudly, assuring me that between "comrades" there was no silver for service. Paris shows the *militaire* a hard, rouged face, and an open palm, all too plainly itching.

—HOWARD O'BRIEN (1918)

⊰FEBRUARY⊱

FEBRUARY 1

*A*t 3 went to a matinee party. . . . I wanted to see the young people & the fashions that have grown up since I was in the gay world. . . . There were five rooms open and they were well filled, everything very handsome. . . . The whole assembly to me had an animal look, this poor human nature seeking to conceal & adorn itself by bits of silk & muslin. I thought of the clothes philosophy—Imagine us all suddenly stripped, the reality of us revealed, how shocked we would be. Cover up our miserable bodies, decorate them by our fancy, and then our minds can have intercourse & we can respect & love. This shows the superiority of mind. Elephants & monkeys, clever as they are, cannot do this.

—SIDNEY GEORGE FISHER (1866)

*A*rranged "Hospital Sketches and War Stories" for a book. By taking out all Biblical allusions, and softening all allusions to rebs., the book may be made "quite perfect," I am told. Anything to suit customers.

—LOUISA MAY ALCOTT (1868)

40

FEBRUARY 2

*S*avannah. Drove out two miles to an auction sale of 180 negroes. They looked serious, and the girls shed some tears. They were sold in families, and after they were knocked off I thought they looked anxious, and I noticed that a mother who was sold with her seven children sobbed very much. It is always a sad sight.

—AMOS A. LAWRENCE (1860)

*R*eports of strikes in Austria, and hopes of early peace. Funny how notions change. Back home we drooled about "democracy" and "glory." Like Burgundy wine, that stuff doesn't stand a sea voyage. Most of the people whom the papers squeak about being "eager for the Front" about as eager for the smallpox.

—HOWARD O'BRIEN (1918)

*L*ast night and night before we had rip-roaring airraids over Bassano, three or four a night—one stands shivering in the window and watches the *searchlights* & the electric sparkle of machine guns and the great red flare of bombs that explode with a thunderous snarl that rips the horizon—and the shrapnel bullets and cases simply rain about our heads. The joke is that you get up in the morning and go about Bassano, just nose in the air for horrors, and try eagerly to find where the bombs exploded, where the widows were made & the orphans bereaved and, nothing,—streets placidly empty—the famous bridge that they are aiming at—arid and untroubled as ever . . . Of course you do find things smashed up a bit here & there, a couple of roofs mashed in or a room turned inside out, or somebody's garden given a new conformation, but it's nothing at all to compare with the wild bril-

41

liance of the airraid the night before that makes you expect smoking ruins & entrails smeared about the paving stones.

—JOHN DOS PASSOS (1918)

T. S. Eliot has been here [Baltimore] all week, lecturing on poetry at the Johns Hopkins. . . . Eliot turned out to be a tall, somewhat ungainly fellow, looking more like an Oxford man than any Englishman. He said that he was having a quiet but tolerable time at Harvard. He lectures once a week, has a weekly tea-party open to undergraduates, and also gives a course in modern English literature—that is, since 1890. He told me that he found the last somewhat difficult, for he seldom reads modern literature, and in the main dislikes it. He said that one of the undergraduates brought a pretty girl to tea one day, and almost broke up the party. Eliot served notice that he'd prefer to have no female guests. . . . An amiable fellow, but with little to say. . . . I drank a quart of home-brew beer, and Eliot got down two Scotches. A dull evening.

—H. L. MENCKEN (1933)

FEBRUARY 3

Mr. Emerson, who returned last week from lecturing, on the Mississippi, having been gone but a month, tells me that he saw boys skating on the Mississippi, and on Lake Erie, and on the Hudson, and has no doubt they are skating on Lake Superior. Probably at Boston he might have seen them skating on the Atlantic.

—HENRY DAVID THOREAU (1856)

$\mathcal{D}$ined at the Frenchman's in order to let Dick see how he does things. Had "Hell-fire" soup and the old regular beans and dish-water. The Frenchman has 4 kinds of soup which he furnishes to customers only on great occasions. They are popularly known among the boarders as "Hell-fire," "General Debility," "Insanity" and "Sudden Death," but it is not possible to describe them.

—MARK TWAIN (1865)

FEBRUARY 4

$\mathcal{T}$he Bostonians are making horrid asses of themselves with Mr. Charles Dickens, poor man. He'll have his revenge, though, when he gets home and takes up his pen again. How people will study his next productions to see if they can find any portraits! However, we shall be fully as bad, with our Boz ball.

—GEORGE TEMPLETON STRONG (1842)

[With black Union troops in Florida] $\mathcal{G}$eneral Scammon our Post-Commander desired to see us so we went to call on him this morning. . . . He [said] that the most intelligent scout and the most effective one at this Post, was a colored man, a former slave—and that he sent in the best reports—in proof of which he read us a long, well-written report in regard to the movements of the rebels in this vicinity—adding that this scout never came in without bringing in prisoners. He also told us that he had written a letter asking for this man a Lieutenancy. . . . High testimony for the poor slave. The rebels have offered three thousand dollars for him—so they know his worth. The Gen. asked him how he had learned to write: to which he replied, "I stole it sir little by little, when I was on the plantation."

—ESTHER HILL HAWKS (1865)

$\mathcal{I}$ woke up at 7. Often I find that I have started praying before I am really awake, just as I fall asleep praying, Lord Jesus, have mercy on us sinners—over and over. Usually I am praying in a state of desperation—certainly not peacefully and confidently as I should. That is to say, during these particular days. So I come back to praying for myself. But it is the misery of waking to the thought of a drunken priest in our midst. Oh God have mercy on Father John. Pope John, pray for him. The priest's name is not John but there are so many Johns I'll call him that and be praying for all priests with their well-stocked bars. "Don't be Jansenistic, Dorothy." "Don't be prudish."

—DOROTHY DAY (1969)

FEBRUARY 5

$\mathcal{G}$o to see father who fails fast. Say good by as he seems nearly gone. In a stupor half the time. Opened his eyes & smiled at me. No pain but so weak. The oil is nearly gone. A sad p.m. Lay still & Dr. read Coleridge, Wordsworth to me so I should not think of sad things. Slept well. Made a poem.

—LOUISA MAY ALCOTT (1888)

$\mathcal{A}$ most excellent day of walking with Van . . . up the Brenta Valley. . . . In the bed of the stream, as the road climbed, were lots and lots of small alpine guns, sitting on their tails and pointing their muzzles up like dogs howling. . . . We kept on up and were produced by a sentry before a bunch of officers. Everybody was very pleasant and wondered who we were. American Red Cross had an exotic flavor to them that was quite entrancing. . . . After much labor & panting, we reached the abode of the commandante, who inside of a little shack in a crevice in the cliff, sat like Old King Cole with his capitanos & tenantes about him, drinking amid a great array of bottles. We drank white wine with him in solemn splendour; He out of a special glass—a sort of curved beaker—while one stood by who continually wiped glasses. . . . Home by road with long loose strides and that feeling of being euzooné that comes from great exercise. Followed by a most delicious dinner of rice & cauliflower and by a reading of poetry in bed afterwards and a sleep of marvellous comfort, punctuated by the usual airraid.

—JOHN DOS PASSOS (1918)

In the crowded subway at 9:15, as I was on my way going to Wall Street, one businessman type said to another, a seat having been vacated at Fourteenth Street, "You sit down. I sat down yesterday." And the other accepted and sat. Perhaps they were friends. In any case, I observed them all the way downtown, and they neither exchanged any further words nor glanced at one another.

—GLENWAY WESCOTT (1955)

FEBRUARY 6

*P*articularly do I feel impressed with sadness when looking on a little girl. I remember the lot of woman which is to be her destiny! . . . To be gifted with quick & sensitive feelings, with warm & passionate affections, with genius, with rare talents perchance—& all this to be crushed & wasted, & borne back upon the heart, till the bitter medecine works at length the healing of the soul.—And is not this blessed healing, this withdrawal of the affections from earth & fixing of them on eternal happiness worth all that must be borne for it?—Doubtless far more—and yet I am sometimes tempted to think with the Indian woman who said "Let not my child be a girl, for very sad is the lot of woman!"

—SOPHIE DU PONT (1838)

$\mathscr{A}$t night went to see the President [Lincoln] on behalf of Mrs Fitz, a loyal widow of Mississippi owning a cotton plantation there, and from whom the U S Army had taken all her slaves amounting to 47, and 10,000 bushels of corn—She is now a refugee in St Louis, reduced to indigence. She asks no compensation for her slaves, but wishes the government to give her a sufficient number of negroes out of those accumulated upon its hands to work her farm the ensuing season, and enable her to raise a crop of cotton, she to pay them out of the proceeds the same wages which the government pays those it employs. I made the proposition to the President thinking it reasonable and just. . . . He became very much excited, and . . . said with great vehemence he had rather take a rope and hang himself than to do it. That there were a great many poor women who had never had any property at all who were suffering as much as Mrs Fitz—that her condition was a necessary consequence of the rebellion, and that the government could not make good the losses occasioned by rebels. I reminded him that she was loyal, and that her property had been taken from her by her own government, and was now being used by it, and I thought it a case eminently proper for some sort of remuneration, and her demand reasonable, and certainly entitled to respectful consideration. He replied that she had lost no property—that her slaves were free when they were taken, and that she was entitled to no compensation. I called his attention to the fact that a portion of her slaves, at least, had been taken in 1862, before his proclamation, and put upon our gun boats, when he replied in a very excited manner that he had rather *throw up,* than to do what was asked, and would not do anything about it. I left him in no very good humor.

—ORVILLE BROWNING (1864)

FEBRUARY 7

$\mathscr{I}$ have been to Plymouth and stood on the Rock, and felt that it was grown more important by the growth of this nation in the minutes that I stood there. But Barnabas Hedge ought not—no man ought—to own the rock of Plymouth.

—RALPH WALDO EMERSON (1834)

*D*reamlike travelling on the railroad. The towns through which I pass between Philadelphia and New York make no distinct impression. They are like pictures on a wall. The more, that you can read all the way in the car a French novel.

—RALPH WALDO EMERSON (1843)

*A*fter dinner I decided to go down to the University of Pennsylvania, my object being to find the free Dispensary and see if I could not obtain treatment for my nervous trouble free of charge. I walked all the way, feeling for all my previous terrors, as if the world were good and lovely and as if I was getting rapidly well. I reached the University at 3 P.M. and went straight to the Dispensary door but when I got there I could not go in. I was ashamed. . . . Accordingly I started toward the city but when I got as far as the bridge that spans the Schuylkill at Walnut street, I recovered my courage and went back. When I reached the sidewalk opposite however a negro was cleaning the windows. I felt as if he would know what I was coming for and so I strolled by again. . . . When I had thought it all over and reasoned with myself once more, I made another effort and this time I succeeded. The negro was still in the window but I walked nervously past. When I reached the hall I found an ambiguous sign which confused me as to the whereabouts of the dispensary, and so I stood about the hall too shamefaced to do anything in particular. Finally I screwed up my courage and went into the drug store and asked. "It's through that door, out in the courtyard there, but your too late said the clerk. It wont be open until Monday." Rebuff, in a way, as this was, it was a relief to me. I strolled comfortably if not gaily out.

—THEODORE DREISER (1903)

47

FEBRUARY 8

*W*omen have less accurate measure of time than men. There is a clock in Adam: none in Eve.

—RALPH WALDO EMERSON (1836)

*M*r. [John Quincy] Adams chose wisely and according to his constitution, when, on leaving the Presidency, he went into Congress. He is no literary old gentleman, but a bruiser, and loves the *melee*. When they talk about his age and venerableness and nearness to the grave, he knows better; he is like one of those old cardinals, who, as quick as he is chosen Pope, throws away his crutches and his crookedness, and is as straight as a boy.

—RALPH WALDO EMERSON (1843)

*W*e went into Bassano to buy vast amounts of food & drink to celebrate. While paying for some condensed milk I noticed the clerk begin to get flustered. He even refused to put paper round the cans—the shutters came down with a bang & Bragg said "they're shelling the town." Whereupon we went out and found the streets full of scurrying people and bang of shutters being pulled down by nervous storekeepers. Sh-sh-Sh-Sh-sss—broom!—overhead and off in the corner of town where the big cement bridge is! We went, laden with bottles & packages to the big piazza—passing the spot where someone had just dropped a chianti bottle in their flight. . . . Other shells. A big French camion full of soldiers passing hurriedly through, stalled in front of us, the driver calling out wildly 'vite—vite'—Another shell. A man jumping out from the back to crank the car slipped on the flagstones and took the most wonderful cropper ever seen of mortal man—Laughter drowned out the next shell—The camion got started at last & scuttled away and the square was empty—except for four foolish ambulance drivers waving bottles & laughing, with

48

their mouths full of chocolate. But by that time the shelling had stopped.

—JOHN DOS PASSOS (1918)

FEBRUARY 9

[In early Carolina] *T*hey brought us 2 Cocks, and pull'd their larger Feathers off, never plucking the lesser, but singeing them off. I took one of these Fowls in my Hand, to make it cleaner than the *Indian* had, pulling out his Guts and Liver, which I laid in a Bason; notwithstanding which, he kept such a Struggling for a considerable time, that I had much ado to hold him in my Hands. The *Indians* laugh'd at me, and told me, that *Eno-Will* had taken a Cock of an *Indian* that was not at home, and the Fowl was design'd for another Use. I conjectur'd, that he was design'd for an Offering to their God, who, they say, hurts them, (which is the Devil.) In this Struggling, he bled afresh, and there issued out of his Body more Blood than commonly such Creatures afford. Notwithstanding all this, we cook'd him, and eat him; and if he was design'd for him, cheated the Devil.

—JOHN LAWSON (1701)

*R*eturned on the horse—found dear Nora there—waltzed a while. I am passionately fond of this exercise—but could I for a moment suppose that my partiality for it would *ever* induce me to attempt it in public, or with a gentleman, I should *never* try it again—Most religious people so decidedly disapprove of dancing that I often have doubts as to its being an innocent amusement—One thing I am sure is that in cities, waltz parties lead to much evil—but I cannot think the mere dancing with Nora for exercise, is any more improper

49

than running a race down the garden walk, or scrambling over the hills.

—Sophie du Pont (1832)

[In Richmond, Virginia] There is to be public speaking in the African Church today, or in the Square, to reanimate the people for another carnival of blood. Mr. Hunter, it is said, has been chosen to preside, and no man living has a greater abhorrence of blood! But, perhaps, he cannot decline.

—John Beauchamp Jones (1865)

Did you read young John D. Rockefeller's plea to the oil men? He implored them to tell the truth, or tell something, whether it was the truth or not, but to please not just sit there, as that made the whole industry not only look dumb, but guilty. Poor young John D! He is trying to do what is right, but his Bible class should include all his holding companies.

—Will Rogers (1928)

FEBRUARY 10

I asked a man today if he would rent me some land, and he said he had four acres as good soil "as any outdoors." It was a true poet's account of it. He and I, and all the world, went outdoors to breathe the free air and stretch ourselves. For the world is but outdoors—and we duck behind a panel.

—Henry David Thoreau (1841)

I have seen the face of the Supreme Court of the United States, and yet live (though with a slight headache). Got home last night at six-thirty, too tired to journalize.

—GEORGE TEMPLETON STRONG (1866)

For some years, ever since the women's lib movement convinced me that I was a heel for having so long been so malely chauvinistic, I have made a point, when, say, buying Christmas presents via telephone from a mail-order catalogue, of asking whomever I'm connected with, after she identifies herself as Joanna or Rosie or Kate or whatever, for her surname. I do this in what I conceive to be the spirit of the Equal Rights Amendment. Whoever heard of a man identifying himself solely as Charlie or George?

—E. J. KAHN, JR. (1987)

FEBRUARY 11

I take great pleasure in viewing and examining the magnificent prospects of Nature that lie before us in this town. If I cast my eyes one way, I am entertained with the savage, unsightly appearance of naked woods, and leafless forests. In another place a chain of broken and irregular mountains throws my mind into a pleasing kind of astonishment. But if I turn myself round, I perceive a wide, extensive tract before me made up of woods and meadows, wandering streams and barren plains, covered in various places by herds of grazing cattle and terminated by the distant view of the town.

—JOHN ADAMS (1756)

When I arrived in France, the French nation had a great many questions to settle. The first was, Whether I was the famous Adams? Le fameux Adams? Ah, le fameux Adams. In order to speculate a little upon this subject, the pamphlet entitled "Common Sense," had been printed in the "Affaires de l'Angleterre et de l'Amerique," and expressly ascribed to Mr. Adams, the celebrated member of Congress—le celebre membre du Congress. . . . When I arrived at Bordeaux, all that I could say or do would not convince anybody but that I was the fameux Adams. . . . But when I arrived at Paris, I found a very different style. I found great pains taken, much more than the question was worth, to settle the point that I was not the famous Adams. . . . I soon found, too, that it was effectually settled in the English newspapers that I was not the famous Adams. Nobody went so far in France or England as to say that I was the infamous Adams. . . . It being settled that he was not the famous Adams, the consequence was plain; he was some man that nobody had ever heard of before, and therefore a man of no consequence—a cipher. And I am inclined to think that all parties, both in France and England,—Whigs and Tories in England, the friends of Franklin, Deane, and Lee, in France,—differing in many other things, agreed in this, that I was not the famous Adams.

—JOHN ADAMS (1779)

Some idea may be formed of the scarcity of food in this city from the fact that, while my youngest daughter was in the kitchen to-day, a young rat came out of its hole and seemed to beg for something to eat; she held out some bread, which it ate from her hand, and seemed grateful. Several others soon appeared and were as tame as kittens. Perhaps we shall have to eat them!

—JOHN BEAUCHAMP JONES (1863)

Raining this morning and very gloomy. . . . Read awhile in Tarbells Life of Lincoln . . . and then went out to luncheon. It was still raining when I got through with that meal, but I decided to go for a walk, so I strolled up to Manayunk along Manayunk Avenue and went across and came down the Schuylkill on the other side. It was raining very hard. The great mills of Manayunk and Pencoyd look like faint outlines in a solid forground of gray. The river was running muddy and deep, the smoke of the factories and engines hanging low. All was sombre and dark to me and yet it had color and was not without beauty. It seemed to me that if I were an artist I could paint a thousend pictures of Manayunk. It so squalid, so poor, so suggestive of all that is artistic and grim in toil. . . . I returned home via the City Ave bridge, wet and rather glum. Took off my cloths and dried them, reading the while in the Life of Lincoln. . . . Ah me—Ah me, who is it that tells the truth and is happy.

—THEODORE DREISER (1903)

FEBRUARY 12

During the afternoon I took a walk. . . . I looked at the trees and the river murmuring along over the stones and my heart was glad. I sang, as I always sing when I am walking, a half dozen different melodies of a minor or plaintive note and at last came to feel as if life were delicious. I was not to remain poor always, I fancied. I was to recover and grow strong and be able to write again. Love was to come back and play its part in my life again. Life, love, sunlight—so I sang and dreamed. . . . I came home, wondering as the twilight fell whether my dreams were to come true and then I found as I always do that I was expecting them too soon. Not now. Not now. Somehow now is almost always commonplace. We see when we return that we have to wait. To be alone, to live alone, to wait, wait, wait, that is the lot accorded us.

—THEODORE DREISER (1903)

*N*o news yet, from home. Hard to be patient. So much can have happened. So powerless to pierce the silence. Nothing much to write about. Lectures, practical maneuvers in field. . . . Thank God for the wine! If pacifists really want to end war, all they have to do is end booze. Without it, everybody'd get so homesick they'd be useless. P——dug up bottle of cognac, and had swell wrangle over Socialism.

—HOWARD O'BRIEN (1918)

*L*incoln's Birthday—and what a break for crossword-puzzle constructors that there are the same number of letters in "abrahamlincoln" and "stephendouglas."

—E. J. KAHN, JR. (1987)

FEBRUARY 13

*T*he meat train did not arrive this evening, and I gave Godey leave to kill our little dog, (Tlamath,) which he prepared in Indian fashion; scorching off the hair, and washing the skin with soap and snow, and then cutting it up into pieces, which were laid on the snow. Shortly afterwards, the sleigh arrived with a supply of horse meat; and we had tonight an extraordinary dinner—pea soup, mule, and dog.

—JOHN C. FRÉMONT (1844)

*H*ome from Chicago and Milwaukee. Chicago grows so fast that one ceases to respect civic growth: as if all these solid and stately squares which we are wont to see as the slow growth of a century had come to be done by machinery as cloth and hardware are made, and were therefore shoddy architecture without honour. 'T was tedious, the squalor and obstructions of travel; the advantage of their offers at Chicago made it necessary to go; in short, this dragging of a decorous old gentleman out of home and out of position to this juvenile career was tantamount to this,—"I'll bet you fifty dollars a day that you will not leave your library, and wade and ride and run and suffer all manner of indignities and stand up for an hour each night reading in a hall"; and I answered, "I'll bet I will." I do it and win the $900.

—Ralph Waldo Emerson (1865)

*W*alking down to the city is not such an easy matter as some might imagine. . . . All the way I hurried so that I did not have much time to grieve and yet I did. Me. Theodore Dreiser. A man who has ideas enough to write and to spare and walking for want of a nickel. . . . Weary, panting, I sat down to supper. . . . After, I came out thinking how I would write all this. What a peculiar story my life would make if all were told, and so sat down in my room alone to read. . . . I took up my life of Lincoln and read eagerly in it, the story of that man of sorrows having much in it that reminds me of my own. That night I slept a little better than usual.

—Theodore Dreiser (1903)

*F*rench very different from us. Been trying ten days to get couple of wooden horses for blackboards, out of French carpenter. Delivered to-day. American would have knocked them together in ten minutes. These all mortised and bolted—last forever. Means so out of proportion to purpose. Like sign over camp gate—work of art—ought to be in museum.

—Howard O'Brien (1918)

FEBRUARY 14

*M*y third hyacinth bloomed this A.M., a lovely pink. So I found things snug. . . . I wrote my tales. Made some shirts for my boys, and went out to buy a squash pie for my lonely supper. It snowed; was very cold. No one paid, and I wanted to send some money home. Felt cross and tired as I trudged back at dusk. My pie turned a somersault, a boy laughed, so did I, and felt better. On my doorstep I found a gentleman who . . . handed me a letter out of which fell a $100 bill. With this bait Mr. B[onner] lured me to write "one column of Advice to Young Women". . . . Thriftily taking advantage of the enthusiastic moment, I planned my article while I ate my dilapidated pie, and then proceeded to write it with the bill before me. It was about old maids. "Happy Women" was the title, and I put in my list all the busy, useful, independent spinsters I know, for liberty is a better husband than love to many of us. . . . So the pink hyacinth was a true prophet, and I went to bed a happy millionaire, to dream of flannel petticoats for my blessed Mother, paper for Father, a new dress for May, and sleds for my boys.

—LOUISA MAY ALCOTT (1868)

*A*fter I had read [the life of Lincoln] until noon . . . I heard [at dinner] how [Clarence] Darrow had closed up the miners case. It was [a] powerful speech, some thought. The lady next to me, however, the only one present who seemed to consider herself somebody, expressed the feeling that she would like to have slapped Darrow. The miners were such wretches in her estimation. . . . This had a most depressing effect on me. Men, working men, a mass of any men desiring something and not being able to get it. . . . Poor, ignorant, leading grimy, narrow lives—oh I know how they fight and quarrel among themselves. I know too full well that they drink and carouse and are like other men, low and corrupt and mean. . . . Are they not like the men who oppress them? Is [J. P.] Morgan pure, is [George] Baer clean? Have they tender hearts, noble souls, fine and beautiful lives? They have money and fine clothes and a pleasant atmosphere of comforts and refinements to move in, but some men are born to degradation and the fault is not theirs after all. Anyhow it grieved me and I went out after dinner and walked about to think of these things. . . . I came to [a] negro fishing by the stream and fell to talking with him. He seemed to be a happy go lucky creature and told me he had place as chief cook at Capon Springs in season and waiting for the season to open. He also told me the society people were very bad at that resort and the women were all immoral. I wondered at this a little but said nothing as I [did] not wish to appear curious or condemnatory of the whites with him. Still I could not think of all that gayety and license without worrying over my own condition. . . . I came away feeling rather depressed over this again, but I tried not to feel too blue.

—THEODORE DREISER (1903)

FEBRUARY 15

*B*y Day we wake with the Silent sight of a Young Fellow in the room getting up from his Girl in the t'other Bed in the Same Room with us. Astonishing Boldness and Impudence! nor could we let the Girl go off without a brief Lecture. But we kept the matter for the Parents for the Time.

—EBENEZER PARKMAN (1744)

*W*ent to a Ball at Alexandria, where Musick and Dancing was the chief Entertainment. However in a convenient Room detachd for the purpose abounded great plenty of Bread and Butter, some Biscuits with Tea, and Coffee which the Drinkers of coud not Distinguish from Hot water sweetned. Be it rememberd that pockethandkerchiefs servd the purposes of Table Cloths and Napkins and that no Apologies were made for either. The Proprietors of this Ball were Messrs. Carlyle, Laurie and Robt. Wilson, but the Doctr. not getting it conducted agreeable to his own taste woud claim no share of the merit of it. I shall therefore distinguish this Ball by the Stile and title of the Bread and Butter Ball.

—GEORGE WASHINGTON (1760)

$\mathscr{I}$ returned to my office, & was planning out with a friend, the probable next proceedings, when we heard a shout from the Court House, continued into a yell of triumph, & in an instant after, down the steps came two huge negroes, bearing the prisoner between them, with his clothes half torn off, & so stupified by the sudden rescue & the violence of his dragging off that he sat almost down, & I thought had fainted; but the men seised him, & being powerful fellows, hurried him through the Square into Court st., where he found the use of feet, & they went off toward Cambridge, like a black squall, the crowd driving along with them & cheering as they went. It was all done in an instant, too quick to be believed, & so successful was it that not only was no negro arrested, but no attempt was made at pursuit.

—RICHARD HENRY DANA (1851)

$\mathscr{R}$ead my life of Lincoln till twelve when I finished it. . . . Lincoln's life moved me deeply as any such tragedy as that always moves me. Lincoln and Christ—somehow these two are naturally associated in my mind. They were both so kind, so tender, so true. Oh that we could all be great, noble and altogether lovely. . . . My sleep this night was not so good owing to my wrought up mental state, the tragedy of [Lincoln's] life staying with me until late.

—THEODORE DREISER (1903)

FEBRUARY 16

$\mathscr{I}$ got a long letter from home and dad says he thinks I ought to be satisfied with what I have made [in the California goldfield] and come home to comfort mother and him. It does not seem as if this was the right sort of a life for a man—no women, no church, nothing of what there was in Norfolk, but then there is a lot in this country that Norfolk hasn't got.

One isn't so cramped and it seems as if there was more room to turn around in. I used to think Squire Battell was the richest man in the world, and he ain't worth more than thirty thousand dollars. If I can go back with that much I would not mind; but I never could settle down again to farm work.

—ALFRED T. JACKSON (1851)

To the Baptist meeting. A stringy, cluttered, packed in, heterogeneous collection of divines and visitors. Noisy, disorderly. Goodall hostile as soon as he saw me. The usual difficulty with the hearing committee, the usual dumb slowness. Why do ministers *have* to walk slow? When—after delays and obstructions, I got a chance to talk—I railed at them for not answering my letters and a brother from the back piped up, "Sister, we didn't know how you look!"

—ALICE DUNBAR-NELSON (1931)

Another beautiful day on the desert and the finest sunset we have seen yet. After a morning on the Civil War, E and I went to lie in an open place among hills. She walked away up into the hills while I stayed below reading. The whole country was so beautiful it hurt.

—SHERWOOD ANDERSON (1936)

FEBRUARY 17

I consume too much time on notes and on *pettinesses* every day. Think more of general effect and impression. Don't quiddle nor twaddle.

—WILLIAM HICKLING PRESCOTT (1842)

*C*roton water bathing pipes just burst, to the consternation of the household who are engaged in solemn consultation somewhere in the basement, up to their necks in water, I suppose. It hasn't flooded my premises, though I think the fatal breach is somewhere inside the wall thereof, which will probably lead to the destruction of my domestic peace and literary seclusion by an irruption of hod-carrying, plaster-mongering Goths, vandals, and Mongrel Tartars. Shall I sue the architect, the plumber, or the Mayor, Aldermen & Co?

—GEORGE TEMPLETON STRONG (1844)

*M*y attention is so much taken up with business during the week that I find it very difficult to give it to the more important duties of Sunday. My mind runs away from its devotions to the plans of business and various engagements. . . . I have enumerated them as follows: 1. My business of commission merchant with a large establishment, clerks, etc., and but one partner. 2. Office of treasurer of a large manufacturing corporation with a capital of a million of dollars. 3. Director in ten corporations: some of them very large. . . . 4. I have charge of all my father's property; also Mrs. Luther Lawrence's and Mrs. Seaver's. 5. Of my own property; including lands in the West, the building of a Seminary and a town (Appleton) in Wisconsin, which is a complicated business. Then there is the business of receiving and paying visits, which I do only as much of as is necessary. The membership of various societies requiring some attention; besides my daily duty of giving two hours of daylight to the business of getting exercise enough to keep my body sound. Some trusts I have given up, but others come in to take their place. . . . Can one be prepared for higher duties when the mind is filled continually with such thoughts as all these things entail?

—AMOS A. LAWRENCE (1850)

*S*pent the day with Mr. Ford in Detroit. When the world is in a hole I go to Ford and ask him. More common sense than

60

all of 'em. Then, too, I know there is more people interested in the new Ford than there is interested in Manchuria; they ain't going to get into Manchuria but they are going to get in these Fords. He said, "Will, you never was as funny purposely as some of our prominent and rich people are acting these days. This is not a panic, it's a side show, watching folks and seeing how scared they can get."

—WILL ROGERS (1932)

FEBRUARY 18

Somebody mentioned housekeeping. I said I hoped that term would not be used where nobody showed the least disposition to such a care. A person then broke out that until I sent Mrs. Woods to take the keys from her every drop of Milk, Spoonful of butter, of fat, every ounce of sugar plumbs, etc. passed regularly through her hands. I laughed at the care we then experienced in Milk, butter, fat, sugar plumbs, soap, Candles, etc. Not one of these innumerations lasted my family half the year. New soap was obliged to be made in June. Fat gone by July. . . . All gone. No body knows how. . . . I never listened to Negroes and therefore gave no ear to the pots of butter, the aprons of plumbs carried away.

—LANDON CARTER (1770)

Finished planting fruit trees at Hascosea. Planted 2 doz Albany Strawberry plants bought in Augusta at Looking Glass. Walked with Frank. Today was inaugurated at Montgomery Jefferson Davis, President of the Confederate States of America. . . . Virginia is jealous because she "the Mother of States" did not lead the movement. She will be the fag end of the Dis united States ere long.

—CATHERINE EDMONDSTON (1861)

$\mathscr{D}$ifference between French and ourselves. Do small things infinitely well. Much more precise in planning. Thorough where we're superficial. But we amaze them the way we dig in. Moved a big howitzer through swamp in 4 hrs. other day. French student officers took a couple of days. We have more ingenuity, more open minds and greater initiative. They find us dumb at mathematics. We find them impractical, wasting time terribly on nonessentials. Humor and exasperation on both sides. Anyway, we're learning a lot—and so are they. Fair exchange.

—HOWARD O'BRIEN (1918)

FEBRUARY 19

$\mathscr{A}$ seaman in the coach told the story of an old sperm-whale, which he called a white whale, which was known for many years by the whalemen as Old Tom, and who rushed upon the boats which attacked him, and crushed the boats to small chips in his jaws, the men generally escaping by jumping overboard and being picked up. A vessel was fitted out at New Bedford, he said, to take him. And he was finally taken somewhere off Payta Head by the *Winslow* or the *Essex*. He gave a fine account of a storm, which I heard imperfectly, only "the whole ocean was all feather white." A whale sometimes runs off three rolls of cord, three hundred fathom in length each one.

—RALPH WALDO EMERSON (1834)

$\mathscr{W}$e are all in high spirits, though we are rather short of provisions, for men who have appetites that could digest anything but oppression; but no matter, we have a prospect of soon getting our bellies full of fighting, and that is victuals and drink to a patriot any day. We had a little sort of convivial party last evening: just about a dozen of us set to work, most patriotically, to see whether we could not get rid of that curse of the land, whisky, and we made considerable progress; but my poor friend, Thimblerig, got sewed up just about as tight as the eyelet-hole in a lady's corset, and a little tighter too, I reckon; for when he went to bed he called for a bootjack, which was brought to him, and he bent down on his hands and knees, and very gravely pulled off his hat with it, for the darned critter was so thoroughly swiped that he didn't know his head from his heels. But this wasn't all the folly he committed; he pulled off his coat and laid it on the bed, and then hung himself over the back of a chair. . . . Seeing the poor fellow completely used up, I carried him to bed.

—DAVY CROCKETT (1836)

$\mathcal{L}$ast evening a short time after the salute was fired a large crowd was seen to assemble at Mrs Morgan's . . . & several soldiers were seen to search the house. We learnt to day that the occasion was this. While the guns were firing Frank Key or as he is called Key Morgan with two or three other boys went to the janitor of the college [Transylvania] and got the key to the door leading on the roof on pretext that a ball had been thrown up there, & hoisted a secession flag on the college. The janitor saw it and cut it down & by order to the teacher Mr. Patterson put it in a cellar till it could be delivered to the authorities, but a Mrs John Dudley who lives near the college told Morgan who got the flag & took it home & having secreted it made the best of his way off. Some soldiers however had seen the flag on the college and came to inquire the cause of its being there, which having learnt they searched Mrs Morgans house found the flag which they tore up and divided among themselves.

—FRANCES DALLAM PETER (1862)

FEBRUARY 20

$\mathcal{M}$y horses freezing, my men discouraged and our utmost exertion necessary to keep them from freezing to death. I then thought of the vanity of riches and of all those objects that lead men in the perilous path of adventure. It seems that in times like those men return to reason and make the true estimate of things. They throw by the gaudy baubles of ambition and embrace the solid comforts of domestic life. But a few days of rest makes the sailor forget the storm and embark again on the perilous Ocean and I suppose that like him I would soon become weary of rest.

—JEDEDIAH SMITH (1828)

*W*hen I am going out for an evening, I arrange the fire in my stove so that I do not fail to find a good one when I return, though it would have engaged my frequent attention, present; so that when I know I am to be at home, I sometimes make believe that I may go out to save trouble. And this is the art of living, too, to leave our life in a condition to go alone, and not to require a constant supervision. We will then sit down serenely to live, as by the side of a stove.

—HENRY DAVID THOREAU (1841)

A big day. Got through stirring chapter of Kit [Carson]. In the afternoon we went to the Rodeo—Indian day. The field, out in the desert, grey sand, Indians very serious and strange. The games much more lovely than that of the circus cowboys.

—SHERWOOD ANDERSON (1936)

FEBRUARY 21

*O*n Jackass Hill again. The exciting topic of conversation in this sparse community just at present (& it always *is* in

dire commotion about something or other of small consequence,) is Mrs. Carrington's baby, which was born a week
ago, on the 14th. There was nothing remarkable about the
baby, but if Mrs C had given birth to an ornamental cast-
iron dog big enough for an embellishment for the State-House
steps I don't believe the event would have created more intense interest in the community.

—MARK TWAIN (1865)

On account of us being a democracy and run by the people,
we are the only nation in the world that has to keep a government four years, no matter what it does.

—WILL ROGERS (1930)

Getting the Sunday *Times* innards on Saturday is not all
gravy. We have looked up the movie's starting time and have
arrived on the dot of six. But that is the Sunday time and
today's was five-fifteen, and we've already missed the scene
where the crocodile grabs the girl and the hero saves her
from something unscreenable, so naturally we have to stick
around for that, and by then it's time to get something to eat.

—E. J. KAHN, JR. (1987)

FEBRUARY 22

After all Religionists, Philosophers and Misanthropes
may say, the sweetest pleasure of this mortal life is the applause of Men—its bitterest grief Their censure. A consciousness that the praise bestowed is not our due may detract
from our enjoyment or that the condemnation is unjust may

mitigate our sufferings. But right or wrong we rejoice in the approbation and wither under the rebuke of our fellows.

—JAMES HENRY HAMMOND (1853)

$\mathcal{T}$he day started fair but ended with a strong cold wind. Fished but no luck. Went for a drive to the oil fields, a wild, strange and terrible place. Men working in mud—the roar and scream of gas, escaping from earth's bowels, the heavy smells. There is the feeling of a vast disorder down below, men profiting by it at terrible risk. Everywhere grey mud and filthy sick smells. They light the escaping gas after conducting it high up in pipes. The dancing flames roar, night and day.

—SHERWOOD ANDERSON (1937)

$\mathcal{W}$ent to Mass at eight, driven by a young man who was going with an intelligent young Lutheran girl and he kept telling me how he argued with her. Did the Protestants have any saints?—No. Did the Blessed Mother visit any of them?— No. Etc. I felt like saying that Catholics needed them more.

—DOROTHY DAY (1959)

FEBRUARY 23

$\mathcal{E}$arly this morning the enemy came in sight, marching in regular order, and displaying their strength to the greatest advantage, in order to strike us with terror. But that was no go; they'll find that they have to do with men who will never lay down their arms as long as they can stand on their legs. We held a short council of war, and finding that we should be completely surrounded, and overwhelmed by numbers, if we remained in the town, we concluded to withdraw to the fortress of Alamo, and defend it to the last extremity. We accordingly filed off, in good order, having some days before placed all the surplus provisions, arms, and ammunition in the fortress. We have had a large national flag made; it is composed of thirteen stripes, red and white, alternately, on a blue ground, with a large white star, of five points, in the centre, and between the points the letters TEXAS. As soon as all our little band, about one hundred and fifty in number, had entered and secured the fortress in the best possible manner, we set about raising our flag on the battlements.

—Davy Crockett (1836)

*T*here is another town down the ridge, called Rough and Ready and it's as lively as Nevada. They hung a nigger there last week for stealing. It's a queer thing how well we get along without any courts or law. Over in Nevada the miners have elected an alcalde, but his decisions are not binding, only as they are accepted by the people. Most of the cases are mining disputes and a miners' jury decides these. Stealing is punished by a whipping and banishment. Outside of a few cutting and shooting scrapes among the gamblers there have been no serious crimes, and it is a fact that we are more orderly and better behaved as a rule than the eastern towns from which we came.

—Alfred T. Jackson (1851)

*T*he grand smash has come. . . . Today I was burning papers all day—expecting a Yankee raid. Gave some silver to Mr. Team—& two books of JC's. Shall try & get them if I go to Greenville. How I have wept this day! My poor heart is weary—& then how it poured—*rain,* rain, rain, & in it all I rushed down to Mrs. Martin. I wanted so to get away. . . . To night Isabella calmly reads beside me—& I am quiet after the day's *rampage.* Oh—my Heavenly Father look down & pity us. Mrs. Johnston told me Mrs. Halsey had sent Mrs. Wigfall a thousand dollars in gold & she sold it for 28,000 in Confeds—so they are living grandly now in Richmond. . . . To day I was thinking of the wretch going to the Yanks named Smith who would not let Mr. C put his head in the car window to tell me good bye. They say I was the last who went in the door. After that the trains were seized by Government—& the flying females even smuggled in by the windows & some, such as dear stout Mrs. Izard, stuck fast & had to be shoved in with a hard push. Helas—for Southern dignity.

—MARY BOYKIN CHESNUT (1865)

FEBRUARY 24

*W*ind. Giles here. Sewed read. Called on Mrs Reed in p.m. *Rub* at night. Clams at noon. Earthquake in Italy.

—LOUISA MAY ALCOTT (1887)

*A*gain am I fallen on evil days—sitting in a dirty courtyard in the front of my car because there is no where else to sit—with a smell of bad pipes, of gasoline, of mule dung and of the Italian army—Then the noises are all unpleasant, sounds of tin cans full of oil, of motors running, of tools jingling, of people hammering iron things . . . and, oh God—we are here for three days. . . . The only thing to do is to watch the camions climbing Grappa—like black cockroaches.

—JOHN DOS PASSOS (1918)

[Corpus Christi] *H*as become a boom town, people crowding in, no rooms to be had. All are to get rich in oil. There are many houses going up, a crazy patchwork, no plan. It is a chance to see, in the raw, how American towns and cities have grown.

—SHERWOOD ANDERSON (1937)

FEBRUARY 25

*D*ined at Mr. [W. C.] Bryant's. . . . B. is to my mind a standing illustration of the truth that in the intercourse of the world good feeling, good principles & intellectual cultivation are not enough to make good manners.

—RICHARD HENRY DANA (1844)

I give up my job at John D. Pringles & went home (at Dawson Ferry) for I have made up my mind to go to the army. I did not feel that I was doing my duty to stay at home when nearly all my comrades and friends was leaving for the seat of war. I went home and told them I was going to the army and was going to Uniontown tomorrow . . . to see what chance I could get.

—SAMUEL A. CLEAR (1864)

*N*ote from Lady Amberly as I sat sewing on my nine-penny dress. She wanted to come and see me, and I told her to do so, and I'd show her how I lived in my sky-parlor,—spinning yarns like a spider.

—LOUISA MAY ALCOTT (1868)

FEBRUARY 26

*W*e are told to-day that civilization is making rapid progress; the tendency is ever upward, substantial justice is done even by human courts. You may trust the good intentions of mankind. You read tomorrow in the newspapers that France is on the eve of going to war with England to give employment to her army. . . . Does the threatened war between France and England evince any more enlightenment than a war between two savage tribes, the Iroquois and Hurons? Is it founded in better reason?

—HENRY DAVID THOREAU (1852)

*G*lory to God! Charleston has fallen! I feel like shouting *all over*. . . . I feel same as old Aunty Brown, who was here when the news came, said she did. "Why," said she, "if I could get hold of dat Gen. Sherman, and all his brave officers I feel as if I could tote dem all ober dis yer place." Our Regt. the 21 U.C.C.Is [Infantry] were the first to enter Charleston. As they marched proudly up Meeting St. with flags flying and drums beating, the excitement among the colored people was at white heat—cheer after cheer greeted them at every turn, as they passed out of Meeting St a fine looking black woman sprang out from the crowd, in front of the officers, and pulling her [shawl] from her shoulders, spread it in front of the soldiers for them to walk on, it seemed the only thing she could do to show her patriotism. The Col. gallantly picked it up and passed it to her, while the soldiers cheered vociferously.

—ESTHER HILL HAWKS (1865)

I am "living an abundant life" with many outside activities ranging from studying the Bible to wrestling, and from saving pictures of famous personalities and semi-nude girls to preparing myself for a rabbinical seminary.

—DAVID S. KOGAN (1945)

FEBRUARY 27

*T*he cannonading began early this morning, and ten bombs were thrown into the fort, but fortunately exploded without doing any mischief. So far it has been a sort of tempest in a teapot, not unlike a pitched battle in the Hall of Congress.

—DAVY CROCKETT (1836)

$\mathcal{O}$ne thing only disgusted me, south of Philad., & that did really so, & to no small degree. I had read in the works of British travelers about the American habits of spitting, & supposed it an exaggeration, for I knew that although we in N. Eng. spit more than the English, yet we did not do it eno' to justify so much fault as the English found. But in the cars between Balt. & Philad., & at Balt., it was disgusting even to a New Englander. There was half a dosen men in the cars who did nothing but spit, they were chewing tobacco with all their might, & when their mouths were full, out it came with all the force long habit could give them. After dark, in the silence, the constant spitting could be heard, now at one end of cars then at the other, like the irregular firing of Militia.

—RICHARD HENRY DANA (1844)

$\mathcal{T}$oday I took a walk to think about Poe—and Americans, all the things in Poe that are not American. It was they that killed him, just as it is the things that are not American in Thoreau that gradually sapped his strength. The chief thing in Poe that sets him apart is that he was a criminal, he was filled with murderous thoughts. Americans are not sadists.

—THORNTON WILDER (1954)

FEBRUARY 28

$\mathcal{S}$anta Anna appears determined to verify his threat and convert the blooming paradise into a howling wilderness. For

71

just one fair crack at that rascal even at a hundred yards distance I would bargain to break my Betsey and never pull trigger again. My name's not Crockett if I wouldn't get glory enough to appease my stomach for the remainder of my life.

—DAVY CROCKETT (1836)

*J*ohn Springer spent the evening at the store. He is a queer hen. Has abundance of cogent and pertinent anecdote. Old Antony Foote of Augusta lost his wife. In relating and enumerating her good qualities and the tremendous loss he observed characteristically that "Her water was excellent to color yarn and he'd rather lost the best cow he had in his barn yard."

—BENJAMIN BROWNE FOSTER (1848)

*S*trange coincidence: William Safire's word-usage department in tomorrow's *Times* magazine reminds us that the past tense of the word "dive" is not "dove" (that, he probably doesn't have to remind us, is a bird) but "dived." On the way out of Borchardt's office, I happen to notice, on one wall, a framed page from a fancy edition of something or other (#16 of 70 copies) signed by the author, Francine Gray. It is a page about a beaver, and what do my wondering eyes perceive but the words "then dove over and came out again and swam."

—E. J. KAHN, JR. (1987)

FEBRUARY 29: LEAP YEAR

*I*t is not wise to talk, as men do, of reason as the gift of God bestowed . . . or, of reasoning from nature up to nature's God. . . . The intellectual power is not the gift, but the presence of God. Nor do we reason to the being of God, but God goes with us into nature, when we go or think at all. Truth is always new and wild as the wild air, and is alive. The mind is always true, when there is mind, and it makes no difference that the premises are false, we arrive at true conclusions.

—Ralph Waldo Emerson (1856)

☙ MARCH ☙

MARCH 1

*H*e was one day last week telling me of the fine opportunity to make money that now offered, of bringing goods from the North to sell . . . and asked me how I thought it would "pay" to bring a lot of hoop skirts to Winchester. I told him that though we were lamentably in need of hoops we could not buy without taking the oath, and I thought the ladies would prefer going hoopless to such an alternative. He tries to be kind, poor old fellow, and knowing our straits invites us secretly to avail ourselves of opportunities to abstract his supplies. He leaves boxes of crackers invitingly open in the hall, and actually proposed to Harry to cut me a supply of wood from his pile in front of my door. It would seem but just to make reprisals, but my poor children seem each day to lose a portion of their respect for the rights of property. They think it no harm to steal or take from those who took all from us, and I often have to interfere and make them carry back things they have appropriated, but we must have wood, so I allow Harry to act on the old man's hint and cut wood for me from the United States woodpile, side by side with a Yankee soldier who does not trouble himself about who gets it.

—CORNELIA PEAKE McDONALD (1863)

*W*hen a Gentleman quoted me on the floor of Congress the other day, another member took exception and said he objected to the remarks of a Professional Joke Maker going into the Congressional Record. Now can you beat that for jealousy among people in the same line?

—WILL ROGERS (1925)

*C*omparing the junior prom of this year with the junior prom of two years ago is grossly unfair—the white naive flat-footed puritanism of the innocent kiss then and the ecstasy of idealism (to topple half a year hence), and the rational exquisitely mature mental and physical heights of *this* promising event elude comparison. I want to be silverly beautiful for him: a sylvan goddess. Honestly, life for me is certainly a gyre, spiraling up, comprehending and including the past, profiting by it, yet transcending it! I am going to make it my job to see that I never get caught revolving in one final repetitive circle of stagnation. . . . I can't stop effervescing: I have so many merry little pots bubbling away in the fire of my enthusiasm.

—SYLVIA PLATH (1953)

MARCH 2

*I*n the last month we have taken a little over four thousand dollars out of the claim and it will take us considerable longer to work it out than we expected. . . . Pard tells me that with what he had before we joined fortunes and what he has made since, he has over ten thousand dollars. He has not sold any of his dust, but has it buried, nobody knows where but himself. He thinks it is too much money to lie idle and has made up his mind to invest it in San Francisco lots. He wants me to join him in the speculation and argues that some day it will be a big city. I haven't got much faith in it and neither has anybody else to whom I have talked about it.

—ALFRED T. JACKSON (1851)

75

*T*o day I have put on my cotton pants and linen coat, and find them more pleasant than my winter garments. I feel like a calico colored butterfly. Guess I'll have to shed again before the season is out.

—David Golightly Harris (1861)

*Th*is morning Mr. George Ruth come to town, and told the pressmen that he would not accept less than $100,000 a year, and I hope he gets it or more, as I think he attracts more money than that to the parks where he plays. But Lord! how weary it maketh me when petty persons compare this salary to the President's, or to their own, saying, "How hard I work, and how little I earn!" But this man chooseth to be a writer or a truckman, and that one a ballplayer, and if so be he is fortunate enough to have the qualities that a great public will pay to see displayed, who is anybody to complain of that? For all I would have to do, I tell myself, to get a larger salary than Babe Ruth's would be to be a greater ballplayer, and if I am not, I have no right to complain, nor do I, but say, "Huzzah for Mr. Ruth!" Heard this afternoon that he hath accepted $70,000 a year.

—Franklin Pierce Adams (1927)

*U*p and greatly shaken at reading of the theft of the Lindbergh baby last night, and I full of fear that the parents will not see him again, for no matter what the immunity offered to any kidnapper might be, it seems to me that he would be so ridden by fright of discovery later that his immunity would be limited. So took my boy Timothy to school, and he told me that I hurt his hand holding it too tight.

—Franklin Pierce Adams (1932)

MARCH 3

*Y*esterday I heard that the Volenteers of Spartanburgh had been ordered to go to Charleston. This will be gratifing to

some of them that are so anxious to make themselves notori-
ous, but I fear that it will be the Death Nell to some others.
The idea of rendering ones name immortal, by some dareing
feat under the walls of Fort Sumter, is very pleasant. But the
thought that one might loose his life, gain no honorable
name, and only leave his boddy as food for the hungry fishes
in the Bay, and an impoverished family at home, is not so
animating. And is calculated to cool ones patriotism.

—DAVID GOLIGHTLY HARRIS (1861)

*T*he attention of the world is on a little curly haired baby.
Till he is found we can't get back to normal. Never since the
two days and a night that this same kid's father was out over
the Atlantic has the attention of everybody been centered so
completely on one thing.

—WILL ROGERS (1932)

*T*hree days since my operation and I am myself again. . . .
Today I threw off my fetters—got up to wash and had my
first laborious goat-shit, changed my hospital pink and red
flapping jacket which left my bum bare to my frilly pink and
white Victorian nightgown. They just wheeled one of the new
women by on a stretcher—the muscular lime-green porter
loaded her on the trolley—the queer flat shape of a drugged
body—the white turban, green blankets, eyes staring up,
dumbly. The other night, they say, "Thelma died." I vaguely
remember a lady in a yellow gown, youngish, wheeling the
tea round. "She died after her op." Outdoors it is sunny,
smelling of wet sweet earth. A few stray airs filter in the windows. I remember luxuriating in these blowing airs on my
first night when I lay wakeful after a day of sleep yet deeply
drugged and invulnerable—it blew sweetly over the sleeping
forms and stirred the curtains.

—SYLVIA PLATH (1961)

77

MARCH 4

*A*nother great day in the political world. To day Mr. Abraham Lincoln takes his seat in the Presadential chair, in opposition to the wishes of many freemen of North Merica. I hope he will be permited to quietly occupy his seat, and as quietly leave it at the expiration of his term.

—DAVID GOLIGHTLY HARRIS (1861)

I saw to day a sale of Negroes—Mulatto women in *silk dresses*—one girl was on the stand. Nice looking—like my Nancy—she looked as coy & pleased at the bidder. South Carolina slave holder as I am my very soul sickened—it is too dreadful. I tried to reason—this is not worse than the willing sale most women make of themselves in marriage—nor can the consequences be worse. The Bible authorizes marriage & slavery—poor women! poor slaves!

—MARY BOYKIN CHESNUT (1861)

I spent the morning at Tuskegee, that living monument to Booker T. Washington. They have a great idea there that some of our schools are copying. They teach the pupils that they are going to have to work, and how to work. Our old mode of college education was teach 'em so they think they won't have to work.

—WILL ROGERS (1928)

*W*ent to a P.T.A. meeting in the school library. The speaker's subject was, "Is Your Child a Norm?" Everybody answered Yes out loud and then questioned it inwardly.

—DOROTHY ROBINSON (1935)

MARCH 5

*P*op, pop, pop! Bom, bom, bom! throughout the day. No time for memorandums now. Go ahead! Liberty and independence forever!

—DAVY CROCKETT (1836)

*Y*esterday dined with the mess. Don't remember any thing they said, but they are all ways witty. . . . The Band was delightful. They were playing "massa's in the cold, cold ground."

—MARY BOYKIN CHESNUT (1861)

*B*uried about three fourths of my equipment to-day at American Express. A *musette* for shoulder and dictionary in pocket, all one needs. Silly, the stuff we took over—soap, folding table, trick lanterns, mess kits, campaign hats—*two* of them, and they're forbidden here! Haven't used any sheets yet, and still on first cake of soap. Wonder how I failed to bring my book on "Diseases of Horse."

—HOWARD O'BRIEN (1918)

*A*merica hasn't been as happy in three years as they are today, no money, no banks, no work, no nothing, but they know they got a man in there who is wise to Congress, wise to our so-called big men. The whole country is with him, just so he does something. If he burned down the capital we would cheer and say "well, we at least got a fire started anyhow." We have had years of "don't rock the boat."

—WILL ROGERS (1933)

$\mathscr{W}$ent to a big party . . . sharecroppers—but didn't stay. Mrs. Roosevelt there, big crowd. Pretty far away from sharecroppers.

—SHERWOOD ANDERSON (1940)

$\mathscr{I}$ feel my mind, my imagination, nudging, sprouting, prying and peering. The old anonymous millionairess seen this morning coming from the ugly boxed orangy stucco house next door, hobbling on one crutch down her path to the gleaming black limousine breathing oh-so-gently at the curb, burdened, bent, she, under the weight and bulk of a glossy mink coat, bending to get into the back of the car, as the rotund, rosy white-haired chauffeur held the door open for her. A bent mink-laden lady. And the mind runs, curious, into the crack in the door behind her: where does she come from, who is she? What loves and sorrows are strung on her rosary of hours? Ask the gardener, ask the cook, ask the maid: all the rough, useful retainers who keep a clockwork ritual of grace in a graceless house, barren-roomed and desolate.

—SYLVIA PLATH (1958)

MARCH 6

$\mathscr{S}$et out from Littleton; came to Sideling Hill, nine miles; thence ten miles to Juniata, which we crossed on the ice; from thence to Bedford, fourteen miles. The snow still continues the same depth. Politics and politicians are as plenty here as in Philadelphia, if great things may be compared to small. I had flattered myself that, as we were going toward the frontiers, we should soon be out of the latitude of politics; but even here two men cannot drink half a gill of whiskey without discussing a point in politics, to the great improvement and edification of the bystanders.

—PETER MUHLENBERG (1784)

I have this moment been up to look at the gorgeous array'd dance and supper-rooms, for the Inauguration Ball, at the Patent Office, (which begins in a few hours;) and I could not help thinking of those rooms, where the music will sound and the dancers' feet presently tread—what a different scene they presented to my view a while since, fill'd with a crowded mass of the worst wounded of the war, brought in from Second Bull Run, Antietam and Fredericksburgh. To-night, beautiful women, perfumes, the violins' sweetness, the polka and the waltz; but then, the amputation, the blue face, the groan, the glassy eye of the dying, the clotted rag, the odor of wounds and blood, and many a mother's son amid strangers, passing away untended there, (for the crowd of the badly hurt was great, and much for nurse to do, and much for surgeon.)

—WALT WHITMAN (1865)

It's wonderful the way the British always apologize for what they have. They say quietly, "Of course, it's not so grand as your Library of Congress." Or, "Of course, it's not so large as the Empire State Building, or so handsome as the George Washington Bridge." And all the time they wouldn't exchange theirs for ours if we diamond-studded ours first. It's the epitome of all self-assurance. When you feel really sure, you don't have to brag. You can admire the other fellow's and at the same time know yours is the best of all possible.

—ANNE MCCAUGHEY (1944)

MARCH 7

*W*all Street is more infested than ever with roving presbyters from the ends of the earth—clerical privateers—each setting forth the claims of his own local Zion, and each declining to stop his noise and move on for anything less than a ten dollar bill. Three of these "freres mendicants" came for me this morning, and my pocketbook feels "as if an elephant had stomped on to it." I object to these centralizing tendencies. The rural districts should have the privilege of doing a little for themselves, instead of making this metropolis their foraging ground.

—GEORGE TEMPLETON STRONG (1872)

I hear colored men speak of their "white friends." I have no white friends. I could not degrade the sacred name of "Friendship" by associating it with any man who feels himself too good to sit at table with me, or to sleep at the same hotel. True friendship can only exist between men who have something in common, between equals in something, if not in everything; and where there is respect as well as admiration. I hope as yet to have a friend.

—CHARLES W. CHESNUTT (1882)

*H*ard to concentrate on simple problems of soldiering. Mind persists in wandering off to why's and wherefore's. . . . So much talk about making world safe for democracy. But when men come in from route-march, fagged, hungry, and some one asks "what the holy hell did we come to this for?" and the answer is "to free the slaves!"—oaths, catcalls. We knew, once, why we came. We've forgotten. Minds are colorless—protection against thinking. Be a machine—the only happiness. . . . The newcomers . . . seem to think it's somehow fine and brave to sleep in mud—despite comfort. Old campaigners different. One here—14 yrs. Regular Army. Goes to bed like lady in beauty parlor. Nuts about cleanliness. Enlisted men pretty well rubbed down, too. Toted rifles and scrubbed harness too long to have any more illusions about soldiering than an office boy has about cleaning gobboons. And all the squawk about "slackers." Too damned much altruism for the other fellow. No especial virtue in being here.

82

Most of us here because we were afraid to stay home—afraid of our women. It's the women who've made all the wars in history.

—HOWARD O'BRIEN (1918)

*G*ood morning of work. . . . Many letters. In the evening to a party of University men. Much singing. The party degenerated into a contest of dirty story telling. Little or no wit. I finally said, "Hell, when you get drunk there is no difference between you and a lot of drunken advertising men."

—SHERWOOD ANDERSON (1936)

MARCH 8

*S*anta Barbara . . . is very cloudy & this decides me to return to L.A. this day. Why stay when it looks like rain. I Go to the barbers for a haircut & then meet Helen at the State cafe. The English according to the papers are just trying to grab Constantinople & the Sweet French to destroy the Bolshiviki. We walk down "Main" street . . . then walk along Sea Shore north, past The Ambassador. Sea weed. I eat some. Sea gulls. A Sandpiper. Rocks & cliffs. The King wave! A "hell diver" or Northern loon. Back by a road known as Alta Vista. The naked Eucalyptus trees. The house so Moorish—a silk rug over a balcony! We come down by the road our driver meant to take. The small houses below. Helens dreams of ours—& what it would be like. We steal some roses. . . . 4 P.M. leave for L.A. The gray clouds. The different kind of crowd. . . . The lights on the road—like long antennae. The danger.

—THEODORE DREISER (1920)

*A*merica wears me, wearies me. I am sick of the Cape, sick of Wellesley; all America seems one line of cars, moving, with people jammed in them, from one gas station to one diner and on. I must periodically refresh myself in this crass, crude, energetic, demanding and competitive new-country bath, but I am, in my deep soul, happiest on the moors—my deepest soul-scape, in the hills by the Spanish Mediterranean, in the old, history-crusted and still gracious, spacious cities: Paris, Rome.

—SYLVIA PLATH (1958)

MARCH 9

*E*ngle came. Went to Carey's with him about the books for the Wisconsin Library. After dinner he came again, & . . . gave me a description of his life in the West, which is rough enough, but will hereafter be more comfortable as he has built a house & will take furniture from Pittsburgh with him. The prospects of that country are immense. There will soon be a water & railroad communication all the way to the Mississippi, & in a few years ships will sail from Milwaukee to England! In another half century settlements, canals, & railroads will be pushed to the Pacific. Could we remain united for another century, imagination can scarcely conceive the prosperity, the happiness which this nation would attain at that time.

—SIDNEY GEORGE FISHER (1837)

*T*he railroad is perhaps our pleasantest and wildest road. It only makes deep cuts into and through the hills. On it are no houses nor foot-travelers. The travel on it does not disturb me. The woods are left to hang over it. Though straight, it is wild in its accompaniments, keeping all its raw edges. Even the laborers on it are not like other laborers. Its houses, if any, are shanties, and its ruins the ruins of shanties, shells where the race that built the railroad dwelt; and the bones they gnawed lie about.

—HENRY DAVID THOREAU (1852)

MARCH 10

$\mathscr{I}$ am hoping with an agony of intensity to reach land today. This afternoon foggy, gulf high. Afraid to trust the yards out in such a sea. A boat came alongside late this evening. The principal inmate, the captain of a vessel lying near, a genteel looking man, told us startling news of late operations in the interior, of the battle of Buena Vista, of a large body of Mexican troops being seen between Matamoros and Brazos, and of the small party at Brazos being in dread of an attack. The latter part of the story was fable, but we didn't know it and were of course somewhat flustered but not scared by the idea of having a fight on our hands before we expected it. There was considerable confusion tonight in getting out and loading up firearms and rubbing up our rusted swords. Many valorous vaunts and some of the tallest talking. A later visitor has knocked our chivalry into a cocked hat, by informing us of the disappearance of the Mexicans and of the fact that the heavy fighting is over, at least for a time—that we are too late for Laurels.

—JAMES LAWSON KEMPER (1847)

$\mathscr{T}$here is a full-page ad in the *Times* for an Advertising Hall of Fame lunch to be held at the Waldorf-Astoria on April first. I do not think this is meant to be April Foolery. The ad is illustrated with a photograph of a Waldorf place setting: knife, fork, spoon, two empty wine glasses, salt and pepper shakers, and a sprig of parsley. Where did I read that the Mafia or somebody insists that hotels and restaurants decorate all their platters with parsley? Do people ever eat the parsley? . . . How high does parsley rank among uneaten foods? These odd musings bring back to mind a fellow I knew years ago, a playboy type, whose hefty unearned income stemmed from a mustard fortune. When somebody asked him how mustard could possibly have generated enough income to support a life-style like his, he replied, "It's not what they eat. It's what they leave on their plate."

—E. J. KAHN, JR. (1987)

MARCH 11

It's said that Susannah Lightfoot and Valentine, two women Friends, sent word yesterday to our Assembly, sitting in Lancaster, that they had a message to them from Heaven. This day near eleven in [the] forenoon, the House adjourned and attended in [the] Court Room to hear her, but I'm informed [it] had but little effect and weight with them.

—CHRISTOPHER MARSHALL (1778)

I do not wish my native soil to become exhausted and run out through neglect. Only that traveling is good which reveals to me the value of home and enables me to enjoy it better. That man is the richest whose pleasures are the cheapest.

—HENRY DAVID THOREAU (1856)

The days all the same here [Acapulco], sun, the sea, a soft breeze. Work and then to eat and then sleep. Awake, bathe, eat again and sleep. The American world seems a million miles off.

—SHERWOOD ANDERSON (1938)

$\mathcal{L}$ate this afternoon I was thinking about Fay Wray in California. Her divorced husband . . . a character out of Hemingway, but much more real since he did what H. characters threaten to do, hung himself in a Florida bungalow. I wanted to telephone Fay, but I was so dead inside that nothing responded. . . . Later in the evening I thought about marrying her. . . . She is mature, adult, a real woman, womanly in a lovely way, very loyal, beautiful. Then what am I waiting for . . . ? Well, I am waiting for guarantees, like any American boob with pragmatic eyes. Will it work? Will we be happy?

—CLIFFORD ODETS (1940)

MARCH 12

$\mathcal{A}$ scheme for the union of the British provinces north of us into a confederacy, somewhat like ours, but with Prince Alfred, a youth of 17 for king & some legal connection left with the mother country, has been determined on, or is now under consideration in England. A monarchy in America & close to the borders of the model Republic! . . . The American people hate monarchy & aristocracy & will permit neither to exist where they have power to prevent it. They arrogate to themselves the right to rule in this respect on this side of the Atlantic, and in fact their influence extends to the other side also, & is so rapidly extending that ere long our boldness may reach the point of dictating forms of government to Europe also.

—SIDNEY GEORGE FISHER (1867)

$\mathcal{I}$n the early morning before daylight we came into the harbor at San Diego, in through the narrow passage, and we followed the lights on a changing course to the pier. All about us war bustled, although we had no war; steel and thunder, powder and men—the men preparing thoughtlessly, like dead men, to destroy things. The planes roared over in formation and the submarines were quiet and ominous. There is no playfulness in a submarine. . . . In San Diego we filled the fuel tanks and the water tanks. We filled the icebox and took on the last perishable foods, bread and eggs and fresh meat. . . . We tied up to the pier . . . got our last haircuts and ate broiled steaks. . . . Strangers came to the pier and stared at us and small boys dropped on our deck like monkeys. Those quiet men who always stand on piers asked where we were going and when we said, "To the Gulf of California," their eyes melted with longing. . . . They were like the men and women who stand about airports and railroad stations; they want to go away, and most of all they want to go away from themselves. For they do not know that they would carry their globes of boredom with them wherever they went. One man on the pier who wanted to participate made sure he would be allowed to cast us off, and he waited at the bow line for a long time. Finally he got the call and he cast off the bow line and ran back and cast off the stern line; then he stood and watched us pull away and he wanted very badly to go.

—JOHN STEINBECK (1940)

MARCH 13

*S*pecial Resolution [by a preacher] . . . To Return or pay for the Books I have some Time agoe borrowed and negligently and unjustly detained for Some years from the owners thereof, at those times purposing to buy them, but to this Day have omitted it; by which I have involved my Self in the Guilt of Unrighteousness.

—EBENEZER PARKMAN (1741)

I just packed my *grip*, borrowed some money from our roomer, Mr. Geo. Brown and left for Chicago at 3 o'clock this afternoon over the Rock Island. I bought a second-class ticket, for $6.50. Was raining a little, when I left Topeka and tonight it is just *pouring*. We are flying thro' Missouri and Iowa and I cannot sleep because I am going to Johnny. Some old *masher* sat in front of me, and tried to flirt with me and I was so glad of the company of a dear old lady, as far as Fairfield Iowa. She said I was too *young* and *pretty* to be *traveling alone*, but I'll bet I can take care of myself against any old fool of a *masher* that shows up. I refused all overtures to talk and would not even look at him. I told him I had a husband and he would not believe it.

—MARTHA FARNSWORTH (1890)

*V*isit from Sec'y Baker. Poked fingers in breech blocks and made usual helpless remarks of layman. Looked about as uncomfortable as he probably was. Gen. Pershing with him. Had honor of saluting him. Seemed more interested in state of my buttons than soul. Generals get that way.

—HOWARD O'BRIEN (1918)

*A*fter dinner we went up to Bonny Hall [in Parker's Ferry, South Carolina] to hear singing. This was a great barony . . . ; Sherman burned the old mansion, but the live oaks were not harmed. . . . We sat out there on a terrace, and the vast cloudy branches, crowned here and there with some stars, made a background for the singers. It was illuminated by a fire on a tall cement block, as if it were a pagan altar; it was almost too flaming. . . . There was fire enough for it to be human sacrifice. It was a choir of four baritones, two basses, and two altos, led by one named Isaiah. . . . I have never heard more velvety voices; somehow virginal. . . . Now and then they began "How dry I am," . . . whereupon the house-man, one named Ephraim, brought a trayful of gin and grape juice. . . . The Negroes here have a quiet and melancholy which is a surprise to me; none of the good spirits and bird chatter and jolly fidgets which we know in the North. I have no idea whether that is voodoo, or malaria, or their memory of injustices.

—GLENWAY WESCOTT (1942)

MARCH 14

*E*nglish tenacity [is] in strong contrast with our facility. The facile American sheds his Puritanism when he leaves Cape Cod, runs into all English and French vices with great zest, and is neither Unitarian, nor Calvinist, nor Catholic, nor stands for any known thought or thing; which is very distasteful to English honour. It is a bad sign that I have met with many Americans who flattered themselves that they pass for English. Levity, levity. I do not wish to be mistaken for an Englishman, more than I wish Monadnock or Nahant or Nantucket to be mistaken for Wales or the Isle of Wight.

—RALPH WALDO EMERSON (1848)

*M*y dear Beth died at three this morning, after two years of patient pain. . . . A curious thing happened, and I will tell it here, for Dr. G. said it was a fact. A few moments after the last breath came, as Mother and I sat silently watching the shadow fall on the dear little face, I saw a light mist rise from the body, and float up and vanish in the air. Mother's eyes followed mine, and when I said, "What did you see?" she described the same light mist. Dr. G. said it was the life departing visibly. . . . On Monday Dr. Huntington read the Chapel service, and we sang her favorite hymn. Mr. Emerson, Henry Thoreau, Sanborn, and John Pratt, carried her out of the old home to the new one at Sleepy Hollow chosen by herself. So the first break comes, and I know what death means,—a liberator for her, a teacher for us.

—LOUISA MAY ALCOTT (1858)

MARCH 15

*R*eturnd to Penningtons we got our Suppers & was Lighted in to a Room & I not being so good a Woodsman as the rest of my Company striped my self very orderly & sent in to the Bed as they call'd it when to my Surprize I found it to be nothing but a Little Straw—Matted together without Sheets or any thing else but only one Thread Bear blanket with double its Weight of Vermin such as Lice Fleas &c. I was glad to get up (as soon as the Light was carried from us) & put on my Cloths & Lay as my Companions. Had we not have been very tired, I am sure we should not have slep'd much that night. I made a Promise not to Sleep so from that time forward chusing rather to sleep in the open Air before a fire as will Appear hereafter.

—GEORGE WASHINGTON (1748)

I sometimes in my sprightly moments consider myself, in my great chair at school, as some dictator at the head of a commonwealth. In this little state I can discover all the great geniuses, all the surprising actions and revolutions of the great world, in miniature. I have several renowned generals but three feet high, and several deep projecting politicians in petticoats. I have others catching and dissecting flies, accumulating remarkable pebbles, cockle shells, &c., with as ardent curiosity as any virtuoso in the Royal Society. Some rattle and thunder out A, B, C, with as much fire and impetuosity as Alexander fought, and very often sit down and cry as heartily upon being outspelt, as Caesar did, when at Alexander's sepulchre he recollected that the Macedonian hero had conquered the world before his age. At one table sits Mr. Insipid, foppling and fluttering, spinning his whirligig, or playing with his fingers, as gaily and wittily as any Frenchified coxcomb brandishes his cane or rattles his snuff-box. At another, sits the polemical divine, plodding and wrangling in his mind about "Adam's fall, in which we sinned all," as his Primer has it. In short, my little school, like the great world, is made up of kings, politicians, divines, L. D.'s, fops, buffoons, fiddlers, sycophants, fools, coxcombs, chimney sweepers, and every other character drawn in history, or seen in the world. Is it not, then, the highest pleasure, my friend, to preside in this little world?

—JOHN ADAMS (1756)

*M*aj. Goodwin falls dead in street-car.—My first thought (& upon talking with others they had had at times similar thoughts) "If it was me I should think with my last gasp, 'So I have had all this dreadful teeth-scraping for nothing'. . . ." I had lately had most all the enamel cleaned off my teeth, by Dr. Riggs, an old fool who helped Dr. Wells, of Hartford, make in 1835, the first application of anesthesia to surgical purposes that was ever made in the world.

—MARK TWAIN (1878)

MARCH 16

*C*hickatabot came with his sannops and squaws, and presented the governor with a hogshead of Indian corn. After they had all dined, and had each a small cup of sack and beer, and the men tobacco, he sent away all his men and women, (though the governor would have stayed them, in regard of the rain and thunder). Himself and one squaw and one sannop stayed all night, and, being in English clothes, the governor set him at his own table, where he behaved himself as soberly, etc., as an Englishman. The next day after dinner he returned home, the governor giving him cheese and peas and a mug and some other small things.

—JOHN WINTHROP (1631)

I made Jack Foster's acquaintance when I first arrived [in St. Augustine, Florida], but he has been away a good deal. He is very homely, & wears shockingly old fashioned clothes, checked pantaloons for instance.—On the other hand, his blood is blue, his connections splendid, his manners excellent; he is polite, kind, attentive, jolly, amusing, & 23. What is more, he has never said or done anything that jarred me in the least. We had a very nice time together at the Tableaux, & he was very attentive. After that I saw him occasionally, & about three weeks ago, he made me a present of a beautiful little alligator, about eight inches long, & just the right size.

—JULIA NEWBERRY (1870)

G ot a copy of *New Republic*. Pacifist leanings. Most of army has, too. War spirit in inverse ratio to proximity to war. Quickest way to end it, put all journalists and politicians under arms. Leave peace arrangements to soldiers, under rank of Lieut. Make talkers fight and fighters talk. . . . Aim of war not to destroy Germans—great people—but make them good citizens of free world. Mr. Wilson sees this. Several laps ahead of the Metternich-Talleyrand school of thought.

—HOWARD O'BRIEN (1918)

S unde, one of our patients, is a Norwegian boy, who is named after the farm in Norway where he was born. He fought against the Nazis in his own country and escaped in a fishing boat. He came to Brooklyn to live with his sister. He is going to be adopted by a couple in Cedar Rapids, Iowa, who will turn their business over to him because they have no children of their own. He is what the war is being fought for.

—ANNE MCCAUGHEY (1944)

MARCH 17

*T*he comet that the Millerites are in such a stew about shone out in great glory tonight. His nucleus was hid below the horizon, but his tail streamed up, a long riband of pale transparent light, like that of an aurora, from the horizon nearly to the zenith. The question of comet or zodiacal light is warmly discussed, but there can hardly be a doubt, I think, but that it's really a comet. If it be the zodiacal light, the respectable functionary has certainly placed itself in a new position before the public.

—GEORGE TEMPLETON STRONG (1843)

I have to be constantly on the watch for fear of my boys doing something to provoke the persecution of the Yankees. Not long since I heard an explosion in the yard loud enough to create some alarm, and on hurrying out saw a squad of soldiers approaching the scene of action, thinking it was an alarm. The noise proceeded from a battery the boys had erected on the top of the cistern and had supplied it with guns they had manufactured out of musket barrels cut into lengths of eight or nine inches, and bored for a touch hole, then mounted on carriages of their own make. I had noticed them very busily engaged about the yard for some time but never dreamed what they were after.

—CORNELIA PEAKE MCDONALD (1863)

*S*t. Patricks Day in the morning, and it is a fine morning, weather beautiful. This is the day of the "Irish Brigade Jubilee". . . . At ten O'Clock the horses and riders came in . . . and arranged themselves in line, and then the word was given and away they go. Some went over the hurdles and ditches, some flew the track and ran through the crowd of soldiers. A sergeant of the 69th New York was trampled to death and half a dozen others badly wounded. The Ambulance was hauling dead and wounded away all day. The second round the Black Stallion of the Dutch Col fell over a hurdle and broke his neck and both arms of the Colonel. They sent the Colonel to the Hospital, rolled the dead horse out of the way and went ahead as if nothing had happened. Corporal Chisholm and myself sit in the Head Quarters carriage of Genl Meade on top of the hill four hundred yards away and we was hardly safe there, as one horse flew the track and nearly run through the carriage we sit in. . . . On they went, horses flying the track, running over the spectators, falling over the hurdles, into the ditches, breaking arms, legs &c. We soon got tired and came back to camp. Never did I see such a crazy time. I will have to alter my mind if I ever go to see another Irish fair.

—SAMUEL A. CLEAR (1865)

*B*efore dinner last night we got the black Isaiah to take us upon the canals in a paddleboat. The perfectly still water is all spotted with last year's lily pads, in a fine variety of rotten colors. Now and then a flock of ducks would whir up ahead of us, splashing the water white; and there were coot and bitterns and one solemnly flying great heron, Herodias. Isaiah says the alligators are still in their winter sleep. We sat close, side by side, in the prow of the narrow damp old craft, with only the faint sound of the paddling behind us, as in a gondola, sliding as if there were a magnet drawing us along. I have been reading A. Huxley's biography of Father Joseph, *L'eminence grise:* a kind of mysticism beautifully written and rather thrilling. . . . So as we slid amid the pale reeds we discussed that.

—GLENWAY WESCOTT (1942)

MARCH 18

*I*n Lucy's confectionary shop I saw a man named Ambler, who is lecturing on "Electro Psychology" in this place, operate

95

upon a boy, arrest his motions instantly, oblige him to follow him, paralyze him, make him feel a hornet's nest around his head, etc. Really, the power of the will of a man over his fellow is surprising and a mystery.

—BENJAMIN BROWNE FOSTER (1850)

I wonder if it be a sin to think slavery a curse to any land. Sumner said not one word of this hated institution which is not true. Men & women are punished when their masters & mistresses are brutes & not when they do wrong—& then we live surrounded by prostitutes. An abandoned woman is sent out of any decent house elsewhere. Who thinks any worse of a Negro or Mulatto woman for being a thing we can't name. God forgive *us*, but ours is a *monstrous* system & wrong & iniquity. Perhaps the rest of the world is as bad. This *only* I see: like the patriarchs of old our men live all in one house with their wives & their concubines, & the Mulattoes one sees in every family exactly resemble the white children—& every lady tells you who is the father of all the Mulatto children in everybody's household, but those in her own, she seems to think drop from the clouds or pretends so to think. . . . Thank God for my country women—alas for the men! . . . Flocks & herds & slaves—& wife Leah does not suffice. Rachel must be *added*, if not *married*. & all the time they seem to think themselves patterns—models of husbands & fathers.

—MARY BOYKIN CHESNUT (1861)

*L*ast night Sara and I dined with F. Scott Fitzgerald and his wife, Zelda. It was a somewhat weird evening. The Fitzgeralds live in an old-fashioned house in the woods near Towson. . . . Its spookiness is not diminished by the fact that Zelda is palpably only half sane. . . . She occupies herself largely in painting, and her paintings are full of grotesque exaggerations and fantastic ideas. Scott himself also begins to show signs of a disordered mind. Sometime ago he had what he now calls a nervous breakdown. . . . He has been trying for six years to write a new novel, but it remains unfinished. . . . Meanwhile, he has sought to raise money by writing dreadful drivel for the *Saturday Evening Post*. . . . Apparently Zelda takes no interest whatever in household affairs. She had not even planned the seating of her guests, and the dinner had apparently been arranged by the cook. After dinner Sara and Zelda sat on a sofa together to talk of their early days in Montgomery. Sara told me that Zelda gritted her teeth during the whole conversation.

—H. L. MENCKEN (1933)

MARCH 19

I rose at 6 o'clock and read the Psalms and four chapters in the Greek Testament. I said my prayers and ate milk for breakfast. My wife continued disordered with her cold. About 11 o'clock I went to church, where I heard that Captain B-r-k was dead suddenly. It rained a little before church. After sermon I invited Colonel Eppes and his wife and the sheriff and Mr. C-s to dinner. I ate fish. In the afternoon the company went away and soon after there came a great gust of wind and rain to punish them for not staying. It likewise thundered a little. In the evening I neglected to say my prayers but had good health, good thoughts, and good humor, thanks be to God Almighty. Nurse was taken sick at church.

—WILLIAM BYRD (1710)

*W*hen I walk in the fields of Concord and meditate on the destiny of this prosperous slip of the Saxon family, the unexhausted energies of this new country, I forget that this which is now Concord was once Musketaquid, and that the *American race* has had its destiny also. Everywhere in the fields, in the corn and grain land, the earth is strewn with the relics of a race which has vanished as completely as if trodden in with the earth. Is it not good to remember the eternity behind me as well as the eternity before? Wherever I go I tread in the tracks of the Indian. I pick up the bolt which he has but just dropped at my feet. And if I consider destiny I am on his trail.

—HENRY DAVID THOREAU (1842)

MARCH 20

*O*ur family, consisting of father, mother, two brothers and one sister, left this morning for that far and much talked of country, California. . . . Our train numbered fifty wagons. The last hours were spent in bidding good bye to old friends. My mother is heartbroken over this separation of relatives and friends. Giving up old associations for what? Good health, perhaps. My father is going in search of health, not gold. The last good bye has been said—the last glimpse of our old home on the hill. . . . Our carriage upset at one place. All were thrown out, but no one was hurt. We were detained several hours on account of this accident. My mother thought it a bad omen and wanted to return and give up the trip.

—SALLIE HESTER (1849)

*T*he secesh are getting pretty high here. The other day when some rebel prisoners passed through here, a great crowd of them went down to the cars & hurrad for Jeff Davis and made a great fuss over the scamps. It is said they expected them for some days & had even got a dinner ready for them. . . . The secesh ladies have also had a sewing society and have been supplying the rebel prisoners. Gen Halleck sent an order here that hurraing for Jeff was not to be allowed.

—FRANCES DALLAM PETER (1862)

*N*oble system, truly. . . . where it is impossible to reward the most illustrious & fittest citizens with the Presidency. Look at the list: Polk, Tyler, Pierce, &c &c, & *almost* Tilden, with a suit pending for swindling the revenue. Half the nation voted for him. Put these things in the mouth of critical foreigner, else they will have no force & teach no lesson. "The Senator" "the Senator"—always "the Senator"—& he a thief. Our adoration of titles. "Hon"—procured in legislature 30 yrs ago. No congressman is entitled to a title.

—MARK TWAIN (1878)

*L*ay longer than I desired to lie, and so hurried to the office, and greatly astonished to read that the late Chief Justice Mr. Taft had said that he considered the result of Prohibition glorious. But all that I could think of was "Glorious! Glorious! One pint of wine among the four of us."

—FRANKLIN PIERCE ADAMS (1930)

*W*henever people talk to me of the incomparable advantages of America, I think of all these broken middle-class lives which I know so well. I think of the fright and the dark rooms in which all these people move. But here we talk of our material advantages over those who live in other countries, never saying that the European, no matter how poor, has a whole inner life built around the facts of his poverty and its acceptance. Here there is only shame and regret, resignation, bitterness, frustration, and an all-abiding sense of inadequacy and anxiety. Here they keep muttering to themselves, "Hopeless, hopeless," and are degraded. In Europe they say, "This is what it is," and they work within the form of poverty and manage to make good rich happy lives for themselves. To meet a happy person in America is to usually meet a person of little or no power, of limited imagination, sensitivity, or perception. From this generalization I exclude certain types

99

of master craftsmen, those who have mastered their work no matter how humble, who have established mastership over materials, things, wood, machines, whatever it may be.

—CLIFFORD ODETS (1940)

MARCH 21

*C*lear, windy, and turning colder. My hands have been hauling leaves, and firewood & working about the new-ground. Hard times is here & worse is coming. Wife, (and me too) are in a peck of trouble about the probability of my being drafted for the war. I confess I did not think that I would be liable to go so soon, but now I think my chance is as good as any ones. If I was to go; I had much rather have gone as a volenteer. Then I could choose my company and arms &c but now, I fear that privaledge is denied me. But if I go, I will try to go as reconciled as well as I can. . . . Somthing has to be done, and I should do my part. . . . Parting with my family will be worse than meeting the yankeys.

—DAVID GOLIGHTLY HARRIS (1862)

*T*he alligator died last night, a most untimely death, & from no apparent cause; I feel dreadfully about it, & especially so, because I did not paint his picture as I might have done.

—JULIA NEWBERRY (1870)

*I*n London, the homosexual circulates everywhere; but in New York he is much more condemned to inhabit an all-homosexual world; and this life of segregation is one of the disadvantages that Wystan (W. H. Auden) has had to accept in coming to live in the United States. But he accepts it and celebrates "celibacy," and . . . makes it a proof of his moral strength.—There was a barman handing out champagne in little tumblers. Wystan told me, in the course of the evening, that he had decided to give them champagne, because whisky often made people quarrelsome. I caught a glimpse of cases of champagne in a bedroom.

—EDMUND WILSON (1955)

MARCH 22

*M*rs. Hutchinson appeared again. . . . After she was excommunicated, her spirits, which seemed before to be somewhat dejected, revived again, and she gloried in her sufferings, saying, that it was the greatest happiness, next to Christ, that ever befel her. Indeed, it was a happy day to the churches of Christ here, and to many poor souls, who had been seduced by her, who, by what they heard and saw that day, were (through the grace of God) brought off quite from her errors, and settled again in the truth. . . . After two or three days, the governor sent a warrant to Mrs. Hutchinson to depart this jurisdiction before the last of this month, according to the order of court, and for that end set her at liberty from her former constraint, so as she was not to go forth of her own house till her departure . . . to Pascataquack; but she changed her mind, and went by land to Providence, and so to the island in the Naragansett Bay, which her husband and the rest of that sect had purchased of the Indians, and prepared with all speed to remove onto.

—JOHN WINTHROP (1638)

*M*y aunt and uncle sit in their front room every night and listen to radio programs for several hours without once turning the machine off. Best of all he likes the news broadcasts, he said. Every time he hears of more people being killed in

Europe he begins to talk to himself as he rocks himself to and fro like a mourner in a synagogue. Mr. Goodman, the star boarder in their house . . . is a shirtcutter by trade. A writer looks at your face, a cobbler at your shoes. Naturally Goodman looks at your shirts. As I shook his hand in greeting he said, "Three-and-a-half dollars."

—CLIFFORD ODETS (1940)

MARCH 23

*W*e got a long sighted government. When everybody has got money they cut taxes, and when they're broke they raise 'em. That's statesmanship of the highest order. The reason there wasn't much unemployment in the last ten years preceding '29 was every man that was out of a job went to work for the government, state or city. It costs ten times more to govern us than it used to, and we are not governed one-tenth as good.

—WILL ROGERS (1932)

I spent the evening quarreling with a young communist. He is an Italian—about 28—school teacher, very superficial education, didactic, self-centered. In person quite charming. He has great physical charm and vitality so the women cluster to him and are sorry for him when he is attacked. They are perhaps thinking of being in bed with him. He may be quite clever there.

—SHERWOOD ANDERSON (1936)

*I*n Europe, I think of New York with a nostalgia I shouldn't have expected. The restaurants in New York of all nations:

French, Italian, German, Jewish-Roumanian, Russian, in which I have sat with friends who, by birth or in the second generation, derived from all those nationalities. We all had it in common that we were struggling with New York, stimulated by New York. More interesting, and perhaps more profitable—after all—than Europe. This is where the new culture, the new civilization, has really been being produced; the new American internationalism.—Bismarck herring and pickles, sauerbraten and beer, zimbalon music, cheese and apple, Orvieto in little straw-basketed flasks.

—EDMUND WILSON (1954)

MARCH 24

*R*eturnd home from my journey to Frederick, etca., and found that the Hound Bitch Maiden had taken Dog promiscuously; That the Bitch Lady was in Heat and had also been promiscuously lind, and therefore I did not shut her up; That Dutchess was shut up, and had been lind twice by Drunkard, but was out one Night in her heat, and supposd to be lind by other Dogs; That Truelove was also in the House, as was Mopsy likewise (who had been seen lind to Pilot before she was shut up).

—GEORGE WASHINGTON (1769)

*T*he fault of [Bronson] Alcott's [utopian] community is that it has only room for one.

—RALPH WALDO EMERSON (1846)

*O*ther spiritual items in the news are that his brother has erected a fourteen-foot statue of Huey Long on the lawn of the capital. Then there is the story of the woman who lifted the American press to seventh heaven. She announced she was expectant of quintuplets. Immediately a fund was created for her, she was given free and wonderful prenatal care. The world has been beating a path to her doorway for several days—her husband and herself have already been photographed in every position but the marital one. Yesterday the bubble burst: only one baby is to be born, according to the latest X-rays. The woman has been dropped like a hot plate loaded with venereal diseases. . . . I was told of a case in Philadelphia. A girl in her early teens was awarded a framed print for honor work in school. The child refused to accept it but burst into tears when the picture was finally forced on her. . . . It was finally revealed that the girl is living in one room with three families sharing it by putting up sheets as walls . . . and there was no place to hang the picture. It seems to me that this sort of violence, so raw and primitive, could happen only in America: a man in Colorado wanted to kill himself. He stood on a box of dynamite and lit the fuse. There was only a partial explosion so the man crawled over to another box, his left leg almost blown off but still dangling, and began to light another fuse but was stopped by friends. . . . I was thinking that when I was a boy the whole promise of American life was contained for me in Christmas cards which showed a warm little house snuggled in a snow scene by night; often little boys or girls were walking up the path of the door and carrying bundles of good things. This represented protection, a home and hearth, goodness and comfort, all things which become increasingly more difficult to attain.

—Clifford Odets (1940)

MARCH 25

$\mathscr{P}$arson Ware sent to me for a pint of canary, he being sick of the gripes with the New England rum, which I sent him, notwithstanding I have but a little, because I should be glad if I were in his condition to receive such a kindness from another.

—WILLIAM BYRD (1709)

I approach the term when my daily journal must cease from physical disability to keep it up. I have now struggled nearly five years, without the interval of a day while mind and body have been wearing away under the daily, silent, but unremitting erosion of time. I rose this morning at four, and with smarting, bloodshot eye and shivering hand, still sat down and wrote to fill up the chasm of the closing days of the last week; but my stern chase after Time is, to borrow a simile from Tom Paine, like the race of a man with a wooden leg after a horse.

—JOHN QUINCY ADAMS (1844)

I wish I could flee into the wilderness as Lot fled from Sodom and take refuge in some dull but decent New England village. No rich and crowded community can long survive universal suffrage.

—GEORGE TEMPLETON STRONG (1872)

*S*hocked this morning to see a picture in the publick prints of A. Woollcott smoking a cigarre [a commercial endorsement] in especiall when not only does he not smoke them save once or twice a year, but last night and the night before at his house he did not even offer me one. At the office all day, and for a walk through the city, and bought some arbutus to take to the ailing poets of the town, Miss Edna Millay and Mr. A. Ficke. And I could not help thinking, I too am an ailing poet, yet no one giveth me so much as a pansy.

—FRANKLIN PIERCE ADAMS (1925)

MARCH 26

*T*he Bitch Musick brought five Puppies, one of which being thought not truc was drownd immediately—the others, being somewhat like the Dog (Lockwood of Mr. Fairfax) which got them, were saved.

—GEORGE WASHINGTON (1769)

*W*e have had a hard fatiguing journey and have just arrived at Pittsburg. . . . We have rode night & day & the roads bad enough. We have now crossed the Allegany Mountains. Witnessed their snow capped tops, been exposed to dangers seen & unseen but an Almighty arm has sustained us. Every variety of scenery has been presented to our view. Lofty mountains, steep declivities, extensive plains, cultivated fields, uncultivated forests, pleasant villages & villages composed of log huts, have alternately met our view. . . . I have not just the opinion of the West I formerly had. . . . The soil I judge to be very fertile, but the people poor & indolent. The buildings look bad & the door yards converted into barn yards. I do not see what could induce any one to leave the refined society of New England for a residence among such a people, unless it be to do them good.

—SARAH WHITE SMITH (1838)

*W*ent . . . to Gordon's furniture plant and was much upset. He is making rather cheap imitations of old hand furniture. It made me ill to see so many men at work, making second rate stuff. The whole experience gave me a queer physical setback.

—SHERWOOD ANDERSON (1937)

MARCH 27

*T*he wife of one William Dyer, a milliner in the New Exchange, a very proper and fair woman, and both of them notoriously infected with Mrs. Hutchinson's errors, and very censorious and troublesome, (she being of a very proud spirit, and much addicted to revelations,) had been delivered of [a] child some few months before, October 17, and the child buried, (being stillborn,) and viewed of none but Mrs. Hutchinson and the midwife, one Hawkins's wife, a rank familist also; and another woman had a glimpse of it, who, not being able to keep counsel, as the other two did, some rumor began to spread, that the child was a monster. . . . At first she [the midwife] confessed only, that the head was defective and misplaced, but being told that Mrs. Hutchinson had revealed all, and that he [the governor] intended to have it taken up and viewed, she made this report of it, viz.: It was a woman child, stillborn, about two months before the just time, having life a few hours before; it came hiplings till she turned it; it was of ordinary bigness; it had a face, but no head, and the ears stood upon the shoulders and were like an ape's; it had no forehead, but over the eyes four horns, hard and sharp; two of them were above one inch long, the other two shorter; the eyes standing out, and the mouth also; the nose hooked upward; all over the breast and back full of sharp pricks and scales, like a thornback; the navel and all the belly, with the distinction of the sex, were where the back should be, and the back and hips before, where the belly should have been; behind, between the shoulders, it had two mouths, and in each of them a piece of red flesh sticking out; it had arms

107

and legs as other children; but, instead of toes, it had on each foot three claws, like a young fowl, with sharp talons.

—JOHN WINTHROP (1638)

*A*nother attack of vertigo. Ill for a week. Sleepless nights. Head worked like a steam engine & would not stop. Planned "Jo's Boys" to the end & longed to get up & write it. Told Dr. W[esselhoeft] that he had better let me get the ideas *out* then I could rest. He very wisely agreed & said, "As soon as you can write half an hour a day & see if it does you good. Rebellious brains must be attended to or trouble comes." So I began as soon as able, & was satisfied that we were right for my head felt better very soon, & with much care about not over doing I had some pleasant hours when I forgot my body & lived in my mind.

—LOUISA MAY ALCOTT (1886)

A dream I had four nights ago. I found myself, in the dream, walking along the edge of a pool with Mr. and Mrs. Roosevelt. Without fuss, quietly, the three of us dropped into the pool with all of our clothes on seemingly with a complete calm faith in the fact that one always drops into a pool with all the clothes on. Mrs. Roosevelt and myself stepped out of the pool, still dressed and dry as before and did not seem surprised at that either. Mr. Roosevelt stayed in the pool, but looked up at me with only his head above water with a mischievous glance, saying, "Oh, you Bolshie you." . . . A moment later the three of us were lying side by side, flat on the stomachs, while many people were passing by us exactly as if we were lying on a boardwalk and sunning ourselves.

—CLIFFORD ODETS (1940)

MARCH 28

*I*t is an old story, but new to me, that there is a deep tragedy in the life of Woodrow Wilson, a first-class play. Perhaps it should be called *The New Freedom*, after his policy and practical effort to make democracy work. In a short time now we may see history repeating itself (this time as "a farce," as Marx puts it) when F. D. R. begins to meddle with America's position in relation to the present quiet war in Europe. Quixotic American presidents scorn socialism; that is why they are quixotic! A Wilson play might open with this statement, made by Wilson perhaps: "Gentlemen, the war is over!" This same play might end when the broken Wilson appears on the balcony of his house on Armistice Day in 1924 and says it was cowardly of America to reject the League of Nations. He is by this time a dying man and is dead shortly afterwards.

—CLIFFORD ODETS (1940)

*O*ne night, late, we walked out and saw the lurid orange glow of a fire down below the high school. I dragged Ted to it, hoping for houses in a holocaust, parents jumping out of the window with babies, but nothing such: a neighborhood burning a communal acreage of scrubby grass field, frames orange in darkness, friendly shouts across the flaming wasteland, silhouettes of men and children fixing a border with tufts of lit grasses, beating out a blaze with brooms as it jeopardized a fence. . . . The fire was oddly satisfying. I longed for an incident, an accident. What unleashed desire there must be in one for general carnage. I walk around the streets, braced and ready and almost wishing to test my eye and fiber on tragedy—a child crushed by a car, a house on fire, someone thrown into a tree by a horse. Nothing happens: I walk the razor's edge of jeopardy.

—SYLVIA PLATH (1958)

MARCH 29

$\mathcal{I}$ met at Mr. Bellows' a Mr. Kay, a Philadelphia bookseller, a man who, though successful in his calling and very conversant in his business, is one of the Fourierites—a queer combination of worldly shrewdness with transcendental flightiness. His face bespoke it all—it was thin and sallow, and comical in the extreme. He exposed the secrets of the bookselling trade, which he thought the most trickish going. The little, contemptible faces—the thin, weak, tottering figures—that one meets here on Broadway, are disgusting. One feels savage with human nature.

—Francis Parkman (1846)

$\mathcal{T}$own Meeting. 20 women there & voted first thanks to father. Polls closed, in joke we thought as Judge Hoar proposed it. Proved to be in earnest & *we* elected a good school committee. Quiet time, no fuss.

—Louisa May Alcott (1880)

$\mathcal{T}$he day at Feibleman's—Jeff and Lillian. Perfect day with everyone nice. The Feibleman house some 50 miles out of New Orleans on a quiet bayou. There is a big swimming pool and we all swam. It was one of those days when many conflicting personalities all seem to blend, something bigger, nicer than any one person in the air.

—Sherwood Anderson (1936)

$\mathcal{J}$anet Flanner telephoned and complained at length in her grand commonsense fashion: the world, the wickedness, Spain, the recession in America; dear little old cold volcano that she is. Today I took her to lunch; but oh, we're not as much alike or in agreement as she seems to think. She has

110

no sense of mystery. . . . Janet and I talked about the Semitic problem. (I remember that when Jean-Michel Frank had his nose fixed, she said she thought circumcision should be local.)

—GLENWAY WESCOTT (1938)

MARCH 30

*P*ray, what things interest me at present? A long soaking rain, the drops trickling down the stubble, while I lay drenched on a last year's bed of wild oats by the side of some bare hill, ruminating.

—HENRY DAVID THOREAU (1840)

[In wartime Richmond] *T*he gaunt form of wretched famine still approaches with rapid strides. . . . It is strange that on the 30th of March, even in the "sunny South," the fruit trees are as bare of blossoms and foilage as at mid-winter. We shall have fire until the middle of May,—six months of winter! I am spading up my garden . . . to raise a few vegetables to eke out a miserable subsistence for my family. My daughter Ann reads Shakespeare to me o'nights, which saves my eyes.

—JOHN BEAUCHAMP JONES (1863)

*W*e got here [Laurel, Mississippi] at 3. Had one puncture. Dirt and gravel roads most of the way. Very hot. The dogwood in bloom. . . . Everywhere along the road the riot of spring and flowers. But it was hot, hot.

—SHERWOOD ANDERSON (1936)

MARCH 31

This time there is no repulse but a heavy fire is poured into us and away we go over our dead and wounded into the and over the Rebel dead and wounded. The rebs fell back slowly disputing every inch of ground, but finally we got them on the fast line and pushed them two miles as near as I could tell. All this time our boys was falling fast and so was the Johnnies. The woods was full of the ghastly Corpses of the dead, and the shrieks of the wounded and dying mingled with the crack of the musket and rumble of the artillery was calculated to impress the whole upon the mind so indelibly that it would last as long as life continued. As I was running past a wounded rebel he caught me by the Pant leg and held me so tight I had to beat his hand lose with my gun. He wanted me to help him off the field. On we went and such cheering as the Old Irish Brigade can only do. . . . There seems to be a great determination throughout all the army to end the war as soon as possible.

—SAMUEL A. CLEAR (1865)

I might as well put in here a note on our seeing Faulkner a few weeks ago. . . . He talked more, and more interestingly, than I had been led to expect. . . . He said that it was significant that one of the Southern generals had written their memoirs of the war. I replied that a number of them had—[James] Longstreet, for example. Longstreet had lived long enough, he answered. He had seen him once, as a child. Longstreet had come to Oxford, and Faulkner had been taken to see him. He remembered an old man with a beard. But

Faulkner had promptly piped up: What was the matter with you at Gettysburg? and his parents had whisked him away. In Charlottesville, a young instructor at the University, a South Carolinian, told me that Longstreet had published three different versions of his memoirs—in each further minimizing his responsibility for the Gettysburg defeat. As the various generals died and could no longer object to what he wrote, he unloaded the blame on others, till, at last, after the death of Lee, he made Lee mainly responsible.

—EDMUND WILSON (1953)

✑ APRIL ✑

APRIL 1

𝒢randmother sent me up into the little chamber to-day to straighten things and get the room ready to be cleaned. I found a little book called "Child's Pilgrim Progress, Illustrated," that I had never seen before. I got as far as Giant Despair when Anna came up and said Grandmother sent her to see what I was doing, and she went back and told her that I was sitting on the floor in the midst of books and papers and was so absorbed in "Pilgrim's Progress" that I had made none myself. It must be a good book for Grandmother did not say a word. Father sent us "Gulliver's Travels" and there is a gilt picture on the green cover, of a giant with legs astride and little Lilliputians standing underneath, who do not come up to his knees. Grandmother did not like the picture, so she pasted a piece of pink calico over it, so we could only see the giant from his waist up. I love the story of Cinderella and the poem, " 'Twas the night before Christmas," and I am sorry that there are no fairies and no Santa Claus.

—CAROLINE COWLES RICHARDS (1853)

𝐼t made me so mad almost beside my self that men can sit up and say to the smartest woman that ever lived "I am the head, I am made by God with more power. My will is the

114

strongest. You are out of your sphere." Oh, I think it's dreadful to be told that *Tom Carey* and *Charles Thomas* have more power than *we* have. Of course they have more *brute* strength but so has a prize fighter more than a gentleman. Oh I can't stand it. . . . I believe that I have as much sense as any boy I know. . . . It seems to me I'd die if I could do *anything* to show that a woman is equal to a man, it is such a burning shame that a woman should have it always poked in their faces. If I have to give up my freedom in the slightest degree, *I'll never marry*—and I don't expect to any how, for if Heavenly Father spares me my senses I'll never be dependent on any one man or woman. . . . Oh, how I wish I had the intellect to do something only to show that all my talk ain't gabble. I am throughly and heartly woman's Right and never expect to change my opinion. I'll *despise*, and *hate* and *abhore* myself if I do. And now if I'm ever going to do anything I must study.

—M. CAREY THOMAS (1872)

APRIL 2

The governor, with advice of some other of the magistrates and of the elders of Boston, caused the said monster to be taken up, and though it were much corrupted, yet most of those things were to be seen, as the horns and claws, the scales, etc. When it died in the mother's body, (which was about two hours before the birth,) the bed whereon the mother lay did shake, and withal there was such a noisome savor, as most of the women were taken with extreme vomiting and purging, so as they were forced to depart; and others of them their children were taken with convulsions, (which they never had before nor after,) and so were sent for home, so as by these occasions it came to be concealed.

—JOHN WINTHROP (1638)

$\mathcal{B}$enjamin Gourd of Roxbury (being about 17 years of age) was executed for committing Bestiality * * * N. B. He committed the filthines at noon day in an open yard. He after confessed that he had lived in that sin a year. The causes he alledged were idlenes, not obeying parents, &c.

—SAMUEL SEWALL (1673)

$\mathcal{C}$rossed the Susquehanna in a flat boat filled with quiet, stupid, stout Dutch-men, women, and pretty girls. Some octogenarian veterans, and two young, fat dandies with checked breeches and frogged wrappers. The whole was a striking contrast to a corresponding group of Yankees. In the wretched cars, too, the same phlegm and stolidity were apparent—their minds were gone to sleep.

—FRANCIS PARKMAN (1846)

$\mathcal{T}$own meeting. Seven women vote. I am one of them & A. another. A poor show for a town that prides itself on its culture & independence.

—LOUISA MAY ALCOTT (1883)

APRIL 3

$\mathcal{E}$vening, Professor Stowe lectured in the Senior Recitation Room. It was an account of his "conversion" through the chapter of *Isaiah* commencing "Ho, everyone," etc. A brutal outrage was perpetrated last night. The medical college was entered, a body, partly dissected, taken from the dissecting room and hung on a tree in the mall.

—BENJAMIN BROWNE FOSTER (1852)

*A*s I have not heard from my parents since the war, they living in New York, I thought I would send a personal advertisement to a New York paper to let them know that my brother and myself are well, and for them to send an answer through the Richmond paper. I gave this to a Yankee picket, who promised me he would send it to New York.

—LEWIS LEON (1864)

*W*alking down Wall Street, I saw something on the *Commercial Advertiser* bulletin board. . . . I read the announcement "Petersburg is taken" and went into the office in quest of particulars. The man behind the counter was slowly painting in large letters on a large sheet of brown paper another annunciation for the board outside: "Richmond is"—"What's that about Richmond?" said I. "Anything more?" He was too busy for speech, but he went on with a capital C, and a capital A, and so on, till I read the word CAPTURED!!! . . . . An enormous crowd soon blocked that part of Wall Street, and speeches began. . . . Never before did I hear cheering that came straight from the heart. . . . These were spontaneous and involuntary and of vast "magnetizing" power. They sang "Old Hundred," the Doxology, "John Brown," and "The Star-Spangled Banner," repeating the last two lines of Key's song over and over, with a massive roar from the crowd and a unanimous wave of hats at the end of each repetition. I think I shall never lose the impression made by this rude, many-voiced chorale. It seemed a revelation of profound national feeling, underlying all our vulgarisms and corruptions, and vouchsafed to us in their very focus and centre, in Wall Street itself.

—GEORGE TEMPLETON STRONG (1865)

APRIL 4

*T*he garden [at the White House] was full all the morning of children & people who had come for the egg rolling. It seems such a needless destruction to the . . . grass.

—EDITH KERMIT ROOSEVELT (1904)

$\mathcal{T}$he . . . small American businessman like my father . . . is always going in and out of some small business, frantically running around to raise a few thousand dollars. Then he opens a loft shop and hires four or six workers. He is going to make a profit on their work, but often he does not get as much out of the business as they do. New York is full of such small unhappy despairing men. Finally they take on the quality of gamblers and racketeers. They borrow money from friends and relatives, from loan corporations. In the year ten they are repaying money they borrowed in the year one. But they never go hungry and they often manage to send a son or two to college. They are not bad men, but this is the only way they know to live, as small entrepreneurs who try not to be in conflict with monopoly capital. They live on a set of illusions that they are not of the working class, above that class. They do not save, for they are so used to being broke that when money comes in they spend it just as fast, so often living in luxurious suites or apartments. Life is a series of predated checks for them, of slipping in and out of traffic as long as the gasoline holds out.

—CLIFFORD ODETS (1940)

$\mathcal{I}$ am a little prejudiced against the higher education; at least present American education. . . . Its concept of and effect on the arts and the humanities are beginning to be questionable. While billions are spent on the millions, television develops, publishing declines, photography flourishes, vocabulary shrinks (except perhaps for humorists). Even great writers express themselves in baby talk or booby talk . . . inarticulateness, for lack of language. Even what our great highbrows utter often is not exactly what I call language—so much of the time it is remote from the dictionary, slack in syntax, careless of pitch, neglectful of cadence, non-clear and unbrief.

—GLENWAY WESCOTT (1953)

APRIL 5

A beautiful spring morning, our first experience of the almost magical change which in a few days comes over the face of Nature. The freshness of every-thing had lured my sister & myself on till we were two miles in the country. . . . Just as we turned to go back, we saw coming on a cross road a man on horseback riding at a quick pace, & by his side a tall negro coming steadily along. We wondered at the perfect uniformity of his steps—until, as they came nearer us, we saw one chain going from his wrists to the saddle, another was around his ancles—giving him just room enough to walk—Following them were two large thick-headed fierce-looking dogs.—The clothes of the negro were badly torn, too. . . . How changed seemed all the sweet things around us, for over them all was thrown the shine of that serpent slavery. . . . The captor was as we were afterwards told a "nigger hunter" by profession— by the side of whom his dogs looked like a far superior race of beings—for they were all their Maker gave them power to be—he a beast with power to be a man.

—CAROLINE SEABURY (1855)

I drowned two of "Hootsie's" kittens this afternoon and it nearly broke my heart; but I don't want so many cats on the place and thought *one* was enough for her; Fred has promised to do so, nearly two weeks, but could not get up courage, so I did it myself, and no one need tell *me* cats *can't count;* our Hootsie cat *can.* I went to her "nest," while she was absent and took out the two kittens, and this evening I went to her home nest, to look at the other kitten and she was curled up happy with all three; she had missed her two babies and hunted for them, found them in the bucket of water, fished them out and carried them back to her nest but they were dead. Oh! it was so dreadfully pathetic and so almost human I *vow* I will *never* do such a thing again. I made Fred bury the kittens while she was again absent from nest.

—MARTHA FARNSWORTH (1895)

The day in a kind of drunkness from the party on the night before. Slept in the afternoon. Steady rain. The wise-cracking authoress left. Talked in the evening with Fletcher McCoy of Duke. Charming wife. Dined with the Dr. Pepper man and Kansas wife. Was sleepy and a bit irritated so tried to irritate others by saying things against the South. Drank coffee—like a fool—and couldn't sleep.

—SHERWOOD ANDERSON (1936)

APRIL 6

*W*rote & sewed. . . . H. in a fuss for L. is saucy. Needs more freedom & she shall have it. A fine active girl shut up too much with quiddly old people. I know how she feels.

—LOUISA MAY ALCOTT (1887)

I took taxi to Morgan Cie to arrange for my boat ticket. Back to apartment in time to take Anne to lunch at the American Embassy at 1:00. Probably forty people there, including some of society's greatest bores. They will *never* get over talking about the time I landed at Le Bourget in 1927, and they all seem to have done the same thing: start to Le Bourget from Paris, get stuck in the traffic jam, see me ride by somewhere in an automobile, and meet me at a lunch at the embassy which Ambassador Herrick invited them to. And they usually want to hold my hand while they tell it all.

—CHARLES LINDBERGH (1939)

The advantages I have in Cambridge [at Harvard University] are partly . . . this study in the Widener Library, where conditions for working are perfect: never any interruptions. . . . The only things that depress me are the window ledges covered with pigeon excrement, and the pictures of Charles Eliot Norton, one of them rather unpleasant, and of his brother with the muttonchop whiskers. I have taken the brother down.

—EDMUND WILSON (1957)

APRIL 7

*O*ur vessels consisted of six small canoes and two large pirogues. This little fleet, although not quite so respectable as that of Columbus or Captain Cook, was still viewed by us with as much pleasure as those deservedly famed adventurers ever beheld theirs, and, I daresay, with quite as much anxiety for their safety and perservation. We were now about to penetrate a country at least two thousand miles in width, on which the foot of civilized man had never trod. The good or evil it had in store for us was for experiment yet to determine, and these little vessels contained every article by which we were to expect to subsist or defend ourselves. However, as the state of mind in which we are, generally gives the coloring to events, when the imagination is suffered to wander into futurity, the picture which now presented itself to me was a most pleasing one.

—MERIWETHER LEWIS (1805)

*C*apt. Wirtz prowls around the stockade with a rebel escort of guards, looking for tunnels. Is very suspicious of amateur wells which some have dug for water. It is useless to speak to him about our condition, as he will give us no satisfaction whatever. Says it is good enough for us ——— Yankees. . . . Prison is all the time being made stronger, more guards coming and artillery looking at us rather unpleasantly from many directions. Think it impossible for any to get away here, so

121

far from our lines. . . . Still fully one-half of all here are constantly on the alert for chances to get away. Foremost in all schemes for freedom is Hendryx, and we are engaging in a new tunnel enterprise. The Yankee is a curious animal, never quiet until dead. There are some here who pray and try to preach. Very many too who have heretofore been religiously inclined, throw off all restraint and are about the worst. . . . Those who find the least fault, make the best of things as they come and grin and bear it, get along the best. Weather getting warmer, water warmer and nastier, food worse and less in quantities, and more prisoners coming nearly every day.

—JOHN RANSOM (1864)

*W*e was up and after the Johnnies bright and early. They took a stand at high bridge on the Lynchburgh Rail Road. This bridge is three thousand feet long, has twenty two piers of brick One Hundred feet high. It is a beautiful bridge. The stream that passes under it could pass through a flour barrel—a small wooden bridge spans the water and is only thirteen feet wide. The rebels fought us for half an hour with great determination but we finally drove them across the high bridge which they set on fire at the farther end. . . . The Rebels retreated on the Rail Road and we followed them closely for about four miles. There they about faced and gave us some shells. . . . Our brigade commander and staff came up and a shell took the head off of the bugler and he stiffened and set in the saddle a few seconds. . . . Another soldier got in the saddle and rode off with the dead mans brains smeared over the horse and saddle.

—SAMUEL A. CLEAR (1865)

122

APRIL 8

*W*e are digging with an old fire shovel at our tunnel. The shovel is a prize; we also use half of canteens, pieces of boards, &c. It's laborious work. A dozen are engaged in it. Like going into a grave to go into a tunnel. . . . Not much faith in the enterprise, but work with the rest as a sort of duty. . . . Great deal of fighting. One Duffy, a New York rough, claims the light-weight championship of Andersonville. Regular battles quite often. Remarkable how men will stand up and be pummeled. . . . I have probably fifty acquaintances here that . . . meet often to compare notes, and we have many a hearty laugh in the midst of misery. I dicker and trade and often make an extra ration. We sometimes draw small cow peas for rations, and being a printer by trade, I spread the peas out on a blanket and quickly pick them up one at a time, after the manner of picking up type. One drawback is the practice of unconsciously putting the beans into my mouth. In this way I often eat up the whole printing office.

—John Ransom (1864)

*T*his morning the troops are all astir early. The Johnnies left during the night, and none to be seen this morning. We ate a hasty breakfast and was soon on their trail like blood hounds. . . . We passed through Stoneville at 9 A.M. . . . Our regiment broke ranks and ransacked the place up in the store-loft, they found a large sugar hogshead full of flour. They jumped in and filled their haversacks without taking them off by scraping them full. It was a general scrabble. When they returned to the Regiment they looked like a lot of Millers for they had flour all over them. They also found several hogsheads of Tobacco and they all had a handful. This they used as whips to whip one another with.

—Samuel A. Clear (1865)

I was once strolling on a walk beside the iron fence of a large orphanage. On the other side of the fence a group of four- and five-year old boys ran parallel with my progress, firing imaginary guns at me. Bang, bang, bang: I was murdered a hundred times. After a time they fell silent, but continued running to keep up with me. Finally, one of them put his hand on the netting and said urgently: "Mister! Mister!" I stopped. Very gravely the boy asked: "Are *you* happy?" The connection was deep, was subterranean. Perhaps the happy do not kill.

—THORNTON WILDER (1956)

APRIL 9

There we stood the two armies facing each other, and we expected to fight the hardest battle of the Campaign. While we was waiting for orders some flags of truce came through our lines and passed to the rear. . . . By this time we had stacked arms on both sides. We were ready for anything . . . but at 3 P.M. our Division got the word attention, and an order was read to the effect that Genl Robt E. Lee had surrendered. . . . When we knew it to be a sure thing what a loud, long glorious shout went up. Then the first thing I knew I was rolling in the mud and several of Co "K" boys piled on top and wallowed me in the mud and themselves too pulled one another about, tripped them up. . . . Such confusion and carrying on was never seen in so short a time. Then the artillery opened. I think there was not one piece but what belched forth the glad tidings, those that were captured and all. It was one continual roar for miles and miles.

—SAMUEL A. CLEAR (1865)

Summoned Bat. Hdqtrs. and ordered to give "lecture" on transmissions and lubrication. Half the men at lecture were the regimental band. Keen interest in transmissions—not!

—HOWARD O'BRIEN (1918)

APRIL 10

*T*he Whigs are more ardent and active, and, they say, better organized than usual, for the charter election, which is to be held on Tuesday. Immense meetings take place every night at the general and ward places of rendezvous. Processions parade the streets at night with music, torches, and banners; the prevailing device for the latter is the *log-cabin;* and we had hard cider, which has become the fountain of Whig inspiration. In an evil hour the Loco-focos taunted the Harrison men with having selected a candidate who lived in a log-cabin and drank hard-cider, which the Whigs, with more adroitness than they usually display, appropriated to their own use, and now on all their banners and transparencies the temple of Liberty is transformed into a hovel of unhewn logs; the military garb of the general, into the frock and the shirt-sleeves of a labouring farmer. The American eagle has taken his flight, which is supplied by a cider-barrel, and the long-established emblem of the ship has given place to the plough. Hurrah for Tippecanoe! is heard more frequently than Hurrah for the Constitution! "Behold old things are passed away, and all things have become new."

—PHILIP HONE (1840)

*P*assed the rapids at Louisville in the steamboat. The English reserve or "offishness" seems to be no part of the western character—though I have had no opportunity of observing a gentleman of high standing. I observe this trait in myself—today, for instance, when a young fellow expressed satisfaction that he should accompany me to St. Louis, I felt inclined to shake him off, though he had made himself agreeable enough.

—FRANCIS PARKMAN (1846)

*T*his morning the news came that the rebel General Lee had surrendered his army and such a time of rejoicing I am sure this town has never seen. Flags of all sizes and descriptions were displayed everywhere this aftn. At 4½ all the bells were rung for almost an hour and the firing of anvils has not ceased since. Now bonfires, burning balls, martial music, and noise and racket. I spent the evening running around with John Probasco, Mattie and Charlie viewing the excitement. Past ten o'c now & the noise as great as ever.

—SALLIE MEIXELL (1865)

APRIL 11

[On the Oregon Trail] *W*e are on the Mississippi, with its rapid muddy current, and low, forest-covered banks. The men of the emigrant party are manly, open, and agreeable in their manners—with none of the contracted, reserved manner that is common in New Englanders. Neither have the women, who are remarkably good-looking, any of that detestable, starched, lackadaisical expression common in vulgar Yankee women. The true philosophy of life is to sieze with a ready and strong hand upon all the good in it, and to bear its inevitable evils as calmly and carelessly as may be.

—FRANCIS PARKMAN (1846)

*A*nd now, old friend, you my Journal, for a time good bye! You are too bulky to be kept out, exposed to prying Yankee eyes and theivish Yankee fingers. You go for a season to darkness & solitude & my record must henceforth be kept on scraps of paper, backs of letters, or old memorandum books which I can secrete. Think how Sheridan's bumming officers would seize upon the "Journal of a Secesh Lady—a complete record of a daily life spent in the Southern Confederacy from

July 1860 to April 65" & how I would feel thus dragged from the recesses of private life & for aught I know published for the amusement of a censorious, curious, and critical public?

—CATHERINE EDMONDSTON (1865)

*E*aster services in an army camp overseas are different from Easter services at Summit church, but somehow better. There are daffodils instead of deep-cupped lilies. There are bare rafters in a Nicean hut instead of oak beams in a high-vaulted arch. There is a piano out of tune with keys that stick, rather than a richvoiced organ. There are o.d. uniforms or blue bathrobes in place of new Easter finery. There are G.I. boots rather than Steigerwalt's latest and finest $22.50 model. But I think the spirit is there in more sincere form.

—ANNE McCAUGHEY (1944)

APRIL 12

*W*ar & Rumors of wars. Great excitement prevails at this time, on account of a report that Fort Sumter is to be bombarded immediately. The volenteers at Spartanburgh has been orderd to repair to Charleston. . . . I came home late & found the following note from Camp, which at wifes request I poste in my journal. . . . "Dear Sir Rub up your Rifle the War has begun. . . . The highest state of Excitement prevails in Spartanburgh Just Now and thare is considerable Slinging of Snott."

—DAVID GOLIGHTLY HARRIS (1861)

*B*efore 4 A.M. the drums beat for parade, & our company was speedily on the march to the batteries which they were to man. At 4.30, a signal shell was thrown from a mortar battery at Fort Johnson, which had been before ordered to be taken as the command for immediate attack—& the firing from all the batteries bearing on Fort Sumter next began in the order arranged—which was that the discharges should be two minutes apart, & the round of all the pieces & batteries to be completed in 32 minutes, & then to begin again. The night before . . . Capt. Cuthbert had notified me that his company requested of me to discharge the first cannon to be fired, which was their 64 lb. Columbiad, loaded with shell. By order of Gen. Beauregard, made known the afternoon of the 11th, the attack was to be commenced by the first shot at the fort being fired by the Palmetto Guard, & from the Iron Battery. In accepting & acting upon this highly appreciated compliment, that company had made me its instrument. . . . Of course I was highly gratified by the compliment, & delighted to perform the service—which I did. The shell struck the fort, at the north-east angle of the parapet. The firing then proceeded, as stated, from 14 different batteries, including Fort Moultrie & the floating battery, which had been placed for this purpose in the cove, back of Sullivan's Island. Most of both shot & shells, at first, missed the fort. But many struck, & the proportion of effective balls & shells increased with the practice. To all this firing, not a gun was fired in return, for two hours or more.

—EDMUND RUFFIN (1861)

To-day I beheld the first secession flag that had met my vision. It was at Polecat Station, Caroline County, and it was greeted with enthusiasm by all but the two or three Yankees in the train. One of these, named Tupps . . . could not sit still a moment, nor keep silence. He had been speculating in North Carolina the year before, and left some property there, which, of course, he must save, if needs be, at the risk of his life. But he cared nothing for slavery, and would never bear arms against the South, if she saw fit to "set up Government business for herself." He rather guessed war was a speculation that wouldn't pay. His volubility increased with his perturbation, and then he drank excessively and sang Dixie. When we reached Richmond, he was beastly drunk.

—JOHN BEAUCHAMP JONES (1861)

At 6:10 p.m. the Vice President called the Cabinet to order and said: "It is my sad duty to report that the President died [at] 5:48. Mrs. Roosevelt gave me this news, and in saying so she remarked that 'he died like a soldier.' " . . . At 6:45 the Chief Justice administered the oath of office to the Vice President, and he became the President of the United States. Mr. Truman responded to the oath firmly and clearly. His only active omission was a failure to raise his right hand when he was repeating the oath with his left hand on the Bible. The Chief Justice had to indicate to him that he should raise his hand—under the circumstances it gave dignity and firmness.

—JAMES FORRESTAL (1945)

APRIL 13

Here begins a new chapter of my journal, entitled WAR. . . . This morning's papers confirmed last night's news; viz., that the rebels opened fire at Sumter yesterday morning. . . . So Civil War is inaugurated at last. God defend the Right. The Northern backbone is much stiffened already. Many who stood up for "Southern rights" and complained of wrongs done the South now say that, since the South has fired the first gun, they are ready to go all lengths in supporting the government. . . . It is said the President will assume the right to call for volunteers, whether the law give it or not. If he does, there will soon be a new element in the fray; viz., the stern anti-slavery Puritanism that survives in New England and in the Northwest. Ossawattomie John Brown

129

would be worth his weight in gold just now. What a pity he precipitated matters and got himself prematurely hanged!

—GEORGE TEMPLETON STRONG (1861)

Came home from the village & found that my hands had not done much work in my absence. Rain last night, the land too wet to plow. The negroes sprouting.

—DAVID GOLIGHTLY HARRIS (1861)

At seven o'clock, I was one of a second batch of prisoners taken from the pen. After marching one and a half miles we were placed on a train of dilapidated boxcars, which broke down just after starting from Appomattox Station. This accident detained us two hours; then we ran down to Pamplin's Station, and were ordered to wait for the up train. I managed to eke out a miserable existence on corn, a few crumbs of hardtack, and some molasses which the guard brought. In return for his kindness, I offered him the use of my blankets. Strange position, a virulent Rebel with his Yankee sentinel sleeping together.

—EUGENE HENRY LEVY (1865)

APRIL 14

Until to-day nothing was ever thought of sacrificing to our country's wrongs. For six months we had worked to capture; but our cause being almost lost, something decisive and great must be done. But its failure was owing to others, who did not strike for their country with a heart. I struck boldly, and not as the papers say. I walked with a firm step through a thousand of his friends, and was stopped, but pushed on. A colonel was at his side. I shouted *"Sic semper!"* before I fired. In jumping, broke my leg. I passed all his pickets, rode sixty miles that night with the bone of my leg tearing the flesh at every jump. I can never repent it, though we hated to kill. Our country owed all her troubles to him, and God simply made me the instrument of his punishment. The country is not . . . what it was. This forced Union is not what I have loved. I care not what becomes of me. I have no desire to outlive my country. This night, before the deed, I wrote a long article and left it for one of the editors of the *National Intelligencer,* in which I fully set forth our reasons for our proceeding.

—JOHN WILKES BOOTH (1865)

The President had been carried across the street from the theatre, to the house of a Mr. Peterson. We entered by ascending a flight of steps above the basement and passing through a long hall to the rear, where the President lay . . . breathing heavily. . . . The giant sufferer lay extended diagonally across the bed, which was not long enough for him. He had been stripped of his clothes. His large arms . . . were of a size which one would scarce have expected from his spare appearance. His slow, full respiration lifted the clothes with each breath that he took. His features were calm and striking. I have never seen them appear to better advantage than for the first hour, perhaps, that I was there. After that, his right eye began to swell and that part of his face became discolored. . . . A double guard was stationed at the door and on the sidewalk, to repress the crowd, which was of course highly excited and anxious. The room was small and overcrowded. The surgeons and members of the Cabinet were as many as should have been in the room, but there were many more. . . . About once an hour Mrs. Lincoln would repair to the bedside of her dying husband and with lamentation and tears remain until overcome by emotion.

—GIDEON WELLES (1865)

131

APRIL 15

A door which opened upon a porch or gallery, and also the windows, were kept open for fresh air. The night was dark, cloudy, and damp, and about six it began to rain. I remained in the room . . . listening to the heavy groans, and witnessing the wasting life of the good and great man who was expiring before me. . . . A little past eleven [a.m.], I . . . took a short walk in the open air. . . . Large groups of people were gathered every few rods, all anxious and solicitous. . . . Intense grief was on every countenance when I replied that the President could survive but a short time. The colored people especially—and there were at this time more of them, perhaps, than of whites—were overwhelmed with grief. . . . A little before seven, I went into the room where . . . the death-struggle had begun. Robert, his son, stood with several others at the head of the bed. He bore himself well, but on two occasions gave way to overpowering grief and sobbed aloud, turning his head and leaning on the shoulder of Senator Sumner. The respiration of the President became suspended at intervals, and at last entirely ceased at twenty-two minutes past seven.

—GIDEON WELLES (1865)

A braham Lincoln died at twenty-two minutes after seven this morning. He never regained consciousness after the pistol ball fired at him from behind, over his wife's shoulder, entered his brain. . . . The temper of the great meeting I found assembled in front of the Custom House (the old Exchange) was grim. A Southerner would compare it with that of the first session of the Jacobins after Marat's death. I thought it healthy and virile. It was the first great patriotic meeting since the war began at which there was no talk of concession and conciliation. . . . No business was done today. Most shops are closed and draped with black and white muslin. Broadway is clad in "weepers" from Wall Street to Union Square. . . . Orations by George Bancroft and by the Rev. (Presbyterian) Thompson of the Tabernacle. Both good; Thompson's very good. "When A. Johnson was sworn in as

President today," said the Rev. Thompson, "the Statue of Liberty that surmounts the dome of the Capitol and was put there by Lincoln, looked down on the city and on the nation and said, 'Our Government is unchanged—it has merely passed from the hands of one man into those of another. Let the dead bury their dead.' "

—GEORGE TEMPLETON STRONG (1865)

*T*he terrible news came that President Lincoln had been assassinated last evening while sitting in his private box in Fords Theater. The bells were tolled. Stores closed, and flags draped in mourning. It has crushed us, saddened every heart. Even strong men shed tears & muttered vows of vengeance have sunk down deep in the hearts. . . . To add to the gloom a dreary, dismal rain set in continuing all day, this evening falling in torrents. We could talk nor think today but of one thing.

—SALLIE MEIXELL (1865)

*A*ll the saloons and major restaurants of Baltimore were closed last night as a mark of respect to the dead Roosevelt, whose body passed through the city at midnight. It was silly, but it gave a lot of Dogberries a chance to annoy their betters, and so it was ordained.

—H. L. MENCKEN (1945)

APRIL 16

*H*ow can I write it? How find words to tell what has befallen us? *Gen Lee has surrendered!* Surrendered the remnant of his noble Army to an overwhelming horde of mercenary Yankee knaves & foreigners. . . . What have we done to be thus visited? That *Lee,* Lee upon whom hung the hopes of the whole country, should be a prisoner seems too dreadful to be realized!

—CATHERINE EDMONDSTON (1865)

*P*assing a leather-goods shop on Fifth Avenue last night, we discovered a mouse in the show window. Too frightened to hide, it clung to the drapery just inside the plate glass, its little eyes terrible in the glaring light. It really had an expression of guilt.

—GLENWAY WESCOTT (1941)

APRIL 17

A dark-colored mulatto man, named Joseph Cartwright, a preacher of a colored Methodist church, came this morning with a subscription book to raise $450 to purchase the freedom of his three grandchildren . . . all under three or four years of age. He told me that he had been upwards of twenty years in purchasing his own freedom and that of his three sons; that, after this, Henry Johnson, late a member of the House of Representatives from Louisiana, had bought his son's wife and her three children, with many other slaves, to carry them away to Louisiana; that after the purchase he had been prevailed upon to consent to leave them here for a short time in the charge of a man to whom he had ostensibly sold them, but with the consent that this Joseph Cartwright should purchase them for $1,025. He had actually purchased and paid for the mother, and was now endeavoring to raise $450 for the three children. There were in the subscription book certificates of two white Methodist ministers, Hamilton and Cookman, to the respectability of this man—a preacher of the gospel! What a horrible exemplification of slavery!

—JOHN QUINCY ADAMS (1840)

*U*pon going down town this morning, every one was speaking of the death of Lincoln, and the *Whig* was in mourning. President Lincoln was killed by Booth (Jno. Wilkes), an actor. I suppose his purpose is to live in history as the slayer of a tyrant; thinking to make the leading character in a tragedy, and have his performance acted by others on the stage.

—JOHN BEAUCHAMP JONES (1865)

*A*t dress parade this evening "The Assassination of President Abraham Lincoln" was read to us. A silent gloom fell upon us like a pall. No one spoke or moved. . . . The "Stars and Stripes" was quietly lowered, and old torn shreds of Flags almost slipped out of the hands of the Color Sargeants. The Regiments was quietly dismissed and we moved away slowly to our quarters, as if we each had lost a near and dear friend at home. Quietly, quietly we went to our rest. Was anybody glad, if he was he made no sign, and well for them they did not, for they never would have reached home alive. No drill, No Dress Parade. No Nothing, all quiet, Flags at half mast, lonesome was no word for us. It was like going from a busy City to a fastness in the mountains, what a hold Old Honest Abe Lincoln had on the hearts of the soldiers of the army.

—SAMUEL A. CLEAR (1865)

*N*o rain to day. Mr. Barnet is so slow & lazy about his work and seems as if he is determined to do nothing. I have to day engaged W Walden to do some work that Barnett had contracted to do. I am worn out & disgusted with his laziness & he is about as good as some of the other baptist broth-

135

ering. I beleive that negroes are more reliable as regards their working contracts than the white men.

—DAVID GOLIGHTLY HARRIS (1868)

*H*ad my first experience today of interviewing the Southern white man. Found him cordial, polite, and just the same as the Northern man, except for the single exception that he would forget and say "nigger" in referring to colored people. Called upon "Col." [Richard L.] Brewer, a lawyer. Seems that every white man is a "Colonel." Southerners like it. I don't mind addressing them as "Colonel," if I can wheedle out of them the information I desire. That is the way the old time Negro secured so many favors from the white man. He feeds upon the latter's vanity, bows reverently, obeisantly, before "Mr. Charley" to make him think he is the greatest man in the world. Poor Negro! He does not fool the white man, for the latter takes tenfold from him; as for the white man, he is deluded into believing the Negro "loves" him. Yet that same genuflecting "darkey" would be his worst enemy were their respective situations reversed.

—LORENZO J. GREENE (1928)

APRIL 18

I am beginning my professional studies. In a month I shall be legally a man. And I deliberately dedicate my time, my talents, and my hopes to the Church. Man is an animal that looks before and after; and I should be loth to reflect at a remote period that I took so solemn a step in my existence without some careful examination of my past and present life. . . . I cannot dissemble that my abilities are below my ambition. And I find that I judged by a false criterion when I measured my powers by my ability to understand and to criticize the intellectual character of another. For men graduate

136

their respect, not by the secret wealth, but by the outward use; not by the power to understand, but by the power to act.

—RALPH WALDO EMERSON (1824)

*D*etails in regard to the funeral, which takes place on the 19th, occupied general attention and little else than preliminary arrangements and conversation was done at the Cabinet-meeting. From every part of the country comes lamentation. Every house, almost, has some drapery, especially the homes of the poor. Profuse exhibition is displayed on the public buildings and the dwellings of the wealthy, but the little black ribbon or strip of black cloth from the hovel of the poor negro or the impoverished white is more touching.

—GIDEON WELLES (1865)

*I*t was a beautiful night [in Boston] and before leaving I leaned out of one of the big windows looking down on the roofs of the tenements and listening to the chimes from Old North Church when I saw the two lanterns hanging out of the belfry above and was fired with a desire to go up and live in the year 1775 for a little while—so, . . . we got the janitor, Mr. Cleveland, . . . and went to rouse the sexton. . . . Soon we saw him returning with what seemed to be an old witch, who held a candle high in her hand and was preceded by a black cat. . . . They were rather aghast at my wanting to go up the spire. . . . The steps were old rotten planks full of holes and there were dangerous corners where there were sometimes no steps at all! . . . There was a full moon which cast weird shadows over us through the old-fashioned small-pained windows. We could just crowd into the little belfry and could look all around and see the same prospect that the sexton saw a hundred and thirty years ago at the same hour. . . . To us it all looked beautiful and prosperous but I wondered what he would have thought of all the warships, the Bunker Hill Monument, and the tall buildings nearer at hand. But the same old moon was shining on it all. Harold tipped the old lady when we had made our perilous descent and we thanked them all gratefully.

—MARIAN LAWRENCE PEABODY (1905)

*F*our years ago today I became a soldier in the American Army. I set out to see what it was all about. Now, as I lay here in this hospital and look out the window on a battle-torn countryside, it isn't real, or doesn't seem real. I feel as if I were returned from the dead. In fact, I was "The Living Dead." I am in no hurry to get home. I don't want to see any friends. I have no plans for the future, no hopes or desires. I am very tired, and about finished, I guess. When I am given food, it is all right. When no food is given, that is alright. When I was captured over two years ago, I weighed one hundred and sixty pounds. Today I weigh one hundred, even.

—THEARL MESECHER (1945)

APRIL 19

*A*t 10 of the clock last night, the King's Troops marched out from the bottom of the Common, crossed over to Phips farm, marched on till they came to Lexington, where they fired and killed eight of our people and proceeded to Concord where they were sent to destroy Magazines of Provisions. After doing some damage by spiking up and destroying cannon &c they halted and were soon attacked by our People, upon which they retreated, being about 800 Men commanded by Major Pitcairn of the Marines. Upon their retreat they were joined by a Brigade commanded by Lord Piercy who continued the retreat and were beat by our People from thence down to Charlestown, which fight was continued till sunset. Our People behaved with the utmost bravery—about thirty of our People were killed and wounded, and fifty of the Kings Troops. The next day they came over to Boston. (Double the

138

number of Kings Troops to our People were in action that day) and blessed be God who most remarkably appear in our favor.

—TIMOTHY NEWELL (1775)

School was hardly open this morning before Mr. Hurley came in and told me that President Lincoln had been assassinated. . . . Several of the large girls who are in classes taught by the white southern teachers, came to me, weeping bitterly and begged to be taken out of their classes. I let them go home at the time and must watch my teachers for any *expression* of disloyalty. The greatest gloom pervades the city. . . . Minute guns have been firing nearly ever since the news came; flags are at half mast. The colored people express their sorrow and sense of loss in many cases, with sobs and loud lamentations! No native whites are seen anywhere on the streets. . . . For me, I am beginning to be strong in the "fatalistic theory." His work was accomplished and he is removed. I will not doubt but God has other men and means, to finish what is yet undone!

—ESTHER HILL HAWKS (1865)

Another Sabbath day has come and gone. . . . I drew a comfortable chair up to a window and spent some time looking out at the farm. But what I saw and thot about was more than just this farm. I saw all of the other farms as well, all of agriculture. The conclusion that I arrived at was that our nation is a careless, thotless nation in so far as our farm folks are concerned. It is true that a great many people are serious in their efforts to better agriculture, but the nation as a whole is not. They take their food and clothing and the source of it as a matter of course.

—ELMER G. POWERS (1936)

$\mathcal{I}$ am in St. Marcel, the largest hospital in Paris. I can walk again, and . . . the ward surgeon insists that I take a pass and see Paris a bit. I do not care about seeing Paris. It's New York that I want to see. . . . Everything seems so noisy. A dropped tin tray, a sharp whistle, a rumble of food carts in the hall, the flap of a window blind, the click of a cigarette lighter, and thousands of sounds unnoticeable to nearly everyone else, paralyze me at times, as they are sharp reminders of various things that in the past spelled danger. If I could quit comparing the click of a cigarette lighter with that of an angry guard releasing the safety on his rifle. The rumble in the halls with sounds made by distant bombing or artillery.

—THEARL MESECHER (1945)

APRIL 20

$\mathcal{B}$ ack to town in the train, Sunday noon. Perhaps no one clever enough to write good fiction could invent or easily recall the real conversation of the lower classes. . . . For example: the cafe-car steward inquires. "And how's the grandmother these days? I don't see her anymore these days." The young woman answers with gusto, "Oh, she's had a few operations but she feels fine." . . . Sipping my black coffee and ice water, I then read the Sunday papers in my systematic way: Virgil Thomson good on brass bands, Dorothy Parker good, deploring Remarque's new novel, the war news bad but really nil. . . . It is overwhelming to know as much as I know, and not to know more. It is my trouble with respect to the war too, and my work, and love, and domestic duty. In the general darkness full of my particular little lightning, heat lightning, my mind and senses grow increasingly passionate.

—GLENWAY WESCOTT (1941)

*W*ystan Auden was sailing for England on Thursday. . . . I told him that, if I were in his place, I should go to Europe and never come back. He said that, even after weeks at Oxford, he did not feel that it was where he belonged, that he belonged over here. I then gave him a tirade about how horrible America was now, said that I had been working in it all my life and was now extremely fatigued. He said that of course it was "hell," that things were "always wrong," but that "the dream" was always there. I replied that the "American dream" was a sickening propaganda phrase, and that the glorification of the American past that had recently been going on was of a kind that made me uneasy, that it reminded me of the glorification of the ancient Roman virtues that became official at a time when they were probably disappearing. He nodded a certain assent, but attempted to raise my morale. "You must remember we depend on you," he said. . . . [James] Thurber had wanted to see me. . . . We arranged to have lunch at the Algonquin, and I invited Dorothy Parker. . . . It was like, as we said, a reunion of Civil War veterans. . . . Dorothy had somewhat deteriorated, had big pouches under her eyes. Thurber seems blinder than ever, one eye is quite gray, and his hair is completely white. I totter around with gout. We at once burst into a confused but animated conversation about *The New Yorker,* the kind of thing of which nobody listening would have been able to understand a word. . . . It depressed me to think we were sitting in the room where the Round Table had once been and where I had arranged for Dorothy to meet the Fitzgeralds for lunch, when Dorothy, on that or some other occasion, sitting at one of the tables along the wall that have chairs on only one side, said that we looked like "a road company of the Last Supper."

—EDMUND WILSON (1958)

APRIL 21

I rose at 5 o'clock and read two chapters in Hebrew and some Greek in Homer. I said my prayers and ate milk for breakfast. I had abundance of people come to see me. About 8 o'clock I went to see the President and then went to court. I settled some accounts first. Two of the negroes were tried and convicted for treason. I wrote a letter to England and then went to court again. About 3 o'clock I returned to my chambers again and found above a girl who I persuaded to go with me into my chambers but she would not. I ate some cake and cheese and then went to Mr. Bland's where I ate some boiled beef. Then I went to the President's where we were merry till 11 o'clock. Then I stole away. I said a short prayer but notwithstanding committed uncleanness in bed. I had good health, bad thoughts, and good humor, thanks be to God Almighty.

—WILLIAM BYRD (1710)

*A*fter being hunted like a dog through swamps [and] woods, and last night being chased by gun-boats till I was forced to return, wet, cold, and starving, with every man's hand against me, I am here in despair. And why? For doing what Brutus was honored for, what made [William] Tell a hero. And yet I, for striking down a greater tyrant than they ever knew, am looked upon as a common cut-throat. . . . I struck for my country, and that at once; a country that groaned beneath this tyranny and prayed for this end. And yet now behold the cold hand they extend to me. . . . The little, the very little I left behind to clear my name, the government will not allow to be printed. . . . I do not repent the blow I struck. I may before my God, but not to man. I think I have done well, though I am abandoned, with the curse of Cain upon [me], when, if the world knew my heart, that one blow would have made me great, though I did desire no greatness. . . . I bless the entire world; have never hated or wronged any one. This last was not a wrong unless God deems it so, and it's with Him to damn or bless me.

—JOHN WILKES BOOTH (1865)

*G*oing out in the afternoon, I found that summer had suddenly come. . . . Along Fifth Avenue, the people were still ply-

142

ing their way as if through the cold and the gray air; their faces were still bleak, boarded up and sharp, as if to cut their way through the city winter. . . . And they seemed stunned and taken unawares by the sudden change in the weather, hardly able to realize that they could permit themselves lighter clothes, an easier and more leisurely pace, and a little natural color.

—EDMUND WILSON (1926)

There is not a Country in the World that can change our outlook as quick as we can. Just a dollar in our pocket makes a different man out of us.

—WILL ROGERS (1935)

APRIL 22

Cold April; hard times; men breaking who ought not to break; banks bullied into the bolstering of desperate speculators; all the newspapers a chorus of owls.

—RALPH WALDO EMERSON (1837)

This afternoon I found Edmund Hosmer in his field, after traversing his orchard where two of his boys were grafting trees; Mr. Hosmer was ploughing and Andrew driving the oxen. I could not help feeling the highest respect as I approached this brave laborer. Here is the Napoleon, the Alexander of the soil, conquering and to conquer, after how many and many a hard-fought summer's day and winter's day, not like Napoleon of sixty battles only, but of six thousand, and out of every one he has come victor. . . . I am ashamed of these slight and useless limbs of mine before this strong soldier.

—R<small>ALPH</small> W<small>ALDO</small> E<small>MERSON</small> (1842)

I made a round-trip to Cambridge for Return to Harvard Day. . . . I take the 8:00 A.M. shuttle up and the 6:00 P.M. back, which means I have to forgo an evening lecture at Memorial Hall by Dr. Ruth on "Safer Sex," sponsored by the Harvard/Radcliffe AIDS Benefit Committee. . . . We homecomers are offered a plethora of courses to audit. One that appeals to me is Afro-American Studies 130, partly because it's being given in a Sever Hall room where once I fought the good battle against irregular Greek verbs. But the young woman instructor can't have been expecting many guests (I am her only one); when she passes out copies of a poem she spends her fifty minutes analyzing line by line, she doesn't have one for me. Her closing words, as chapel bells next door began to peal, are "Love poems tomorrow." All this and Dr. Ruth, too! . . . . Donald Fleming, the doyen of History 1690b, quotes Bill Buckley to the effect that he'd rather be governed by the first two hundred names in the Boston phone book than by the Harvard faculty.

—E. J. K<small>AHN</small>, J<small>R</small>. (1987)

APRIL 23

The "Great Western" . . . came up from Sandy Hook about two o'clock . . . the largest vessel propelled by steam which has yet made her appearance in the waters of Europe. . . . The Battery and adjacent streets were crowded with curious spectators, and the water covered with boats conveying obtrusive visitors on board. . . . Everybody is so enamoured of it, that for a while . . . our countrymen, "studious of change, and pleased with novelty," will rush forward to visit the shores of Europe instead of resorting to Virginia or Saratoga Springs; and steamers will continue to be the fashion until some more dashing adventurer of the go-ahead tribe shall demonstrate the practicability of balloon navigation, and gratify their impatience by a voyage *over,* and not *upon,* the blue waters in two days, instead of as many weeks, thereby escaping the rocks and shoals and headlands which continue yet to fright the minds of timid passengers and cautious navigators. . . . As for me, I am still skeptical on this subject. . . . I should hesitate to trust to the powers of the air or the firegod for my transportation and safe-conduct over this rivulet of blue water of three thousand miles in width, which separates us from the land of our fathers.

—PHILIP HONE (1838)

This is the day upon which Father Miller first pitched for the grand conflagration, but as the time approached he altered it, and now says that the world will certainly be burned between March 1843 and March 1844! The weather to-day was somewhat unusual; being something like the Irishman's hog, streaks of contraries—now a little sunshine, and now a little thunder and lightning.

—ISAAC MICKLE (1843)

Breeding, brains, and beauty—another trio of Bs—seem to be the English upper-class ideal of a perfect woman. I learned this tonight when . . . I went to see *Rebecca* at Radio City. It is a sensationally successful movie, but it is just a well-tailored piece of hokum directed by the English [Alfred] Hitchcock. I have yet to see an American movie which was not "canned" and I exclude no picture made in this country.

—CLIFFORD ODETS (1940)

APRIL 24

A sever Storm of rain. I was Calld at 1 hour pm from Mrs Husseys by Ebenzer Hewin. Crosst the river in their Boat. A great sea A going. We got safe over then sett out for Mr Hewins. I Crost a stream on the way on fleeting Loggs & got safe over. Wonder full is the Goodness of providence. I then proseeded on my journey. Went beyond Mr Hainses & a Larg tree blew up by the roots before me which Caused my hors to spring back & my life was spared. Great & marvillous are thy sparing mercies O God. I was assisted over the fallen tree by Mr Hains. Went on. Soon Came to a stream. The Bridg was gone. Mr Hewin took the rains waded thro & led the horse. Asisted by the same allmighty power I got safe thro & arivd unhurt. Mrs Hewins safe delivd at 10 h Evn of a Daughter.

—MARTHA BALLARD (1789)

*W*ish I had the man here that invented the polka—I'd scrape him to death with oyster shells. Probably, though, he's dead already, and polking everlastingly through another and a *worser* world, and so beyond my vengeance.

—GEORGE TEMPLETON STRONG (1848)

*W*e attended the monthly meeting of our Township Farm Bureau this evening. No strangers or outside speakers were present. Just a meeting of the good home farm folks. One of the occasions that develops sympathy, creates understanding and binds folks together to work for the good of the community, State and Nation. The young folks were in town for their music lesson while wife and I were at the Meeting.

—ELMER G. POWERS (1931)

APRIL 25

This morning Mr. Gilbert Hamilton (at whose house my dear little daughter Susannah has been ever since her last illness) sent me an account of her death Certainly approaching, and he says in his letter, although her face, feet and hands are all cold and her pulse quite gone and reduced to the bones and skin that cover them and dying very hard under the Severe agonys of her disorder, Yet does she preserve her Usual Patience to such a degree that he never saw such an Example before. Severe stroke indeed to A Man bereft of a Wife and in the decline of life because at such periods 'tis natural to look out for such Connections that may be reasonably expected to be the support of Greyhairs and such an one I had promised myself in this child in Particular.

—LANDON CARTER (1758)

My Assistant Secretary, [Theodore] Roosevelt, has determined upon resigning, in order to go into the army and take part in the war. He has been of great use; a man of unbounded energy and force, and thoroughly honest, which is the main thing. He has lost his head to this unutterable folly of deserting the post where he is of most service and running off to ride a horse and, probably, brush mosquitoes from his neck on the Florida sands. His heart is right, and he means well, but it is one of those cases of aberration—desertion—vain-glory; of which he is utterly unaware. He thinks he is following his highest ideal, whereas, in fact, as without exception every one of his friends advises him, he is acting like a fool. And, yet, how absurd all this will sound if, by some turn of fortune, he should accomplish some great thing and strike a very high mark.

—JOHN D. LONG (1898)

Went with Katy and Mims to a German place in Philadelphia. Danced. It was hot and I took off my coat. They saw my brown shirt and cheered. They thought me a Nazi.

—SHERWOOD ANDERSON (1936)

APRIL 26

*A*s far as I notice what passes in philanthropic meetings and holy hurrahs there is very little depth of interest. The speakers warm each other's skin and lubricate each other's tongue, and the words flow and the superlatives thicken and the lips quiver and the eyes moisten, and an observer new to such scenes would say, Here was true fire; the assembly were all ready to be martyred, and the effect of such a spirit on the community would be irresistible; but they separate and go to the shop, to a dance, to bed, and an hour afterwards they care so little for the matter that on slightest temptation each one would disclaim the meeting. "Yes, he went, but they were for carrying it too far," etc., etc. The lesson is, to know that men are superficially very inflammable, but that these fervors do not strike down and reach the action and habit of the man.

—RALPH WALDO EMERSON (1838)

[Esther Arther] *H*ad seen Hemingway sometime fairly lately and had been astonished at the way in which he kept up his boyishness; remembered how, when he had said that he would like to die in the bullring, Zelda Fitzgerald had said, "You're more likely to die in the marble ring!"—There are so few of my old friends left that it does me good to see Esther and talk about the Fitzgeralds, the Seldeses, the Bishops, Muriel Draper, Dos and Hemingway and all that. She said that the more she lived in Europe, the more American she became. . . . It made me reflect on the difference, now, between Europeans and Americans. Esther and I, in conversation, have a much wider range, but probably don't go into anything as deeply as the intellectuals in England and on the Continent do. But they are all more provincial now than we. This is the great shift that has taken place during my time. I felt in connection with her, too, the special characteristics of our race of the twenties: habit of leisure and at least enough money . . . , freedom to travel and read, to indulge and exhaust curiosities, completely uninhibited talks, resistance to challenge of the right to play, to the idea of growing

148

old, settling down to a steady maturity. We made fun of the puerility of Hemingway. . . . He lives in an adventure book for boys, but there is something in myself that responds to it. There may be an element of this in my pursuit of the Dead Sea Scrolls, my visits to Zuni and Haiti, my love of acquiring new alphabets.

—EDMUND WILSON (1954)

*T*he utter sordidness of my NY worklife now that I am 28. . . . Impossible to regard the great garbage pile of the future (which I see as clearly sitting there on the skyline as if it were the Empire State) with any timid favor. In Europe I hope to dream about Asia. In Asia I shall dream about the death of Home States. I hope to circumnavigate the globe before the spirit gives out.

—ALLEN GINSBERG (1954)

APRIL 27

*H*ere we are at last, safe and sound. We expect to remain here several days, laying in supplies for the trip and waiting our turn to be ferried across the river. As far as eye can reach, so great is the emigration, you see nothing but wagons. This town presents a striking appearance—a vast army on wheels—crowds of men, women and lots of children and last but not least the cattle and horses upon which our lives depend.

—SALLIE HESTER (1849)

*M*r Emerson died at 9 p.m. suddenly. Our best & greatest American gone . . . and the man who has helped me most by his life, his books, his society. I can never tell all he has been to me from the time I sang Mignon's song under his window, a little girl, & wrote letters a la Bettine to him, my Goethe, at l5, up through my hard years when his essays on Self Reliance, Character, Compensation, Love & Friendship helped me to understand myself & life & God & Nature. Illustrious & beloved friend, good bye!

—LOUISA MAY ALCOTT (1882)

F. Scott Fitzgerald and his wife were here to lunch yesterday. Mrs. Fitzgerald is a patient at the Phipps Clinic [in Baltimore] . . . and is still plainly more or less off her base. She managed to get through lunch quietly enough, but there was a wild look in her eye. . . . [Fitzgerald] told me that he had dropped out deliberately, on the ground that he needed time to think things out anew. He began to write at 22, and had quickly exhausted all his store of experience. To that end he went to Paris. . . . Unfortunately, Fitzgerald is a heavy drinker, and most of his experience has been got in bars. . . . He is a charming fellow, and when sober makes an excellent companion. Unfortunately, liquor sets him wild and he is apt, when drunk, to knock over a dinner table, or run his automobile into a bank building.

—H. L. MENCKEN (1932)

APRIL 28

Landed at New Orleans this a.m. about 8. Took a carriage after breakfast and drove about the old French part of the city. Visited the old "St Louis Hotel." Reminds one of a vast privy. Place where the legislature has met. Hasn't been swept for 40 years. . . . One old pirate buried here. Was a fine pi-

150

rate, an ornament to his profession. But he fell by mixing in ward politics & finally sunk so far from his former estate as to be elected alderman. But his grave is remembered to this day—more because of his early record.

—MARK TWAIN (1882)

*E*very invention during our lifetime has been just to save time, and time is the only commodity that every American, both rich and poor, has plenty of. Half our life is spent trying to find something to do with the time we have rushed through life trying to save. Two hundred years from now history will record: "America, a nation that flourished from 1900 to 1942, conceived many odd inventions for getting somewhere, but could think of nothing to do when they got there."

—WILL ROGERS (1930)

*A*t a luncheon in a fine house, sitting atop a steep incline, so it seems to be in the treetops, we had a hot discussion about aggression in men and women. Mr. Daniels, the hostess' husband . . . appeared to take the view that women are just as aggressive and brutal as men. Yet it is surely on the whole husbands who beat their wives. On the whole it is men who torture . . . other men and women, though there have been exceptions—in the Nazi camps we now know women were as brutal as the Nazi men. On the whole it is men who indulge in blood sports. Are women just as bloodthirsty? I had been mildly needled for some time, but finally the worm turned, and I said, "Men rape women. There is no way out of that!"

—MAY SARTON (1976)

APRIL 29

*M*r. Cotton Mather dined with us, and was with me in the new Kitchen when this was; He had just been mentioning

151

that more Ministers Houses than others proportionably had been smitten with Lightening; enquiring what the meaning of God should be in it. Many Hail-Stones broke throw the Glass and flew to the middle of the Room, or farther: People afterward Gazed upon the House to see its Ruins. I got Mr. Mather to pray with us after this awfull Providence; He told God He had broken the brittle part of our house, and prayd that we might be ready for the time when our Clay-Tabernacles should be broken. Twas a sorrowfull thing to me to see the house so far undon again before twas finsh'd.

—SAMUEL SEWALL (1695)

*W*arm. I arrived in Savannah at 1:00 A.M. I never before knew what it is to be a stranger, nor would I be now conscious of the absence of "those I love now far away," could I read without pain; but a man in my situation [with a diseased eye] what can he do? Write, *c'est tout* ["that's all"]. And though I have never seen this book before, I feel as if restored to the conversation of a sincere friend, whilst imparting my feelings to the unconscious paper. I have not journalised for some months past, though I have witnessed more novelty during that [period than] any time . . . in all my preceding existence. I will give a retrospective review of all that when I am more in the humor. Here I am in a new land and have an opportunity of being what I will.

—JOSEPH LYONS (1833)

*O*n board the boat are a party of Baltimoreans—flash genteel—very showily attired in "genteel undress," though bound for California. They make a great noise at table, and are waited on by the Negroes with great attention and admiration. Also a vulgar New Yorker, with the moustache and the air of a Frenchman, bound for Santa Fe. . . . A young man on board from St. Louis, bound for Santa Fe, has one brother on the Atlantic, another on the Pacific, and a third on the

Mississippi, while he is going to the [Rio Grande] del Norte. So much for American wandering.

—FRANCIS PARKMAN (1846)

APRIL 30

[In the first session of Congress] *T*his is a great, important day. . . . The Vice-President [John Adams] rose in the most solemn manner. . . . "Gentlemen, I wish for the direction of the Senate. The President will, I suppose, address the Congress. How shall I behave? How shall we receive it? Shall it be standing or sitting?" . . . Mr. Izard got up and told how often he had been in the Houses of Parliament. He said a great deal of what he had seen there. He made, however, this sagacious discovery, that the Commons stood because they had no seats to sit on. . . . Here we sat an hour and ten minutes before the President [George Washington] arrived. . . . As the company returned into the Senate chamber, the President took the chair and the Senators and Representatives their seats. He rose, and all arose also, and addressed them. This great man was agitated and embarrassed more than ever he was by the leveled cannon or pointed musket. He trembled, and several times could scarce make out to read, though it must be supposed he had often read it before. He put part of the fingers of his left hand into the side of what I think the tailors call the fall of the breeches, changing the paper into his right hand. After some time he then did the same with some of the fingers of his right hand. When he came to the words *all the world*, he made a flourish with his right hand, which left rather an ungainly impression. I sincerely, for my part, wished all set ceremony in the hands of the dancing-masters, and that this first of men had read off his address in the plainest manner, without ever taking his eyes from the paper, for I felt hurt that he was not first in everything.

—WILLIAM MACLAY (1789)

*S*ince my removal to the Presidential mansion I rise about five; read two chapters of Scott's Bible and Commentary, and the corresponding Commentary of Hewlett; then the morning newspapers, and public papers from the several departments; write seldom, and not enough; breakfast an hour, from nine to ten; then have a succession of visitors, upon business, in search of place, solicitors for donations, or from mere curiosity, from eleven till between four and five o'clock. The heads of departments of course occupy much of this time. Between four and six I take a walk of three or four miles. Dine from about half past five to seven, and from dark till about eleven I generally pass the evening in my chamber, signing land-grants or blank patents, in the interval of which, for the last ten days, I have brought up three months of arrears in my diary index. About eleven I retire to bed. My evenings are not so free from interruption as I had hoped and expected they would be.

—JOHN QUINCY ADAMS (1825)

[On a wagon train west] *S*ometimes we ladies ride behind the whole, sometimes, between the hindermost waggon and the mules; as circumstances may be. It is not safe for any to be far in the rear, because they are always exposed to be robbed of their horses and, if not killed by wild Indians, themselves left to wander on foot.

—MYRA FAIRBANKS EELS (1838)

[In North Dakota] *S*aturday we baked, washed, ironed, scrubbed floors, churned, and painted the kitchen. In the late afternoon I rode to the lake to see Grover, who was seeding his land up there, went one round with him, and then had to come home to milk cows. The thought now filters into my dim brain that I should never have learned to milk. Mama and Ethel never did.

—ANN MARIE LOW (1928)

154

MAY

MAY 1

I rose about 8 o'clock and read a chapter in Hebrew and some Greek in Lucian. I said my prayers, and had boiled milk for breakfast. The weather was cold and cloudy. My tailor brought me some rich waistcoats but I liked none of them. About 11 o'clock I went to visit my cousins Horsmanden again and drank tea with them. I sent for my daughter to see them, but about 1 o'clock I took my leave and went to Pontack's, where I dined and ate some boiled beef. After dinner I went to Garraway's Coffeehouse and read the news, and about 4 o'clock went home, and about six went to Will's Coffeehouse, where I saw my Lord Dunkellen, who told me he left my mistress crying and had not eaten anything all day. I lost two guineas in betting to my Lord Orrery. Then I went to Mrs. B-r-n, who told me she had consulted Old Abram about me and he promised I should succeed. Then I went to Mrs. FitzHerbert's and sat with her till 10 o'clock and then walked home but took a woman into a coach and committed uncleanness. Then I went home and prayed to God to forgive me.

—WILLIAM BYRD (1718)

I wish one could live without eating, for myself I would willingly resign all the pleasure I derive from it to escape the suffering it produces. Eating, shaving, dressing, heat, cold & one or two other periodical bores make us constantly sensible of our animal nature, brings us back to earth from our high imaginative flights, and prevent or disturb that calm, pure, intellectual serenity, which sometimes for a few moments & by short glimpses we enjoy, & which is certainly far preferable to any sensual gratification. Temperance, & exercise, & regular habits are very fine things, but of no easy acquisition to persons of keen senses & quick imaginations. It is so difficult to enjoy *by rule*, & women & wine & the luxury of indolence are such temptations.

—SIDNEY GEORGE FISHER (1837)

*F*ine weather, to the great comfort of the locomotive public. Never knew the city in such a chaotic state. Every other house seems to be disgorging itself into the street; all the sidewalks are lumbered with bureaus and bedsteads to the utter destruction of their character as thoroughfares, and all the space between the sidewalks is occupied by long processions of carts and wagons and vehicles omnigenous laden with perilous piles of moveables. We certainly haven't advanced as a people beyond the nomadic or migratory stage of civilization analogous to that of the pastoral cow feeders of the Tartar Steppes.

—GEORGE TEMPLETON STRONG (1844)

MAY 2

*Y*orktown. About half after one, died the negro woman Dinah, without sign or groan; she had lain very quiet for a day or two; scarcely any pain, as she, I heard say, told her mistress. She was between fifty and sixty years of age. I was engaged part of this day in [the] orchard and likewise in hunting out a proper person to lay out the negro woman, as all

156

the poor women here are rich in imagination, so that it was with difficulty one could be procured at any rate.

—CHRISTOPHER MARSHALL (1778)

The landing at Independence—the storehouses—the Santa Fe waggons—the groups of piratical-looking Mexicans, employees of the Santa Fe traders, with their broad, peaked hats—the men with their rifles seated on a log, ready for Oregon. Among the waggons behind, some of the Mexicans were encamped. The Baltimoreans got shamefully drunk, and one of them, an exquisite in full dress, tumbled into the water. . . . C. W. of St. Louis, who harnessed his mule into his waggons, and drove off for Santa Fe, bent on seeing. He seemed about eighteen years old, open, enterprising, and thoughtless. He will come back a full-grown man.

—FRANCIS PARKMAN (1846)

Mr Benton came in & read Poetry to us all the afternoon. My mind was far away, and when he appealed to me for an opinion, or asked if I had read such & such a thing, I could not for my life collect either my thoughts or my memory sufficiently to give him an intelligible answer. In fact it comes to me as strange that I have ever taken any interest in anything but the War & the state of the country. Ages seem to have past over me & all my sense been so long absorbed in one thing that I have forgotten aught else. God help me! Here I am sewing on Uniforms which may ere long be drenched in Blood, the blood of my neighbors, yes perhaps of my own husband, & yet I am petty enough to be provoked at this well meant but ill timed Poetry! Away with it! It no longer interests me! The time for it is past! I feel as tho' I could *live* poetry, poetry of the sternest & most heroic cast.

—CATHERINE EDMONDSTON (1861)

$\mathcal{S}$uddenly, bang!—out of the blue I have begun to work on a Wilson play. . . . For two days and nights, sleeping by day, I haven't left the house and have remained in my pajamas, reading and writing notes for scenes and characters. My main impulse for the play is the growing sentiment for war in this country. Some sections of so-called liberals are making calls for U.S. intervention in the European war in the name of the old crusade for democracy. Robert Sherwood, the fine espouser of popular causes, has just opened a play in which the Lunts are acting, a theatre piece call to arms. The Wilson play will do the opposite if I am any sort of writer at all; it will show that our present president is treading the dangerous path already bloodied up by Wilson and company. What I personally think of Wilson himself is not clear to me yet.

—CLIFFORD ODETS (1940)

MAY 3

$\mathcal{O}$ne of the foreign ambassadors said to me, "You have been often in England." "Never, but once in November and December, 1783." "You have relations in England, no doubt." "None at all." "None, how can that be? you are of English extraction!" "Neither my father or mother, grandfather or great grandmother, nor any other relation that I know of, or care a farthing for, has been in England these one hundred and fifty years; so that you see I have not one drop of blood in my veins but what is American." "Ay, we have seen," said he, "proof enough of that." This flattered me, no doubt, and I was vain enough to be pleased with it.

—JOHN ADAMS (1785)

$\mathcal{F}$irst job, negotiating lease of field from Frenchman, for artillery purposes. American method, decide what you want, ask "how much?" and come across or get out. French work differently. Visited field, Frenchman and I discussed syndicalism and war aims for ten minutes, while Americans fidgeted. From that into mutual congratulations on the Alliance. All sorts of topics canvassed. Then back to house, where he served up some extra-special Burgundy. More conversation on this and that . . . and to-morrow we'll go on with matter. "Wasted" time, doubtless, but to-morrow we'll settle it, every blade of grass itemized. Done American fashion, owner would get sore, and we'd have to resort to condemnation.

—HOWARD O'BRIEN (1918)

I saw a soldier in a tall guardhouse near the barbed wire fence and did not like it because it reminds me of a concentration camp. I am just wondering what the effects will be on the Japanese so cut off from the world like this. Within the confines of Tanforan our radios and papers are the only touch with reality. I hardly know how the war is going now. . . . Sometimes I feel like a foreigner in this camp hearing so much Japanese although our family uses English almost exclusively.

—CHARLES KIKUCHI (1942)

*A*n image of the modern man . . . is this: he stands before the mirror, talking to himself, sneering. Then he pulls out a gun and shoots at the hated image in the mirror—the glass smashes all around his feet and he thinks he has done something or made a point!

—CLIFFORD ODETS (1940)

MAY 4

I am too nervous, too wretched to-day to write in my diary, but that the employment will while away a few moments of this trying time. Our friends and neighbors have left us. Everything is broken up. . . . Mr. —— and myself are now the sole occupants of the house, which usually teems with life. . . . The closed piano, the locked bookcase, the nicely-arranged tables, the formally-placed chairs, ottomans and sofas in the parlor! Oh for some one to put them out of order! . . . I heard my own footsteps so plainly, that I was startled by the absence of all other sounds. . . . Why did we think it necessary to send off all that was so dear to us from our own home? I threw open the shutters, and the answer came at once, so mournfully! I heard distinctly the drums beating in Washington. . . . I looked at the Capitol in the distance. . . . That Capitol of which I had always been so proud! Can it be possible that it is no longer *our* Capitol? And are our countrymen, under its very eaves, making mighty preparation to drain our hearts' blood? And must this Union, which I was taught to revere, be rent asunder? Once I thought such a suggestion sacrilege; but now that it is dismembered, I trust it may never, never be reunited. We must be a separate people—our nationality must be different, to insure lasting peace and goodwill. Why cannot we part in peace?

—JUDITH McGUIRE (1861)

The negro movement is still a most vexatious and mischievous one and its effects are painfully felt in every Southern household. This morning Cy came to high words with George and John, insisting he had a right to stay here, to bring here whom he pleases, to keep his family here. He is, he said, entitled to a part of the farm after all the work he had done on it. The kitchen belonged to him because he had helped cut the timber to build it. He also insists that the land belongs to the U.[nited] States, and that it is to be divided among the negroes, etc. Willie told him that he would give him three days to find a place to move to, a thing which he declared his intention of doing three weeks ago.

—EMMA MORDECAI (1865)

Oh, I sure could go for a hamburger now: the big juicy kind. I've eaten so much canned food the past week that it becomes tasteless. Many of the boys are worried about being fed saltpetre because they think it will ruin their manhood. A contrasting reaction is the number of victory gardens that are being planted; these industrious Japanese! They just don't seem to know how to take it easy—they've worked so hard all of their lives that they just can't stand idleness—or waste. They are so concerned that water is not left running or that electricity is not being wasted.

—CHARLES KIKUCHI (1942)

MAY 5

*T*his morning, without giving any warning of their intentions, *all* the servants were discovered to be packing up to go. . . . Cyrus has rented a house on the turnpike, near the battery, and is moving there with the rest of his family. They all seem anything but joyous at the change. . . . His wife, Sara, has behaved as well as possible the whole time, and we all respect her for it. She does not seem to approve of Cy's arrangements. They will now begin to find out how easy their life as *slaves* had been, and to feel the slavery of their freedom.

—EMMA MORDECAI (1865)

*O*n arising at eleven in the morning, I called Bill and Lee and suggested a ride through the countryside. . . . It becomes increasingly difficult to find any country. Everywhere there are smooth roads and intensive traffic. We got off the beaten track though and landed out near Long Island Sound, at Freeport. It was so summery that we quickly decided to have dinner at a place right on the water. . . . When the evening began to come we started for home, this time, sadly . . . , listening to all manner of disturbing news on the radio. England has been given a staggering blow in the belly by the

Nazis. The House of Commons is being "common" and questioning the leadership of Munich and after. How interesting it was to see all the people standing around at the water's edge there. What everyone was doing was snatching at the real spring, standing in the warm sun, happy to be living, filled with simple but mysterious urges—it was like a French painting, perhaps by Seurat.

—CLIFFORD ODETS (1940)

MAY 6

This is a beautiful day and all the boys are up early and fussing around as we cross over to the late rebel Capitol on our Pontoon Bridges as the Rebs had burned their Bridge. This day one year ago we was pelting away at the Johnnies in the battle of the wilderness. There we go, we pass over the Pontoons, the taut stretched lines that hold them give back and fourth. As the current strikes the boats the men all stagger like as if we were intoxicated. We finally strike the graded stretch, pass the burned district and find that few streets look like streets now. We pass Old Libby Prison and Castle Thunder, now the windows are filled with miserable looking faces. . . . Our friends [are] the Colored People, the poor darkies carrying water and give us to drink. All ages, sex and sizes all busy as nailers. The day is warm and we drink much and they bring more and more. How pleased they look, how happy they seem to be. We's glad you's cum! We's glad you's cum is their shout all along our line of march. It seems to me I could pick the Union people from rebels by the look on their faces, but on we go, the side walks and hills crowded all along the line with a motley crew. We could not see far back for the crowd was jammed up close and we merely had room to pass. We marched to the outskirts of the city, halted, stacked arms and rested for three hours.

—SAMUEL A. CLEAR (1865)

*I*n reading Mark Antonine last night, it was pleasant to be reminded, by some of his precepts, of a living example in a dear person near me. We are such vain peacocks that we read in an English journal, with joy, that no house in London or in Paris can compare with the comfort and splendour at Delmonico's in New York. But I was never in Delmonico's.

—RALPH WALDO EMERSON (1865)

MAY 7

I rose at 6 o'clock and read two chapters in Hebrew and two chapters in the Greek Testament. I said my prayers and ate milk for breakfast. I danced my dance. Then I read a sermon of Dr. Tillotson's which affected me very much and made me shed some tears of repentance. The weather grew very hot. The sick boys were a little better. I ate of roast beef for dinner. In the afternoon my wife and I took a long sleep which discomposed me. Then I read another sermon in Dr. Tillotson, after which we took a walk and met Mr. C-s who walked with us and told us several strangers were come to my cousin Harrison's. He stayed here till 9 o'clock. I neglected to say my prayers but had good health, good thoughts, and good humor, thanks be to God Almighty.

—WILLIAM BYRD (1710)

[En route to Oregon territory] *S*tarted as early as usual. Stopped to dinner. Travelled 20 miles. Suffered much a few days past from loss of appetite, a sickness at the stomach. This evening at camp, took an emetic given me by brother Smith. Its operation was great and powerful. Was consoled from the thought that my friends at home were assembled & praying for me.

—ELKANAH WALKER (1838)

There is no wood to be had to build a fire, and we have to depend on dried buffalo chips. That means that the cook and one other at least for every wagon must range the prairie—sometimes for miles—looking for the droppings of buffalos. . . . I had no idea of this before I came on this expedition, or I would have thought twice again before leaving home. Everybody values dried buffalo chips almost as highly as precious gems.

—ANDREW GORDON (1849)

MAY 8

We met two wagons coming back from the Promised Land today. The men with them looked pretty well down in the mouth. . . . They stopped and we had a long powwow. We gave them some liquor and grub. They had not been to California—never got there. It seemed that the Humboldt Desert had almost ruined them, and they turned back. Two of their men died of cholera; they had three left, and these survivors had hollow eyes and caved-in cheeks, and looked as if they were about done for. . . . They had three oxen left, but they pulled the wagon easily, for it was almost empty. They had painted on the white cover of the wagon the words, "Going for Gold." It was not funny, but sad.

—ANDREW GORDON (1849)

The Biblical absurdity of the Almighty's being only six days building the universe and then fooling away 25 years building a towhead in the Mississippi. "Towhead" means infant, an infant island, a growing island, so it is said.

—MARK TWAIN (1882)

_M_rs. R., one of the loveliest women in our community, was struck by lightning during the storm last evening. She had always had a great terror of lightning, though in every other respect she was a fearless woman, so that her family always gathered round her during a storm and tried as much as possible to shut out the sight and sound. On this occasion her husband and daughter were sitting one on each side of her on an old-fashioned mahogany sofa, she with her handkerchief thrown over her face. When the fatal flash came the husband and daughter were thrown forward to the floor and were stunned; as soon as they recovered consciousness they turned to reassure the mother as to their not being seriously hurt. She was still sitting straight up on the sofa with the handkerchief over her face; they lifted the handkerchief as they received no answer and found life extinct. . . . There was only one small spot at the back of the neck.

—ELIZABETH PRINGLE (1905)

MAY 9

_P_reachd to 8 Indians, at Schoolhouse, from Heb: 12.14. _Follow holiness, without which etc._ . . . Askd _Sarah_, an old Indian Woman, who commonly attends my Lecture, if She knew the Reason why the Indians Were So generally Set against coming to My Lecture? She told me, She Supposd they dare not come; for _Sam Niles_ warnd and Solemnly Chargd them, not to hear Any of Our Ministers, that wore great White Wigs.

—JOSEPH FISH (1774)

_R_eceived today the first despatches from Grant. The President thinks very highly of what Grant has done. He was talking about it today with me and said, "How near we have been to this thing before and failed. I believe if any other general

165

had been at the head of that army it would have now been on this side of the Rapidan. It is the dogged pertinacity of Grant that wins." It is said that Meade observed to Grant that the enemy seemed inclined to make a Kilkenny-cat fight of the affair, & Grant answered, "Our cat has the longest tail."

—JOHN HAY (1864)

Morn'g 1st Div. passed from Warren's right to his left to rejoin Corps—We had just arrived when Whittier rode up to Gen. W. with news that Sedgwick was killed—we had been with him a moment before—he was in an exposed angle between Warren's front & ours & had just been chaffing a man for ducking at the bullets of a sharpshooter; saying "Why man they couldn't hit an elephant here at this distance"—he was struck on one side of the nose & sunk senseless & soon died—MacMahon & Whittier were with him at the time.

—OLIVER WENDELL HOLMES (1864)

Up early and left at eight. . . . Fog and rain—but later clear. Went only to Ithaca. Kiwanis, dressed as cowboys, shooting guns in the hotel lobby.

—SHERWOOD ANDERSON (1939)

MAY 10

The ladies are postponing all engagements until their lovers have fought the Yankees. Their influence is great. Day after day they go in crowds to the Fair ground where the 1st S. C. Vols. are encamped, showering upon them their smiles, and all the delicacies the city affords. They wine them and cake them—and they deserve it. They are just from taking

166

Fort Sumter, and have won historic distinction. . . . By closing our ports it is thought we can be subdued by the want of accustomed luxuries. These rich young men were dressed in coarse gray homespun! We have the best horsemen and the best marksmen in the world, and these are the qualities that will tell before the end of the war. We fight for Existence—the enemy for Union and the freedom of the slave. Well, let the Yankees see if this "new thing" will pay.

—JOHN BEAUCHAMP JONES (1861)

*B*eing curious about the handwriting of Woodrow Wilson, I called Mrs. Eastman on the phone and had her come down here. . . . She said the main contradiction of his nature was his extreme idealism combined with a very thin skin and an inability to face discord or vulgarity. Also that he had, whoever he was, a very painful necessity of preserving "face," Oriental in its strength. She did not say so, but she gave me enough bits and fragments to make me see that Wilson had a progressive nature built up on a reactionary base. If he lost face, she said, it was very possible he would break down or do something violent, even killing himself.

—CLIFFORD ODETS (1940)

*A*t the Associated Press meeting in New York last week I fell in with a general in the army whose name I don't recall. He was in the air arm and appeared to be a Southern cracker—a tall, slim, somewhat evil-looking fellow with pale blue eyes, set too close together. When I let fall the fact that I have yet to make my first trip in an airship he almost fainted: it was simply impossible for him to imagine anyone falling so far behind the march of Christian enlightenment. I thereupon added that I own no automobile, never listen to the radio, see a movie no more than once a year, object to air-cooling, and am just getting used to a horse and buggy. By this time he was almost in collapse. If I had added that I buy no war bonds, and never contribute to either the Red

Cross or the Community Fund I suppose that he'd have needed medical attention.

—H. L. MENCKEN (1944)

MAY 11

*T*he first day of Court. Nature and truth, or rather truth and right are invariably the same in all times and in all places; and reason, pure unbiased reason, perceives them alike in all times and in all places. But passion, prejudice, interest, custom, and fancy are infinitely precarious; if, therefore, we suffer our understandings to be blinded or perverted by any of these, the chance is that of millions to one, that we shall embrace errors. And hence arises that endless variety of opinions entertained by mankind.

—JOHN ADAMS (1756)

*Y*ou wire the State or the Federal Government that your Cow or Hog is sick and they will send out experts from Washington and appropriate money to eradicate the Cause. You wire them that your Baby has the Diphtheria or Scarlet Fever and see what they do.

—WILL ROGERS (1924)

I'll probably never execute my old plan to do a model funeral service for agnostics, admittedly damned. I am now too near my own need for it to give it the proper lightness of touch. Some day somebody else will do one. . . . An agnostic's

funeral, as things stand, consists mainly of idiotic speeches—
that is, when there is any ceremony at all.

—H. L. MENCKEN (1940)

MAY 12

A Night Battle, over a week since.—We already talk of
Histories of the War . . . but shall we ever get histories of the
real things? . . . Who know the conflict hand-to-hand—the
many conflicts in the dark, those shadowy-tangled, flashing-
moonbeam'd woods—the writhing groups and squads—hear
through the woods the cries, the din, the cracking guns and
pistols—the distant cannon—the cheers and calls, and
threats and awful music of the oaths. . . . Of scenes like
these, I say, who writes—who e'er can write, the story? . . . .
No history, ever—No poem sings, nor music sounds. . . . No
formal General's report, nor print, nor book in the library,
nor column in the paper, embalms the bravest, North or
South, East or West. . . . Likely, the typic one of them . . .
crawls aside to some bush-clump, or ferny tuft, on receiving
his death-shot—there, sheltering a little while, soaking roots,
grass and soil with red blood. . . . And there, at last, the Bravest Soldier crumbles in the soil of mother earth, unburied
and unknown.

—WALT WHITMAN (1863)

*C*olumn after column charged up to the works and while
our colors was sticking on our side they planted theirs on
the other, but we would mow them down and they would fall
back and make room for others to meet the same fate. Our
artillery made gaps in their lines from dawn until after dark,
the roar of the guns was ceaseless. A tempest of shells
shrieked through the forests and plowed through the fields;
I went over the works and seen the Johnnies laying in piles,

the dead laying on the wounded holding them tight, and hundreds torn into pieces by shells after they was dead. It was an awful sight, and our boys, they laid dead and wounded by the hundreds.

—SAMUEL A. CLEAR (1864)

*A*ll day we have been fighting & are banging away still—bullets are now whistling round these H.Q. & meanwhile a flock of little chickens are peeping & cheeping—their mother no doubt being in the belly of some soldier.

—OLIVER WENDELL HOLMES (1864)

*S*o after supper at my work, and then heard that little Charlie Lindbergh's body had been found, and that he had been murdered within a day or two after he had been kidnaped, and I think that the murder occurred within two hours of the kidnaping, and my feeling of insensate rage was so great that I felt like going out and killing the first person I met.

—FRANKLIN PIERCE ADAMS (1932)

MAY 13

I rose at 6 o'clock and read a chapter in Hebrew and some Greek in Josephus. I said my prayers and ate milk for breakfast. I danced my dance and settled my accounts. I ate red herring and sallet for dinner. In the afternoon I settled my accounts again. Nurse came home from the wedding where she had stayed all night, contrary to her mistress' orders, for which I was in too great a passion with her, but she gave me as good as I brought and she was so impudent to her mistress that she could not forbear beating her. In the evening I took a walk about the plantation and in the garden where I ate abundance of cherries. My horse Star got a thorn in his foot and was lame. I had good health and good thoughts but was out of humor with Nurse.

—WILLIAM BYRD (1709)

[At Mount Harmon] *T*his evening Mrs. Lester came in to tell me that there was great trouble among the men. Mr. Bryan has arrived at Rose Hill, & has sent some of the Negroes off to Baltimore, on their way to his estate in Georgia. The Negroes here dread nothing on earth so much as this, and they are in great commotion about it. Two of the women sent are the wives of two of my hands, & the poor fellows, who heard it only this even'g are in terrible distress & have gone over to take leave of them. . . . The Negro is capable of strong affection & local attachment. Here these people have lived all their lives & their parents also, for generations. All their friends & relations are here. They regard the South with perfect horror, and to be sent there is considered as the worst punishment. . . . When to all this is added the separation of husband & wife, parent & child, the case is very hard. But they are *property,* & Mr. Bryan has a right to do as he pleases with his own. Only it requires a Southern education to enable a man to bring his mind to the point of exercising such a right in such a manner.

—SIDNEY GEORGE FISHER (1846)

MAY 14

I rose about 8 o'clock and read a chapter in Hebrew and some Greek in Lucian. I said my prayers, and had boiled milk for breakfast. The weather was clear and warm, the wind southwest. About 11 o'clock I went to Mr. G-n-y but he was out. Then I went to Sir Wilfred Lawson's and drank a dish of chocolate. Then I went to William L-m and stayed with him about half an hour; then to the coffeehouse and read the news, and about 2 o'clock went to my cousins Horsmanden to dinner and ate some fish. After dinner we took a nap by consent and about 5 o'clock I went home, and from thence to the coffeehouse, where I quarreled with a woman because she would not change me a guinea. Then I went to the play and stayed it out. After the play I picked up a woman and carried her to the tavern and ate some roast chicken and lay with her, for which God forgive me. About 12 o'clock I walked home and neglected my prayers.

—WILLIAM BYRD (1718)

*T*he favors of our government are . . . distributed without regard to moral character.

—SIDNEY GEORGE FISHER (1859)

*A*mericanization process. Draft men, of foreign blood, scattered through all units. Located Italian, speaking French, in ——th. Protested when ordered for duty as interpreter. Didn't want to speak French for fear people might think him not Amurrican. Acquaintance growing up among different regions of U.S. Oregon reg't and outfit from Boston on same ship. Mass. boys at first dubious of "wild" Westerners—which had highest percentage of college men and generally *vien eleve* of any outfit I've seen. Most refractory bunch yet encountered, from Alabama. Pistol toters. . . . Negro troops— *salutingest* crowd! Very smart, but need extra-strong officers. Liquor their undoing. . . . Americans may gain new independence out of this experience. Those who began by blushing at candor with which Gaul of both sexes goes about processes of excrementation, may return to U.S. converted to sensible notion that distended bladder less pleasing in sight of Lord than reasonable, natural, and comfortable figure of man against convenient if only nominally sheltering tree. If it jolts Puritan tradition to that extent, this war will not have been in vain.

—HOWARD O'BRIEN (1918)

$\mathcal{I}$ left Paris with a certain reluctance, had moments . . . when I could almost imagine myself, as I had never done before, becoming a mellow old expatriate discussing world literature and history, and explaining America to Europeans, in some comfortable cafe. I had begun, before I left, to have again something of my old feeling for Paris.—A few days in New York, followed by New Haven and Boston . . . had me back in the American jitters again—too many cocktails, too many engagements, too many things to do. . . . I felt that the tension at home was infinitely worse than anything in Israel, even with their troubles with the Arabs. Failure of Dulles at Geneva, the McCarthy investigation all over the papers and people getting it on radio and television. All messy and hysterical; makes no sense.

—EDMUND WILSON (1954)

MAY 15

$\mathcal{D}$ined out with E. It may be that the whole illness is due to the thing going on in Europe. It is in my mind all day and my dreams at night.

—SHERWOOD ANDERSON (1940)

$\mathcal{A}$ drunk in the dining car, trying to engage me in conversation while I was trying to work. "I see you are a busy man. I am a seaman. I sail the seven seas." . . . These were his exact words. . . . Then to my surprise he and the dining-car steward spoke in French. I questioned the latter about it a little afterward. He had learned French in the other war, the world war. The drunk, he said, was Belgian, a merchant mariner discharged for some psychoneurosis; he used the world-war term for it, shell shock.

—GLENWAY WESCOTT (1944)

$\mathscr{P}$layed golf with Eisenhower Sunday and dined with him last night at Bunny Carter's. . . . He said that it was a sad thing that nowadays so many people mistook "bad deport-ment" for strength. They consider that a man who beats upon the table is a strong man when really tact is more important and often depicts a much stronger attitude.

—C. L. SULZBERGER (1951)

MAY 16

$\mathscr{A}$lfred Knopf and I are here [Bethlehem, Pennsylvania] for the Bach festival. All day yesterday . . . we tried in vain to get some beer. This morning, having given up all hope of getting any help from the hotel staff, I tackled a taxi driver and he took us to a low dollar-a-day hotel in the region behind the railroad station. When we rapped at the door the bartender stuck his nose through a crack and regarded us suspiciously. He said, "What do you want?" I answered, "Some beer." He then asked, "Who are you?" I said, "Two poor musicians." Then he asked, "Where are you from?" I said, "New York." He still seemed dubious, and so I held up a score of the B Minor Mass. Apparently he recognized it, for he at once opened the door and brought us in. His beer turned out to be excellent, and we got five glasses of it and a ham sandwich for 65 cents. . . . I am sorry that we discovered this excellent place so late. If we had known of it last night we might have put in a couple of pleasant hours drinking the beer. As it was,

174

we sat in our hotel room drinking Scotch highballs. Scotch does not suit Bach. His music demands malt liquor.

—H. L. MENCKEN (1931)

*C*old and clear and I managed to get back to creative work— a big day. In the evening took a long slow drive with Funk who was in one of the moods in which a man talks for hours of past adventures with women. Alas, I joined in it.

—SHERWOOD ANDERSON (1938)

*A*gain unable to work because of weakness. Went to the doctor and to Mary. It was a dark rainy day. The whole city seems sick and depressed over the war in Belgium. It is a world sickness.

—SHERWOOD ANDERSON (1940)

MAY 17

*R*ev. Ralph Waldo Emerson preached . . . in the afternoon, from the text, "The wisdom that cometh from above is gentle." His sermon was on the value and importance of the Christian grace of gentleness. It was a beautiful exemplification of the spirit he was desirous of diffusing aboard. He and his brother [Charles] came to tea, and were very agreeable.

—MARY WILDER FOOTE (1829)

*L*ondon was a shock. I hadn't been here since 1914 except for a few hours passing through in 1921—and I find that I can hardly find my way around. London is now just like Chicago: the same enormous neon signs plastered over the front of the buildings; the same movie palaces with gaudy decorations and people waiting to get in, in long lines; the same tabloids and cheap newspapers with no news in them—nothing but rather sickish crimes; the same cheap-looking window displays of drugstores and five-and-ten-cent stores—the same men and women sitting in doorways and digging in garbage cans as in New York. . . . Strong as I am for America, I have always thought it was nice for the English to have their own institutions. When I go to the theater, I find that the most successful gags are Americanisms, now already slightly stale, such as— "Oh yeah?". . . . Nothing has ever made me feel so keenly that I grew up in one world and am living now in another. It is queer to reflect that the London I knew . . . was the old London.—Still, the city has a kind of smartness, with its brass signs and well-dressed men, that no American city has. In fact, I believe that during this period it has grown smarter. The English have been through the war, the dole, the General Strike, all the gaiety and hollowness of after the war. . . . The gulf between the United States and Europe is already so great that it would take an American his whole life to get readjusted to England, and then he could never get back to the American thing again.

—EDMUND WILSON (1935)

*A*merican memoirs are very boyish, raw, uncooked, no matter what the age of the writer. Straightforwardness is the rule, but it is that very quality which eludes depth. . . . One of the distinguishing marks of the American, unless he be [a] businessman, is that of not giving an intention to the mind and its thinking.

—CLIFFORD ODETS (1940)

MAY 18

*T*ravelled 27 miles. This morning received a visit from some of the Pawnee Indians. Curiosity I suppose prompted their visit. They love to look at us & examine all we have about us & would gladly steal a little if they could. They encamped at noon with us. I sat a little distance from the company watching my saddle &c. when a company of them came around me. They would look at me & laugh & talk to each other. One came & looked under my umbrella as I was sitting on the ground. I looked up to him & smiled & said ha, ha. He was pleased with the attention & quickly said ha, ha, shook hands with me & passed off.

—SARA WHITE SMITH (1838)

*I*n the early evening . . . we sat in the deepening twilight, listening to war news, drinking ourselves drowsy with sherry wine. The German war machine is driving through the famed Maginot Line, on to Paris. No one, Marxist or not, is going to tell me that France and England are as bad in this fight as Hitler's Germany. I am not sure at all about America's future role in this war. Things are moving so rapidly that the opinion of today is worse than useless tomorrow.

—CLIFFORD ODETS (1940)

*T*his is the kind of thing that is disgusting and dismaying in America—I notice it especially getting back [from Europe]. Good abilities degenerate, go to waste—I think of all the friends of my school and college years who showed promise and didn't pan out. There are moments when I feel like that myself. The vulgarity of life in the United States shows up in one of its very bad aspects in the inability of professional men to persist beyond youthful years in living up to any high standard of civic conscience of science or art. Since the standards are not there in clear sight, since they are not supported by a hierarchy, the individual has to make more of a moral effort, which, combined with the effort involved in mastering any field with its skills, is likely to prove too much for him.

—EDMUND WILSON (1954)

MAY 19

Mr. Adams went out a swimming the other day into the Potomac, and went near to a boat which was coming down the river. Some rude blackguards were in it, who, not knowing the character of the swimmer, amused themselves with laughing at his bald head as it poppled up and down in the water, and, as they drew nearer, threatened to crack open his round pate if he came nigh them. The President of the United States was, I believe, compelled to waive the point of honour and seek a more retired bathing place.

—RALPH WALDO EMERSON (1828)

They are beginning to pull down old St. George's in Beekman Street, a venerable landmark. All the west side of Broadway between Eighteenth and Nineteenth Streets is coming down—a row of twopenny little two-story shops. Cheever's Meetinghouse, west side of Union Square, is in course of rapid demolition. Tiffany & Co. are to build on its site. It will be an improvement—the change will. Real jewels will be sold there instead of bogus ones. Cheever's pew-holders paid high prices for their bogus acquisitions. Tiffany's customers will pay still larger sums, but they will secure a genuine article.

—GEORGE TEMPLETON STRONG (1868)

We went at twilight to walk in the green park. . . . I took a pair of silver-plated scissors in my raincoat pocket with the intent to cut another rose. . . . I leaned to snip a pink bud, one petal uncurling, and three hulking girls came out of the rhododendron grove, oddly sheepish, hunched in light manila-colored raincoats. . . . I saw . . . with a shock, a newspaper loaded with scarlet rhododendron blossoms neatly tucked behind a bush . . . and saw another newspaper crammed full of bright pink rhododendrons. . . . "Why are you picking them?" Ted asked. "For a dance." . . . They half-thought we would approve. "Don't you think you'd better stop?" Ted

178

asked. "This is a public park." Then the little one got brassy and fairly sneered, "This isn't your park." "Nor yours," I retorted. . . . We saw them hurrying down to a waiting car and loading the rhododendrons into the open back trunk. . . . I wondered at my split morality. Here I had an orange and a pink rosebud in my pocket and a full red rose squandering its savors at home. . . . but these girls were ripping up whole bushes—that crudeness and wholesale selfishness disgusted and angered me. I have a violence in me that is hot as death-blood.

—SYLVIA PLATH (1958)

MAY 20

This day left Columbia's River, and stood clear of the bars, and bore off to the Northward. The men, at Columbia's River, are strait lim'd, fine looking fellows, and the Women are very pretty. They are all in a state of Nature, except the females, who wear a leaf Apron—(perhaps 'twas a fig leaf). But some of our gentlemen, that examin'd them pretty close, and near, both within and without reported, that it was not a leaf, but a nice wove mat in resemblance!! and so we go—thus, thus—and no War!—!

—JOHN BOIT (1792)

Driving along the highway [in Iowa], I picked up a young man who said that he was from the east. He described conditions there, as he sees them, and commented on the bitterness of many of those people. Replying to his question about people here, I told him that the farm folks here always have something to eat and, of equal importance, we always have our minds occupied and our hands busy. Two things that help much to keep people contented. He admitted that if the "Industrial East" were given many of the things they are now

179

asking for, they would soon find that changing conditions would prove this sort of relief to be exceedingly burdensome.

—ELMER G. POWERS (1931)

I was lying in bed this morning—too lazy to arise—and listening to the radio telling about the dangers of B. O.; how wonderful it was to eat Wheaties; please smoke Chesterfields; and Ladies, wouldn't you like to have a cheap skunk fur coat? When the thought struck me: Here we are living at the end of an epoch in a great transitional stage and a great war in progress which will mean much to humanity, and yet most of us don't feel much differently. Even I feel this way at times. I can see and hear and read signs of the change all around me, but life seems to go along in its well-worn rut. Even the war is an event that one is deeply aware of yet so distant. The American public has not yet reacted fully to the significance of the whole catastrophe. We must be hard hit—directly—before this happens, and this will be soon. Maybe we are too human.

—CHARLES KIKUCHI (1942)

[In Italy] *The* ruined towns between Rome and Ninfa: whole villages left as empty walls and rubble—pink houses—all the buildings looked soft, so that you thought of tearing the paper off a cardboard box and also tearing, by mistake, the gray underneath, or of slicing a part of the crust off a loaf of bread. In one place, a family of children were sitting in a room of which only two corners were left. They had little pots of flowers in the room, and seemed to be sitting around in their bright—black, green, and red—Sunday clothes. . . . I saw "W ROOSEVELT" written on one wall.

—EDMUND WILSON (1945)

MAY 21

[On the Oregon Trail] *W*e passed the recent grave of one of the Mormons, who had been buried near the road. The other party were in advance, and discovered a cow, straggled, no doubt, from the Mormons. They gave chase and drove her back on the road, where we headed her, and various awkward attempts were made to noose her. . . . A tremendous gust of rain come down suddenly upon us . . . and the cow ran off. . . . A rifle ball was sent after her ineffectually; and the Captain, in defiance of the storm, cocking one of his huge buffalo pistols, galloped off in pursuit, and both soon vanished in the diagonal sheets of rain. Presently he and the cow appeared looming through the storm, the Capt. shouting to us that he had shot her. He rode behind her, driving her along, which was very easy as she was shot through the body. . . . We feasted on her at night.

—FRANCIS PARKMAN (1846)

*P*oor, old journal—it doesn't like Yankee raids. It came so very near being consigned to the flames last Friday . . . when we thought the Yanks were coming, but Ma hid it away in the folds of an old dress—and so 'twas left to tell its tale to generations yet unborn. That same Friday was quite an exciting day. . . . Some soldiers had brought intelligence that the enemy were at New Castle. We went to work and hid silver and everything of value that could be put away in our room, thinking that the wretches would hold our dormitory sacred. About 30 wagons and 500 horses stopped here, running away from the Yankees, and we feared they would attract them, but Pa persisted in saying there was no danger. . . . On Sunday we heard all the danger was over and commenced to get out an occasional silver spoon. . . . On Monday everything was so peaceful that we began to think of future happiness, and I ruffled a chemise.

—LUCY BRECKINRIDGE (1864)

$\mathcal{N}$ow more war news on the radio. Here is a voice coming from Paris. Next is apt to be followed by direct telephone message from London and Berlin. The distressing magic of the twentieth century! France and England are losing every move so far. Germany has driven its way clean through to the channel coast. Also holding Amiens and a direct road on to Paris. France is naturally in a panic: premiers and commanding generals are being changed. An announcer on the radio just said, touting up America and its products, "King Solomon in all his glory did not have even a toothbrush!"

—CLIFFORD ODETS (1940)

MAY 22

$\mathcal{I}$ rose about 6 o'clock and read two chapters in Hebrew and some Greek in Lucian. I said my prayers and ate boiled milk for breakfast. I danced my dance. It rained a little this morning. My wife caused Prue to be whipped violently notwithstanding I desire not, which provoked me to have Anaka whipped likewise who had deserved it much more, on which my wife flew into such a passion that she hoped she would be revenged of me. I was moved very much at this but only thanked her for the present lest I should say things foolish in my passion. I wrote more accounts to go to England. My wife was sorry for what she had said and came to ask my pardon and I forgave her in my heart but seemed to resent, that she might be the more sorry for her folly. She ate no dinner nor appeared the whole day. I ate some bacon for dinner. In the afternoon I wrote two more accounts till the evening and then took a walk in the garden. I said my prayers and was reconciled to my wife and gave her a flourish in token of it. I had good health, good thoughts, but was a little out of humor, for which God forgive me.

—WILLIAM BYRD (1712)

The loss of life by steamboats in this country, and especially on the Western waters, is shocking in the extreme, and a stigma on our country; for these accidents (as they are called) seldom occur in Europe, where they do not understand the art and mystery of steam devices, or, indeed, of shipbuilding, better than we do. But we have become the most careless, reckless, headlong people on the face of the earth. "Go ahead!" is our maxim and pass-word; and we do go ahead with a vengeance, regardless of consequences and indifferent about the value of human life. What are a few hundred persons, more or less? There are plenty in this country, and more coming every day; and a few years in the life of a man makes very little difference in comparison with the disgrace of a steamboat being beaten in her voyage by a rival craft.

—PHILIP HONE (1837)

I read all the papers about the great success of Charles Lindbergh in flying his airplane across the Atlantic, and could not read enough of it, the whole story being the most thrilling and happy-endingest story I could imagine, and I doubt that any one ever will look upon its like again. And this is the first great thing I can recall when there is no dissenting or doubting voice, no one to whisper that perhaps it was "framed," or that it all was done by Wall Street men to further the interest of some stock or other. I saw no flaw in the entire proceeding, save what I imagine America, and especially New York, will try to do this young man in the way of making him listen to so much oratory that he will probably long for the comparatively unwindy stretches of the air above the Atlantic.

—FRANKLIN PIERCE ADAMS (1927)

MAY 23

I cannot avoid observing on a most outrageous inconsistency governing between those who have unanimously declared for an Independency, and all the half pay writers on that side of the present question, from the famous author of *Common Sense* down to the E. F. of the 17th inst., said to be Dr. Jones. . . . Why then is a limited monarchy objected to on account of some possible arbitrariness that may be introduced into it, and the same tendency or precedent for such a tendency, established only because it can be confidently advanced that these Republican distractions have arisen from Monarchical Principles; for my part I see no difference; an evil begot how it will and necessity is no better plea in a Republican form than it is or can be in a monarchical form. In both it is bad, and is such a payment to extravagant power that I dread its effects wherever I hear it mentioned. A State had better run in debt or do anything to engage a free consent to Part with a thing than ever countenance the taking it by force; besides do military men know the proper boundary to any action in which their own Power is to judge of? I never knew but one man who resolved not to forget the citizen in the soldier or ruler and that is G[eorge] W[ashington] and I am affraid I shall not know another.

—LANDON CARTER (1776)

*C*otton thread holds the union together; unites John C. Calhoun and Abbott Lawrence. Patriotism for holidays and summer evenings, with music and rockets, but cotton thread is the Union.

—RALPH WALDO EMERSON (1843)

*T*ime was when holidays fell on holidays. But this Saturday seems to be the onset of the Memorial Day weekend, and the day itself is going to be celebrated on Monday the twenty-fifth. I suppose the parades will be held then. I am glad Tony has grown up, because otherwise it might be hard to explain to him why the firemen and police and Legionnaires no longer strut their stuff on the thirtieth—in honor, Jinny and I used to pretend, of his birthday. This arbitrary fooling around with the calendar can have unexpected, even cruel, consequences.

184

When I go to the tailor's at 1:00 P.M. today to have my dinner jacket cleaned and put into hibernation for the summer, two very elderly women with canes are walking—hobbling rather—down Lexington Avenue toward a fast-food joint that is almost always open. When they reach it, it is closed. The looks they exchange are almost as painful to watch as it must be for them to make their slow way back to wherever they came from.

—E. J. KAHN, JR. (1987)

MAY 24

We have struck upon the old Oregon Trail, just beyond the Big Blue, about seven days from the Platte. The waggons we saw were part of an emigrant party, under a man named Kearsley. They encamped about a mile from us behind a swell in the prairie. The Capt. paid them a visit, and reported that the women were damned ugly. Kearsley and another man came to see us in the morning. We had advanced a few miles when we saw a long line of specks upon the level edge of the prairie; and when we approached, we discerned about twenty waggons, followed by a crowd of cattle. This was the advanced party—the rest were at the Big Blue, where they were delayed by a woman in child-bed. They stopped a few miles farther to breakfast, where we passed them. They were from the western states. Kearsley had complained of want of subordination among his party, who were not very amenable to discipline or the regulations they themselves had made. Romaine stayed behind to get his horse shod, and witnessed a grand break-up among them. The Capt. [of the train] threw up his authority, such was the hurly-burly—women crying—men disputing—some for delay—some for hurry—some afraid of the Indians.

—FRANCIS PARKMAN (1846)

*T*he romance of boating is gone now. In Hannibal the steamboatman is no longer a god. The youth don't talk river slang any more. Their pride is apparently railways—which they take a peculiar vanity in reducing to initials—an affectation which prevails all over the West. They roll these initials as a sweet morsel under the tongue.

—MARK TWAIN (1882)

*I*n modern America there are few women. Instead females are hard, driving, nervous, not a restful spot in them. (They do not know how to flirt. . . .) Joan Crawford has always typified to me the modern American woman and for my taste I know of no woman so ugly and desexed as Joan. They are Sears, Roebuck women, pushed into a certain mold, made to order, tailored, neat, and oh so hard!

—CLIFFORD ODETS (1940)

*P*leasant lying in bed reading last night under that old distinguished pink-and-white checkerboard quilt, with, in the white squares, its varied patterns. The weather is not unlike autumn, and reminds me of lying in bed, in my youth, and reading the novels of Hardy.

—EDMUND WILSON (1957)

MAY 25

*M*onday morning I left my father's to return to my circuit with much weeping around me. My father told some of the family he never expected to see me again in this world. It caused trouble on my mind as he was out of the ark of safety but I felt determined to serve God and call Sinners to repentence. I went on my way, crying, to Lynchburg, twelve miles.

—JOHN EARLY (1807)

*S*aw in the post office today a little boy apparently four or five years of age smoking a cigar with all the ease and nonchalance of an experienced smoker. Unenviable precocity. Perhaps by another year the little three foot one, may have donned a swallow tail and be transmogrified into a driver of blood horses and perchance fashionable gamester.

—BENJAMIN BROWNE FOSTER (1847)

*T*he day of suspense is at an end. Alexandria and its environs, including, I greatly fear, our home, are in the hands of the enemy. . . . Poor Jackson (the proprietor) had always said that the Confederate flag which floated from the top of his house should never be taken down but over his dead body. It was known that he was a devoted patriot, but his friends had amused themselves at this rash speech. He was suddenly aroused by the noise of men rushing by his room-door, ran to the window, and seeing at once what was going on, he seized his gun, his wife trying in vain to stop him; as he reached the passage he saw Colonel Ellsworth coming from the third story, waving the flag. As he passed Jackson he said, "I have a trophy." Jackson immediately raised his gun, and in an instant Ellsworth fell dead. One of the party immediately killed poor Jackson. . . . He is the first martyr. I shudder to think how many more there may be.

—JUDITH McGUIRE (1861)

*A*gainst good manners and tact of French, *gaucherie* and excessive self-confidence of some Americans show to sorry advantage. We need a few hundred years more of civilization to make us understand that etiquette is not mere effeminacy, and that skyscrapers, bath-tubs, quick lunch counters and express elevators do not in themselves justify our belief that we are a superior race.

—HOWARD O'BRIEN (1918)

MAY 26

Spent the evening at Mr. Edmund Quincy's . . . [who] told a remarkable instance of Mr. Benjamin Franklin's activity and resolution to improve the productions of his own country. . . . Mr. Franklin mentioned [during Quincy's visit to Germantown] that the Rhenish grape vines had been introduced into Pennsylvania, and that some had been lately planted in Philadelphia, and succeeded very well. . . . Within a few weeks, Mr. Quincy was surprised with a letter from some of Franklin's friends in Boston, that a bundle of these Rhenish slips were ready for him; these came by water. Well, soon afterwards he had another message that another parcel of slips were left for him by the post. The next time Mr. Franklin was in Boston, Mr. Quincy waited on him to thank him for his slips; "but I am sorry, sir, to give you so much trouble." "O, sir," says Franklin, "the trouble is nothing to me, if the vines do but succeed in your province. However, I was obliged to take more pains than I expected, when I saw you. I had been told that the vines were in the city, but I found none, and was obliged to send up to a village, seventy miles from the city, for them." Thus, he took the trouble to hunt over the city, and not finding vines there, he sends seventy miles into the country, and then sends one bundle by water, and, lest they should miscarry, another by land, to a gentleman whom he owed nothing and was but little acquainted with, purely for the sake of doing good in the world by propagating the Rhenish vines through these provinces.

—JOHN ADAMS (1760)

$\mathcal{N}$ooned on Black Walnut Creek. . . . Afternoon, not well—sat slouching on horse, indulging an epicurian reverie—intensely hot—dreamed of a cool mountain spring, in a *forest* country—two bottles of Champagne cooling in it, and cut-glass tumblers, full of sparkling liquor. A wide expanse of perfectly flat prairie—rode over it hour after hour—saw wolves—and where they had dug up a recent grave. Turkey buzzards and frequent carcasses of cattle; camped on Wyatt's Creek. Twenty miles or so.

—FRANCIS PARKMAN (1846)

$\mathcal{W}$e sure are a-living High. Our Children are delivered to the schools in Automobiles. But whether that adds to their grades is doubtful. There hasent been a Thomas Jefferson produced in this country since we formed our first Trust. Rail splitting produced an immortal President in Abraham Lincoln; but Gold, with 29 thousand courses, hasent produced even a good A Number-1 Congressman. There hasent been a Patrick Henry showed up since business men quit eating lunch with their families, joined a club and have indigestion from amateur Oratory. Suppose Teddy had took up putting instead of horseback riding. It's also a question what we can convert these 4 billion filling Stations into in years to come.

—WILL ROGERS (1928)

MAY 27

$\mathcal{A}$fter dinner at St. John's Church . . . There were scarcely thirty persons in the House. The neglect of public worship in this city is an increasing evil, and the indifference to all religion throughout the whole country portends no good. There is in the clergy of all the Christian denominations a time-serving, cringing, subservient morality as wide from the spirit of the Gospel as it is from the intrepid assertion and vindication of truth. The counterfeit character of a very large portion of the Christian ministry of this country is disclosed in the dissensions growing up in all the Protestant churches on the subject of slavery. The abolitionists assume as the first principle of all their movements that slavery is sin. Their opponents, halting between the alternative of denying directly this position and of admitting the duty binding upon them to bear their own testimony against it, are prevaricating with their own consciences, and taxing their learning and ingenuity to prove that the Bible sanctions slavery; that Abraham, Isaac, and Paul were slaveholders; and that St. Paul is the apostle of man-stealers, because he sent Onesimus back to his master Philemon. These preachers of the Gospel might just as well call our extermination of the Indians an obedience to Divine commands because Jehovah commanded the children of Isreal to exterminate the Canaanitish nations.

—JOHN QUINCY ADAMS (1838)

*W*onder how the grand Democratic Palaver is getting on at Baltimore about this time. They've a pretty tangled skein to wind and I suppose the consumption of cobblers and brandy smashes, loud lying and hard swearing throughout today has kept the dealers in those commodities pretty actively employed.

—GEORGE TEMPLETON STRONG (1844)

*I*n the vast empty courtyard of the Winter Palace [in Leningrad], little children in pink pinafores . . . were playing. . . . We were admitted to rooms of Nicholas I—first, a large bathroom, very queer—it made the little girl guide laugh—with a deep deep tub sunk in the floor and great stove in the next room to heat the water—then upstairs the Tsar's tiny rooms—he had some kind of agoraphobia, it seems—with their ugly nineteenth-century furniture, rather Victorian and middle-class . . . and a lot of photographs, slightly faded, of places they'd been to and evidently liked. The little guide wanted to know whether Roosevelt wasn't a great man.

—EDMUND WILSON (1935)

MAY 28

*C*aptain John Brown of Osawatomie called to see me with one of his rangers. He has been stealing negroes and running them off from Missouri. He has a monomania on that subject, I think, and would be hanged if he were taken in a slave State. He has allowed his beard to grow since I saw him last, which changes his appearance entirely, as it is almost white and very long. He and his companion both have the fever and ague, somewhat, probably a righteous visitation for their fanaticism.

—AMOS A. LAWRENCE (1859)

*A*ll Boston turned out to see the first regiment of negroes that had ever been raised in the Northern States. The officers are all educated gentlemen, and Shaw rode with Lieutenant-Colonel Hallowell (whose arm was still in a sling) at the head of the column. He was splendid. I stationed myself outside the window on a projection of one of the stone stores in Franklin Street, and as they came up with the bands playing and the people cheering from the street, and from the houses, with the flags flaunting, it was indeed a grand and novel sight. The troops marched beautifully. When Shaw and his staff came opposite I hailed him and bid him adieu. He raised his hat to me, and waved it toward me twice, at the same time speaking to Hallowell, who did the same. May God bless these dear youths. May God save our country from its foes. May God help this government to crush rebellion, and to crush its cause with it—slavery. Would to God, would to God, I could fight these battles for these young men.

—AMOS A. LAWRENCE (1863)

$\mathcal{I}$ learned, fishing for war news on the radio, that Reynaud, the French premier, was scheduled to make a speech in Paris. . . . Sure enough, a French voice came in, zooming up and down, gliding, shattering—a very poor distance reception. . . . "We must expect certain limitations on our future life." Immediately John Gunther appeared at the microphone, there to interpret the speech. . . . He is trying not to be sensational, but says the Allies are under a "dreadful stress." . . . The Germans have a million Allied troops encircled in a trap. . . . Both London and Paris report that the German dead are piled up in heaps. . . . Suddenly his voice jumps up. "This IS News!" he says. . . . The Belgian force has just capitulated. . . . King [Leopold] ordered a surrender against the unanimous advice of his ministers; they are on their chairs in London and he is on the battlefield—he sees the slaughter and they are probably being cajoled and threatened by the frantic English. For this means that all of the channel ports on the French and Belgian coasts are now open to the Germans; it means fearful attack on England; it means hell let loose in every shape, by every means of expulsion and impulsion that man can leash to gasoline and gunpowder. . . . An organ plays "The Star-Spangled Banner," and the air is silent but for the low, powerful humming of the radio set.

—CLIFFORD ODETS (1940)

MAY 29

$\mathcal{A}$ notion has got footing here that "Southern gentlemen" are a high-bred chivalric aristocracy, something like Louis XIV's noblesse, with grave faults, to be sure, but on the whole, very gallant and generous, regulating themselves by "codes of honor" (that are *wrong,* of course, but very grand); not rich, but surrounded by all the elements of real refinement. Whereas I believe they are, in fact, a race of lazy, ignorant, coarse, sensual, swaggering, sordid, beggarly barbarians, bullying white men and breeding little niggers for sale.

—GEORGE TEMPLETON STRONG (1856)

I could fill my journal with much that has transpired since I last wrote, if I were only inclined to undergo the labor of writing in this *dead book*. I don't know why it is that I write in this, even at such long intervals. It don't give me any satisfaction while I write and I never look back to see what has been written. Nor do I relish the idea of scribbling for the benefit of those who will seize upon this fragmentary history of my life after I am gone. It is, after all, the dislike of giving up what I have so long been in the habit of doing, more or less.

—John William Sterling (1870)

*E*llie has never been to Yellowstone Park, so we drive up there, in part to talk to the leader of Nicola's climbing expedition, in part to see Old Faithful. There's a lot of faith out here in the mountains. Ken Johnson, the helicopter pilot, was telling us that although a Baptist by birth he is now a Mormon and that his beeper always seems to go off in church. Steve Adkinson, whom we've come to Yellowstone to interview, started off as a Catholic but is now, he says, pantheistic. "I can't look out of a window and see a storm without seeing the face of God behind it," he says. . . . Back at the Colter Bay bar, we have a drink with a man who may well be the only Illinois banker in history who was Elvis Presley's army sergeant and whose wife is the daughter of a Czechoslovakian who served in Hitler's army.

—E. J. Kahn, Jr. (1987)

MAY 30

*T*his day a voluntary Bee or Spinning Match at my house. Begun by Break o'day, & in fornoon early were sixty-four Spinning Wheels going. Afternoon seventy wheels going at the same Time for part of the time. Ninety-two daughters of Liberty spun and reeled, respiting and assisting one another. Many brought their flax, especially of my Society—the Spinners were all Denominations, Chh., Quakers, Bapt. & Cong. &c. They spun One hundred & seventy Skeins (fourteen-knotted) and seven Knots.

—EZRA STILES (1770)

[In Kansas] *A*m wearing the Bloomer dresses now; find they are well suited to a wild life like mine. Can bound over the prairies like an antelope, and am not in so much danger of setting my clothes on fire, while cooking when those prairie winds blow.

—MIRIAM DAVIS COLT (1856)

*M*y journal contains but little except the war news of the day, & my speculations on the subject. . . . It absorbs the thought & conversation of every person, men, women & children. The newspapers have scarcely a paragraph that is not connected in some way with its progress & the women & children have become politicians. . . . All are staunch patriots & would like to become soldiers. This feeling of intense devotion to our cause & the enthusiasm which pervades all classes & conditions, all sexes & ages & colour, gives us assurance of ultimate victory under the blessing of an over ruling Providence.

—HENRY RAVENEL (1861)

*B*egan today to teach Nanny to fire a gun, & to load & manage it. Could not prevail on Jane to join us. I am trying to persuade all the ladies of my acquaintance in this neighborhood to learn to shoot, & to become familiar with using guns & pistols. If this practice & usage was general, & it was known that every female, as well as male, kept fire-arms always ready, & knew how to use them, it would remove all of the small existing danger of insurrectionary or other attacks, of negroes—& would render our women an important portion of a "home-guard."

—EDMUND RUFFIN (1861)

$\mathscr{I}$t dismayed me to find how nervous and uneasy I was made all afternoon by the prospect of having dinner with Mrs. Roosevelt. . . . Several times I thought I'd send a telegram pleading illness. This is no different from not going to a grammar-school graduation party because a girl, a certain girl, was there. Finally I dressed carefully and went there, to a place called the Cosmopolitan Club. I took some vermouth first but my mouth was parched. Mrs. Roosevelt was standing in the reception room on the fourth floor. I walked forward and introduced myself in such a low voice that she had to ask me to repeat the name. We shook hands and I walked to one side so she might continue to meet the others who were rapidly arriving. There I was able to get over my amazement at her size—she is over six feet tall, I think. She moved around the room, introducing people, chatting here and there a few sentences—she has the hostess form down to an art and science combined.

—CLIFFORD ODETS (1940)

MAY 31

$\mathscr{J}$ust as I dismounted att Tradaway's [an inn in Maryland], I found a drunken club dismissing. Most of them had got upon their horses and were seated in an oblique situation, deviating much from a perpendicular to the horizontal plane, a posture quite necessary for keeping the center of gravity within its proper base for the support of the superstructure; hence we deduct the true physicall reason why our heads overloaded with liquor become too ponderous for our heels.

Their discourse was as oblique as their position; the only thing intelligible in it was oaths and God dammes; the rest was an inarticulate sound like Rabelais' frozen words a thawing, interlaced with hickupings and belchings. I was uneasy till they were gone, and my landlord, seeing me stare, made that trite apology—that indeed he did not care to have such disorderly fellows come about his house; he was always noted far and near for keeping a quiet house and entertaining only gentlemen or such like, but these were country people, his neighbours, and it was not prudent to dissoblige them upon slight occasions. . . . While he spoke thus, our bacchanalians, finding no more rum in play, rid off helter skelter as if the devil had possessed them, every man sitting his horse in a see-saw manner like a bunch of rags tyed upon the saddle. I found nothing particular or worth notice in my landlord's character or conversation, only as to his bodily make. He was a fat pursy man and had large bubbies like a woman.

—ALEXANDER HAMILTON (1744)

*D*rove in town early to see the procession [to dedicate the St. Gauden monument to Robert Gould Shaw and the 54th Massachusetts Regiment, in Boston]. The Governor rode through the lines and after him came Battery A on the dead run. Then Jake Peabody and Charlie Dabney on horseback. Others less fortunate were riding on the back of the heavy artillery wagons, clinging on for dear life and looking as if they were being shaken to jelly. The N.Y. Seventh marched wonderfully and had a splendiferous band. Lorimer Worden towered above the crowd. The Veterans of the old 54th (Shaw's Regiment) came in for great applause, especially when the torn but still bright colors went by held up by a lame old Negro. . . . Papa went to the Music Hall and said it was a fine meeting. Booker T. Washington made the best speech.

—MARIAN LAWRENCE PEABODY (1897)

I am very severe with myself. Perhaps I am almost a prude in that respect. I scarcely allow a man to touch me. If our hands meet accidentally I draw mine away, almost unconsciously because it has become a habit. And yet, sometimes I have all I can do to keep myself in this self-adjusted straitjacket. For at times I find myself thinking recklessly and blindly, "What does it matter? There is so much love being given and taken in the world. Why should I guard mine so rigidly?" I would so love to run my hands thru people's hair sometimes or give someone a little, little caress. You see I am very conventional about these things. Or perhaps I should say, "I am extremely reserved." But I can't help that. Principles are principles you know. Yet, as I have said, sometimes I feel very much like saying, "Principles go hang." I am not such a cold, flapping fish as I may seem.

—WANDA GAG (1915)

The New York Times is a blistering rash of war news, war hysterias, war plans, screams for democracy. It seems from their pages that tomorrow the Nazis will be here with a mechanized invasion of our forty-eight states. But look inside the financial page. There it tells that the Germans are quietly making payments of interest to American banks on almost fifty millions of loans. There one learns that Italy, urgently requested on the front page of Roosevelt not to enter the war, has just shipped four millions in gold here. And the *Times* financial expert tells the moneymen not to worry—Roosevelt has given assurances that he will not close the market, will not make artificial prices, etc., etc. Meaning that the usual channels of profits and gambling in war woe are open to all, as usual, at the old stand.

—CLIFFORD ODETS (1940)

☙ JUNE ☙

JUNE 1

*T*he lower ferry of Susquehanna, which I crossed, is above a mile broad. It is kept by a little old man whom I found att vittles with his wife and family upon a homely dish of fish without any kind of sauce. They desired me to eat, but I told them I had no stomach. They had no cloth upon the table, and their mess was in a dirty, deep, wooden dish which they evacuated with their hands, cramming down skins, scales, and all. They used neither knife, fork, spoon, plate, or napkin because, I suppose, they had none to use. I looked upon this as a picture of that primitive simplicity practiced by our fore-fathers long before the mechanic arts had supplyed them with instruments for the luxury and elegance of life.

—ALEXANDER HAMILTON (1744)

[In California] *W*e gather up the fresh pine needles occa-sionally and renew our mattress filling, and the pine smell is not only very pleasant but also seems to be a regular sleeping tonic. The longer one lives here the more the country grows on one. When I was at San Francisco, where it was foggy, windy and disagreeable, my thoughts turned to the moun-tains and I longed to get back to Rock Creek again. Pard has his theory about it and in his learned way says the main charm is that we go back to nature, where we belong; throw off our artificial civilization and turn Pagans, and that the closer we get to Mother Earth the more we are in accord with what the Great Cause intended for us. This all may be, but pork and beans get monotonous just the same as having none but the society of men makes one wish for the sight and companionship with a woman. Still, I am afraid I am getting spoiled for I do not feel as if I could take up again the drudgery and hard work of my old life, and if it was not for the old folks I should care very little about going back to New England again.

—ALFRED T. JACKSON (1851)

$\mathcal{O}$ur streets today have been ringing with the sounds of war—one regiment leaving for Virginia—afterwards the cars brought another crowd of sick & wounded—among them are some prisoners—I could not but look anxiously into the face of everyone to see whether there was a familiar countenance—captive in a strange land—When will this agony be over—From the hour where I first saw the Confederate flag flying to this evening there has been a conflict of feeling—personal attachments—struggling against inborn principles—As I heard some prisoners this evening singing Yankee Doodle, the old familiar tune, so long unheard thrilled me with strange emotion—I was alone, & the tears fell thick & fast—when they in loud tones sent forth "The Star Spangled Banner"—I cannot cease to love it.

—CAROLINE SEABURY (1862)

$\mathcal{G}$rand procession of mourning for Mr. Lincoln. . . . Many officers and men scarred and browned with their campaigns were in the procession; but as interesting as any were the great vans filled with soldiers who had lost their lower limbs and who could not walk. These were cheered more than any.

—AMOS A. LAWRENCE (1865)

*W*e had dinner at the Algonquin, then went to the Ziegfeld Follies. [Adelaide Walker] said she hadn't done anything like that in years, and I said it was just like the twenties; but it was not really at all like the twenties. At the show, I was tired and dull: I realized that the Follies could not be revived, that Beatrice Lillie was really too old, that I was really too old. . . . I afterwards had the idea of doing a *New Yorker* story with the title " 'This Is Just Like the Twenties,' He Croaked."

—EDMUND WILSON (1957)

JUNE 2

*W*asted the day with a magazine in my hand. As it was artillery election, it seemed absurd to study; and I had no conveniences or companions for pleasure, either in walking, riding, drinking, hustling, or any thing else.

—JOHN ADAMS (1760)

*Y*esterday (Thursday) was observed by the Nation as a day for humiliation, etc., on account of the death of Lincoln. McLean and myself attended Dr. Bacon's church, where we heard a commemorative discourse on the life of Lincoln. The mercury stood at 82—the church was crowded—everyone was picking off these worms which have stript bare all the fruit and elm trees.

—JOHN WILLIAM STERLING (1865)

*D*r. F. E. Townsend, the old age pension man. . . . told me a long tale about his cousin, a man of his own age, who lately came down with cancer of the prostate. He said that at his advice the cousin submitted to castration and that the effects

200

were magnificent. The cancer vanished and the patient put on 40 pounds of flesh. . . . Townsend told me that his cousin is now strong enough to operate a three-acre chicken farm and is otherwise in prime condition. He said that he was thinking seriously of getting castrated himself. His prostate is normal, but he believes that he is underweight and that adding 30 or 40 pounds would improve his general health. He said somewhat primly: "My reproductive stage is now over, and I see no reason why I shouldn't sacrifice a couple of useless glands." Meanwhile, he is giving himself regular injections of some sort of testosterone preparation. He told me that it is the most effective stimulant he has ever discovered. . . . He didn't mention any specific effect upon his gonads and I didn't ask him.

—H. L. Mencken (1943)

JUNE 3

As came home saw one Elisabeth Nash, born at Enfield, about 25 Years old, just about Three foot high, not the breadth of my little finger under or over. Her Hands show Age more than anything else. Has no Brests. By reason of her thickness and weight can goe but very sorrily. Can speak and sing but not very conveniently, because her Tongue is bigger than can be well stowed in her Mouth. Blessed be God for my Stature, unto which neither I, nor my Dear Mother, my Nurse, could add one Cubit.

—Samuel Sewall (1689)

I rose at 6 o'clock and as soon as I came out news was brought that the child [his infant son] was very ill. We went out and found him just ready to die and he died about 8 o'clock in the morning. God gives and God takes away; blessed be the name of God. Mrs. Harrison and Mr. Anderson and his wife and some other company came to see us in our affliction. My wife was much afflicted but I submitted to His judgment better, notwithstanding I was very sensible of my loss, but God's will be done. Mr. Anderson and his wife with Mrs. B-k-r dined here. I ate roast mutton. In the afternoon I was griped in my belly very much but it grew better towards the night. In the afternoon it rained and was fair again in the evening. My poor wife and I walked in the garden. In the evening I neglected to say my prayers, had indifferent health, good thoughts, and good humor, thanks be to God Almighty.

—WILLIAM BYRD (1710)

*B*etween the time of my A.M. and meridian, Captain Clark and myself strolled out to the top of the heights in the fork of these rivers, from whence we had an extensive and most enchanting view. The country, in every direction around us, was one vast plain in which innumerable herds of buffalo were seen, attended by their shepherds, the wolves. The solitary antelope, which now had their young, were distributed over its face. Some herds of elk were also seen. The verdure perfectly clothes the ground. The weather was pleasant and fair.

—MERIWETHER LEWIS (1805)

*S*uch a lovely June evening had come that I was charmed into a quiet passive state, thinking ahead of a stroll down Fourteenth Street and Second Avenue. . . . In my little walk, so pleasurable because so rare . . . , I enjoyed the shop windows. . . . I thought that some of these side streets were as strange to me as the side streets of Havana, as interesting, as full of life, as varied. . . . Later I proposed another walk with Morris. We walked across the square, admiring very keenly the night stillness which stood among the leafy trees there. Homeless men were sleeping on the benches; we lowered our voices. And now a healthy morning is at the windows, near six. . . . The morning is misty but the sun is coming over a Fourteenth Street building like a fat red orange, or, if you like, a hot nickle.

—CLIFFORD ODETS (1940)

JUNE 4

[En route to the California gold fields] *I* got out to walk and was soon in advance of the train. . . . I lay down to await the coming of our carriage and was soon in a sound sleep. When I awoke I found two hours had elapsed and our company had passed me long since. . . . I struck out on foot. After having travelled till the perspiration stood in big drops on my brow and . . . mounting a small eminence . . . I saw our team and mess in the bottom of the valley. . . . The whole top and body of the carriage was literally crushed to atoms. . . . Another of our teamsters was taken with cholera today at noon and is now a corpse.

—NILES SEARLS (1849)

[In Hollywood] *The* movie girls in startling costumes, selling cigarettes. . . . Ted Shawn and his dancers. Bebe Daniels. Mary Pickford and her dog. Douglas Fairbanks. The beautiful Russian wolf-hound that peed on the stage. And the shudder of offended propriety that went of the good American audience. Dozens of stars appear. Fire works afterward. The genial audience yelling "who," when it couldn't catch the names. . . . The lights. The cool night air. L.A. always looks like a huge valley of diamonds at night—twinkling orange diamonds.

—THEODORE DREISER (1921)

This morning the third grade held their classes in the Buddhist Church up at the end of our barracks. Could hear them singing "God Bless America" at the top of their voices. It was interesting to hear one Issei say something about his little daughter was in there because she was an American while he was a Japanese. He said it with a smile and no trace of any bitter feelings. Most of the families around here are that way. They feel so sorry for the Nisei because we are in a tough situation. These married men keep more or less quiet on their feelings about the war in public whereas the single men are more outspoken. The married men are more stable because they have benefited more from America.

—CHARLES KIKUCHI (1942)

JUNE 5

After dinner we fell upon politicks, and the expected French war naturally came in, whence arose a learned dispute which was about settling the meaning of the two words, declaration and proclamation. Mr. Smith asserted that a proclamation of war was an impropper phraze, and that it ought to be a declaration of war, and on the other hand a proclamation of peace. Mr. Morison affirmed with a bloody oath that there might be such a thing as a proclamation of a declaration and swore heartily that he knew it to be true both by experience and hearsay. They grew very loud upon it as they put about the bowl, and I retired into a corner of the room to laugh a little, handkerchief fashion, pretending to be busied in blowing my nose.; so I slurd a laugh with nose blowing as people sometimes do a fart with coughing.

—ALEXANDER HAMILTON (1744)

Visited a bigger and better Super Market, which has just been opened on the outskirts. Wonderful layout, including a

Beauty Shoppe, Lending Library, and Post Office Station. Big parking lot, with six cars on it, but more people than that inside. . . . But, Lord, what an exhibit the whole place makes of the high standard of American living. We don't know our wealth.

—JAMES WEBB YOUNG (1942)

*S*tepson David once asked me when I thought the New Age had begun. I think it began this morning, when I board a Lexington Avenue bus that's air-conditioned and has an empty seat and, to cap it all, a driver who greets new fares with "Good morning, passengers," who announces each stop, who stops without jerking, and who releases us all to the outside world with a "Have a good day." Or am I dreaming?

—E. J. KAHN, JR. (1987)

JUNE 6

*E*urope is a dream . . . while hotels, bad eating, & sea-sickness, are things of the past. I know that it wont last but a few months, nevertheles I am home, yes actually at home. Here I am in the old house, where I was born, & where I wish I could always live; it is the dearest place on earth to me, & worth all London Paris & New York put together; Sister & Mother may talk, & say what they like, still I shall persist in my opinion, that there is no place equal to Chicago, & no place like home.

—JULIA NEWBERRY (1869)

*I*nvasion! At last the day we all knew was coming has arrived. Everyone is grim as we listen to the news on the radio.

—DONALD J. WILLIS (1944)

The invasion: the sixth hour of the sixth day of the sixth month of 1944. What have our astrologists and numerologists to say about this?

—Glenway Wescott (1944)

And where were you on D-Day? I was in a peaceful hospital in that most peaceful of all peaceful countries, Scotland. I was in a room with four or five patients who were on their way back to the States, some of them having already done their part and some of them n.p. cases who didn't have what it takes to do the job and whose only concern was that the invasion might hold up their departure for home. . . . It's a day when all sorts of emotions well up within you—mental pictures of those ships as they loaded up, what was going on in the minds of the men, the fear that must have been in them, and yet the dogged determination to get this messy business over with.

—Anne McCaughey (1944)

JUNE 7

At 2 O'clock this morning they made a long determined charge, but the boys never wavered. We could hear the Reb officers shouting forward, forward. On they came but it was only to be mowed down by the Thousand. We never thought of getting drove out, I rather enjoyed it and I believe the rest of the boys did also. At daylight this morning all was quiet. The enemy advanced a white Flag, asking permission to bury their dead, which was granted. We had an armistice of two hours. The quietness was really oppressive, It positively made us feel lonesome, after a continual racket day and night for so long. We sit on the works and let our legs dangle over on the front and watch the Johnnies carry off their dead comrades in silence, but in a great hurry. Some of them lay dead within twenty feet of our works—the live Rebel looks bad enough in his old torn, ragged Butternut suit, but a dead Rebel looks horrible all swelled up and black in the face. After they were through there was nothing left but stains of Blood, broken and twisted guns, old hats, canteens, every one of them reminders of the death and carnage that reigned a few short hours before. When the 2 hours was up we got back in our holes and they did the same.

—SAMUEL A. CLEAR (1864)

*V*igell here . . . fixed fences, mowed some in yard & then hoed in currant and R.[raspberry] bushes. But the old chap discovered the strawberry patch & from thenceforth occupied his time equally between watching for chances for forays into said patch, and the said dashes & excursions. If noticed, he was forthwith eagerly engaged in culling large pig-weeds. His plunder he rendered invisible. . . . Picked 4 qts. strawberries this evening—all drying up.

—SARAH CHRISTIE STEVENS (1894)

[At Cape Cod, Spectacle Pond] *P*ond pale slate among greenery—laurel growing bright with purplish pink, first pale adder's mouths, water-lily buds bobbing up (on stalks) like the yolks of hard-boiled eggs. The roads of soft sand.

—EDMUND WILSON (1949)

JUNE 8

*A*t 823 today was an Andersonville prisoner who said he had seen his brethren there on their hands and knees around the latrines of that infernal pen, grubbing among faeces for

207

undigested beans and grains of corn wherewith to mitigate the pains of slow starvation.

—GEORGE TEMPLETON STRONG (1865)

I have in school a woman of this name [Susan Black] whose history has greatly interested me. She is about thirty six years of age, quite black. . . . The first notice taken of her, which she remembers, by her old master, was when she was about twelve yrs old. One day he called her to go into the shed with him. . . . When there, he caught hold of her, held her and in spite of her frightened resistance—with his handkerchief stuffed in her mouth, committed *rape* on such a child. . . . [She] married a fellow-slave, had a "real wedding" in church as she expressed it, and until the breaking out of the rebellion had no serious troubles. . . . Her Master . . . on learning that her husband had gone [to see the Yankees], undertook to console her by offering her joint stock, in his affections with his wife. Tried entreaties, money, which she threw in his face, and lastly whippings and threats. . . . till one day, after exhausting all his powers to make her yield to his desires, he had her stripped naked, tied up and then with his own hands beat her 'till the feaver of passion had subsided. Susan said he would take particular pains to beat her over the pubis; until she was terribly swollen and the blood run down her legs and stood in pools on the floor. . . . She succeeded in reaching this City [Charleston] and was secreted in a small room, by her father. . . . When our soldiers marched into the city Susan was wild with delight. . . . Susan's husband came over to Port Royal and enlisted in the 1st S.C. Regt, was a good soldier, got disabled was discharged and came back here with the "Yankee soldiers" to find his wife, which he was not long in doing and they are now living here as quietly and happily as though they had only lived prosy ordinary lives like other people. Susan goes to school— her husband goes a fishing.

—ESTHER HILL HAWKS (1865)

JUNE 9

At six in the evening I went to my lodging, and looking out att the window, having been led there by a noise in the street, I was entertained by a boxing match between a master and his servant. The master was an unwieldy, pott-gutted fellow, the servant muscular, rawbon'd, and tall; therefor tho he was his servant in station of life, yet he would hav been his master in single combat had not the bystanders assisted the master and help him up as often as the fellow threw him down. The servant, by his dialect, was a Scotsman; the names he gave his master were no better than little bastard, and shitten elf, terms ill apply'd to such a pursy load of flesh.

—ALEXANDER HAMILTON (1744)

When I made that promise to Robert Booker three months ago, I did not expect that I would ever have to keep it. Yet at 11:15 this morning I found myself—a white, bespectacled college professor at the usually conservative age of thirty-six—advancing to my baptism by fire as a sit-in demonstrator! With me was Robert Booker, a tall dignified Negro youth who is president of the student body of our college. As we approached the basement lunch counter in Rich's [in Knoxville, Tennessee], the city's largest department store, Booker showed no fear; I was secretly terrified. . . . Booker brushed by the astonished guard and took a seat at the counter. . . . Leaving Rich's, we walked up the street to the Todd & Armistead Drug Store, where we knew another group had been sitting-in. This group had left and the counter was now reopened. Robert and a Negro girl sat down at the rather small counter. I sat down next to the young lady. Immediately a waitress put up a cardboard sign on which was scrawled in crayon, "counter closed." The counter employees went into the back room and no one said anything to us.

—MERRILL PROUDFOOT (1960)

JUNE 10

*M*y daily duties sometimes press hard. First I rise and dress, say my own prayers, and prayers with some of my children. Before seven the triangle is struck for family prayers in the library. Breakfast at seven. Lay out work for men afterwards. Off on horseback at eight. Visit the contractors who are building for me about here and the laborers on the grounds. Then to Cambridge, oftenest to look after new work or old—just now the new house for president, and refitting the Brattle House; or to meet the president or steward or some one of the professors on their business; or to review the college 'troops.' Then to Boston by half past nine. Here are all sorts of business, commercial, philanthropic, political; besides building of three large stores, and a carriage factory, and drilling my company daily. This pushes me hard till after three, when I get on my horse again and reach home a little late for dinner. Then read the news, and rest until I turn out to inspect my garden and workmen, or to take my wife to drive in my country wagon. All assemble at quarter before eight o'clock at tea. Children's bedtime and prayers with them at half past eight. Then a nap, and reading or writing till eleven or twelve. There is a great scarcity of employment, and I have taken about thirty-five men to dig my marshes, then to haul gravel from them, then to cover with loam, and sow grass seed.

—Amos A. Lawrence (1861)

*M*iss Philip, Whistler and Kennedy to dinner to celebrate Whistler's *Grand Prix* and J's. Gold Medals, Whistler, of course, treating the occasion with all solemnity and distinction—arriving with Miss Philip, both in evening dress—we were not, which he evidently thought a slight on our part. "Shocking! Shocking!—your want to ceremony," he said. Just before we sat down to dinner, Cole came in most unexpectedly; as the other Gold Medallist, it was appropriate, but things did not go quite as they ought to have gone to begin with. Cole was still full of the diet question. He now lives chiefly on rhubarb tops—they have such a "foody" taste, his son thinks. "Dear me! Poor fellow!" Whistler told him, "it sounds as if once long, long

210

ago he had really eaten, and still has a dim memory of what food is!" "And spinach," Cole added, "it's fine. We eat it raw. It's wonderful, the things it does for you!" "But what does it do for you?" Whistler asked. And Cole began a dissertation on the juices of the stomach. But that was enough. Whistler would have no more. "Well, you know, when you begin to talk about the stomach and its juices it's time to stop dining." As he talked Cole was eating meat and drinking wine quite heartily. The evening was not over successful.

—ELIZABETH AND JOSEPH PENNELL (1900)

$\mathcal{I}$n Washington the other day, at the convention of the Workers' Alliance of WPA workers, I heard Mrs. Roosevelt address the delegates. . . . There was a palpable touch of patronage in her friendliness. She spoke, not as one who has observed them politely from afar. She was excessively amiable, but there was something fixed and artificial about her smile. I don't think she made much impression on the poor fish before her. They cheered when she came in and they applauded politely when she finished, but it was plain that she left them as hopeless as they were before she spoke to them. They had been listening for three or four days to a long succession of palpable quacks, beginning with General Jacob S. Coxey and running down to Congressman John M. Coffee, of the State of Washington. Compared to these transparent mountebanks, Mrs. Roosevelt at least looked sincere, but her sympathy for the poor shovel-leaners was plainly that of a kindly doctor, not that of a suffering fellow patient.

—H. L. MENCKEN (1939)

JUNE 11

$\mathcal{O}$ne thing was very grievous unto us at this place; There was an old woman, whom we judged to be no less than an hundred yeeres old, which came to see us because shee never saw English, yet could not behold us without breaking forth into great passion, weeping and crying excessively. We demaunding the reason of it, they told us, she had three sons, who when master *Hunt* was in these parts went aboord his Ship to trade with him, and he carried them Captives into Spaine . . . by which meanes shee was deprived of the comfort of her children in her old age. We told them we were sorry that any English man should give them that offense, that *Hunt* was a bad man, and that all the English that heard of it condemned him for the same: but for us we would not offer them any such injury, though it would gaine us all the skins in the Countrey. So we gave her some small trifles, which somewhat appeased her.

—WILLIAM BRADFORD AND EDWARD WINSLOW (1621)

*B*eing encamped on low clay soil, there is mud & water all around us & some water within. Our tent is 10 feet long & 8 wide on the ground. Sometimes have a curtain to separate the families that we may be more retired as yesterday & today. . . . In our part we have this morning our two saddles & blankets, my work basket, our India rubber valise, Mr. Smith's gun & shaving apparatus, long box that holds the clothes, my cloak, bonnet &c. Not having chairs, we are sitting on the blankets writing on our laps. All our things are very damp. The ground soaked with water. We have a buffalo hide spread down but that is now wet & I have been taking the water off it with the sponge & the water is now dripping through upon us & we can't help it. We sit with our India rubber shoes, shawls & hoods on, it is so cold. Mrs. Walker has been crying. I asked her why she cried. She said to think how comfortable her father's hogs were. This made us both laugh & cry together.

—SARAH WHITE SMITH (1838)

*N*ow the Prairie life begins! We left "the settlements" this morning. Our mules travel well and we joged on at a rapid pace till 10 o'clock when we came up with the waggons. We crossed the branch and stretched our tent. It is a grand affair indeed. 'Twas made in Philadelphia by a regular tent-maker of the army, and every thing is complete. Our bed is as good as many houses have; sheets, blankets, counterpanes, pillows &c. We have a carpet made of sail duck, have portable stools. Well after a supper at *my own table* and *in my own house* I can say what few women in civilized life ever could, that the first house of his own to which my husband took me to after our marriage was a *tent;* and the first table of my own at which I ever sat was a cedar one, made with only *one leg* and that was a tent pole.

—SUSAN MAGOFFIN (1846)

JUNE 12

As the trail gets rougher we encounter piles of things that people have thrown away to lighten their loads. This was a day of scenes of abandoned property; stoves, blacksmith tools, mattresses, cooking utensils, and provisions of every kind strung along the road. There was also an abandoned wagon with broken axles. We have been seeing dead animals from the first day.

—ANDREW GORDON (1849)

I'm full of sorrow and contrition tonight. A poor little mouse had been caught alive and unharmed, which I tended very carefully through the evening, and supplied with food and water. Its little eyes and whiskers were delightful, and I fully intended to set it at large in the street in front of somebody else's dwelling house after making it the subject of a slight scientific experiment, often heretofore tried on myself and rather pleasurable than otherwise—inebriation by chloroform. So he was "taken up tenderly, lifted with care" by the

213

tail and lodged beneath a spacious bell-glass with a rag wet with a sufficient dose of that beneficent fluid. First he ran about vigorously, then his footing grew uncertain, then he tumbled down and kicked. Then I lifted the bell-glass and took him out, and he kicked more feebly and lay still and did not come to. I became alarmed. I exhausted the remedial agents within my reach, cold water, artificial respiration, and friction of the extremities. Ammonia and galvanism were not at hand. But it was unavailing. "The vital spark had fled." It makes me unhappy, for though mice are vermin, I hate to kill them.

—GEORGE TEMPLETON STRONG (1856)

The President left for Long Branch at 8 o'clock yesterday, leaving a great many Congressmen with fingers in their mouths, waiting to complete business at the executive Mansion. The President has done much to show with how little personal attention the Government can be run. Perhaps this is the drift of modern thought. It is said that Queen Victoria's retirement from public affairs has proved to England how unnecessary a sovereign is to the wants of a people. We can say as the Methodist shouter did in Bedford, "The same thing over here."

—JAMES A. GARFIELD (1872)

The case of F. Scott Fitzgerald becomes distressing. He is boozing in a wild manner, and has become a nuisance. . . . Several years ago . . . he caused a town sensation by arising at the dinner table and taking down his pantaloons, exposing his gospel pipe. . . . He was lately laid up at the Johns Hopkins, suffering with a liver complaint. The young doctors of Baltimore avoid him as much as possible, for he has a playful habit of calling up those he knows at 3 a.m. and demanding treatment, i.e., something to drink. How he manages to get any work done I can't imagine. . . . He calls up the house now and then, usually proposing that Sara and I go automobiling

214

with him, but he is always plainly tight, and Sara always puts him off. His automobile driving is fearful and wonderful.

—H. L. MENCKEN (1934)

[At the Park of Culture and Rest, Moscow] The Russians never squeal or shriek as we do at Coney Island—frightful paleness and rawness—peculiar effect of nothing having any color, neither their clothes, nor their faces, nor the signs on the buildings of the park—they have no dyes . . . except a little indispensable red for the flag. . . . Park makes our country fairs look like mad orgies of gaiety and color.

—EDMUND WILSON (1935)

JUNE 13

I attempted to cross the [Potomac] river with Antoine in a small canoe, with a view to swim across it to come back. . . . My son John, who was with us, thought the boat dangerous, and, instead of going with us, went and undressed at the rock, to swim and meet us in midway of the river as we should be returning. I thought the boat safe enough. . . . Before we had got half across the river, the boat had leaked itself half full, and then we found there was nothing on board to scoop up the water and throw it over. Just at that critical moment a fresh breeze from the northwest blew down the river as from the nose of a bellows. In five minutes' time it made a little tempest, and set the boat to dancing till the river came in at the sides. I jumped overboard, and Antoine did the same, and lost hold of the boat, which filled with water and drifted away. We were as near as possible to the middle of the river, and swam to the opposite shore. . . . While struggling for life and gasping for breath, [I] had ample leisure to reflect upon my own indiscretion. . . . My son John joined me, having swum wholly across the river, expecting to meet us returning with the boat. . . . While Antoine was gone [for help], John and I were wading and swimming up and down on the other shore, or sitting naked basking on the bank.

—JOHN QUINCY ADAMS (1825)

The President [Jackson] is certainly the most popular man we have ever known. Washington was not so much so. His acts were popular, because all descriptions of men were ready to acknowledge him the Father of his Country; but he was superior to the homage of the populace,—too dignified, too grave for their liking; and men could not approach him with familiarity. Here is a man who suits them exactly. He has a kind expression for each. . . . His manners are certainly good, and he makes the most of them. He is a gourmand of adulation, and by the assistance of the populace has persuaded himself that no man ever lived in the country to whom the country was so much indebted. Talk of him as the second Washington! It won't do now. Washington was only the first Jackson. Poor Adams used to visit New York during his presidency. The papers, to be sure, announced his arrival; but he was welcomed by no shouts, no crowd thronged around his portals, no huzzas rent the air when he made his appearance, and yet posterity, more just than ourselves, will acknowledge him to have been . . . twenty times superior to Jackson.

—PHILIP HONE (1832)

I had my first sit-in in a variety store today, and also my first experience as group leader. My group was sent to Grant's. The counter was closed as soon as the first Negroes sat down. . . . One customer left a full plate of food, explaining to the waitress that she was unable to eat it. . . . (I remember how, when I first came to the South seventeen years ago, the thought of eating food that had been *prepared* by Negroes turned my stomach; this woman would no doubt be elated to be able to afford a Negro cook, but was nauseated by the thought of eating *with* a Negro. The fact that I have

216

grown beyond my own prejudice gives me hope for her.) The others quietly completed their refreshments and left.

—MERRILL PROUDFOOT (1960)

JUNE 14

*O*ne Abraham Shurd of Pemaquid, and one Capt. Wright, and others, coming to Pascataquack, being bound for this bay in a shallop with 200 work of commodities, one of the seamen, going to light a pipe of tobacco, set fire on a barrel of powder, which tare the boat in pieces. That man was never seen: the rest were all saved, but the goods lost. That man, that was blown away with the powder in the boat at Pascataquack, was after found with his hands and feet torn off. This fellow, being wished by another to forbear to take any tobacco, till they came to the shore, which was hard by, answered, that if the devil should carry him away quick, he would take one pipe. Some in the boat were so drunk and fast asleep, as they did not awake with the noise.

—JOHN WINTHROP (1632)

I descended the hill and directed my course to the bend of the Missouri near which there was a herd of at least a thousand buffaloe. . . . I selected a fat buffaloe and shot him very well, through the lungs; while I was gazing attentively on the poor anamal dischargin blood in streams from his mouth and nostrils . . . a large white, or rather brown bear, had perceived and crept on me within 20 steps before I discovered him; in the first moment I drew up my gun to shoot, but at the same instant recollected that she was not loaded and that he was too near. . . . I ran about 80 yards and found he gained on me fast, I then run into the water. . . . He sudonly wheeled about . . . , declined the combat on such unequal grounds, and retreated. . . . It now seemed to me that all the

217

beasts of the neighborhood had made a league to destroy me. . . . Three bull buffalo, which were feeding with a large herd about a half a mile from me on my left, separated from the herd and ran full speed toward me. . . . When they arrived within a hundred yards they made a halt, took a good view of me, and retreated with precipitation. I then continued my route homeward, passed the buffalo which I had killed, but did not think it prudent to remain all night at this place, which really, from the succession of curious adventures, wore an impression on my mind of enchantment. At some times, for a moment, I thought it might be a dream, but the prickly pears which pierced my feet very severely once in a while, particularly after it grew dark, convinced me that I was really awake, and that it was necessary to make the best of my way to camp.

—MERIWETHER LEWIS (1805)

JUNE 15

*A*fter supper they set in for drinking, to which I was averse and therefor sat upon nettles. . . . Two or three toapers in the company seemed to be of opinion that a man could not have a more sociable quality or enduement than to be able to pour down seas of liquor and remain unconquered while others sunk under the table. I heard this philosophical maxim but silently dissented to it.

—ALEXANDER HAMILTON (1744)

*W*ent with Miss Dora Howells to the Court House to hear Mrs Gage lecture on womans rights. She is a woman of a good deal of talent—an easy fluent, & rather impressive speaker, but a little too ornate. She uttered some truths upon the subject of female education, but her leading idea, a change of places & pursuits between men & women is an absurdity. . . . I couldn't help asking myself, & shrinking from the question, how I would like to see mother, sister or wife make such an exhibition. It is too great a violation of my instincts of female decorum & delicacy to admit of any enjoyment. . . . If women must lecture I prefer to patronize good curtain lectures, & think them far less offensive and injurious than these public displays.

—ORVILLE BROWNING (1854)

*S*ince we were short of workers this morning (for now the novelty has worn off and it has become a day-by-day grind), we economized by sending only two Negro persons and myself to Sears'. Since they are going to close when one or two Negroes come in, why bother to send more? . . . We don't seem to bother getting one another's full names. This is an impersonal enterprise, since we come from many different groups and do not expect to be associated after the sit-ins are over; nevertheless there is a deep sense of comradeship among us because of our common jeopardy. In both these respects we are like an army battalion at the front lines.

—MERRILL PROUDFOOT (1960)

JUNE 16

*W*hen the train started Brewster and I went back to the hunting ground to search for the lost pistol and blanket. Hunted for more than 3 hours in vain, then set out to overtake the train. . . . The sun was hot, the road dusty and the wind blew almost a tornado. It was impossible to keep my hat on. I had to walk bent against the wind to keep from being blown off the trail. It was hard walking, and as it was over a dreary sand waste without water, we suffered such thirst that we had to drink out of a muddy stagnant pool. We overtook the train at 1:15 p.m., encamped on a high table land above the river bottom. . . . Once at home, as the camp really seemed to be, we prepared a good drink of lemonade to quench our thirst, and regaled ourselves on a dish of pinola mush and molasses, hard bread, cold coffee and buffalo steak. The train had travelled 12 miles.

—BERNARD J. REID (1849)

*S*tiring news this morning from Pennsylvania, the rebels are going into the state as fast as they can. Hooker is at Fairfax with his army. likely this move of lees is the last or death strugle of the rebels. we went out and had a mess of cherries this afternoon. weather warm health good.

—FRANKLIN HORNER (1863)

I here declare my unmitigated hatred to Yankee rule—to all political, social & business connection with Yankees—& to the Yankee race. Would that I could impress these sentiments, in their full force, on every living southerner, & bequeath them to every one yet to be born! May such sentiments be held universally in the outraged & down-trodden South, though in silence & stillness, until the now far-distant day shall arrive for just retribution for Yankee usurpation, oppression, & atrocious outrages—& for deliverance & vengeance for the now ruined, subjugated, & enslaved Southern States!

—EDMUND RUFFIN (1865)

*G*rant's counter stretches in a straight line along one entire side of the store. A conveyor belt behind the counter carries orders out from the kitchen and dirty dishes back in. As we sat at the counter today, the white male cook got an idea for a big joke. He put large slices of watermelon on three plates and sent them out on the belt. One of the waitresses he alerted to stand at the far end of the belt to catch them and

220

send them back on the return belt. They circulated the water-melon in front of us eight or ten times. They were right—we were hungry, and for some who like watermelon better than I do, it must have been a successful torture. The implication in the choice of watermelon was obvious, but our group took it in good humor.

—MERRILL PROUDFOOT (1960)

JUNE 17

*L*ast night our men cast up an intrenchment on Bunker's hill, Charlestown & at Dorchester point—This morning about Sunrise the *Lively* man of War, flung herself down near the Ferry, & fired several Cannon at the Breastwork & killed one man——he imprudently exposed himself, lying on the ground—The Army made ready for a sudden alarm—About 4 oC. P.M. a general Battle ensued at Charlestown—The Regulars landed, & sat fire to the meeting house, & took the advantage of the Smoke which covered them. . . . our men gave the Enemy a brisk fire at a distance from the fort—& not long before the Regulars came with a bold front & scailed the Walls & took possession of the fort—our men retreated & fled in confusion. We lost five field pieces—& of the killed about 50 & of the wounded about 50—we lost several officers—— Prayed with Regt. in the fort.

—DAVID AVERY (1775)

*T*his was the day of the great celebration of the completion of the monument on Bunker Hill. . . . What a name in the annals of mankind is Bunker Hill! what a day was the 17th of June, 1775! and what a burlesque upon them both is an oration upon them by Daniel Webster, and a pilgrimage by John Tyler and his Cabinet of slave-drivers. . . . I have throughout my life had an utter aversion to all pageants and public dinners, and never attended one when I could decently avoid it. . . . But now, with the ideal associations of the thundering cannon, which I heard, and the smoke of burning Charlestown, which I saw, on that awful day, combined with this pyramid of Quincy granite, and Daniel Webster spouting, and John Tyler's nose, with a shadow outstretching that of the monumental column—how could I have witnessed all this at once, without an unbecoming burst of indignation, or of laughter? Daniel Webster is a heartless traitor to the cause of human freedom; John Tyler is a slave-monger. What have these to do with the Quincy granite pyramid on the brow of Bunker Hill? What have these to do with a dinner in Faneuil Hall, but to swill like swine, and grunt about the rights of man? I stayed at home, and visited my seedling trees, and heard the cannonades of the rising, the meridian, and the setting sun, and answered a letter from the Rev. Joseph Emerson.

—JOHN QUINCY ADAMS (1843)

*W*ent to Byberry. On the boat met Miss Peabody, and Mattie Griffiths, the author of "Autobiography of a Female Slave." . . . We spent the day very pleasantly at Byberry. . . . Our conversation was almost entirely about prejudice. The ladies expressed themselves very warmly against it. On reaching the city, Mrs. P[utnam] and I were *refused* at *two* ice cream saloons, successively. Oh, how terribly I felt! Could say but few words.

—CHARLOTTE FORTEN (1857)

JUNE 18

*W*ent to Independence Hall.—The old bell with its famous inscription, the mottoes, the relics, the pictures of the heroes of the Revolution—the *saviours* of their country,—what a

222

mockery they all seemed,—*here* where there breathes not a freeman, black or white.

—CHARLOTTE FORTEN (1857)

*I*n one of the Hospitals I find Thomas Haley, Co. M, Fourth New York Cavalry—a regular Irish boy. . . . came over to this country from Ireland to enlist—has not a single friend or acquaintance here—is sleeping soundly at this moment, (but it is the sleep of death) has a bullet-hole straight through the lung. . . . I often come and sit by him in perfect silence. . . . Poor youth, so handsome, athletic, with profuse beautiful shining hair. One time as I sat looking at him while he lay asleep, he suddenly, without the least start, awaken'd, open'd his eyes, gave me a long, long steady look, turning his face very slightly to gaze easier—one long, clear silent look—a slight sigh—then turn'd back and went into his doze again. Little he knew, poor death-stricken boy, the heart of the stranger that hover'd near.

—WALT WHITMAN (1862)

*C*alling on Dorothy Parker. . . . my depression at finding her and her circle the same—she still sitting around very pretty but in slightly dowdy dressing gown, drinking gin and ginger ale. . . . little intelligent sensitively responsive cocker-spaniel puppy which keeps peeing on things; Dorothy's unwillingness to hear anybody else's stories, wisecracks. . . . The Algonquin Circle had grown social, their humor no longer quite so low-down—but for Dorothy . . . the little humorists' world seemed smaller than before.

—EDMUND WILSON (1933)

JUNE 19

*Y*esterday I amused myself and boys by shooting bull-frogs at the fishpond. I killed ten last night, we had them for supper. They made a delicate dish. I shall be a frogeater after this. I eat so much frogs that last night I jumped in my sleep.

—DAVID GOLIGHTLY HARRIS (1860)

*W*e struck tents this morning and packed up and all are ready to move, when the order was countermanded and the boys tried which could get off the most cuss words to the square inch.

—SAMUEL A. CLEAR (1865)

*A*t the great San Diego Worlds Fair yesterday, Mr. Hoover received a tremendous ovation. There is no country in the world where a person changes from hero to a goat, and a goat to a hero, or visa versa, as they do with us. And all through no change of them, the change is always in us. Its not our public men that you cant put your finger on, its our public. We are the only fleas weighing over 100 pounds. We dont know what we want, but we are ready to bite somebody to get it.

—WILL ROGERS (1935)

*A*ll right, so the headlines blare the two of them [the Rosenbergs] are going to be killed at eleven o'clock tonight. So I am sick at the stomach. . . . The tall beautiful catlike girl who wore an original hat to work every day rose to one elbow from where she had been napping on the divan in the conference room, yawned, and said with beautiful bored nastiness: "I'm so glad they are going to die." She gazed vaguely and very smugly around the room, closed her enormous green eyes, and went back to sleep. The phones are ringing as usual, and the people planning to leave for the country over the long weekend, and everybody is lackadaisical and rather glad and nobody very much thinks about how big a human life is. . . . They were going to kill people with those atomic secrets. It is good for them to die. So that we can have the

224

priority of killing people with those atomic secrets which are so very jealously and specially and inhumanly ours. . . . The execution will take place tonight; it is too bad that it could not be televised . . . so much more realistic and beneficial than the run-of-the-mill crime program. . . . The largest emotional reaction over the United States will be a rather large, democratic, infinitely bored and casual and complacent yawn.

—SYLVIA PLATH (1953)

JUNE 20

*P*reachd at Indian Meeting house, to 20 Indians . . . From Matth: 22:39. *Thou Shalt love they Neighbour as Thy Self*—A grace and Duty much Wanting and greatly Neglected Among these Indians. In the Fore part of My Discourse, Indians Seemd Sleepy and Careless—Digressed and rousd them, by Awakening Touches. Towards the Close of my Discourse, A Molatto (Ammon,) a Lusty Man, . . . fell into great distress, manifested by Crying out bitterly, which continued through the Remainder of Sermon. Finishd off with a fervent Prayer, trembling as he Spoke. Found upon Speaking to him after Sermon, that the Word reachd his Conscience, Wakd up a Sense of his Guilt, in late evil Conduct, having been long reputd a Christian, but of late Years or Months, walkd unbecoming his Profession. Several other Indians, manifested Some deep Impressions from the *Word*.

—JOSEPH FISH (1768)

*J*ust before leaving the hollow and entering the valley of the North Fork, I was behind the train reading some names on trees, when a very fine looking indian came across the hollow towards me on a dun pony. He was naked down to the waist and his long black hair was plaited in a queue behind. He was armed with bow and arrows and spear. Could

225

talk no English. We shook hands and made signs, but to little purpose. He rode and moved with dignity and agility. Soon Francisco came up and tried to talk to him but could not except by signs. Soon leaving us he started up the precipitous bluffs, which his pony climbed like a mountain goat.

—BERNARD J. REID (1849)

There appears to be quite a sensation in regard to gold discoveries near the Canada line, and several persons from this place have gone up and others are going. The excitement seems to be spreading rapidly and the wise ones say there is something in it. But after all, the "Bloomer Costume" is the grand topic of the day. Its chief features seem to be short, snug dresses and loose trousers, a sort of compound of the harem and circus. . . . Somebody calls it the "knee plus ultra of fashion."

—BENJAMIN BROWNE FOSTER (1851)

Visited with an old country woman, over seventy, who praised the Lord and blessed His Name. For the first time in her life she has running water in her house. It's just a cold water spigot in her kitchen sink, with another outside for her flowers, but it means no more toting from the old well. Riches.

—JAMES WEBB YOUNG (1942)

JUNE 21

Plenty of soldiers pass by every day after dress parade. One man came yesterday to buy a chicken for a sick soldier, but I gave it to him. I am so unused to such things, that I felt as if I were doing a *cruel act*, to put the innocent *live* chicken in the big soldier's power. " 'Tis excellent to have a Giant's strength, 'tis tyrannous to *use* it as a Giant." I've no doubt we were cruel Giants in the chicken's idea!

—JOSEPHINE CLAY HABERSHAM (1863)

*W*ounded men are seen everywhere; in the streets, on the railroad cars, at the railroad station. Some badly maimed. Certainly there were never so many maimed men of one nation before, and the graves! And the sorrowing hearts! O God, how long?

—AMOS A. LAWRENCE (1864)

*I*n Boos Brothers Cafeteria 723 Broadway [Los Angeles] we feel our first real Earthquake. The floor & walls rock. I have a sense of the mystery & terror of it. A sense of huge merciless forces supersedes that of life. There is hush—a slight sense of nausea—then a babel of voices. I am like one in a dream—standing tray in hand ready to pick up an order of string beans. Helen is white & shaking. Since it is a long way to the door & there is a crowd—we wait instead of trying to run out. No one leaves—no panic—but there is a sense of possible death imminent. It all very wonderful & different, so remote from the mood of ordinary life.

—THEODORE DREISER (1920)

JUNE 22

A great number of Bills for Prayer and Thanks—but p.m. I happen'd to forget to take Notice of two of them that were put up then. They were Lieutenant Bruce's for his Wife; and Mr. Eliphalet Adams on occasion of the Death of his Mother: Lieutenant Bruce came into my House, and the Storm abroad was great, Thunder, Lightening, and Rain. Yet the Storm of Brother Bruce's Passions was more grievous. . . . He went away talking and in a Rage, notwithstanding it was the Sabbath, and the Storm which Should have Struck Terror, into each of our Hearts. I could not Suffer him to go away in Such a Frame. I put on my Great Coat, and went to the Meeting House . . . Somewhat out of Breath by my running through the Rain. . . . He being Still at the Stables, I Stop'd there again and there labour'd to pacifie him: but all was in Vain. . . . This was a just Chastizement from God upon me, for my own Sloth and Negligence! the Lord be mercifull to me a Sinner!

—EBENEZER PARKMAN (1755)

*P*roceeding up the valley, objects were seen on the opposite hills, which disappeared before a glass could be brought to bear upon them. A man, who was a short distance in the rear, came spurring up in great haste, shouting Indians! Indians! He had been near enough to see and count them, according to his report, and had made out twenty-seven. I immediately halted; arms were examined and put in order; the usual preparations made; and Kit Carson, springing upon one of the hunting horses, crossed the river, and galloped off into the opposite prairies, to obtain some certain intelligence of their movements. Mounted on a fine horse, without a saddle, and scouring bareheaded over the prairies, Kit was one of the finest pictures of a horseman I have ever seen. A short time enabled him to discover that the Indian war party of twenty-seven consisted of six elk, who had been grazing curiously at our caravan as it passed by and were now scampering off at full speed. This was our first alarm, and its excitement broke agreeably on the monotony of the day.

—JOHN C. FRÉMONT (1842)

H. L. Mencken, the undesirable element of Literature, was sitting by me at the [Democratic party] convention and he suggested the singer follow "Dixie" with "Marching through Georgia." I knocked him under the press table, before Cap-

tain Hickman, my Texas Ranger Friend, could get out his gun
to totally dispose of him.

—WILL ROGERS (1928)

The Army photographers disrupted our day by taking a
moving picture of our pressroom in action. These official docu-
mentary films will probably be used to show the "bigwigs" how
well off we are and they will also be kept for the record of the
"greatest mass migration in American history." . . . We were
excited about being in the movies. They put the huge klieg lights
in and it made us sweat like hell. I had on Jack's Hawaiian
shirt and typed out a letter while they took some shots. The
director made us go through the motions of being busy.

—CHARLES KIKUCHI (1942)

JUNE 23

No visitors were allowed in today because of Army orders
to search all barracks for contraband. Rushed home to hide
all the knives and tools. . . . [Chief Easterbrooks] had a whole
pile of saws, hatchets, knives, and Japanese literature in his
office. He said that the tools . . . were "potentially dangerous
weapons." Who in the hell would we attack anyway—the Japs
surrounding us? . . . Only the more timid gave up articles.
The others figured that nothing could happen to them anyway since they were already prisoners. . . . Lately I've been
getting that restless feeling again. I feel so useless at times.
And I resent the term "white bastards" which I hear many of
the Nisei using. And E. T. refers to the Jewish people as the
"Kikes" who gypped hell out of the Japanese in the evacua-
tion. Won't minority groups ever learn not to hate another
minority group because of their seeking some scapegoat?
This sort of thing can only lead to further hatreds and the
Japanese here are in a swell position to get it right in the

neck unless all of the minority American groups learn that their problems are common and should be worked out together for the future good of this country.

CHARLES KIKUCHI (1942)

*A*s dawn breaks, I see the beach directly ahead of our convoy. It is unusually quiet, which gives me an eerie feeling. There are more sunken ships than ships afloat in these waters. Many things are in the water that should not be there. Smashed tanks, broken equipment, and metal fragments are laying in the brine of Omaha Beach. Behind us in the moist air of the English Channel is the invasion armada, an unbelievable display of power. Warships of all sizes are offshore, now silent, but mute testimony of the terrible battle which took place here. They are grim reminders of what is yet to come. Barrage balloons sway in the air as P-47 Thunderbolt fighter-bombers zoom from a newly built airstrip close to the beach.

—DONALD J. WILLIS (1944)

*T*oday, for what I suspect is the first time in history, a nuclear physicist participated in a lunch counter sit-in! Dr. Robert Ellis . . . . is a Negro . . . developing peaceful uses for thermonuclear energy. He and Harvey sat near one end of the counter and discussed—of all things—nuclear physics! . . . No matter how many degrees you earn, no matter how many books you write, even if you become a college president or a United Nations Secretary, you still cannot eat at the nicest restaurants, stay at the best hotels, see the new movies, own a business on Main Street, or buy a home in the fashionable part of town. The class system of medieval Europe never had the finality which race strictures have today in portions of the United States, for in feudal society the religious vocation offered a way of escape even to the peasant. Our segregated Church fulfills no such democratizing function.

—MERRILL PROUDFOOT (1960)

JUNE 24

$\mathcal{W}$e . . . traveled up a long, gradual slope, or plain, free of rocks, trees, or gullies, and came at half past eleven o'clock to the summit of the South Pass of the Rocky Mountains. We could hardly realize that we were crossing the great backbone of the North American Continent. . . . The ascent was so smooth and gentle, and the level ground at the summit so much like a prairie region, that it was not easy to tell when we had reached the exact line of the divide. . . . Near the summit, on each side of the road, was an encampment, at one of which the American flag was flying. . . . To see the old flag once more strongly reminded us of home. There was a hailstorm at noon, but that did not prevent the assembled company from having an off-hand celebration of our arrival at the summit. Music from a violin with tin-pan accompaniment, contributed to the general merriment of a grand frolic.

—MARGARET A. FRINK (1850)

$\mathcal{B}$ooker T. Washington received an honorary degree [at Harvard] and made the finest speech of all, receiving tremendous applause. . . . When they all left Sanders Theatre for lunch, Papa saw Mr. Washington turning to the left and hurrying off towards Harvard Square so he called after him and said, "This way, Mr. Washington—the lunch is over this way," but Mr. Washington just waved and said, "Yes, I know, I'll be there shortly." President Alderman of Tulane University had received a degree too and Mr. Washington had thought he and possibly other Southerners might not like being at the table with him so he got his lunch in Harvard Square somewhere, and came in quietly a little late, though he was to be the chief speaker of the day.

—MARIAN LAWRENCE PEABODY (1896)

$\mathcal{I}$n the paper today there was an interesting letter to the editor. The man ranted and raved that the Nisei should be

disfranchised because they could never assimilate by inter-
marriage "because the Japs will always have those short
arms." He stated that the Nisei have high birth rates and
would soon outnumber and outvote the Caucasions unless
they were all disfranchised and deported. Just can't understand the utter stupidity of some people. They would make
good Fascist stooges.

—CHARLES KIKUCHI (1942)

JUNE 25

*R*eached the Arkansas [Great Bend, Kansas] at 4 o'clock,
encamped and replenished our shot pouches. "Keep your
eyes skinned now," said the old trapper. "We are entering
upon the most dangerous section of the trace, the war ground
of the Panis [Pawnees] Osages, and Kansas." This is likewise
a fine buffalo country, but we have no hump! no marrow
bones and no tongues, except our own parts of speech. Our
hunters have brought in an antelope.

—ALPHONSO WETMORE (1828)

*T*his evening there is heavy canonading by the enemy.
Skirmish firing still going on all the time. Sometimes it nearly
amounts to a fight, then it eases off to the same old bang,
bang, bang, like water dropping off the eaves of a house. The
bullets go zip zip over our breastworks day and night, making
the men bow their heads.

—SAMUEL T. FOSTER (1864)

*L*ooking out through the window . . . I saw the white gawky
and graceful figure of a girl moving across the wide black

232

open doorway of a new white garage, just framed in the green fronds of summer trees.

—EDMUND WILSON (1927)

JUNE 26

I rose about 8 o'clock and read a chapter in Hebrew and some Greek in Lucian. I said my prayers and had milk for breakfast. The weather was clear and cold, the wind west. I wrote some verse. About eleven came Daniel Horsmanden and stayed half an hour, and about one I went to Ozinda's, where I lost four guineas and about two returned home and ate some battered eggs for dinner. After dinner I put some things in order and then took a nap till 5 o'clock, when Daniel Horsmanden came and we went to the park, where we had appointed to meet some ladies but they failed. Then we went to Spring Gardens where we picked up two women and carried them into the arbor and ate some cold veal and about 10 o'clock we carried them to the bagnio, where we bathed and lay with them all night and I rogered mine twice and slept pretty well, but neglected my prayers.

—WILLIAM BYRD (1718)

M——s and I returned to town where M——s, having a generall acquaintance, for he had practised physick ten years in the city and was likewise the Church of England minister there, he introduced me into about 20 or 30 houses where I went thro' the farce of kissing most of the women, a manner of salutation which is expected (as M——s told me) from strangers coming there. I told him it was very well, if he led the way I should follow, which he did with clericall gravity. This might almost pass for a pennance, for the generality of the women here, both old and young, are remarkably ugly.

—ALEXANDER HAMILTON (1744)

233

*N*ext door to us lives a young man who is learning to drum. He studies hard at his science every night. I should like to reward his music with a wreath of *Smilax peduncularis* [catbriar].

—RALPH WALDO EMERSON (1834)

JUNE 27

*V*ery fine, likely to be hot; at my office early. The only way to compose myself and collect my thoughts, is to sit down at my table, place my Diary before me, and take my pen into my hand. This apparatus takes off my attention from other objects. Pen, ink, and paper, and a sitting posture, are great helps to attention and thinking.

—JOHN ADAMS (1770)

3 miles then brought us to the beawtiful town of *"Greencastle"* on the *"Harrisburg"* R. R. This is a fine town larger than Washington Ga houses large & fine, shady streets. This town like others in this State have never felt the affect of war. The R. R. runs down Main Street. People strong Unionist & looked mad & sullen at our apperance a great many closed doors; stores all closed the Streets & Hotels crowded with young men just out of service. Some nice looking girls dressed very fine as evry thing is cheap. Several Federal Flags were seen the girls had them on their bonnets. We marched through quick time with music. . . . After leaving town we had the plain mud road to march, very muddy, but we marched through fields of wheat & corn tearing down fences & not respecting scarsly any thing. The soldiers hardly respecting any thing, robing bee gums & poultry yards. We were gathering up all the horses & beeves in the country. People all very much frightened along the road.

—THOMAS WARE (1863)

*J*ust now Surrealism is very much the fad. I remember how Dali, hanging on to a fur-lined bathrobe, leapt or fell through Bonwit Teller's window. The result was that his exhibition was crowded for weeks, and for the first time he sold all his pictures. Eight or nine out of every ten persons in that crowd surely thought that Bonwit Teller performance very cheap and false. But six or seven out of ten would not have come to the exhibition at all if there had been no performance. We hate cheap publicity—we also hate alarm clocks, but they wake us up.

—GLENWAY WESCOTT (1939)

*T*he big day! By 9:15 we were downtown. . . . While our number was far short of a hundred, there were enough to put twenty-five picketers on each of the two fronts of Rich's. . . . I feel very conspicuous; I have always thought picketers looked silly. . . . Traffic is increasing as the curious drive by to see what is going on. Some young fellows with a convertible have obtained huge Confederate and Tennessee flags and are riding round and round the store giving rebel yells and occasionally firing blank cartridges. . . . I am carrying this afternoon my favorite sign, "We Are All Brothers in Christ." A young grown man passes behind me and growls in my ear, "You damn sonofabitch!" I think of the legend on the sign and get a thrill as I realize, "Christianity is still powerful! I know, because it still has enemies!"

—MERRILL PROUDFOOT (1960)

JUNE 28

*T*he celebration [of the opening of the railroad in Charleston] is over and no body hurt. . . . Baker the *cuisiner* made the best speech. When all had nearly finished, he mounted the table and requested the waiters to bring back the empty dishes as there was 1500 lbs of meat yet untouched. The dishes or rather trays were then full. The crowd was immense. Probably not less than 3000 persons in all, women, children and negroes included. I do not think I ever saw so many persons assembled together. So the Rail Road is finished. . . . Nothing could be heard, save the cannon, by all.

—JAMES HENRY HAMMOND (1842)

$\mathcal{G}$rass & hard work but that does not account sufficiently for the heavy gloom which seems settled on all the negro faces. I have seen this gradually thickening ever since the Richmond battles of last year & more especially since the late repulse at Charleston. They seem utterly subdued as if by blasted hopes. Yet there is a peculiar furtive glance with which they regard me & a hanging off from me that I do not like. I have no doubt they have all along been well apprised with the Abolition version, of what is going on, & may thus shut up their faces & cease their cheerful greetings in view of the future, not the past. They would wish to be passive & take what comes. But the roar of a single cannon of the Federal's would make them frantic—savage cutthroats & incendiaries.

—JAMES HENRY HAMMOND (1863)

JUNE 29

$\mathcal{A}$ Democrat never adjourns. He is born, becomes of voting age, and starts right in arguing over something, and his first political adjournment is his date with the undertaker. Politics is business with Democrats. He don't work at it, but he tells what he would do if he was a working at it. It's been a fine convention, nobody nominated, nothing done. But what difference does it make? After all we are just Democrats.

—WILL ROGERS (1932)

236

$\mathcal{A}$s I go about the country, talking with a good many kinds of people, I find that the subject matter for conversation does not vary much, percentage-wise. First, and properly so, comes the weather—sure instinct for the importance of our physical environment. Then comes man, quite literally embracing woman, with all the ramifications thereof. Most of the rest can be summarized under food and drink, business and war. Beyond this I am reminded of what William James' carpenter said—that there is not much difference between one man and another, but what little there is, is important.

—JAMES WEBB YOUNG (1943)

$\mathcal{I}$ remember [Djuna Barnes] attacking me years ago for insisting that American writers should stay in the United States. Why shouldn't they live in Paris, where it was so much pleasanter? Today I detest the American cities and would gladly spend a good deal of my time in Paris.

—EDMUND WILSON (1958)

$\mathcal{S}$purred by the rising excitement, between sixty and seventy came to sit-in today, enough to hit nearly all the stores whose counters remain open. . . . Walgreen's is the only place we go that has booths; Logan and I occupy one together. A man in a white jacket . . . conspicuously spits on the floor. The next time he tosses a lighted cigaret on me; it rests in a fold of my coat. . . . A group of white boys who appear to be high school age come up to our booth and begin to tantalize me. . . . As they continue their heckling, I look straight ahead at Logan. Suddenly I feel myself drenched with . . . liquid. My glasses are filmed over. . . . My eyes smart. . . . Logan utters quiet words of encouragement; he is a great strength to me. . . . Suddenly I am jolted by a severe blow on the left side of my face. My first thought is of being hit by a batted tennis ball when I was six years old—it stings like that. . . . Failing to get any response, one or two of the boys grab me and start pulling me from the booth. . . . At precisely this moment a young white man who has been eating in a booth near ours

237

rises. . . . Sternly he says to the boys, "You fellows have gone far enough and now you'd better get out of here! Look, I'm neutral in this, but this fellow was just sitting here." . . . Here is a clear example of the effectiveness of the non-violent approach. It has caused this "neutral" to declare himself for decency and order.

—MERRILL PROUDFOOT (1960)

JUNE 30

It has been my fate to be acquainted in the way of my business with a number of very rich men. . . . But there is not one of all these who derives more pleasure from his property than I do from mine; my little farm, and stock, and cash afford me as much satisfaction as all their immense tracts, extensive navigation, sumptuous buildings, their vast sums at interest, and stocks in trade yield to them. The pleasures of property arise from acquisition more than possession, from what is to come rather than from what is. These men feel their fortunes; they feel the strength and importance which their riches give them in the world; their courage and spirits are buoyed up, their imaginations are inflated by them. The rich are seldom remarkable for modesty, ingenuity, or humanity. Their wealth has rather a tendency to make them penurious and selfish.

—JOHN ADAMS (1772)

I know of nothing in society so beneficial in its influence upon young men as to be thrown into intercourse with married ladies much older than themselves. . . . The fopperies & affectations which they are liable to contract from being *beaux* to young ladies they feel to be out of place & they insensibly fall into a respectful style of address, tax their sense & knowledge to appear to advantage & pay attentions from which they know they can have no return but increased self respect & the esteem of a superior woman.

—RICHARD HENRY DANA (1842)

*N*ow, about dark, we came into the musquito regions, and I found to my great *horror* that I have been complaining all this time for nothing . . . for some two or hundred or even thousands are nothing compared with what we now encountered. . . . About 10 o'clock the mules became perfectly frantic. . . . They were turned out to shift for themselves, and Magoffin . . . tied his head and neck up with pocket handkerchiefs and set about having the tent stretched. I drew my feet up under me, wraped my shawl over my head, till I almost smothered with heat, and listened to the din without. Millions upon millions were swarming around me, and their knocking against the carriage *reminded me of a hard rain.* It was equal to any of the plagues of Egypt. . . . Magoffin came to the carriage and told me *to run if I could* . . . (and without opening my mouth Jane said, for they would *choke* me) straight to bed. When I got there they pushed me straight in under the musquito bar . . . and oh, dear, what a relief it was to breathe again. . . . I tried to sleep and toward daylight succeeded. On awakening this morning I found my forehead, arms and feet covered with knots as large as a pea.

—SUSAN MAGOFFIN (1846)

JULY

JULY 1

*M*r. Hezekiah Willet slain by Naragansets, a little more than Gun-shot off from his house, his head taken off, body stript. Jethro, his Niger, was then taken: retaken by Capt. Bradford the Thursday following. He saw the English and ran to them. He related Philip to be sound and well, about a 1000 Indians (all sorts) with him, but sickly: three died while he was there. Related that the Mount Hope Indians that knew Mr. Willet, were sorry for his death, mourned, kombed his head, and hung peag in his hair.

—Samuel Sewall (1676)

*D*uring this day's march, the caravan *bachi* shot his own mule through the head in a buffalo chase. Stearne's lament over the dead ass repeated.

—Alphonso Wetmore (1828)

*A*t about 6 o'clock I received a telephone call. . . . Mr. Dehn of course. . . . We talked a long while and he said he'd come at 7 p.m. to see me. Which he did accordingly. He was obviously glad to see me. So was I glad to see him. He looked at my new sketches and then we took a walk. To Loring Park as of old. We kept up a bantering sort of conversation for a while and then he suggested that we stop talking nonsense. So we talked Socialism.

—WANDA GAG (1915)

*O*utside I can hear the swish of the cars as they go by down the highway. The barbed wire fence way below us reminds us that we are on the inside. On the other side of the highway there is a huge glass hothouse where they raise chrysanthemums and dahlias. The tiny men working hard way in the distance look like ants, but they are free men. The armed soldier, some lonely boy from the middle west, paces back and forth up by the main gate. In the sentry boxes, the soldiers look bored. They probably are more bored than the residents here.

—CHARLES KIKUCHI (1942)

JULY 2

*M*iss Nancy Carter last Night or this morning, in some whimsical freak, clipt off her Eye-Brows; She has a very good Skin; exceeding black hair, & black-well arched, full Eye-brows, which, as I said the other day are much esteemed in Virginia—She denies positively that She cut them her self, & swears some mischievous person has done it when She was sleeping. But I am inclined to think it is an experiment She has been making on herself to see how she can vary the looks of her face. It made me laugh when I saw it first, to think how early & how truely She copies Female absurdities.

—PHILIP VICKERS FITHIAN (1774)

*H*ere at the foot of the mountain the engagement became general & fierce & lasted until 8 O'clock at night. And in the third & last charge the fatal blow was struck. My Brother: You have offered your life as a sacrifise upon your country's Altar. Today concludes the term of life of my Brother. He now sleeps upon the battle field of Gettysburg with

> *There Brothers, Fathers, small & great,*
> *Partake the same repose*
> *There in peace the ashes mix*
> *Of those who once were foes*

Many of our brother soldiers whose life was made a sacrifise upon our country's altar. There the weeping willow gently waves over his grave. And there we prayed that God would guard and protect that little mound.

—ROBERT WARE (1863)

*W*hat does the American now feel about the situation in which he finds himself—rich-poor, handsome-ugly, healthy-weakly, white-black? His situation was formerly accepted by him as "God's will"; his improving such elements as were improvable was approved and even aided by God; his reverses and illnesses were sent him from Above. What goes on in his mind now when he [is] fortunate and unfortunate, i.e., victim of hazard?

—THORNTON WILDER (1960)

JULY 3

*A*bout ten an old Negro Man came with a complaint to Mr Carter of the Overseer that he does not allow him his Peck of corn a Week—The humble posture in which the old Fellow placed himself before he began moved me. We were sitting in the passage, he sat himself down on the Floor clasp'd his Hands together, with his face directly to Mr Carter, & then began his Narration—He seem'd healthy, but very old, he was well dress'd but complained bitterly—I cannot like this thing of allowing them no meat, & only a Peck of Corn & a Pint of Salt a Week, & yet requiring of them hard & constant Service. We have several Rains this day so that the Ground is sufficiently wetted—I spent the greater part of the day writing at my Sermon.

—PHILIP VICKERS FITHIAN (1774)

*O*ur march to-day is through a plane and rolling prairie, surrounded with buffalo. A herd of these attempted to break through our column of teams. "It will take a smart scrimmage and sprinkle of shots," said the old trapper, "to turn them aside," and the leader fell at the flash of his rifle. Marched 20 miles, and encamped without timber—our supper dressed as usual, over buffalo fuel.

—ALPHONSO WETMORE (1828)

A fine cloudy day. The rebs all left last night about midnight. They were uneasy about the Yankees. They stole all the bees & chickens in the neighborhood. We have heard rumors of a great battle going on about Gettysburg. The rebs are in a tight place and I think will leave thousands in this state to be buried. General Mead has superceded Hooker, he being unwell. The troops are offered so fast that transportation cannot be afforded fast enough.

—AMOS STOUFFER (1863)

I left Charlotte yesterday on the freight-train, which carries an "accommodation coach." The accommodation was wretched. The car was old and dirty, and full of dust. The cinders flew in the windows, and in all it was pretty disagreeable. . . . There was a lady on board. She was faded and wrin-

243

kled, highly painted, wore false teeth and was very talkative. She had a little girl along who was very precocious, and was always uttering some pert but seldom smart remark. The lady, I have since learned, is "Miss Belle Boyd, the confederate spy." The girl was "Miss Elmo Boyd." The lady lectures, and the little girl recites verses of "original poetry."

—CHARLES W. CHESNUTT (1875)

*F*lew down here [Claremore, Oklahoma] to recuperate from one straight month of speeches. Heard a mule braying a while ago out at the farm and for a minute I couldn't tell who he was nominating. Roosevelt made a good speech yesterday and he did aviation the biggest boost it ever had. Took his family and flew out there. That will stop these big shots from thinking their lives are too important to the country to take a chance on flying. But it was a good thing the convention broke up. Times was hard. Some of the delegates had started eating their alternates. Cannibalism was about to be added to other Democratic accomplishments.

—WILL ROGERS (1932)

JULY 4

*W*here the deuce the enjoyment or sense or recreation or enthusiasm of going about the streets all night exploding petty fireworks, discharging guns and pistols, yelling, singing, making night hideous in the most uncouth and unbecoming mode and keeping a poor devil half awake—where the excuse is I don't discover.

—BENJAMIN BROWNE FOSTER (1850)

A very sad affair occurred at Shelter's this morning. Absalom Shelter hung himself. He has been in trouble for a good while. The rebels took all his horses and told him when they came back they would take all the crops along. It made him very uneasy. His wife found him. He was not quite dead yet, but soon died. I went up directly. He was quite warm yet and looked quite natural.

—AMOS STOUFFER (1863)

The insolent *Yankees* in our neighborhood are firing their guns in honor of *the day!* Little do *they* know or appreciate the precious *boon of Liberty* left us by our fathers on that glorious day, 1776! God grant that we Southerners, as a nation, may yet show the world an example of a refined and Christian nation who, having dearly bought this priceless boon, may know how to enjoy and value it!

—JOSEPHINE CLAY HABERSHAM (1863)

[Asbury Park] *The* girls were wearing long dresses and light coats lined with fur at the bottom and the men white knickerbocker trousers and sweaters checked tan and white. Hot dogs, dabbed with mustard from the common bowl with a little long-handled wooden trowel, and buttermilk; salt-water taffy, hot buttered popcorn. . . . As the sky darkened, the fireworks were started, and a rocket streamed violet and silver against the deepening gray—then it burst in brooches of red, gold and green, great bouquets that unfolded and shriveled, growing out of one another; the loud detonation of a cluster of white electric stars. Children held the bristling brass of their toy sparklers out to the enormous darkening sea.—Before night, little blond bob-haired girls and boys, in pink and yellow pinafores, slid squealing down the smooth bumpy slides in an interminable succession.—The last random pops and shots of the Fourth.—The smell of gunpowder.

—EDMUND WILSON (1925)

245

[In a German POW camp] *W*ould like to see some fireworks on this Independence Day, but was just another day's work. Sure hope we can get out of here before long. We have clothing and food. We aren't suffering for anything except freedom. . . . Many of the fellows are looking forward to big things when this war is finally over. . . . I have no wife, no home, no job, no auto or any of the things the fellows speak of. If I can once again have my freedom in my own country, I will be satisfied.

—THEARL MESECHER (1944)

JULY 5

A wet rainy day. Last night it rained very hard. The waters are all very high. It will be impossible for the rebs to cross the Potomac for a while now. Last night and this morning we heard their trains going along the Waynesboro road to get back to Virginia. The Rebs have been terribly cut up. Over the mountains a force of our men captured about a dozen wagon loads of their wounded and had them to town. Some had their legs and some their arms shot entirely off. It is reported that they are retreating this way. . . . There is every now and then a few rebels going along the pike, but they are all prisoners.

—AMOS STOUFFER (1863)

*Th*e Revolutionary Dames celebrated the Fourth in a new hall. I made the speech of the occasion, which they all said was very good. A gentleman read a paper on the American flag. The first one, he informed us, was made out of a sailor's blue coat and a woman's red petticoat and white apron. So the petticoat was in the beginning and waved over the cornerstone of the Republic, while all the men of the thirteen colonies were tied metaphorically to an apron-string.

—ELIZABETH CADY STANTON (1897)

That liberty that we got 159 years ago Thursday was a great thing, but they ought to pass a law that we could only celebrate it every 100 years, for at the rate of accidents yesterday we wont have enough people to celebrate it every year, and the speeches? Did you read them? Never was as much politics indulged in under the guise of "Freedom and liberty." They was 5 percent what George Washington did, and 95 percent what the speaker intended to do, what this country needs on July the Fourth is not more "Liberty or more freedom" its a Roman candle that only shoots out of one end.

—WILL ROGERS (1935)

I forgot to note the principal event of yesterday: Every year on the Fourth a softball team of the kids of Mulhocaway play against a team of the girls of the jail: at sunset, Tchelitchew-pink, on the institutional greensward in front of its toy church against its languid flag—the spectator girls, Cadmus-faced, all around sitting squat or lolling but at the high points of the game bursting up onto their feet, jitterbuggy and ear-splitting. Ethel Sahl, the Marijuana murderess, pitching to my young nephew, for example. A tall young Negress . . . famous for her bad temper; dangerous with a baseball bat. My brother arriving late from the hayfield. . . . played an inning just before dark, towering over farm children and slum women; not just for fun . . . but as a kind of gesture of Americanism. . . . Dear America, poetical Fourth.

—GLENWAY WESCOTT (1945)

JULY 6

Last night twelve white men came, dressed and painted in Indian style, and gave us a dance. No pen can describe the horrible scene they presented. Could not imagine that white men, brought up in a civilized land, can appear to so much imitate the Devil.

—Myra Fairbanks Eells (1838)

The head of Washington hangs in my dining-room for a few days past, and I cannot keep my eyes off it. It has a certain Appalachian strength, as if it were truly the first-fruits of America, and expressed the Country. The heavy, leaden eyes turn on you, as the eyes of an ox in a pasture. And the mouth has gravity and depth of quiet, as if this MAN had absorbed all the serenity of America, and left none for his restless, rickety, hysterical countrymen.

—Ralph Waldo Emerson (1852)

Lord! how tired I am of all this tendency to ballyhoo the war. Magazine editors, newspaper columnists, radio commentators, and Washington headline hunters all seem determined to dramatize it and jazz it up. They act like press agents for a "Roosevelt & Hopkins' Greatest Show on Earth." It is true that for awhile we had ringside seats at history. But now we are in the ring, with a serious, dirty, and dangerous job to do. We ought to cut out the showmanship and get on with it.

—James Webb Young (1942)

JULY 7

Been in town [Nevada, California] all day. The citizens had a celebration Thursday, but it did not amount to much. Lawyer McConnell made a speech and another fellow read the Declaration of Independence. Then everybody fell into line, marched up and down the street, hurrahing and firing off pistols, and that was all there was to it. The town was jammed with outsiders and the hotels and restaurants ran short of grub. The saloons and gambling houses were chock-a-block and half the men in sight were full of rot-gut whiskey. Went in to see the pretty French woman, but could not get near the table where she was dealing. She's a handsome woman and the boys say she's straight as a string. That may be, but it is strange, considering the company she keeps and her occupation. Went home early, as I couldn't get a meal.

—ALFRED T. JACKSON (1850)

*W*e went out to Lake Minnetonka. I was very peevish when we started out, and . . . the fact that two feather-headed couples were walking before us may have been responsible for part of my disgust. They would fool around, grabbing each other's hands or managing to touch each other as if by accident, and it irritated me. Of course I know it is as old as the world is old, but just that afternoon I couldn't bear to think of such a thing as physical attraction. . . . Not that I would despise a girl for allowing a man to take little liberties—I suppose it isn't her fault that she is so primitively constructed. But that day it did seem so irritatingly *"animalisch."* As I sat there I was filled with revolt at the thought of any man except a relative touching me. I don't know what I would be like if I were a man. If my feelings would be the same as they are now, I certainly would be able to have good morals.

—WANDA GAG (1915)

*A*morous and wretched, pacing the town as if it were all one vacuous bedroom, but still patiently pacing. Newsreel theater, a most unpleasant program: The Braddock-Louis fight. A broken-toothed old clubwoman opining that, instead of banning dogs from Manhattan, we should get rid of three hundred thousand "useless humans." The new bobsled run at Palisades Park, seventy-two miles an hour on ballbearings. The clubbing and killing of irritating picketers by huge serene policemen in Chicago on Decoration Day: the reel that was

249

suppressed for a while. Then dreamy views of places in Virginia associated with George Washington, with accompaniment of "Carry Me Back" and "My Country 'Tis of Thee"—from which I fled.

—GLENWAY WESCOTT (1937)

JULY 8

*N*ew Meeting House: In Sermon time there came in a female Quaker, in a Canvas Frock, her hair disshevelled and loose like a Periwigg, her face as black as ink, led by two other Quakers, and two other followed. It occasioned the greatest and most amazing uproar that I ever saw.

—SAMUEL SEWALL (1677)

I quartered in a trader's cabbin [by the Allegheny River] and about midnight the *Indians* came and called up him and his squaw. . . . She sold the *Indians* rum, with which being quickly intoxicated, men and woman began first to sing and then dance round the fire. . . . which continued all the next day. An *Englishman* when drunk will fall fast asleep for the most part, but an *Indian*, when merry, falls to dancing, running, and shouting, which violent action probably may disperse the fumes of the liquor, that had he sat still or remained quiet, might have made him drowsy. . . . As soon as we alighted they shewed us where to lay our baggage, and then brought us a bowl of boiled squashes cold; this I then thought poor entertainment, but before I came back I had learnt not to despise good Indian food.

—JOHN BARTRAM (1743)

250

$\mathscr{W}$arm sunshine morning. At eleven, went and met Committee of Inspection at Philosophical Hall; went from there in a body to the lodge; joined the Committee of Safety (as called); went in a body to State House Yard, where, in the presence of a great concourse of people, the Declaration of Independence was read by John Nixon. The company declared their approbation by three repeated huzzas. The King's Arms were taken down in the Court Room, State House [at the] same time. From there, some of us went to B. Armitage's tavern; stayed till one. I went and dined at Paul Fooks's. . . . Fine starlight, pleasant evening. There were bonfires, ringing bells, with other great demonstrations of joy upon the unanimity and agreement of the declaration.

—CHRISTOPHER MARSHALL (1776)

$\mathscr{R}$omance in its broad sense is the most wanted product in the world. So many people lead lives of "quiet desperation" that any advertising which offers them escape, and any product which offers them utility plus color, performs a profound service.

—JAMES WEBB YOUNG (1942)

JULY 9

$\mathscr{M}$y Husband & I were awake at 3 hour this morning by Mrs Heartwel and Gillbard who brot us the horrible tydings that Captain Purington had murdered all his famely Except his son James who must have shared the same fate had he not been so fortunate as to make his Escape. . . . My son went in and found . . . said Purington, his wife, & six Children Corps! and Martha he perceived had life remaining who was removd to his house. Surgical aid was immediately calld and she remains alive as yet. . . . The Corps were removd to his Barn where they were washt and Laid out side by side. A

251

horrid spectakle which many hundred persons came to behold. I was there till near night when Son Jonathan conducted me to his house and gave me refreshment. The Coffins
were brot and the Corps carried in a Waggon & deposited in
Augusta meeting hous.

—MARTHA BALLARD (1806)

*W*ithin twenty yards of my gun stands a solitary locust
tree, the sole representative of a once noble grove which
graced the graceful lawn. Charred from the burning of the
mansion and torn by relentless cannon balls, truly "grand,
gloomy, and peculiar," its glory has not all departed. Amidst
a tuft of foliage which graces the topmost bough, there daily
sits a mockingbird which, with the rising of the sun, carols
forth its superb madrigal until the first gun fires. What a
subject for contemplation, this "gleam of heaven," in the
midst of the "pomp, pride, and circumstance" of glorious war!
How painfully am I reminded by the winged messenger of
peace of my once happy home in the South!

—EUGENE HENRY LEVY (1864)

JULY 10

*M*y husband and I attended at the sollom funeral of
James Purington & his famely which he murdered. There was
a prayer made by Reverend Mr. Stone, a discoarse delivered
by a Mr Taylor from Proverbs 25 C 28 V—he that hath no
rule over his own spirit is like a city broken down and without
walls. There were a vast number of people attended. The performance was on a stage which was Erected before the meeting house. The houses near were Crowded, the street
Crowded & the tops of Buildings covered with people. Said
Puringtons remains were Lodged in the Porch with the ax &
raisor which he made use of to deprive his famely & himself

252

of life on his Coffin, his Dear wife & 6 Childrens remains laid in the ally before the Boddy Pews. . . . The funeral proseeded from the meeting hous, went over Kenebeck Bridg, then turned and went up the hill south and down second street, turned at the Jail, & went to the grave yard. He was interd without the wall.

—Martha Ballard (1806)

Have bought of a new prisoner [in Andersonville] quite a large (thick I mean,) blank book so as to continue my diary. Although it's a tedious and tiresome task, am determined to keep it up. Don't know of another man in prison who is doing likewise. Wish I had the gift of description that I might describe this place. . . . Nothing can be worse or nastier than the stream drizzling its way through this camp. And for air to breathe, it is what arises from this foul place. On all four sides of us are high walls and tall trees, and there is apparently no wind or breeze to blow away the stench, and we are obliged to breathe and live in it. Dead bodies lay around all day in the broiling sun, by the dozen and even hundreds.

—John Ransom (1864)

Roosevelt announces that we positively will not send soldiers abroad. An Italian woman in the Bronx killed her six children by gas; she feared she was going insane!

—Clifford Odets (1940)

JULY 11

It is now the season at which the buffalo begin to copulate, and the bulls keep a tremendous roaring. We could hear

253

them for many miles, and there are such numbers of them that there is one continual roar. Our horses had not been acquainted with the buffalo. They appeared much alarmed at their appearance and bellowing. When I arrived in sight of the White Bear islands, the Missouri bottoms on both sides of the river were crowded with buffalo. I sincerely believe that there were not less than 10 thousand buffalo within a circle of 2 miles around that place.

—MERIWETHER LEWIS (1806)

$\mathcal{S}$omeday I want to develop this point and use it in a play: the sharp and dramatic cleavage between appearance and reality in American life; how one lives in conformist patterns here; and the weird fruit of this inner disunion and dislocation.

—CLIFFORD ODETS (1940)

$\mathcal{S}$pent the morning picking apricots, whose lovely color makes them the pleasantest of all fruits to handle. Wished again that our civilization could be so organized that every man could have some such outdoor work part of every day. There is mental as well as physical health in it.

—JAMES WEBB YOUNG (1942)

JULY 12

$\mathcal{W}$e lodged . . . [near] a hunting cabin, where there were 2 Men, a Squaw and a child, the men came to our fire and made us a present of some venison, and invited *Mr Weisar, Shickalamy* and his son, to a feast at their cabin. It is incumbent on those who partake of a feast of this sort, to eat all

254

that comes to their share or burn it: now *Weisar* being a traveller was intitled to a double share, but he being not very well, was forced to take the benefit of a liberty indulged him, of eating by proxy, and called me, but both being unable to cope with it, *Lewis* came in to our assistance, notwithstanding which we were hard set to get down the neck and throat, for these were allotted us; and now we had experienced the utmost bounds of their indulgence, for *Lewis* ignorant of the ceremony of throwing the bone to the dog, tho' hungry Dogs are generally nimble, the *Indian* more nimble, laid hold of it first, and committed it to the fire, religiously covering it over with hot ashes. This seems to be a kind of offering, perhaps first fruits to the Almighty power to crave future success in the approaching hunting season.

—JOHN BARTRAM (1743)

I wish I could never hear the word *lousy* again. I am willing to bet that Tommy Plunkett uses it fifty times a day, but he is no worse than the others. It is "lousy" this and "lousy" that. The rain is lousy, the trail is lousy, the bacon is lousy, some of the drivers are lousy, and Gus Thorpe, losing in the card game, has just said that he has had a lousy deal. Sometimes I think that I am going on a long journey with a traveling insane asylum, and that I am crazy myself. The thought of California—still far away—makes me want to puke.

—ANDREW GORDON (1849)

*H*olzer is going to use the old laboratory for the purpose of hatching chickens artificially by an electric incubator. Just think, electricity employed to cheat a poor hen out of the pleasures of maternity. Machine-born chickens! What is home without a mother? I suggested to H that he vaccinate his hens with chicken-pox virus. Then the eggs would have their embryo hereditarily inoculated and none of the chickens would have the disease. For economy's sake he could start with one hen and rooster. He being a scientific man with no

255

farm experience, I explained the necessity of having a rooster. He saw the force of this suggestion at once.

—THOMAS ALVA EDISON (1885)

*L*ike a disgusted owl [Helena Rubinstein, the beautician] keeps arching her neck back over her shoulder with a little jerk, squinting forcefully; and in those doleful tones of hers she confides . . . her determination to marry a title. . . . "The name Rubinstein means nothing, only business, business. Lots of money now; can have good title, French. Old bachelor, maybe widower, nice (you know): never married Jew'sh before." A realist, stoically scornful of herself, she hastens to be the first to point out that in any case it could be only for her money. Around over her bosom studded with a selection of her famed hoard of jewels, and over the silken sackful of her old body as a whole, she, rigidly agitated, waves her dark hand to emphasize this point: oh, not for her looks, not now anymore! She admits having in mind, for example, the Duc de Vendome.

—GLENWAY WESCOTT (1937)

JULY 13

I carried my ticket from Mr. Warden to the Cabinet of Natural History in the Garden of Plants. How much finer things are in composition than alone. 'Tis wise in man to make cabinets. . . . to form a cabinet of natural history. . . . Here we are impressed with the inexhaustible riches of nature. . . . the hazy butterflies, the carved shells, the birds, beasts, fishes, insects, snakes, and the upheaving principle of life everywhere incipient, in the very rock aping organized forms. Not a form so grotesque, so savage, nor so beautiful but is an expression of some property inherent in man the observer,—an occult relation between the very scorpions and man. I feel the centipede in me,—cayman, carp, eagle, and fox. I am moved by strange sympathies; I say continually "I will be a naturalist."

—RALPH WALDO EMERSON (1833)

*W*ent to New York via Desbrosses Street ferry. Took cars across town. Saw a woman get into car that was so tall and frightfully thin as well as dried up that my mechanical mind at once conceived the idea that it would be the proper thing to run a lancet into her arms and knee joints and insert automatic self-feeding oil cups to diminish the creaking when she walked.

—THOMAS ALVA EDISON (1885)

*O*n an impulse we jumped into a cab and told the startled dozing driver to get us to the World's Fair in a hurry, to the Aquacade to be exact. Landed in Eleanor Holm's dressing room in back of the pool. It was interesting back there— scores of young boys and girls, summer, swimming, a whole tent town, shacks, budding romances, night, firework displays on the fair lagoon next door, music from portable radios, some boys and girls playing Ping-Pong, playing jokes, languid long-legged girls, naked bodies bronzed by the sun. When Eleanor passed us in through the gate we saw a show that was real and attractive only because of the young human bodies using themselves in swimming and diving. It is really the summer that puts on the show, and I could not help remarking that the huge audience was more of a show than what took place on the stage.

—CLIFFORD ODETS (1940)

JULY 14

*W*e departed New London att seven a'clock in the morning, crossing the ferry, and rid eight miles thro a very stonny

257

rough road where the stones upon each hand of us seemed as large as houses, and the way it self a mere rock. This is propperly enough called Stonnington. We breakfasted att one Major William's and proceeded 10 miles farther to Thomson's where we baited our horses. Here we met one Captain Noise, a dealer in cattle, whose name and character seemed pritty well to agree, for he talked very loud, joaked and laughed heartily att nothing. The landlady here was a queer old woman, an enormous heap of fat. She had some daughters and maids whom she called by comical names. There was Thankfull, Charity, Patience, Comfort, Hope.

—ALEXANDER HAMILTON (1744)

*W*e can never forget this campaign. We had hard marching, hard fighting, suffered hunger and privation, but our general officers were always with us, to help the weary soldier carry his gun, or let him ride. In a fight they were with us to encourage. Many a general have I seen walk, and a poor, sick private riding his horse, and our father, Lee, was scarcely ever out of sight when there was danger. We could not feel gloomy when we saw his old, gray head uncovered as he would pass us on the march, or be with us in a fight. I care not how weary or hungry we were; when we saw him we gave that Rebel yell, and hunger and wounds would be forgotten.

—LEWIS LEON (1863)

*S*unday, Bastille Day in France. They celebrated with tears. Out of bed at five. The long Sunday afternoons of the New York summer are beautiful: the placidity, the hushed quiet, the sun falling softly, the people strolling calmly through the untrafficked streets . . . like a Japanese print.

—CLIFFORD ODETS (1940)

JULY 15

*H*ave been very busy to-day.—On my return from school did some sewing, and made some gingerbread.—Afterwards adopted "Bloomer" costume and ascended the highest cherry tree, which being the first feat of the kind ever performed by me, I deem worthy of note.—Obtained some fine fruit, and felt for the time "monarch of all I surveyed," and then descended from my elevated position.

—CHARLOTTE FORTEN (1854)

*O*ne day he and I went over into the pasture to read a book on Anarchism and Socialism. We read it too, but got very little out of it. . . . It was written in an exceedingly involved manner, and . . . he seemed to be much more interested in me than in the book. . . . There was a long puddle which had to be crossed by way of unsteady stones. Adolph took my hand to help me and when, after we had crossed it, our little fingers were still interlocked I made no move to alter the arrangement. I had often wondered what I *would* do when I loosened the reins on myself. I find that my demonstrations are very mild. I curled my fingers around his hand and bent his fingers, one by one. I could see that he was glad about it and that he regretted we were so near home. I am not a bit sorry I did it either.

—WANDA GAG (1916)

*W*as rude to rude young Harvard kid. Went to hear Robert Penn Warren on poetry. Liked him, the cut of his jaw, his quality. . . . Katherine Ann Porter cold woman. Too many middle aged women about.

—SHERWOOD ANDERSON (1940)

*W*hy these dreams? These last exorcisings of the horrors and fears beginning when my father died and the bottom fell out. I am just now restored. I have been restored for over a year, and still the dreams aren't quite sure of it. They aren't for I'm not. And I suppose never will be. Except that we will be living a safe life, no gin parties, no drunk ego-panderings. If I write stories, poems, and the novel. All I need to do is work, break open the deep mines of experience and imagination, let the words come and speak it all, sounding themselves and tasting themselves.

—SYLVIA PLATH (1957)

JULY 16

*H*eard Mr. Whitney from I Corinthians xv. 19: "If in this life only we have hope in Christ, we are of all men most miserable." A discourse somewhat occasional upon the decease of my father. . . . I have at no time felt more deeply affected by that event than on entering the meeting-house and taking in his pew the seat which he used to occupy, having directly before me the pew at the left of the pulpit, which was his father's, and where the earliest devotions of my childhood were performed. The memory of my father and mother, of their tender and affectionate care, of the times of peril in which we then lived, and of the hopes and fears which left their impressions upon my mind, came over me, till involuntary tears started from my eyes. I looked around the house with enquiring thoughts. Where were those whom I was then wont to meet in this house? The aged of that time, the pastor by whom I had been baptized, the deacons who sat before the communion-table, have all long since departed. Those then in the meridian of life have all followed them. Five or six persons, then children like myself, under the period of youth, were all that I could discern, with gray hairs and furrowed cheeks, two or three of them with families of a succeeding generation around them. The house was not crowded, but well filled, though with almost another race of men and women. It was a comforting reflection that they had the external marks of a condition much improved upon that of the former age.

—John Quincy Adams (1826)

A New York radical was present, & he said, among other things, that all our office holders were the servants of the majority, & that if a custom officer or a postmaster charged him more than he thought he ought to, or refused to accommodate him, he had only to say to him "Sir, recollect I meet you at the polls."

—Richard Henry Dana (1842)

Today I made a bouquet of wild carrot: which was the thing to wear in your hair at an Elizabethan party; which the Pilgrims brought over for their gardens but which ran wild. I made it beautiful but there was something wrong with it: it was like a lot of idealism gone wrong, it was too white, too pale green, it was like some unwarranted, pity-worthy passion.

—Glenway Wescott (1945)

The convention was a show of almost incredible obscenity. Truman, when he arrived to accept his nomination, looked scared, despite his truculence. . . . It was plain that he was not sure of himself. Old Alben Barkley, a political hack of the most dismal sort, took the Vice-Presidential nomination without any apparent enthusiasm. When he and Truman appeared on the platform to accept, Truman had his wife and daughter with him. Barkley had only one daughter with him, though he has two. . . . The Truman women and Barkley's daughter are all homely, and they did not stay on the platform long.

—H. L. Mencken (1948)

261

JULY 17

*O*h! England my heart yearns towards thee as to a loved and loving friend! I long to behold thee, to dwell in one of thy quiet homes, far from the scenes of my early childhood; far from the land, my native land—where I am hated and oppressed because God has given me a *dark skin*. How did this cruel, thus absurd prejudice ever exist? How can it exist? When I think of it a feeling of indignation rises in my soul too deep for utterance. This evening I have been thinking of it very much. When, Oh, when will these dark clouds clear away? When will the glorious light of Liberty and Justice appear? The prospect seems very gloomy. But I will try not to despond.

—CHARLOTTE FORTEN (1854)

*H*ottest day of season. Hell must have sprung a leak. At two o'clock went out on yacht—cooler on the water. Sailed out to the Rock-buoy. . . . Dropped anchor in a shady part of the open bay. I acted as master of the fish lines, delivered them baited to all. . . . Fish seem to be rather conservative around this bay. One seldom catches enough to form the fundamental basis for a lie. Dante left out one of the torments of Hades. I could imagine a doomed mortal made to untangle wet fish lines forever. Everybody lost patience at the stupidity of the fish in not coming forward promptly to be murdered.

—THOMAS ALVA EDISON (1885)

*T*he beach: too late, after a hot walk along a gravelly, sunny sidewalk on Route 6, the deathly pink, yellow and pistachio colored cars shooting by like killer instruments from the mechanical tempo of another planet. . . . A great blue span of Atlantic under the cliff at Nauset Light, and a swim in the warmish green seaweeded water, rising and falling with the tall waves at tide turn. Lay in sun far up beach, but the sun

262

was cold, and the wind colder. The boom, boom of great guns throbbing in the throat, then the ride back, bad-tempered.

—SYLVIA PLATH (1957)

JULY 18

*I*n the evening, our road lies up an inclined plane, towards the Rocky mountains; seven miles to our camp, on the bank of a muddy pool around which one hundred and sixty mules are pressing; a puddle is reserved for ourselves, which is deemed a luxury, after having drank unto pickling the salt waters of the Semiron, our long eared stoics opened their konks half an hour before we halted, inviting this humane measure.

—ALPHONSO WETMORE (1828)

*A*fter many days of anxious waiting the news came, "Prepare immediately to receive 500 wounded men," indeed they were already at the dock! . . . 150 of the brave boys from the 54th Mass. Col. Shaw's Regt. were brought to us and laid on blankets on the floor all mangled and ghastly. What a terrible sight it was! It was 36 hours since the awful struggle at Ft. Wagner and nothing had been done for them. We had no beds, and no means even of building a fire, but the colored people came promptly to our aid and almost before we knew what we needed they brought us buckets full of nice broth and gruels, pitchers of lemonade, fruits, cakes, vegetables indeed everything needed for the immediate wants of the men was furnished—not for one day but for many. . . . and in 24 hours the poor fellows were lying with clean clothes and dressed wounds in comfortable beds, and we breathed freely again.

—ESTHER HILL HAWKS (1863)

*T*oday we spent 6 hours deciding on Court Martials, the President, Judge Holt, & I. I was amused at the eagerness with which the President caught at any fact which would justify him in saving the life of a condemned soldier. He was only merciless in cases where meanness or cruelty were shown. Cases of cowardice he was specially averse to punishing with death. He said it would frighten the poor devils too terribly, to shoot them.

—JOHN HAY (1863)

*W*alking down and looking at the Shrewsbury and going into the woods on the road past our old house to the Rumson, where I used to go as a child. *America:* It still seems even to us a country strange and wild. It is as if we had just sailed into this estuary and found the quiet little harbor with its pale opaque blue-gray waters, half brackish and half salt, tranquilly rippled with evening and the little white moored launches, with the birds flying over the water and the grassy and wooded banks—as if the little white sailing boats against the gold sun had just found themselves there themselves. . . . the country which we still found so wild and to which we were still new.

—EDMUND WILSON (1944)

JULY 19

*L*ast evening we had one of the most severe showers of rain, ever known; it continued almost the whole Night, with unremitted violence; many of their tents were ancle deep in water. many of the sick Lay their whole lengths in the water, with one blankett only to Cover them. One man having the small pox bad, & unable to help himself, and being in a tent alone, which was on ground descending; the Current of water, came thro his tent in such plenty, that it covered his head, by which means he drowned, this is the care that officers take of their sick. such attention is paid to the distrest, who are destitute of friends. Buried two yesterday, and two more today Cursing and Damning to be heard, and Idleness to be seen throughout the army as usual.

—LEWIS BEEBE (1776)

*T*here is no such thing as delicacy here. Nine out of ten would as soon eat with a corpse for a table as any other way. In the middle of last night I was awakened by being kicked by a dying man. He was soon dead. In his struggles he had floundered clear into our bed. Got up and moved the body off a few feet, and again went to sleep to dream of the hideous sights. I can never get used to it as some do. Often wake most scared to death, and shuddering from head to foot. Almost dread to go to sleep on this account. I am getting worse and worse, and [Andersonville] prison ditto.

—JOHN RANSOM (1864)

*S*till lying at anchor, and I am full of ennui. We've pumped the whole of Chesapeake Bay through this ship. But I always feel blue on the dark of the moon. Went ashore yesterday with a feeling of "oh boy, oh joy" but almost fainted when the physician said I was not pregnant but had eaten too many soft-shelled crabs. Bought a black leather handbag to console me, and how I do enjoy swinging it like any sailor's dolly. Was to meet Fred at the Crown for lunch, but the handbag delayed me and I was late. . . . Spent the afternoon adding to my compilation of sea-going lingo: a holiday is a spot left unpainted. . . . It's a language unto itself. The animal kingdom enters strongly into the speech of men who seldom see animals. A heaving line is thrown with a monkey's fist; a decorated knot is a catspaw; a back splice is, heavens be, a dog's cock; a knot to hold a line on a gangway is a Turk's head; ratlines are part of the standing rigging; holding the anchor from paying out is a claw. An incompetent seaman "ain't worth a fart in a gale of wind"; a deaf one "can't hear

265

himself fart." Poor, dear Mama, pray for your wayward
daughter! To heave a line in just a bit is "a cunt's hair."

—DOROTHEA MOULTON BALANO (1911)

JULY 20

$\mathcal{O}$ur way hence, lay over fine rich level land as before, but
when we left it, we enter'd a miserable thicket of spruce, opu-
lus, and dwarf yew, then over a branch of *Susquehanah,* big
enough to turn a mill, came to ground as good as that on the
other side the thicket; well cloathed with tall timber of sugar
birch, sugar maple, and elm. In the afternoon it thunder'd
hard pretty near us, but rained little: We observed the tops
of the trees to be so close to one another for many miles
together, that there is no seeing which way the clouds drive,
nor which way the wind sets: and it seems almost as if the
sun had never shone on the ground, since the creation.

—JOHN BARTRAM (1743)

$\mathcal{O}$ur poor cat was sick, and [Molly] proposed sending to
Mr. Driver's, to see if we could beg some catnip for him. Henry
exclaimed that he did not know what Mr. Driver would say,
if we sent *on Sunday,* for catnip to give our cat. "Then he
ought to read his Bible," said Molly, "and he would find out
that if his sheep fall into a pit on the Sabbath day, he must
lay hold on it, and lift it out." Mary's constant reference to
Scripture is very striking. She convinces me that it is adapted
to children's needs, and its standard is not too high for their
comprehension.

—MARY WILDER FOOTE (1851)

*M*rs. G has placed fly paper all over the house. These cunning engines of insectiverous destruction are doing a big business. One of the first things I do when I reach heaven is to ascertain what flies are made for. This done, I'll be ready for business. . . . Mrs. G has promised for three consecutive days to have some clams a la Taft. She has perspired her memory all away.

—THOMAS ALVA EDISON (1885)

*C*ountry details: When our housekeeper, Mrs. Smith, lived at Stoneblossom thirty years ago, there was such a plague of rats at the barn that they gnawed the horses' feet just above the hoof, until the blood ran. Not every horse, however: "There's something different about some that draws them." Lately calves in the pasture ate off the tail of Dr. Case's spotted riding horse, so that he had to crop it close, like a mule's.

—GLENWAY WESCOTT (1937)

JULY 21

*T*here appeared in the world, as Civilization advanced, a marked character which was its creature—a fashionist. He never laughs, he never weeps, is never surprised, never moved. He is completely selfish. By his self-command he aspires to an influence over society which owes nothing to rank, wealth, office, talents or learning—the command of fashion. He derides and is cool, and so reigns. This person has been shown to the public under several names. . . . But 't is all one rascal with all his *aliases.*

—RALPH WALDO EMERSON (1829)

$\mathcal{I}$ arrive at Boss Rushs at 2 A.M. this morning. I threw myself down on the floor and at daylight our old friend Boss woke me up. I could smell the ham cooking in the kitchen and the coffee. . . . After doing full justice to the breakfast I start for the Ohio Pyle Falls, nearly all down hill. I arrive between 8 and 9 A.M. I find them all in good shape, and I get a warm reception. I take off the old Army Blue and put on the Citizen Clothes and feel well satisfied with myself, and feel that I would do it again if they should want three hundred thousand more. After dinner I go down to the saw mill, I file the saw and start the old saw mill and make the saw dust fly. Buckwheat Cakes and honey (wild) has to suffer and all else that is eatable, that appetite of mine still continues. . . . Hardtack a thing of the past.

—SAMUEL A. CLEAR (1865)

$\mathcal{S}$ ince last night a cow on the adjacent farm has been bellowing as periodically as a foghorn on a ship picking its way through fog. Yesterday they took its calf away and this regular expressionless bellow is its cry. A stricken but stupid mother standing in a world of grass, mourning by instinct between chews of the grass. It is a characterization to carry over into human life.

—CLIFFORD ODETS (1940)

JULY 22

$\mathcal{A}$ fter dismissing [from church] I went to Change and, returning from thence, dined with Mr. Lechmere. There was a lady att table of a very masculine make but dres'd fine a la mode. She did not appear till dinner was almost over, pretending she could not endure the smell of the vittles and was every now and then lugging out her sal volatile and Hungary water, but this I observed was only a modish air, for she made a shift betwixt times to swallow down as much beef and pudding as any body att the table; in short her teeth went as fast as her tongue, and the motion of both was perpetuall.

—ALEXANDER HAMILTON (1744)

*I*n passing through towns and villages, and even on the high-roads, we naturally attracted a good deal of attention. . . . The remarks we heard from the bystanders as we marched along often became by-words in the regiment. We were no exception to the generality of mankind, of liking to see a pretty face, even if it did belong to a woman of "secesh" sentiments. When the boys at the head of the column discovered a pretty girl, if she was on the right side of the road, *"guide right"* would be passed along the line; and *"guide left"* if on the left side of the road.

—CHARLES E. DAVIS (1862)

I am listless with the heat, dull, apathetic, immediately reaching for a cigarette, not sure that I am awake or asleep. Coffee, more cigarettes, the newspapers. Then the eminent appeasing Lord Halifax on the radio to answer Hitler's speech. No peace, says the Lord, and with the help of God the English will carry the day. If all the English are like Lord Halifax it is to be feared that the Germans have already won the war! After the other guests left Luther and frau and I stretched out on the front lawn and looked up at the sky for a half hour of starry consideration. At one time stars, the sky, trees, birds, all were very important to my world. . . . In these last seven years they have become almost meaningless to me. . . . "What is this world, if full of care we have no time to stand and stare?" . . . It is wrong to lose the desire to stare at the silent powerful things of nature. American life tends to make us too rationalistic, too anxious to spend our time "usefully"—the mooning goes out of life for most of us, and with it the meaning.

—CLIFFORD ODETS (1940)

JULY 23

*D*ragged day and night continually through the water by this steam engine, at the rate of near twelve knots, or fourteen statute miles, the hour; in the nearing America my inviting port, England loses its recent overweight, America resumes its commanding claims. . . . In the cabin conversations about England and America, Tom Appleton amused us all by tracing all English performance home to the dear Puritans, and affirming that the Pope also was once in South America, and there met a Yankee, who gave him notions on politics and religion.

—RALPH WALDO EMERSON (1848)

*T*he portion of the battlefield I examined was the part nearest to the turnpike road & the Stone Bridge. . . . In this open ground, & on the highest level, was the humble dwelling house in which . . . occurred the killing of the old woman who owned it, by a cannon shot, as she lay sick in bed, & incapable of being removed, while the battle was raging around her residence. It was a horrible sight. The dead (nearly all then left being of the Yankee army) were scattered over this whole open ground. . . . Clotted blood, in what had been pools, were under or by almost every corpse. From bullet holes in the heads of some, the brains had partly oozed out. The white froth covering the mouths of others was scarcely less shocking in appearance. . . . Hundreds of our soldiers were indulging their curiosity in viewing the dead, as I was, & many accosted the living . . . to ask why they came to invade & to fight us, who had never offended them. . . . No one more bitterly hates the northerners as a class than I do, or would be more rejoiced to have every invading soldier killed—but all my hatred was silenced for the wounded, seen in this long continued & wretched state of suffering.

—EDMUND RUFFIN (1861)

*W*e cook and eat, talk and laugh with the enemys dead lying all about us as though they were so many logs.

—SAMUEL T. FOSTER (1864)

JULY 24

*I*n camp all day. Trains crossing over and camping about us in great numbers. Growing city of wagons, tents, men, women and children, whites, indians, negros, horses, oxen and mules. Motley crowd. After breakfast, rigged my lines and went fishing. Out till 3. Lazy work. No luck.

—BERNARD J. REID (1849)

*T*he morning was quite cool and we had a fire, the children amusing themselves popping corn. I was taken sick as I always am. . . . I took cloroform for the first time and was pleased with the result at the same time not altogether satisfied as to its safety. . . . Ma who is afraid of it did not apply it as often as [the doctor] told her to. At one time after a long inhalation everything became indistinct. I appeared to see Dr Eve who was just before me as tho in a dream. Everything seemed dim and distant. I appeared to be floating off—A feeling of lightness which I cannot discribe came over me. At the same time I was conscious enough to tell Ma to "take it away" and then in recovering from the effect I felt just as one does in being aroused from a dream—Its effect in lulling pain is magical and of all the ways to select for committing suicide I should think it preferable.

—ELLA THOMAS (1863)

*E*miko, Alice, and Miyako went out for a walk this evening. They went way down to the far end of camp—near the fence where the highway goes by. They were watching the cars go by when a very "high class car" drove by. A "high toned" lady was sitting in back with a chauffeur in front. Emiko said that she suddenly stuck her head out of the window and with a look of hatred stuck her tongue out at them. It was so funny that it made them laugh. Then they got mad so they thumbed their noses at the fast departing limousine! Miyako asked me tonight why the white people did not like the Japanese.

—CHARLES KIKUCHI (1942)

JULY 25

There is no remedy for love but to love more.

—HENRY DAVID THOREAU (1839)

Emiko is so much more Americanized than most Nisei girls. . . . Everything she does is western. . . . Tonight she said that she got to thinking about the woman that stuck her tongue out as she passed in a car and the possibility occurred to her that a more fanatic person may even go as far as to throw a bomb sometime. It disturbs her to think that the Nisei are considered as "Japs" by the majority of the population and she wondered if we will ever become accepted on an equal basis.

—CHARLES KIKUCHI (1942)

The artist's life nourishes itself on the particular, the concrete: that came to me last night as I despaired about writing poems on the concept of the seven deadly sins and told myself to get rid of the killing idea. . . . Start with the mat-green fungus in the pine woods yesterday: words about it, describing it, and a poem will come. Daily, simply, and then it won't lower in the distance, an untouchable object. Write about the cow, Mrs. Spaulding's heavy eyelids, the smell of vanilla flavoring in a brown bottle. That's where the magic mountains begin.

—SYLVIA PLATH (1957)

JULY 26

$\mathscr{H}$enry Ford is 66 years old today. He has had more influence on the lives and habits of this nation than any man ever produced in it. Great educators try to teach people, great preachers try to change people, but no man produced through the accepted channels has moved the world like Henry Ford. He put wheels on our homes, a man's castle is his sedan. Life's greatest catastrophe is a puncture, everybody is rushing to go somewhere where they have no business, so they can hurry back to the place where they should never have left.

—WILL ROGERS (1929)

$\mathscr{T}$his morning, it being Sunday, there were services on the port promenade. Benches had been arranged on the deck, facing a canvas backdrop on which a Red Cross flag was pinned. Father Francis W. Kelly of Philadelphia, a genial smiling fellow with a faculty for plain talk, gave the sermon. It was his second for the day. He had just finished the "first shift," which was for Catholics. This one was for Protestants. It was pleasant to stand and sing on the rolling deck with the blue panel of the moving sea, on our left, to watch. There we could see two others of our fleet of transports rolling over the long swells, nosing into white surf. The sermon dealt with duty, and was obviously pointed toward our coming landing somewhere in Japanese-held territory. Father Kelly . . . pounded home the point. After the services, ironically, many of the men turned to the essential job of loading machine-gun belts. Walking around the deck in the bright morning sun, I had to step around lads sitting on the former shuffleboard court, using a gadget which belted the cartridges automatically. All you had to do was feed them in.

—RICHARD TREGASKIS (1942)

$\mathscr{T}$he express buses, Clinton to New York, bypass Newark when they haven't any passengers for it. Today I heard the

273

driver say roughly to a small elderly man, gray-haired, gray-skinned, "Are you going to make me go all the way into Newark on a hot day? You're the only Newark passenger I've got." "Oh dear, oh dear," said the man. "Don't you see, I've got to get home somehow. But it's too bad, it's silly, I'm sorry. I just went to Clinton for the ride, round trip, to cool off!"

—GLENWAY WESCOTT (1955)

JULY 27

*T*here was a meeting of the Special Board for Public Works at two o'clock and . . . I had asked Chief of Staff MacArthur to come in on some Army projects. He had presented a very large list running into the hundreds of millions, out of which the President allowed him $6 million for coast defenses in the Canal Zone and Hawaii, in addition to $6 million previously allowed for ammunition. MacArthur is the type of man who thinks that when he gets to heaven, God will step down from the great white throne and bow him into His vacated seat, and it gave me a great kick to have him in and break the news to him. While he was here though, two or three of the members foolishly asked him some questions which gave him a chance to deliver a lecture on the subject of the necessity for the little old peanut Army posts that we have scattered around the country.

—HAROLD L. ICKES (1933)

*B*illy [Rose] said he had bought some new paintings, so we drove over to his house to see them. And there they were on his florid walls, a very fine Titian, a Rubens, a small Holbein, and, best of all to my taste, a very small Renoir filled with fragrance and Gallic charm, this last piece on Eleanor's dresser! Eleanor, Billy said, told him, when he said he was

274

going to put a Renoir in her bedroom, "Don't you go banging any nails in my wall!"

—CLIFFORD ODETS (1940)

I have named our new receptionist Miss Malaprop. When I asked her this morning how she liked her job, she said it was fine; the gentlemen from the publications told her such funny antidotes.

—JAMES WEBB YOUNG (1942)

JULY 28

I think, taking the government, the social influences, the climate, & the unhealthiness of this country together, that it certainly is the most God-forsaken region that civilized beings were ever compelled to dwell in. If you go to the South you have disease, the heat of Africa, mosquitoes, slavery, ferocious & vicious manners, a low & degraded standard of morals and opinion; if you go to the North you find the cold of Iceland during half the year, a society without refinement or elevated feelings, absorbed in money-getting & living without social intercourse in selfish isolation, and democracy with its mobs, riots, demagogues & corruption. Which of the two to choose is difficult to determine.

—SIDNEY GEORGE FISHER (1844)

*T*his evening we anticipated having "divine service" but just before the time to commence the rebs. sent us a couple of *shells* by way of showing their affectionate remembrance of us—and the meeting is defered much to the relief and satisfaction of Chaplain Jones who is a great coward—and whenever there is any noise of shells near he is taken with an intense desire to visit the P.O. or 'Christian Commission,' both of which are situated out of the reach of rebel *compliments!*—The peculiar noise of a shell tearing through the air is enough to upset the *nerves* of a *novice*, but we old *campaigners* get used to them!

—ESTHER HILL HAWKS (1864)

*I*n the vestibule or piazzi of the church I saw something covered up but did not know what it was until told that the dead man was there. He was resting on a soiled straw bed covered with a common blue blanket with the flies swarming over it. A gentleman . . . lifted the blanket from off his face remarking "that it was very much such a face as Stonewall Jackson's." There lay the man around whom had clustered all the endearing associations of home. A mother—a wife—a sister had loved him. Perhaps now around the family altar a group of children pray "please bring Pa home safe and well," happily unconscious how he died. God grant they never may know! A crowd of children and servants were around him at times, all privileged to lift the blanket from his careworn but intellectual face—and there he lay unknown & uncared for, prepared for the hasty burial which awaited him.

—ELLA THOMAS (1864)

JULY 29

*T*he date of the last entry made in this Journal will be one ever memorable in the history of our Southern Confederacy—Upon the 21st of July was fought the battle of Manassas. But *today* is one still more memorable to me—Today Mr Thomas leaves home for months—perhaps forever! . . . Upon his telling [the Negroes] that he was going off for such an indefinite time they appeared very much affected. Aunt Patience burst into tears and sobbed bitterly. When the cars came by every Negro from both places followed him and shook hands with him as he bid them farewell—It was too much for me and I rose from the table excited beyond control. Turner joined me and for a time we sat in the front Piazzi, all of us feeling the bitterness of parting—My darling husband how I love him. Oh God shield him in the hour of danger.

—ELLA THOMAS (1861)

*I*f anything should happen to me now in these air raids, which I don't take seriously enough, I want all and sundry to know that the game was worth the candle, that I'd be sorry to go because I'm not ready to die (not for about fifty years) but that I had a lot of fun, that I'd recommend life to anyone who was considering its purchase and hesitating because they weren't sure it was worth all the effort it cost. Even in the midst of this terrible war and the suffering I have seen and heard described, I would say that life is wonderful, the world is a miraculous sort of place and filled with never-ending surprises and new sensations. Like the morning you wake up after a rough night and it's raining and miserable and the first news that breaks upon your ears is that you have to move and everybody in the tent is being very bitchy and annoying, so you get up and make the preparations to move in a generally disgusted state. Then, after a hit-or-miss breakfast of leftover K rations, you stroll outside the tent and the sun bursts forth in all its glory, warm and bright and soul-filling and blue sky comes through all around and suddenly the world is a beautiful place and the people in it are gay and charming.

—ANNE McCAUGHEY (1944)

JULY 30

I rose at 5 o'clock and wrote a letter to Major Burwell about his boat which Captain Broadwater's people had brought

277

round and sent Tom with it. I read two chapters in Hebrew and some Greek in Thucydides. I said my prayers and ate boiled milk for breakfast. I danced my dance. I read a sermon in Dr. Tillotson and then took a little [nap]. I ate fish for dinner. In the afternoon my wife and I had a little quarrel which I reconciled with a flourish. Then she read a sermon in Dr. Tillotson to me. It is to be observed that the flourish was performed on the billiard table. I read a little Latin. In the evening we took a walk about the plantation. I neglected to say my prayers but had good health, good thoughts, and good humor, thanks be to God. This month there were many people sick of fever and pain in their heads; perhaps this might be caused by the cold weather which we had this month, which was indeed the coldest that ever was known in July in this country. Several of my people have been sick, but none died, thank God.

—WILLIAM BYRD (1710)

I don't think much of Hawaiian royalty. Years ago when the late King and the present King were only Princes—youths—they traveled in U.S. with the premier of the kingdom, Dr. Judd, an American. On one occasion, on board a southern steamer they did not go in to dinner as soon as the bell rang, and then there was no room for them. They were offended. . . . Other accounts say they went in to dinner, but observing their black faces, and uninformed of their rank, the steward enforced the rule of the boat excluding colored persons from the cabin table. They were naturally incensed and all that could afterwards be done failed to wipe from their minds the memory of the affront. Yet, at its worst, it was one which was offered to them as unknown and merely private individuals, and being entirely unofficial could not affect them as Princes or their country through them, and should have been so received and so valued. The men only were insulted, not the Princes, and thus their country was no more insulted than if the affront had been offered to the commonest Kanaka in the realm.

—MARK TWAIN (1866)

*E*xpected to see Gen. Pershing like Napoleon at Friedland, on white charger, spy glass under arm, surrounded by gold laced officers in swords and high boots. Found instead group huge stone barracks, around court, with million typewriters all clicking at once. Reminded me of Sears Roebuck.

—HOWARD O'BRIEN (1918)

JULY 31

[On a visit to Valley Forge] *W*hilst Mr. Morris was fishing, I rid over the old Cantonment of the American [Army] of the Winter, 1777 and 8, visited all the Works, wch. were in Ruins; and the Incampments in woods where the grounds had not been cultivated. On my return . . . observing some Farmers at Work, and entering into Conversation with them, I received . . . information with respect to the mode of cultivating Buck Wheat, and the application of the grain. . . . On my Return to Mrs. Moore's I found Mr. Robt. Morris and his lady there. Spent the day there fishing &ca and lodged at the same place.

—GEORGE WASHINGTON (1787)

[As the presidential election approaches] *I* rise between five and six, and, when the tide serves, swim between one and two hours in the Potomac. Breakfast about nine, then write or meditate or receive visitors till one or two. Attend at my office till six, then home to dine. Take an evening walk of half an hour, and from ten to eleven retire to bed. There are eight or ten newspapers of extensive circulation published in various parts of the Union acting in close concert with each other and pouring forth continual streams of slander upon my character and reputation, public and private. No falsehood is too broad, and no insinuation too base, for them, and a great portion of their calumnies are of a nature that no person could show or even assert their falsehood but myself. . . . The result is a great waste of time and of mental occupation upon subjects personal to myself, to the necessary neglect of public business and detriment to the public service. I have no reason to hope to be released from this state of trial for many months to come. To pass through it with a pure heart and a firm spirit is my duty and my prayer.

—JOHN QUINCY ADAMS (1824)

How damned ridiculous it all is! The long generations toiling—skimping, lashing themselves screwing higher and higher the tension of their minds, polishing brighter and brighter the mirror of intelligence to end in this—My God what a time—All the cant and hypocrisy, all the damnable survivals, all the vestiges of old truths now putrid and false infect the air, choke you worse than German gas—The ministers from their damn smug pulpits, the business men—the heroics about war—my country right or wrong—oh infinities of them! Oh the tragic farce of the world.

—JOHN DOS PASSOS (1917)

It is good to go through the Middle West at this season of the year and see the fruits of the rich earth. In spite of the early floods, the fields of shocked wheat, the stands of corn, the orchards, and pastures, all give an effect of peace and plenty beyond our deserts in a war-torn world. Anybody looking for an America worth fighting for can see it here.

—JAMES WEBB YOUNG (1943)

≈AUGUST≈

AUGUST 1

*A*fter thirty a man wakes up sad every morning excepting perhaps five or six until the day of his death.

—RALPH WALDO EMERSON (1835)

*W*e commenced our journey to Walla Walla. . . . The Flathead and Nez Pierce Indians and some lodges of the Snake tribe accompany us to Fort Hall. Have travelled two months. . . . We have plenty of dry buffalo meat. I can scarcely eat it, it appears so filthy, but it will keep us alive, and we ought to be thankful. Do not think I regret coming. No, far from it. I would not go back for the world; am contented and happy. Feel to pity the poor Indian women. Am making some progress in their language; long to be able to converse with them about the Saviour.

—NARCISSA WHITMAN (1836)

*D*uring the day one of the boys brought in a Virginia paper in which it was stated that one "Southerner could lick five Northern mudsills." It was not so very comfortable to feel that

281

we were to be killed off in blocks of five. . . . Some time during the night an alarm was sounded by the beating of the "long roll," and we were ordered into line to drive the terrible foe, who was thought, even then, to be in our midst. Immediately everything was excitement and confusion. . . . When it was discovered, as it shortly was, that all this excitement was caused by a pig who strolled into camp and was mistaken by the officer of the guard for the rebel army, many of us were imbued with a courage we hardly felt before.

—CHARLES E. DAVIS (1861)

[In North Dakota] The country is overrun with surveyors these days. The Missouri River Diversion Project has three automobiles full of them running around. Others are here about this game refuge idea, and some on a shelterbelt project. The Missouri D. P. people are going to turn this area into a huge lake. The game refuge people are going to let it revert to the wild. The shelterbelt people intend to put in a lot of trees to keep the wind from doing damage to the farms the other two outfits intend to eliminate. The geodetic survey has built a tower on a hill south of us to flash lights all night long, though I don't know why. . . . Our bountiful and interfering government sometimes creates awful messes.

—ANN MARIE LOW (1934)

AUGUST 2

Traversed today the most remarkable country. . . . Nature some day long ago was in agony here and the traces of her convulsive writhings are left forever. . . . The plain and the hill sides are strewn with volcanic rock,—black, heavy and porous, like cinder. Mineral or gaseous springs spout up in hundreds of places. . . . The soda well on the bank of a little stream to the right of trail sparkles with a bead as pure and strong as that of any soda fountain. I drank nearly three pints. . . . Steamboat Spring . . . boils up furiously with a fitful pulse through an aperture a foot in diameter in the solid rock. Its water is warm, and it takes its name from the noise it makes.

—BERNARD J. REID (1849)

*R*ode up to parade in ev., found Mr. Baker in his tent, & introduced him to S. He invited us to the Cadets' "hop" . . . in the Academic Hall . . . lighted by a few tallow candles, with no refreshments but two buckets of water with four tumblers to drink from. . . . The ladies always attend, as a favor to the cadets, & because the young soldiers are so popular. . . . The dancing was more lively & animated than any I have ever seen before, in America. . . . At the tap of the drum, for tattoo, the dance ceased, instantly, in the midst of a polka, & each cadet left his partner on the floor & hurried to the camp, the ladies finding their own way, or with the aid of their friends, to their carriages.

—RICHARD HENRY DANA (1850)

*T*his afternoon I found an acre of thistles, the heavy Scottish kind, such beautiful flowers with large dark butterflies over them everywhere. I also found blackberries that hang down the bank of the Mulhocaway above the old swimming hole . . . dead ripe so that whenever I touched a bush some fruit went plop and downstream. I stood in the water to pick them. I had to break great spiderwebs between me and the best clusters; it was enchanting.

—GLENWAY WESCOTT (1945)

AUGUST 3

*A*ll the martins of the vicinity have deserted their customary pole-elevated tenements and, in obedience to the law of progress, which has attained to "Socialism" with them, have colonized in the belfry of the Universalist Church, and every morning make the air vocal.

—BENJAMIN BROWNE FOSTER (1849)

A very hot day. Shortly after breakfast we left for Pleasant Valley, sixteen miles, where we arrived in the afternoon, and where we bivouacked for the night. A good many of the men were overcome by the heat, and . . . the size of the knapsack was too heavy for men unused to carrying such a weight. It must be reduced, and there were no more Bibles.

—CHARLES E. DAVIS (1861)

*K*atherine Anne [Porter] to Monroe one day: "Do you know why I have lost my husbands and lovers, and now have to conclude my life all soul alone? Because I have always talked too much at breakfast time."

—GLENWAY WESCOTT (1955)

*T*he great fault of America—this part of it—is its air of pressure: expectancy of conformity. . . . I find myself horrified at voicing the American dream of a home and children—my visions of a home, of course, being an artist's estate, in a perfect privacy of wilderness acres, on the coast of Maine. . . . I must work for an inner serenity and stability . . . which does not depend on a lifelong street address within easy driving distance of an American supermarket.

—SYLVIA PLATH (1958)

284

AUGUST 4

$\mathcal{I}$ left my horses att Barker's stables and drank tea with my landlady, Mrs. Guneau. There was in the company a pritty young lady. The character of a certain Church of England clergiman in Boston was canvassed, he having lost his living for being too sweet upon his landlady's daughter, a great belly being the consequence. I pitied him only for his imprudence and want of policy. As for the crime, considdered in a certain light it is but a peccadillo, and he might have escaped unobserved had he had the same cunning as some others of his brethern who doubtless are as deep in the dirt as he in the mire.

—Alexander Hamilton (1744)

$\mathcal{A}$fter the rain the day came off clear and beautiful. Worked on the story and then hurried off to town for supplies. In the evening we had a big feast, for all the county officials of Smyth County. Fifteen men sat down, all great eaters. They did eat.

—Sherwood Anderson (1939)

$\mathcal{L}$istening to Colonel Charles Lindbergh on the radio delivering a speech in which he urged cooperation with Hitler on America. There, the meeting chairmanned by Mr. Avery Brundage, are the beginnings of a real American Fascist Party. . . . Fortunately Lindbergh's personality lacks richness and depth. There is something sulky and vinegary about him.

—Clifford Odets (1940)

$\mathcal{T}$oday is my father's birthday. I had asked them to dine, and Mother suggested my having a birthday cake—which reminded me that formalities must be good for ailing old souls. . . . We exchanged honey and peaches and tomatoes, which made it like some olden time.

—GLENWAY WESCOTT (1945)

AUGUST 5

$\mathcal{O}$ne of the most difficult things to 'have a *realizing sense*' of, in this climate, is the *change* of *seasons*. April and August are so much alike it is hard knowing when one ends and the other begins—but *birthdays* will come round, and ones mirror is a more faithful friend than memory. If *mirrors* could be abolished I could not believe that I am *growing old*—but with these faithful friends present, before me I cannot forget the rolling years even if I would.

—ESTHER HILL HAWKS (1864)

$\mathcal{L}$OVE is something the efficacy of which is believed in by all good Americans. It is a cure for all aches and pains, for toothache, looseness of the bowels, timidity, and all profound depressions of the spirit. If only Americans (and I yield to no one my Americanism!) could believe in companionship, as the Europeans do. In that simple believing, half of our national superficiality would vanish. This is the truth.

—CLIFFORD ODETS (1940)

$\mathcal{I}$ could *smell* land. Prairie-born one that I am, I'd never before believed that land can be smelled. . . . At 5 p.m., junked up with carbine, gas mask, pack, canteen, etc. I floundered over a rail and swayed down a cargo net into a landing craft. A smoke screen was whooshed around us. . . . With salt spray blurring my expectant eyes, I strained toward

286

this bloodiest battleground of the Pacific. It looked like a country club. . . . There was a look of cultivated precision about the island. . . . As I hauled my White Knight paraphernalia onto that coral, I muttered, to mark the occasion, the single word, "Okinawa."

—EDWARD ROBB ELLIS (1945)

AUGUST 6

Two men servants to one Moodye, of Roxbury, returning in a boat from the windmill, struck upon the oyster bank. They went out to gather oysters, and, not making fast their boat, when the flood came, it floated away, and they were both drowned, although they might have waded out on either side; but it was an evident judgment of God upon them, for they were wicked persons. One of them, a little before, being reproved for his lewdness, and put in mind of hell, answered, that if hell were ten times hotter, he had rather be there than he would serve his master, etc. The occasion was, because he had bound himself for divers years, and saw that, if he had been at liberty, he might have had greater wages, though otherwise his master used him very well.

—JOHN WINTHROP (1633)

The mysteries of a new world have been shown to me since last Thursday. In a few short months I should have been a happy mother . . . but the ruling hand of a mighty Providence has interposed and by an abortion deprived us of the hope. . . . After much agony and severest of pains, which were relieved a little at times by medicine given by Dctr. Mesure, *all was over*. I sunk off into a kind of lethargy. . . . My situation was very different from that of an Indian woman in the room below me. She gave birth to a fine healthy baby, about the same time, *and in half an hour after she went to the River*

287

and bathed herself and it, and this she has continued every day since. . . . It is truly astonishing to see what customs will do. No doubt many ladies in civilized life are ruined by too careful treatments during childbirth. The Fort is quite desolate. Most who are here now of the soldiers are sick. Two have died, and have been buried in the sand hills.

—SUSAN MAGOFFIN (1846)

[On his last visit with Edna St. Vincent Millay] *I* felt a certain satisfaction in the idea that I was outlasting her, but at the same time was troubled and depressed at finding the metamorphosis she had undergone. She seemed to have ceased to care about her looks. . . . I kept looking away and out the window.—At the same time, the strength of her character and her genius overcame me, as the visit went on, just as it always had. . . . I reflected in dismay . . . on the tendency of the writers of my generation to burn themselves out or break down: Scott and Zelda, John [Bishop], Phelps Putnam (just dead), Paul Rosenfeld, Elinor Wylie, Edna. One didn't really believe till one saw it demonstrated that giving oneself up completely to art, to emotion, to enjoyment, without planning for the future or counting the cost, produced dreadful disabilities and bankruptcies later.

—EDMUND WILSON (1948)

We have been afflicted by drought for the third successive summer, the worst. The meadows are withered, as they used to be in Wisconsin when I was a boy—the crops are tragic, the flowers dwarfish. But the skies are glorious, azure, with vain immaculate clouds; the swimming holes are clean and deep, full of boys.

—GLENWAY WESCOTT (1954)

AUGUST 7

I dined with Mr. Fletcher in the company of two Philadelphians, who could not be easy because forsooth they were
in their night-caps seeing every body else in full dress with
powdered wigs; it not being customary in Boston to go to dine
or appear upon Change in caps as they do in other parts of
America. What strange creatures we are, and what triffles
make us uneasy! . . . I was my self much in the same state
of uneasiness with these Philadelphians, for I had got a great
hole in the lappet of my coat, to hide which employed so
much of my thoughts in company that, for want of attention,
I could not give a pertinent answer when I was spoke to.

—ALEXANDER HAMILTON (1744)

G arnett brought Taz Anderson and Dr. McMillan home to
dinner. It seemed just like the quiet antebellum days, before
Washington [Georgia] had become such a thoroughfare, and
our house a sort of headquarters for the officers of two Confederate armies. It was almost as if the last four years had
been blotted out. . . . Everything relating to the dear old Confederate times is already so completely dead and buried that
they seem to have existed only in imagination. . . . The frightful results of its downfall are all that remain to tell us that
there ever was a Southern Confederacy.

—ELIZA ANDREWS (1865)

W hat am I going to do with the rest of my life? . . . From
what I've observed of race relations during the war, of what
the Southern white boys say they are going to do to the colored boys after the war, I think maybe the best place for me
would be working for Negro rights in the U.S.A. Yesterday,
listening to Chaplain England's sermon, standing leaning
against the plank that serves as a table in the mess hall,
when he was talking of the necessity of having convictions, I
thought of my own convictions and those of the other people

289

who were standing in the tent, and I thought I probably ought to use my convictions to combat their convictions, or lack of them. . . . I just would hate to go home and have to fight another civil war through our own ignorance and feeling of insecurity and inadequacy when I feel the whole thing could be avoided with a lot of education and a lot of tolerance and a lot of people working together toward that end.

—Anne McCaughey (1944)

With nearly everyone who came in to see me on August 7 the first topic of conversation was the atomic bomb. Everyone seemed to feel that a new epoch in the world's history had been ushered in. The scramble for the control of this new power is going to be one of the most unusual struggles the world has ever seen.

—Henry A. Wallace (1945)

AUGUST 8

In the early afternoon I gathered up myself . . . and rode out to Luther and Sylvia's farm. . . . Sylvia was watching the baby . . . and planting strawberry plants in rows. Luther was bustling around . . . watching the men . . . thresh and pack the ripe oats in one operation. Not only that, but the straw is baled at the same time, chaff flying all over. Men work like that—five of them here—planting, reaping, packing, carting, and we do not see it. Right in the fields, right in the sun, and we in the city are ignorant of everything but the greedy eating! . . . Their baby is charming. So are Sylvia's breasts when I see them, when she bends to play with the baby or plant more little strawberry plants. So are the odorous green plants heavy with ripening tomatoes. So are the four dogs drawing close to the house as evening comes and the country world grows still.

—Clifford Odets (1940)

A news-letter which I get from England says that the Russians are beginning to worry about American economic imperialism in the post-war world. I wouldn't have given it a thought if I had not recently talked with a woman who has made a fortune writing soap operas. She says the next big development in [soap operas] is in the export field—that American advertisers will eventually take them around the world, just as American movie producers did Mickey Mouse. No wonder the Russians are worried!

—JAMES WEBB YOUNG (1943)

*S*truck by the number of people in the literary world of England who seem to be *illegitimate sons or the products of misalliances.* . . . This is all a gesture of the English system. Imagine Ezra Pound or Walt Whitman concealing his parentage or birthplace! Lincoln seems to have hoped that he was an illegitimate child, but everybody knew his background. . . . On the part of the more intelligent people [in Europe], there is a curious contradiction in the attitude toward America. On the one hand, they are always pumping you about what they consider outrageous happenings . . . McCarthy and the Rosenbergs . . . a black-and-white bus incident in the South. . . . But, on the other hand, they expect America to do something wonderful for them, and they apply to us standards of integrity, humanitarianism, and political wisdom that they never would expect of themselves. They cannot seem to imagine that we are just like everybody else.

—EDMUND WILSON (1956)

AUGUST 9

*T*he Southerner asks concerning any man, "How does he fight?" The Northerner asks, "What can he do?"

—RALPH WALDO EMERSON (1837)

$\mathcal{T}$he ride back to the city a chore. . . . The moment one so much as approaches the city, the rhythm of all the cars becomes very distinctive—one sits up nervously, watchfully. Here everything runs together, as if through a funnel. . . . Once you have driven through the funnel you are in the bottle called Manhattan. . . . [Then,] moving . . . from room to room, the windows all thrown open, the broad summer night slowly munching the heart away. It's not easy to be alone and go to sleep in this wide summer night.

—CLIFFORD ODETS (1940)

$\mathcal{W}$e have been visiting the cemetery several times a week. . . . Little Charlie Smith's grave is in the far left-hand corner. . . . There is a park bench beside the Catholic Worker plot, and when we have arranged our vases of flowers, we sit on the bench and eat the pears we have gathered from the next field and say the rosary. . . . It is quiet but for the sound of crickets, katydids and an occasional cicada, and the August sun covers everything with a dusty gold. . . . Life and death are so close together. Little Charlie Smith was drowned July 11. Baby Margaret was born exactly 4 weeks later. "The spaces of our life, set over against eternity, are brief and poor."

—DOROTHY DAY (1953)

$\mathcal{I}$n England, I kept myself down to the English quietness and flatness and fell into the English conversational rhythm, in which, for example, in asking a question, one emphasizes the first word: *Do* you . . . ?, *Can* you tell me . . . ?, *Have* you read the program?, etc. We Americans emphasize the main verb: Have you *read* the program?, etc., which seems more natural from the point of view of the meaning. There is evidently, for the English, some principle of underemphasis involved. . . . I have felt on this trip particularly the great difference between *Europe and America,* that we have always had something to build, to win, whereas they have too much to look back on. I can see with my own family . . . and my

292

own career, how we have always been going somewhere. This involves a certain constant pressure, from which I relax when I come abroad.

—EDMUND WILSON (1956)

AUGUST 10

$\mathcal{T}$he Indians that deal at our Store, often want to stay in ye House at Nights while they remain here, & often want Victuals; they also want to bring their Squas to lie with at Night, which I Object against, letting them know that they shall bring none such to Sleep in our House, & having shut out two Squas last Night, they kept throwing Stones on ye House & Door after we went to bed, untill we went out & threaten'd them away. So many Roberies Commited here at Nights that all Noise tends to keep me from Sleep & ye fleeas together, that I get but little Sleep.

—JAMES KENNY (1761)

$\mathcal{T}$he town was in a great bustle today to witness the death of a young man named Richard Smith, who was hung on the commons for murdering a Captain Carson whose wife this Smith married during the Captain's absence, and on his return, a dispute taking place about the lady, Smith went to Carson's house, having previously bound him over to keep the peace, and on his refusal to leave the house, discharged a pistol into his mouth, which caused his death after lingering some days in great pain. The crowd (which however I did not join) to witness his death was excessive. . . . Vast numbers of well dressed and delicate looking girls were hurrying to the scene, and those who would weep over a sick bed could stand in a scorching sun for hours to see a hearty man strangled! Smith was a native of Ireland.

—SAMUEL BRECK (1816)

*H*aving the wounded of our Div. Hospital properly cared for, Dr. White and I resolved to go over the battle-field to see if there were any of our men not brought off. . . . I met with one poor fellow who was some distance from any of his companions and asked him what regiment he belonged to? "The 73rd N.Y." was the reply. "What's your name?" "P. Sullivan." "Are you a Catholic?" "Yes, I am." "Pat, what brought you here?" "O! Misfortune," was the poor fellow's answer.

—JAMES SHEERAN (1863)

AUGUST 11

I went to Change att 12 o'clock and dined with Mr. Arbuthnott. I had a tune on the spinett from his daughter after dinner, who is a pritty, agreeable lady and sings well. I told her that she playd the best spinett that I had heard since I came to America. The old man, who is a blunt, honest fellow, asked me if I could pay her no other compliment but that, which dashed me a little, but I soon replied that the young lady was every way so deserving and accomplished that nothing that was spoke in the commendation could in a strick sense be called a compliment. I breathed a little after this speech, there being something romantick in it and, considering human nature in the propper light, could not be true. The young lady blushed; the old man was pleased and picked his teeth, and I was conscious that I had talked nonsense.

—ALEXANDER HAMILTON (1744)

*T*he truth is not injured nor touched though thousands of them that love it fall by the way.

—RALPH WALDO EMERSON (1832)

$\mathcal{A}$gain and again the only verity I can turn to is this journal, thumbing the pages backwards, hoping, wondering, waiting to turn outwards once more. On a day, a night, in some future week or month it will happen. One never dies of this. . . . There is a tendency in this journal . . . of smoothly writing only what is known and rational to you, writing what you can handle and be superior to. Keep out of that dangerous groove if you can.

—CLIFFORD ODETS (1940)

AUGUST 12

$\mathcal{I}$ went to a house to see if God lived in the hearts of the people. . . . I found two young women living together. I asked if they feared God. Their answer was as though they never heard of God for the devil had a palace there and one of them asked me if I wanted a wife without a fortune to court her. I told her the devil would have her here and in hell hereafter.

—JOHN EARLY (1807)

$\mathcal{I}$ see the President almost every day, as I happen to live where he passes to or from his lodgings out of town. He never sleeps at the White House during the hot season, but has quarters at . . . the Soldiers' Home, a United States military establishment. I saw him this morning. . . . He always has a company of twenty-five or thirty cavalry, with sabres drawn, and held upright over their shoulders. . . . Mr. Lincoln, on the saddle, generally rides a good-sized easy-going gray horse, is dress'd in plain black, somewhat rusty and dusty; wears a black stiff hat, and looks about as ordinary in attire, &c., as the commonest man. A Lieutenant, with yellow straps, rides at his left, and following behind, two by two, come the cavalry men in their yellow-striped jackets. They are generally going at a slow trot, as that is the pace set them by the One they wait upon. The sabres and accoutrements clank. . . . I see very plainly ABRAHAM LINCOLN's dark brown face, with the deep cut lines, the eyes, &c., always to me with a deep latent sadness in the expression. We have got so that we always exchange bows, and very cordial ones.

—WALT WHITMAN (1863)

This morning Grandma went down with Mother and Aunt Lilly to be sworn in as an American citizen. She resented being fingerprinted as an alien, and studied diligently for the forthcoming exam. She did quite well, until questioned whether she belonged to a subversive society. Grandma, not understanding, nodded her head. The clerk inquired if she were a Communist, and Grandma exclaimed indignantly: "God forbid!" She is very proud and happy.

—DAVID S. KOGAN (1943)

AUGUST 13

I made the tour thro the town . . . and, att a certain lady's house, saw a white monkey. . . . It was about a foot long in its body and, in visage, exceeding like an old man, there being no hair upon its face except a little white, downy beard. It laugh'd and grinned like any Christian (as people say), and was exceeding fond of his mistress, bussing her and handling her bubbies just like an old rake. One might well envy the brute, for the lady was very handsome. . . . It is strange to see how fond these brutes are of women, and, on the other hand, how much the female monkeys affect men. The progress of nature is surprizing in many such instances. She seems by one connected gradation to pass from one species of creatures to another without any visible gap, intervall, or *discontinuum* in her works; but an infinity of her operations are yet unknown to us.

—ALEXANDER HAMILTON (1744)

[Crossing the Rockies] *T*his morning started through a canon that is seven miles long ascending all the way. . . . Dobbins' wagons are always in the lead, then ours, and father's last. With three or more yokes of cattle to each wagon, there is a lot of dust at any time, but today it was worse than ever and seemed to permeate everything. The food was supposed to be put away securely but had its full share. Snuggled up in uninviting beds, with hands and faces unwashed. Weariness and discomfort were soon forgotten in sound sleep that was refreshing even though dust coated.

—HELEN CARPENTER (1857)

*A*t last a whole day for myself! I lifted my head just now after typing for an hour, and heard the absolute silence— there is not a breath of wind, the sea the most radiant pale blue. The lobster boats creep by, hardly making a sound. And then I heard the slight gentle whirring of crickets, that sound of late summer with autumn already in it.

—MAY SARTON (1975)

AUGUST 14

*I*n the morning rode a single horse, in company with Mrs. Cranch and Mrs. Adams in a chaise, to Marblehead. . . . Returned and dined at Cranch's; after dinner walked to Witchcraft hill, a hill about half a mile from Cranch's, where the famous persons formerly executed for witches were buried.

Somebody within a few years has planted a number of locust trees over the graves, as a memorial of that memorable victory over the "prince of the power of the air."

—JOHN ADAMS (1766)

$\mathscr{D}$ined with three hundred and fifty Sons of Liberty, at Robinson's, the sign of Liberty Tree, in Dorchester. We had two tables laid in the open field, by the barn, with between three and four hundred plates, and an awning of sailcloth over head. . . . We had also the Liberty Song—that by the farmer, and that by Dr. Church, and the whole company joined in the chorus. This is cultivating the sensations of freedom. . . . Otis and Adams are politic in promoting these festivals; for they tinge the minds of the people . . . with the sentiments of liberty; they render the people fond of their leaders in the cause, and averse and bitter against all opposers. To the honor of the Sons, I did not see one person intoxicated, or near it.

—JOHN ADAMS (1769)

$\mathscr{E}$nemy aircraft dropped their first bombs on Guadalcanal today. . . . The air-raid alarm, a dilapidated dinner bell, jangled, and there was a general scurrying for protective foxholes. A few of us, however, went to a clearing to watch the excitement. . . . In a few seconds, someone shouted, "There they are!" and pointed, and we all looked. Then I saw three of the Japs, silvery and beautiful in the high skys. They were so high that they looked like a slender white cloud moving slowly across the blue. But through my field glasses, I could see the silvery-white bodies quite distinctly: the thin wings, the two slim engine nacelles, the shimmering arcs of the propellers. I was surprised that enemy aircraft, flying overhead with the obvious intention of dropping high explosives upon us, could be so beautiful.

—RICHARD TREGASKIS (1942)

298

AUGUST 15

*H*ere on the summit, where the stillness was absolute, . . . we thought ourselves beyond the region of animated life; but while we were sitting on the rock a solitary bee . . . came winging his flight from the eastern valley, and lit on the knee of one of the men. It was a strange place, the icy rock and the highest peak of the Rocky Mountains, for a lover of warm sunshine and flowers; and we pleased ourselves with the idea that he was the first of his species to cross the mountain barrier—a solitary pioneer to foretell the advance of civilization. I believe that a moment's thought would have made us let him continue his way unharmed; but we carried out the law of this country, where all animated nature seems at war; and, seizing him immediately, put him in at least a fit place— in the leaves of a large book, among the flowers we had collected on our way.

—JOHN C. FRÉMONT (1842)

*I*n Europe the blitzkrieg is on—thousands of planes battling each other, the American newspapers cra-a-zy with excitement. In the American people? Restlessness, avidity for any scraps of information . . . anxiety, uneasiness, and, sadly, superficiality. Never again in our time will there be an ease of living, for none of us.

—CLIFFORD ODETS (1940)

*M*rs. McCormick telephoned her [New York *Times*] office and I overheard this sentence: "Yes, there on my desk; it's my end-of-the-war piece, but of course if the war has not ended, you can't run it." . . . Then we went for a stroll . . . and by good fortune . . . got back just two minutes ahead of the news [that the war had ended]. I am always interested in the circumstances in which great news is brought to one, scarcely less than in the news itself. . . . I was glad to be, not out anywhere amid the excitement, but in a mere sitting room

299

with little old individuals whom I know well enough to situate in the history lesson. Of course the radio brought us nation-wide hubbub, *ad nauseam.*

—GLENWAY WESCOTT (1945)

AUGUST 16

*T*his evening I had a conversation with Mr. N about the "spiritual rappings."—He is a firm believer in their "spiritual" origin. He spoke of the different manner in which the different "spirits" manifested their presence,—some merely *touching* the mediums, others thoroughly *shaking* them, etc. I told him that I thought I required a very "thorough shaking" to make me a believer. Yet I must not presume to say that I entirely disbelieve that which the wisest cannot understand.

—CHARLOTTE FORTEN (1854)

*J*ames Harris & wife is with us to day and last night. David Miller & Wilford Harris has come to bid us farewell before they go to the wars (and to eat watter-melons).

—DAVID GOLIGHTLY HARRIS (1861)

[In Provincetown, Massachussetts] *O*ne saw through the space between the cottages the plain dense blue, gray, or sepia of the blunt shapes of little boats . . . Along the horizon lay a row of red gunboats, all pointed in the same direction, toward the town, and with their smokestacks toward the forward end, like the last remaining jagged teeth of the lower jawbone of the skull of some link between the human and the animal.

—EDMUND WILSON (1930)

AUGUST 17

*C*ame to salmon fishing; obtained some fish and boiled for breakfast; find it good eating. They are preparing to cross Snake river. I can cross the most difficult streams without the least fear. There is one manner of crossing husband has tried, but I have not. Take an elk skin and stretch it over you, spreading yourself out as much as possible, then let the Indian women carefully put you in the water and with cord in the mouth they will swim and drag you over.

—NARCISSA WHITMAN (1836)

*A*fter a long ride in the humid air, the sky so dark (as if it has been relating itself somehow to the war during the past weeks), Bette and I landed here, looked at newspapers, took cool showers, spoke lightly in the heavy morning. I found myself pacing back and forth, nervous, restless, so tired.

—CLIFFORD ODETS (1940)

*T*alked with the domestic science editor of one of the women's magazines. She told me that she had tested literally thousands of recipes, covering almost every kind of food. Asked her what, after all this, she considered the best eating.

She thought it was pretty hard to beat a good sirloin steak, washed down with straight whisky. Western gal.

—JAMES WEBB YOUNG (1942)

AUGUST 18

We proceeded on & crossed Bushy Run, the banks were mud & mire, the stream up to the horses bellies, & such was the darkness that we could scarcely see the water. By good providence we got safely through & soon arrived at another Dutchman's, one Tegart. . . . At first he declined letting us in, alleging that the house was full of indian traders from Pittsburgh &c. At last we wrought a little upon his humanity, & he unbared the door. . . . Around the dirty room of the Log house lay asleep and snoaring, a number of men. No bed or bedding was to be had. We persuaded the fellow who let us in, to make up a fire. . . . He also brought us two dirty blankets, & spreading them on the muddy floor, before the fire, we lay down supperless to try to sleep. But such swarms of fleas from the blankets attacked us on all quarters, that sleep refused us its oblivious soothing comforts. The Dutchman, with a beard an inch in length, sat on a block in the corner of the chimney place smoking his pipe . . . We quitted our uneasy couch at dawn.

—DAVID McCLURE (1772)

In the after part of the day, the party with the Indians arrived. We met them under a shade near the boat, and after a short talk we gave them provisions to eat and proceeded to the trial of Reed. He confessed that he "deserted and stole a public rifle, shot-pouch, powder and ball," and requested that we would be as favorable with him as we could, consistently with our oaths, which we were, and only sentenced him to run the gauntlet four times through the party, and that each

302

man with 9 switches should punish him, and for him not to be considered in future as one of the party. The three principal chiefs petitioned for pardon for this man. After we explained the injury such men could do them by false representations, and explained the customs of our country, they were all satisfied with the propriety of the sentence, and were witnesses to the punishment. After which we had some talk with the chiefs about the origin of the war between them and the Mahas, &c. Captain Lewis' birthday. The evening was closed with an extra gill of whiskey, and a dance until 11 o'clock.

—WILLIAM CLARK (1804)

*W*e Americans worship the almighty dollar! Well, it is a worthier god than Heredity Privilege. Better a deity that represents the labor of your hands and your contribution to the world's wealth than a deity which represents not a contribution, but a robbery; for no king or noble has ever lived who was not a robber, and the successor of robbers, since no kingship or nobility was ever yet conferred by the one and only authority entitled to confer it—the mass of the nation.

—MARK TWAIN (1889)

AUGUST 19

*A*nswered General Dearborn's letter, and received one from my wife, chiefly upon an attack against me in one of the Philadelphia newspapers on account of the negligence of my dress. It says that I wear neither waistcoat nor cravat, and sometimes go to church barefoot. . . . In the Washington *City Gazette,* some person unknown to me has taken the cudgels in my behalf, and answered the accusation gravely as if the charge were true. It is true only as regards the cravat, instead of which, in the extremity of the summer heat, I wear round my neck a black silk riband. But, even in the falsehoods of this charge, what I may profitably remember is the perpetual and malignant watchfulness with which I am observed in my open day and my secret night.

—JOHN QUINCY ADAMS (1822)

*A*nother week is numbered with the past and finds us toiling down the Humboldt or St. Mary's River. . . . Our men are becoming emaciated and querulous. Luxuries in the way of foods are among the things to memory dear. Rancid bacon with the grease fried out by the hot sun, musty flour, a little pinoles and some sacks of pilot bread, broken and crushed to dust and well coated with alkali, a little coffee without sugar—now constitutes our diet. The men need more and must have it or perish. Yet at our present rate of progress, even these supplies must fail long before we can reach California. A deep gloom prevails in camp.

—NILES SEARLS (1849)

A scientific morning: Newton Harvey took us all over the Marine Biological Laboratory. . . . There are ice-cold rooms, furnace-hot rooms, pitch-black rooms . . . as well as vast witches' kitchens for combinations of researchers. There is one great warehouse for everything out of the sea alive and kicking; another for ditto dead, pickled in barrels, stinking. . . . The human researchers are almost as diverse and bizarre as the marine researchees: lovely-looking nuns, tiny tottering old men. . . . an extreme hunchback, his face situated at just about the juncture of his collarbones, with a husky helper, and, mysteriously seated on the floor, a little golden-haired child. In the sub-basement storeroom we found the most beautiful youth in minimum shorts up on a stepladder working along the shelves: waistline as slender as the stalk of something, muscles of his back rippling, legs stretch-

304

ing—and sprawled down below, underneath the shelves, another not so beautiful, taking a rest, reading *Life* magazine.

—Glenway Wescott (1955)

AUGUST 20

Everybody is going around half-naked on account of the heat. Even old Mrs. Goudy. She shed her outer garments and appeared in her petticoat. "I'm going around in my shimmy tail," she called out, "and it's cooler." Later on, when we stopped for nooning, and to eat a little, I saw her grandson throwing buckets of river water over her. He threw it over while she wore her under clothes, so the old gal must have been soaking wet for hours.

—Andrew Gordon (1849)

The emigrants are a woe-begone, sorry-looking crowd. The men, with long hair and matted beards, in soiled and ragged clothes . . . have a half-savage appearance. . . . The once clean, white wagon tops are soiled and tattered. . . . The rickety wheels are often braced up with sticks. . . . They go creaking along the dusty roads . . . drawn by weary beasts hardly able to travel, making up a beggardly-looking caravan. . . . The great, splendid trains of fifteen, twenty, or thirty wagons have shrunk to three, four, or at most half a dozen, with three-fourths of their animals missing. Their former owners now trudge along on foot, packing on their backs the scant provisions left, with maybe a blanket, or leading skeleton horses that stagger under their light burdens. . . . One only hope sustains all these unhappy pilgrims, that they will be able to get into California alive . . . where the gold which they feel sure of finding will repay them for all their hardships and suffering.

—Margaret A. Frink (1850)

$\mathcal{W}$ent with Otis and Fern to the Lowville Fair [Upstate New York] in the evening. . . . We threw away some nickels on the glassware game of chance, where the coins skim right out of the dishes, and there is no chance of winning anything except, as I once did, a glass. . . . We had hot dogs and iced tea, and went into the grandstand to see the drum corps competition. . . . As we left, I saw the big swing that turns you upside down slowly whirling its blunt-ended bright-lighted spoke against the dark upstate sky, and there seemed to me something grand and wild about even this transient amusement park: the fun that the people were having against the immense dark sky in the mountain-horizoned countryside. A gaiety which, though healthy, was lonely and contrasted with their rural lives. Some, they told me, went every night.

—EDMUND WILSON (1955)

AUGUST 21

$\mathcal{R}$ose at 6 for the first time in six months. Dreamed engaged to marry a huge ugly beast. . . . Deliberated whether to blow out brains or perform engagement; waked by the striking of 6. . . . Every person of every sex and grade comes in [to my room] without knocking; plump into your bedroom! They do not seem at all embarrassed, nor think of apologizing at finding in bed or dressing or doing—no matter what—but go right on and tell their story as if it were all right. . . . It took me six weeks to teach my old Anna [his maid] not to come in without knocking and leave and finally it was only by appearing to get into a most violent passion and threatening to blow out her brains, which she had not the least doubt I would do without ceremony.

—AARON BURR (1809)

$\mathcal{A}$ new kind of war risk came home to me today. On a steep, winding, mountain road the hydraulic brakes of my son's car suddenly went haywire, and it ended up as a pile of junk in a ditch. Fortunately, the driver crawled out with only a broken shoulder. But the cause of the failure, investigation disclosed, was in the work of a completely inexperienced mechanic, to whom a hitherto reliable garage had entrusted a recent checkup. The manpower shortage can be inconvenient in such things as laundry service, but it is murderous in the garages.

—JAMES WEBB YOUNG (1943)

*Y*esterday: the weird spectacle of fiddler crabs in the mud off Rock Harbor Creek. . . . At our approaching footsteps, the crabs near the bank scuttled up it, into holes in the black mucky earth, and into the grass roots, and the crabs in the soggy black center of the dried pool dug themselves into the mud, under little mud lids until only claws jutted from the little cliff of the bank, and elbows and eyes looked out of the myriad holes among the roots of the dry grasses and the drying clustered mussel shells, like some crustaceous bulbs among the tussocks. An image: weird, of another world, with its own queer habits, of mud, lumped, underpeopled with quiet crabs.

—SYLVIA PLATH (1957)

AUGUST 22

I decline invitations to evening parties chiefly because, besides the time spent, commonly ill, in the party, the hours preceding and succeeding the visit are lost for any solid use, as I am put out of tune for writing or reading. That makes my objection to many employments that seem trifles to a bystander, as packing a trunk, or any small handiwork, or correcting proof-sheets, that they put me out of tune.

—RALPH WALDO EMERSON (1838)

307

$\mathscr{A}$fter leaving the book at Mr. Emerson's I returned through the woods, and, entering Sleepy Hollow, I perceived a lady reclining near the path which bends along its verge. It was Margaret [Fuller] herself. She had been there the whole afternoon, meditating or reading. . . . We talked about autumn, and about the pleasures of being lost in the woods, and about the crows, whose voices Margaret had heard; and about the experiences of early childhood . . . ; and about the sight of mountains from a distance, and the view from their summits; and about other matters of high and low philosophy. In the midst of our talk, we heard footsteps above us, on the high bank; . . . and, behold! it was Mr. Emerson. He appeared to have had a pleasant time; for he said that there were Muses in the woods today, and whispers to be heard in the breezes. It being now nearly six o'clock, we separated,— Margaret and Mr. Emerson towards his home, and I towards mine.

—NATHANIEL HAWTHORNE (1842)

$\mathscr{T}$he stench of bodies strewn along Hell Point and across the Tenaru spit was strong. Many of them lay at the water's edge, and already were puffed and glossy, like shiny sausages. Some of the bodies had been partially buried by wave-washed sand; you might see a grotesque, bloated head or twisted torso sprouting from the beach. It was not pleasant to look at the piles of bodies on the spit. But that carnage was a pale painting, compared to the scene in the grove across the spit. That was a macabre nightmare. . . . Everywhere one turned there were piles of bodies; here one with a backbone visible from the front, and the rest of the flesh and bone peeled up over the man's head, like the leaf of an artichoke; there a charred head, hairless but still equipped with blackened eyeballs; pink, blue, yellow entrails drooping; a man with a red bullet-hole through his eye. . . . There is no horror to these things. The first one you see is the only shock. The rest are simple repetition.

—RICHARD TREGASKIS (1942)

$\mathscr{L}$istened to Janet [Flanner]'s broadcast from Paris; then walked home. The summer dust on the lower leaves of the roadside makes them silvery. The night insects are going so that if one stops to listen it seems unendurable. The freight of war still passing through High Bridge reverberates—rain tomorrow?

—GLENWAY WESCOTT (1945)

AUGUST 23

$\mathscr{Y}$esterday evening we reached our encampment at Rock Independence. . . . Not unmindful of the custom of early travellers and explorers in our country, I engraved on this rock of the Far West a symbol of the Christian faith. Among the thickly inscribed names, I made on the hard granite the impression of a large cross, which I covered with a black preparation of India rubber, well calculated to resist the influence of wind and rain. It stands amidst the names of many who have long since found their way to the grave, and for whom the huge rock is a giant grave stone.

—JOHN C. FRÉMONT (1842)

$\mathscr{W}$hile at Sandy Hook we received the hats and uniform coats issued to us by the State. . . . The hats were neither useful nor ornamental . . . made of black felt, high-crowned, with a wide rim turned up on one side, and fastened to the crown was a brass eagle containing the figure 13. Now it so happened that the person who selected the sizes was under the impression that every man from Massachusetts had a head like Daniel Webster—a mistake that caused us much trouble, inasmuch as newspapers were in great demand to lessen the diameter of the crown. Those of us who failed to procure newspapers made use of our ears to prevent its falling on our shoulders.

—CHARLES E. DAVIS (1861)

I had a ten-thirty appointment with the President [Roosevelt] this morning. . . . When I got up to his study, his valet ushered me into his bedroom, telling me that the President was shaving. He waved toward the bathroom and the President called out to me to come in. There he was, sitting before a mirror in front of the washstand, shaving. He invited me to sit on the toilet seat while we talked.

—HAROLD L. ICKES (1935)

AUGUST 24

*S*ome old man said the great injury the war would do us, that it would take forty years to get rid of the *heroes* it made. He said the war had proved one thing the pest of civil life: the *heroes* who tormented every body with their *courage* were the first to leave the battle field.

—MARY BOYKIN CHESNUT (1861)

*S*eated in the garden, where I've been sleeping all the afternoon en repos—It is the most charming of gardens with what was once a pool of water with a fountain, at one end in front of the shell of the little pink stuccoed house the garden belonged to. We use it now as a dug out and dive into it when the shells the Germans persist in tossing into this blessed village get too close. It is just the sort of garden a pensive little French boy with large brown eyes & premature scepticisms should play in, a garden full of such plaisance with its white roses and its fat-juiced pears and its white blotches of phlox-flowers among evergreens that it makes one hate still more all the foolishnesses with which men try to disturb the rich ease of life. . . . Death, that should come tranquilly, like the dropping of an over ripe pear, brimming with sweetness, why should it come in the evil shriek of a shell?

—JOHN DOS PASSOS (1917)

310

*G*ertrude Stein kindly invited me to tea: a fat, most amiable old woman who lives in a strange combination of sloppy comfort and a modern art museum with her friend, the cozy, hideous Alice Toklas. Stein is writing a new novel, *Brewsie and Willie,* about GIs and how they worry and how she worries about them and how they worry together about their worrying: "Are we isolationists or are we isolated is what I want to know," she said, munching excellent cookies.

—C. L. SULZBERGER (1945)

AUGUST 25

[In Virginia] *S*till stormy. The Gentlemen who are sailing up the Bay to the Congress have a disagreeable time—This is a true August Northeaster, as we call it in Cohansie—*Ben* is in a wonderful *Fluster* lest he shall have no company to-morrow at the Dance—But blow high, blow low, he need not be afraid; *Virginians* are of genuine Blood—They will dance or die! . . . All the Evening Toddy constantly circulating—Supper came in, & at Supper I had a full, broad, sattisfying View of *Miss Sally Panton*—I wanted to hear her converse, but poor Girl any thing She attempted to say was drowned in the more polite & useful Jargon about Dogs & Horses!—For my Part, as I was unwilling to be singular, if I attempted to push in a word, I was seldom heard, & never regarded, & yet they were constantly refering their Cases to me, as to a supposed honest fellow, I suppose because I wear a black Coat, & am generally silent; at Home I am thought to be noisy enough; here I am thought to be silent & circumspect as a Spy—How different the Manners of the People!

—PHILIP VICKERS FITHIAN (1774)

*G*rew cold before morning. Went northward 5 miles, where the river turns first west then S.W. . . . Camped for noon at

311

10 miles. Bo't [bought] a pair of coarse boots from ox train for $3.95. Had a good swim. Afternoon, kept down the river. Picturesque mountains on either side. Towards sundown the air becalms and the dust after rising a few feet high overspreads the plain like a lake of smooth muddy water. Along our line of wagons some are completely submerged in it. Others show only their tops, which seem to go floating along like little boats in the water. Here and there the heads of the men on foot stick up and glide along in rows and groups like ducks on a pond. Passed the grave of Melinda, wife of Henry Cain, of Platte County, Mo. Total today 18 miles.

—BERNARD J. REID (1849)

The Ficklens sent us some books of fashion brought by Mr. Boyce from New York. The styles are very pretty, but too expensive for us broken-down Southerners. I intend always to dress as well as my means will allow, but shall attempt nothing in the way of finery so long as I have to sweep floors and make up beds. It is more graceful and more sensible to accept poverty as it comes than to try to hide under a flimsy covering of false appearances. . . . I feel, with perfect sincerity, that my faded calico dress has a right to look with scorn at the rich toilettes of our plunderers. Notwithstanding all our trouble and wretchedness, I thank Heaven that I was born a Southerner,—that I belong to the noblest race on earth—for this is a heritage that nothing can ever take from me.

—ELIZA ANDREWS (1865)

AUGUST 26

We collected our horses and set out at sunrise. We soon arrived at the extreme source of the Missouri. Here I halted a

312

few minutes. The men drank of the water and consoled themselves with the idea of having at length arrived at this long-wished-for point. . . . One of the women who had been assisting in the transportation of the baggage halted a little run about a mile behind us, and sent on the two pack horses which she had been conducting by one of her female friends. I inquired of Cameahwait the cause of her detention and was informed by him, in an unconcerned manner, that she had halted to bring forth a child and would soon overtake us. In about an hour the woman arrived with her newborn babe and passed us on her way to the camp, apparently as well as she ever was.

—MERIWETHER LEWIS (1805)

J wish I'd kept this beastly diary up. . . . I want to be able to express, later—all of this—all the tragedy and hideous excitement of it. . . . The grey crooked fingers of the dead, the dark look of dirty mangled bodies, their groans & joltings in the ambulances, the vast tomtom of the guns, the ripping tear shells make when they explode, the song of shells outgoing, like vast woodcocks—their contented whirr as they near their mark—the twang of fragments like a harp broken in the air—& the rattle of stones & mud on your helmet—And through everything the vast despair of unavoidable death of lives wrenched out of their channels—of all the ludicrous tomfoolery of governments.

—JOHN DOS PASSOS (1917)

*P*arty of Congressmen to Front. . . . Chief interest of party—souvenirs. Half the time spent collecting iron. Only thing they had more of was misinformation. Got so tired of their digging through rusty scrap iron, asking "And what's this, Lieutenant?" I'd answer: "Oh, part of fuse on German 4000 millimeter shell." Probably piece of jam-tim. . . . But it's their God damned *frivolity* that infuriates. Treat the war as circus, put on for their especial benefit. Most of them here as nothing but curiosity seekers, getting material for re-election campaigns, and be able

313

to talk familiarly of "the brave boys Over There." Keen for getting pictures snapped "on the battlefields."

—HOWARD O'BRIEN (1918)

AUGUST 27

I rose at 5 o'clock and read two chapters in Hebrew and some Greek in Josephus. I said my prayers and ate milk for breakfast. I danced my dance. I had like to have whipped my maid Anaka for her laziness but I forgave her. I read a little geometry. I denied my man G-r-l to go to a horse race because there was nothing but swearing and drinking there. I ate roast mutton for dinner. In the afternoon I played at piquet with my own wife and made her out of humor by cheating her. I read some Greek in Homer. Then I walked about the plantation. I lent John H-ch 7 in his distress. I said my prayers and had good health, good thoughts, and good humor, thanks be to God Almighty.

—WILLIAM BYRD (1709)

*W*e have passed through some two or three little settlements today. . . . It is truly shocking to my modesty to pass such places with gentlemen. The women slap about with their arms and necks bare, perhaps their bosoms exposed (and they are none of the prettiest or whitest). If they are about to cross the little creek that is near all the villages, regardless of those about them, they pull their dresses, which in the first place but little more than cover their calves—up about their knees and paddle through the water like ducks, sloshing and spattering every thing about them. . . . And it is repulsive to see the children running about perfectly naked. . . . I am constrained to keep my veil drawn closely over my face all the time to protect my blushes.

—SUSAN MAGOFFIN (1846)

314

*M*y grandfather, I believe, made a mistake when he came to this country. He was an unhappy man himself and his descendants have had many troubles. I believe, in truth, that immigration is always unwise—that is, when it is not enforced. I believe my chances in Germany would have been at least as good as they have been in America, and maybe a great deal better. I was born here and so were my father and mother, and I have spent all of my 62 years here, but I still find it impossible to fit myself into the accepted patterns of American life and thought. After all these years, I remain a foreigner.

—H. L. MENCKEN (1942)

AUGUST 28

*M*y Lott is Singular but with patience I wish to Conform to it. My husband returned at Evening from Ballstown much fatagued with his Journey. Had a fitt of shakeing. I heat a Blankett and put it about him at about 3 hour morning. He being relaxed dirtied the Bed. I rose, shirted him and removed the dirty lining. Went to Bed again but was so Cold that I Could not sleep. I rose again before the sun rose. Washt the things which were unclean but felt so unfitt to attend worship that I tarried at home. My famely all attended. O my God when will the Time be when I may have it in my power to go to thy house to worship again?

—MARTHA BALLARD (1802)

*Y*esterday in town talked with George Sennott, Esq., who hoped the rumour true that Sigel had shot McDowell, for he liked that any man should shoot any other, as that showed character, whilst most men would do nothing, either good or bad, but only compromise and neutralize.

—RALPH WALDO EMERSON (1862)

315

$\mathcal{A}$nd so the yarning went on, and finally somebody told the classic story about the two marine jeep drivers on Guadalcanal, supposedly a true story, very true, anyhow, in its essential American psychology. It was about two jeeps passing in the night, one with proper dim-out headlights, the other with glaring bright lights. So the driver of the dim-light car leans out as they pass and shouts to the other driver: "Hey! Put your f——g lights out!" To which the other replies: "I can't. I've got a f——g colonel with me!"

—RICHARD TREGASKIS (1942)

AUGUST 29

[In a spell of insomnia] $\mathcal{G}$ot up and attempted to light candle, but in vain; had flint and matches but only some shreds of punk which would not catch. Recollected a gun which I had on my late journey; filled the pan with powder and was just going to flash it when it occurred to me that though I had not loaded it someone else might; tried and found in it a very heavy charge! What a fine alarm it would have made if I had fired! Then poured out some powder on a piece of paper, put the shreds of punk with it, and after fifty essays succeeded in firing the powder; but it being dark, had put more powder than intended; my shirt caught fire, the papers on my table caught fire, burnt my fingers to a blister (the left hand, fortunately); it seemed like a general conflagration. Succeeded, however, in lighting my candle and passed the night till 5 this morning in smoking, reading, and writing this.

—AARON BURR (1809)

$\mathcal{W}$e are living high on rosting corn & melons at this time, and will have them until frost. Our boy is doing very well, constantly smiling & occasionaly crowing. His voice is as pleasant as a gobler's in the Spring. At this time Emily is *quite* busy whipping Maria. She gets mad, that makes me cross, then she fights all the plantation. Oh! these women. They pretend to be working for the soldiers. I wish they would work for the soldiers, and not work on me.

—DAVID GOLIGHTLY HARRIS (1861)

*O*ur women are now in a nice condition—traveling, your false hair is developed & taken off to see if papers are rolled in it—& you are turned up instantly to see if you have pistols concealed—not to speak of their having women to examine if you are a *man*—in disguise. I think *these* times make all women feel their humiliation in the affairs of the world. With *men* it is on to the field—"glory, honour, praise, &c, power." Women can only stay at home—& every paper reminds us that women are to be *violated*—ravished & all manner of humiliation. How are the daughters of Eve punished.

—MARY BOYKIN CHESNUT (1861)

[In Hollywood] *T*he man makes of his wife something mechanical here, a mechanism. It is exactly what he does in a story conference, with the characters of a movie he is building. The characters are titled with names, boy and girl, but they are not human beings; instead they are dead bodies which can be slung around and moved to and fro to further the plot progression. Real life, in other words, is subordinated to device, cliché, and plot movement—to the supermechanism!

—CLIFFORD ODETS (1940)

AUGUST 30

*M*onday rode to Braddock's field. . . . It was a melancholy spectacle to see the bones of men strewed over the ground, left to this day, without the solemn rite of sepulture. The fact is a disgrace to the british commanders at Fort Pitt. The bones had been gnawed by wolves, the vestiges of their teeth appearing on them. Many hundreds of skulls lay on the ground. I examined several, & found the mark of the scalping knife on all. I put one, & a jaw bone, in my portmantau, which I afterwards presented to Mr. Stewart's Museum in Hartford. The harness of the horses remained unconsumed on the ground. A man who lives near the field of battle, & whose corn field takes in a part of it, had humanely collected a great number of the bones & laid them in small heaps.

—DAVID McCLURE (1772)

*C*alifornia always did have one custom that they took serious. . . . That was in calling everything a "ranch." Everything big enough to spread a double mattress on is called a "ranch." Well, up here is these mountains where there is lots of fishing, why every house you pass they sell fishing worms, and it's called a "worm ranch." Well, I always did want to own a "ranch," so I am in the market for a good worm ranch.

—WILL ROGERS (1932)

*T*alked with a man who has made his living selling high-priced but mediocre art to the rich. He says that nowadays the newly rich, and especially those in the small towns and western states, are his best picking. The older rich are hugging their decreased incomes to their chests; but the newer rich are still anxious to establish themselves as patrons of the arts and of learning. For them he puts on a regular J. Rufus Wallingford front, complete with Rolls Royce, cane and spats.

—JAMES WEBB YOUNG (1943)

AUGUST 31

[In Santa Fe] *I*t is really hard to realize it, that I am here in my own house, in a place too where I once would have thought it folly to think of visiting. I have entered the city in a year that will always be remembered by my countrymen; and under the "Star-spangled banner" too, the first American lady who has come under such auspices, and some of our company seem disposed to make me the first under any circumstances that ever crossed the Plains.

—SUSAN MAGOFFIN (1846)

[In a Confederate prison in Richmond] *The* feeling of animosity against the people of the North is to me unaccountable, when I reflect how closely have been all our relations of commerce and society. . . . To-day a patriarchal citizen, whose long locks, extending over his shoulders and whitened by the snows of more than seventy winters, respectful in his demeanor and intelligent in conversation, called upon the prisoners, and stated, among other matters, that he resided in Charleston, South Carolina, and was the person who fired the *first* gun at Fort Sumter. The gentleman was the *Reverend* Edward Ruffin. He did not meet with a cordial reception among the officers after such an avowal; they were not disposed to cheer a minister of the gospel in his exultant boast of being the first to shoot down the flag of his country.

—ALFRED ELY (1861)

*C*oming into New York on the Sandy Hook boat. The bridges and the buildings painted light . . . against the gray sky—and from that dimness, a tug swimming to distinctness and to the vulgarity of day, dark, practical and hard, as it approached the boat.—The harsh honk of the boat blew behind me, scratching raucously my eardrums—there was honking and howling on the harbor, and the prolonged diapason of a small steamer with one smokestack, just off the brown cliffs above the Battery—our boat answered with another honk.— The shipping all quiet and deserted, just before the dinner hour—only early points of light on the quiet tugs.—When I got started in the taxi, the sun was farther down, and suddenly everything was a gray blot: docks, sky and street.

—EDMUND WILSON (1929)

∽ SEPTEMBER ∽

SEPTEMBER 1

*A*rrived at Fort Walla Walla. . . . After breakfast was over we were shown . . . in the room Mr. Pambrun prepared for us, on hearing of our approach. It was the west bastion in the fort, full of portholes in the sides, but no windows, and was filled with firearms. A large cannon, always loaded, stood behind the door by one of the holes. These things did not move me.

—NARCISSA WHITMAN (1836)

*A*fter breakfast I washed dishes, and ran on the hill till nine, and had some thoughts,—it was so beautiful up there. Did my lessons . . . and Mr. Lane read a story, "The Judicious Father": How a rich girl told a poor girl not to look over the fence at the flowers, and was cross to her because she was unhappy. The father heard her do it, and made the girls change clothes. The poor one was glad to do it, and he told her to keep them. But the rich one was very sad; for she had to wear the old ones a week, and after that she was good to shabby girls. I liked it very much, and I shall be kind to poor people. . . . As I went to bed the moon came up very brightly and looked at me. . . . I get to sleep saying poetry,—I know a great deal.

—LOUISA MAY ALCOTT (1843)

321

$\mathscr{I}$ must record as a matter of curiosity the results of my silly experiments with Hashish. . . . Tried it very cautiously and warily in small successive doses . . . and made up my mind that the drug was inert. . . . Thursday night at twelve, just before retiring, I treated myself to a larger bolus, as big as two peas perhaps, and went to bed and to sleep as usual. At two A.M. I woke from a perturbed, dreamy slumber. . . . The prominent feature of my mental condition was that I was . . . two gentlemen in one night shirt: G. T. Strong No. 1 was in an agreeable, mild delirium. . . . G. T. Strong No. 2, rather languid and lazy, looked on. . . . There seemed slowly to present itself . . . bodily death with its accessories. It was as if a corpse in its cerements was drawing near me, and I knew that with its first touch, I should be *It*. There was no illusion of sense, but a hideous horror of loathing and shrinking such as I never felt before.

—GEORGE TEMPLETON STRONG (1856)

$\mathscr{W}$e are . . . becoming a little more comfortable in our island quarters. A few elementary necessities like privies have been slammed together, mostly made from prefabricated Japanese housing sections. . . . We also have an oven which has been fashioned from a captured Japanese safe. . . . It is startling to think how one's standards of values change under the continued impetus of living conditions such as ours on Guadalcanal. Things like bread and privies, considered the barest necessities at home, become luxuries. One thinks of warm water, the smooth water-closet seat of civilization, and a bed with sheets as things that exist only in a world of dreams.

—RICHARD TREGASKIS (1942)

SEPTEMBER 2

$\mathscr{I}$n the course of the day, we landed to shoot at pidgeons; the moment a gun was fired, some Indians, who were on the

shore above us, ran down and put off in their peroques with
great precipitation; upon which Mr. Blondeau informed me,
that all the women and children were frightened at the very
name of an American boat, and that the men held us in great
respect, conceiving us very quarrelsome, and much for war,
and also very brave. . . . We stopt at an encampment, about
three miles below the town, where they gave us some excellent plums. They despatched a peroque to the village, to give
notice, as I supposed, of our arrival. It commenced raining
about dusk, and rained all night. Distance 40 miles.

—ZEBULON PIKE (1805)

$\mathcal{R}$ide to see the divine service of the Shaking Quakers. . . .
We have a short address of invitation to us . . . to become
members of their fraternity, after which they sing a hymn to
the tune of 'Jolly mortals, fill your glasses,' and dance,
moving backwards and forwards to the tune of an old country-
dance. . . . After two dances . . . a young preacher comes forward and addresses us in a sensible discourse (disfigured,
indeed, by useless repetition), the object of which is to prove
that we ought to abandon worldly pursuits, pleasures, and
enjoyments, and, more especially, the conjugal pleasures, for
the sake of that pure felicity which attends celibacy. . . . How
ridiculous the notion, entertained by some, of the perfectabil-
ity of human nature.

—GOUVERNEUR MORRIS (1810)

$\mathcal{L}$iz Taylor is getting Eddie Fisher away from Debbie Reynolds, who appears cherubic, round-faced, wronged, in pin
curls and house robe—Mike Todd barely cold. How odd these
events affect one so. Why? Analogies? would like to squander
money on hair styling, clothes. Yet know power is in work
and thought. The rest is pleasant frill. I love too much, too

wholly, too simply for any cleverness. Use imagination. Write and work to please.

—SYLVIA PLATH (1958)

SEPTEMBER 3

In [the Constitutional] Convention. Visited a Machine at Doctr. Franklin's (called a Mangle) for pressing, in place of ironing, clothes from the wash. Which Machine from the facility with which it dispatches business is well calculated for Table cloths and such articles as have not pleats and irregular foldings and would be very useful in all large families. Dined, drank Tea, and spent the evening at Mr. [Robert] Morris's.

—GEORGE WASHINGTON (1787)

Peaceful happy fine day with guests until evening, when E came from Troutdale full of war news. Reports actual war begun. I had to flee the house to be in darkness.

—SHERWOOD ANDERSON (1939)

Leland Hayward, the agent, sent his car and driver for me to take me to see his wife, Margaret Sullavan, at their house . . . [before] they had to be off to dinner (I thought it unfair of them to have invited me there for an hour). . . . She is very intuitive, still restless underneath. . . . afraid somewhat of the outer world, of being put up in a high place to be slapped by the outrageous slings of fortune. When we walked to the door, her husband half-dressed in dinner clothes, I felt very depressed and she knew it, although I hadn't shown my face. She said for me to come again. . . . She said it again, insistently, herself feeling depressed. . . . A third time she said this . . . and I drove away, the air chilly, the night so suddenly dark. . . . I wanted to burst into tears and didn't speak to the driver all the way home, although we had chatted about everything going out there, about Roosevelt versus Wilkie, English fascists, and whatnot.

—CLIFFORD ODETS (1940)

SEPTEMBER 4

*H*ad a trying time crossing [the desert]. . . . The mooing of the cattle for water, . . . the cry of "Another ox down," the stopping of train to unyoke the poor dying brute, . . . and the weary, weary tramp of men and beasts . . . will never be erased from my memory. Just at dawn, in the distance, we had a glimpse of Truckee River, and with it the feeling: Saved at last! Poor cattle; they kept on mooing, even when they stood knee deep in water. The long dreaded desert has been crossed and we are all safe and well . . . grass green and beautiful, and the cattle are up to their eyes in it.

—SALLIE HESTER (1849)

I bought my worm ranch. The man is to turn over 2000 yearling worms, 2000 2-year olds, 500 bull worms and the rest a mixed herd. Now I find in these Sierra Nevadas they are fishing with grasshoppers, so got a grasshopper ranch adjoining. Am going to do a Luther Burbank, cross my grass-hoppers and worms and produce an animal that if the fish don't bite him, he will bite the fish, so you get your fish anyhow.

—WILL ROGERS (1932)

*P*ut story aside to work on speech for Salem and Cornell. The threshers are in the neighborhood and we stopped work on the barn. The war in Europe is on again. I was sick thinking of it. Bob, Mary, John with his Eleanore and Anne came to dine. There was a heavy thunder shower. The war in everyone's mind.

—SHERWOOD ANDERSON (1939)

SEPTEMBER 5

I have great Reason to fear that I have had too Strong a Reliance and Dependence upon Form; and my Soul may have been led away by the snare. . . . I have especially been afraid of my Birth Day Formalitys; and have often omitted to write down any Thing of the 2 last years; but indeed might well omitt it to write since there was So little done; and what was done, was done so lamely, brokenly and sinfully. But now it has pleas'd the glorious and gracious God . . . to grant me this Day, having now been continued Forty Years. I cannot but take some Distinct Notice of it.

—EBENEZER PARKMAN (1743)

I have suffered much to-day,—my friends Mrs. P and her daughters were refused admission to the Museum, after having tickets given them, solely on account of their complexion. Insulting language was used to them—Of course they felt and exhibited deep, bitter indignation; but of what avail was it? none, but to excite the ridicule of those contemptible creatures, miserable doughfaces who do not deserve the name of men. . . . No words can express my feelings. A day of retribution must come. God grant that it may come very soon!

—CHARLOTTE FORTEN (1854)

$\mathscr{T}$o the county fair: uncrowded . . . yokels and yokelesses, the year in and year out professionals, mysterious riffraff in family groups . . . how they live in their trailers and trucks . . . all in a glaring electricity, a howling amplification of the Andrews Sisters and "Lilli Marlene." Bertha Bert, the "ha-morpha-dite" (as the barker said it). . . . The one comic detail was *her* maltreating *him* to prove that *it* had no nerves; the mysterious detail was his-her-its having had a dearly beloved husband in the Marines, killed on Saipan.

—GLENWAY WESCOTT (1945)

SEPTEMBER 6

$\mathscr{T}$o Gray's, six miles. There came a man there, one of the neighbors. I prayed for him and he was afraid, he said, to go home by himself for fear the devil would get him alive. He started bellowing like a bull.

—JOHN EARLY (1807)

$\mathscr{A}$ beautiful sou'east breeze yesterday. Fred lame but dousing his Florida celery in salt and I embroidering on deck. Cloudy today and just a day for soogying [washing with soap powder] the after cabin, which is what the sailors are doing. I see from the *Saturday Evening Post* that while my back was turned New Mexico became a state. President Taft has vetoed their attempt to provide recall of undesirable officials, says the *Post* in an overly righteous lecture down to the western-ers, who it is said are called by easterners "Sons of the bray-ing jackass."

—DOROTHEA MOULTON BALANO (1911)

327

SEPTEMBER 7

*A*t Night, a Man of the name of Purdie, came to offer himself to me as housekeeper, or Household Steward. He had some testimonials respecting his character, but being intoxicated, and in other respects appearing in an unfavorable light, I informed him that he would not answer my purposes, but that he might stay all night.

—GEORGE WASHINGTON (1785)

*I*n descending this cupola, discovered a village of small animals that burrow in the ground. . . . Killed one, and caught one alive, by pouring a great quantity of water in his hole. We attempted to dig to the beds of one of those animals. Were not halfway to his lodge. We found 2 frogs in the hole, and killed a dark rattlesnake near with a ground rat [or prairie dog] in him. . . . The village of those animals covered about 4 acres of ground on a gradual descent of a hill, and contains great numbers of holes on the top of which those little animals sit erect, and make a whistling noise, and, when alarmed, step into their hole. We poured into one of the holes 5 barrels of water without filling it.

—WILLIAM CLARK (1804)

A letter from M. M. Noah, editor of the New York *Advocate* . . . like all the editors of newspapers in this country who have any talent, an author to be let. There is not one of them whose friendship is worth buying, nor one whose enmity is not formidable. They are a sort of assassins who sit with loaded blunderbusses at the corner of streets and fire them off for hire or for sport at any passenger whom they select.

—JOHN QUINCY ADAMS (1820)

SEPTEMBER 8

*I*t is painful to see how very few educated men we have, able to think, to write, to instruct & guide in difficult times. A consequence of democracy.

—SIDNEY GEORGE FISHER (1856)

[In Paris] *I*t was very interesting the other day to have K. come across a young American girl who is studying at one of the colleges here, and to have her confirm in every respect Miss Clough's opinion of the unspecialized, unprepared, intelligent American student. She had done very well indeed at home, but found herself overwhelmed with mortification of her ignorance of what she supposed her chosen branch of knowledge. She found her fellow students kind and friendly and desirous to help her, but the dullest companions; for outside of their special interests their minds were perfectly blank and indifferent and absolutely without any general curiosity, one of them recommending as a novelty of which she probably had not heard, and by which she might be shocked, *Jane Eyre* to read; another, whose name is known in two hemispheres, asked her what she spoke when she was in Paris, English or American, and whether New York is a seaport.

—ALICE JAMES (1891)

[At the Maryland State Fair] *I*t's a marvel of a fair: Hundreds of species of pigeon. . . . Hundreds of pigs, with teenagers maneuvering them with walking sticks . . . with movement rather like a hockey game, this way and that, to and fro, to and fro, over the golden straw of the judging area. A great showing of Shetland ponies; they have revolutionized the breed: no longer tranquil and clumsy and dwarfy as they used to be: wild fairy-tale creatures, as slender as greyhounds, and not much bigger; with an exaggeratedly long cut of hoof like ballet shoes, and long profuse ringletted seven-

teenth-century hair . . . to be watched and judged made the
mares weep and gave the stallions erections.

—GLENWAY WESCOTT (1955)

SEPTEMBER 9

*S*ink of the Humboldt—sink of everything that is human
and humanizing! We have absolutely used up a good-sized
river! Have run it into the ground! . . . The thermometer indi-
cates 140 on this arid plain. . . . Reclining under the wagon,
I look out over an arid, burning waste. The whole atmosphere
glows like an oven. The water is bitter and nauseous. Off to
the southwest, as far as the eye can extend, nothing appears
but a level desert. This we must cross! . . . Fate decrees it! A
hundred dead animals around us admonish haste! Not a particle of food for our stock! We only pause here until night, to
start for the Carson.

—NILES SEARLS (1849)

*W*arnings from home against Demon Rum. Unnecessary.
Defendu. Beer out, also Colored liquid of indifferent taste and
no potency. Wine a blessing. . . . Earnest old ladies in pants
over here "investigating" must be disappointed. Less drunk-
enness in all France than N.Y. can show on one Saturday
night. We're strong on bath tubs, Pullmans, express elevators, etc. But for temperance in food and drink French have
us scratched at post. . . . Sent home Boche helmet. Make
novel and commodious gobboon.

—HOWARD O'BRIEN (1918)

oward the shank of the day, caught the Governor of our state off duty, and we had a little snifter together while he told me of the cares of office in war time. This morning he was gotten out of bed by a lady who telephoned him to please have a dead horse removed from the highway in front of her estate, at once. This was followed by a call from another lady, recently moved into the state, who thought maybe the Governor's wife might get her a cook. A good part of the rest of the day had been spent in long distance telephoning, at his own expense, to persuade the medical authorities who control a rare new drug to furnish some of it for the dying husband of a woman constituent. Votes for women?

—JAMES WEBB YOUNG (1943)

SEPTEMBER 10

idweek, sentenced a woman that whip'd a Man, to be whip'd; said a woman that had lost her Modesty, was like Salt that had lost its savor; good for nothing but to be cast to the Dunghill: 7 or 8 join'd together, call'd the Man out of his Bed, guilefully praying him to shew them the way; then by help of a Negro youth, tore off his Cloaths and whip'd him with Rods; to chastise him for carrying it harshly to his wife.

—SAMUEL SEWALL (1707)

assed a small island near the center of the river, of a mile in length, and camped on one above, separated from the other by a narrow channel. Those islands are called Mud Islands. The hunters killed 3 buffalo and one elk today. The river is falling a little. Great number of buffalo and elk on the hillside, feeding. Deer scarce.

—WILLIAM CLARK (1804)

The Lord knows that I am not a handsome man, nor one gifted with social graces. So in my youth the Apollos of this world often awed me. Tonight, out to dinner, I met one of them again. When I first met him, twenty years ago, he was already a high government official, and exuded success at every pore. I remember how he dazzled me. But since then I have learned that it pays to examine this type with particular attention to their mental horse power. This one proved to be just another Body by Fisher.

—JAMES WEBB YOUNG (1942)

SEPTEMBER 11

*H*ere, the man who left us with the horses, 22 days ago, . . . joined us, nearly starved to death. He had been twelve days without anything to eat but grapes and one rabbit, which he killed by shooting a piece of hard stick in place of a ball. This man, supposing the boat to be ahead, pushed on as long as he could. When he became weak and feeble, determined to lay by and wait for a trading boat, which is expected, keeping one horse for the last recourse. Thus a man had like to have starved to death in a land of plenty for the want of bullets or something to kill his meat.

—WILLIAM CLARK (1804)

*O*n the Mississippi broad turbin stream. Sand bars, low alluvial shores with forests . . . streaming files of ducks & geese . . . corn field where crops of corn have been raised for 28 years successively, without manure—rich covering. . . . Travellers—some adventurers embark without money—are put ashore at wood piles—remain till next boat comes along—hoist a handkerchief on pole—taken on board boat under way—too late to set them ashore, carry them to next pile. So they work their way from wood pile to wood pile. . . . Go to

332

farm house. Woman spinning—young lad sitting idle—their beds in room full of negro children. Fat little gourd shaped one cries—the lad tells another child to amuse it by rolling ball on floor. Have lived here 33 years. Man says he never struck a negro since he was a boy [and] would not sell one unless the negro wished to go away.

—WASHINGTON IRVING (1832)

*L*ast night a gallows was erected in front of William Lloyd Garrison's house in Brighton St, with two nooses, headed "by order of Judge Lynch": it drew many people to it, and at 10 oclock was taken down.

—BRADLEY N. CUMINGS (1835)

*B*idding all good bye at dusk we took to the road again. The road becomes terribly heavy with sand. No wonder the exhausted mules could not drag the train along. The stench of dead oxen still assails us at frequent intervals. . . . At about 10:30 we caught sight of trees that denoted water and soon came to the river bank. . . . The desert was past at last and we were in paradise. While we were resting on the bank McCollum struggled up crying "water! water!" I called him to come to us, took our large canteen to the water's edge, filled it and brought it up to him. He grasped it convulsively—and to my caution to drink judiciously he replied—"Yes, I will drink judiciously, *but I will drink it all,*"—and he did. . . . Guided by a light in a grove of cottonwoods, we found the advanced "Pioneers," bivouacked and mostly asleep. . . . Got some hard bread, broiled a slice of bacon on the coals and ate a slight repast. Then spread our blankets under the trees near the fire, and slept soundly, with fatigue for an effectual opiate.

—BERNARD J. REID (1849)

*I*n an odd mood all day. I did not want others. I tried to keep a laughing outside. I went along as though I was part of others but was not. I worked. I went with Paul for a walk. I dug up some roots of butterfly weed. I played cards with the others in the evening. All of my association with others was on the surface only.

—SHERWOOD ANDERSON (1937)

SEPTEMBER 12

I wonder that every colored person is not a misanthrope. Surely we have everything to make us hate mankind. I have met girls in the schoolroom—they have been thoroughly kind and cordial to me,—perhaps the next day met them in the street—they feared to recognize me; these I can but regard now with scorn and contempt. . . . These are but trifles, certainly, to the great, public wrongs which we as a people are obliged to endure. But to those who experience them, these apparent trifles are most wearing and discouraging; even to the child's mind they reveal volumes of deceit and heartlessness, and early teach a lesson of suspicion and distrust.

—CHARLOTTE FORTEN (1855)

*2*50th anniversary of settlement of C[oncord]. grand rally. Dinner & reception. Lowell, Curtis, Evarts, Gov. Robinson & the town dignitaries out in full force. I wished thier manners & grammer better, but beside Lowell & Curtis few would shine. . . . Outsiders asked why Miss A[lcott] was never invited to sit among the honored ones at such times? C[oncord] cant forgive her for not thinking it perfect.

—LOUISA MAY ALCOTT (1885)

*R*ead Browning last night in a private house to 130 people, the ladies in the majority. Have made speeches several times at banquets where half were ladies. Have read & lectured a good many times at matines, where of course ladies were largely in the majority. In all such cases, failure may be counted upon. . . . For several reasons. To begin with, ladies are cowards about expressing their feelings before folk; men *become* cowards in the presence of ladies. . . . The Elmira Reformatory contains 850 convicts, who are there for all manner of crimes. People go there & lecture, read, or make speeches. . . . Afterward, they always say that for a splendid audience give them a housefull of convicts. . . . The whole secret lies in the absence of ladies. Any 850 men would be just as inspiring, where no dampening female person was in sight, with her heart full of emotion & her determined repression choking it down & keeping the signs of it from showing on the outside. There is more inspiration in an audience of male corpses than in a packed multitude of the livest & brightest women that ever walked.

—MARK TWAIN (1888)

SEPTEMBER 13

I should think that the good people of this little town [in Kansas] never saw a woman dressed in the short dress before. . . . One lady, in a very friendly manner, has advised me to lay off my short dress while I remain here, as it is not fashionable. But fashion and show hold so small a place in my mind now, that to please a few fastidious ladies for the few days I may remain here, would not recompense me for the bondage I should submit myself to in wearing long dresses, when I can go so nimbly around in my short, loose, and easy dress, to bring water, pick up chips, bring in wood, milk, *to get milk*, cook in the kitchen, wait upon the sick. . . . Long dresses will do for afternoons, when all the work is done up, for drawing-rooms, parlors, and the inactive—but to energetic, active women, who want to live for health, and the good that they can do, I would say, don the Bloomer!

—MIRIAM DAVIS COLT (1856)

I have just returned from attending the evening service at the "Mutes" church in 18th St. near corner of 5th Avenue. The services were conducted by Revd. Mr Gallaudet in the sign language. . . . a most impressive & solemn service. . . . It is said to be the only church of the kind in the world. It is a wonderful thing & intensely interesting to see these poor unfortunates, by these humane institutions brought into communion with their maker through the instrumentality of those holy scriptures, which otherwise would have been to them "a sealed book & a dead letter." Before service began they were conversing freely among themselves by their silent sign language but after it commenced, all were attentive and apparently absorbed in what was going on.

—HENRY RAVENAL (1860)

*L*ast Friday morning Mr Harris left his home for the hard and perilous life of a soldier. This is the first time since he started that I have felt sufficiently composed to write a sentence. Why should I tremble so? His life is in the hands of God in all cases and surely he is safer at the post of duty than elsewhere. Last night we had thunder, lightning and a little rain.

—EMILY HARRIS (1863)

SEPTEMBER 14

*Y*esterday Mr. Mann's Address on Education . . . was full of the modern gloomy view of our democratical institutions. . . . Sad it was to see the death-cold convention . . . as they sat shivering, a handful of pale men and women in a large church, for it seems the Law has touched the business of Education with the point of its pen, and instantly it has frozen stiff in the universal congelation of society. . . . We are shut up in schools and college recitation rooms for ten or fifteen years, and come out at last with a bellyful of words and do not know a thing. We cannot use our hands, or our legs, or our eyes, or our arms. We do not know an edible root in the woods. We cannot tell our course by the stars, nor the hour of the day by the sun. It is well if we can swim and skate. We are afraid of a horse, of a cow, of a dog, of a cat, of a spider. Far better was the Roman rule to teach a boy nothing that he could not learn standing.

—RALPH WALDO EMERSON (1839)

Mr. Parker Pillsbury came, and we talked about the poor slaves. I had a music lesson with Miss P. I hate her, she is so fussy. I ran in the wind and played be a horse, and had a lovely time in the woods with Anna and Lizzie. We were fairies, and made gowns and paper wings. I "flied" the highest of all. In the evening they talked about travelling. I thought about Father going to England. . . . It rained when I went to bed, and made a pretty noise on the roof.

—LOUISA MAY ALCOTT (1843)

We arrived at the place where the Donner Party perished, having lost their way and being snowed in . . . and died from want of food . . . in 1846. Two log cabins, bones of human beings and animals, tops of the trees being cut off the depth of snow, was all that was left to tell the tale of that ill-fated party, their sufferings and sorrow. . . . We crossed the summit of the Sierra Nevada. It was night when we reached the top, and never shall I forget our descent to the place where we are now en-

337

camped—our tedious march with pine knots blazing in the darkness and the tall, majestic pines towering above our heads.

—SALLIE HESTER (1849)

*A*s we came out of the St. Regis there were millions awaiting [General Jonathan] Wainwright; and motorcycles streaking and screaming up the avenue. I was sorry not to stay to see it; now there is only MacArthur left for me to observe the welcome of.

—GLENWAY WESCOTT (1945)

SEPTEMBER 15

*H*arry Meigs had made up his mind to give up the law & to study divinity. . . . No wonder, for beyond general principles, the learning necessary for practice is a dry mass of details of no interest and the practice itself has become little better than a mere trade under the degrading influence of democracy. . . . The bar & the bench, too, have fallen very far below the dignified & respectable position it held when I knew it thirty years ago. . . . The courtroom, in those days, every morning when the bar assembled, was like a drawingroom, filled with elegantly dressed gentlemen of courtly & refined manners. . . . All is now changed—culture, elegance, refinement, courtesy, eloquence, wit, scholarship have vanished.

—SIDNEY GEORGE FISHER (1869)

I had a tooth out the other day, curious and interesting, like a lifetime; first, the long-drawn drag, then the twist of the hand and the crack of doom! The dentist seized my face in his two hands and exclaimed: "Bravo, Miss James!" and

338

Katherine and Nurse, shaking of knee and pale of cheek, went on about my "heroism," whilst I, serenely wadded in that sensational paralysis which attends all the simple rudimentary sensations and experiences common to man, whether tearing of the flesh or of the affections, laughed and laughed at 'em. As long as one doesn't break in two in the middle, I never have been able to see where the "heroism" comes in.

—ALICE JAMES (1890)

*M*ost of the morning on correspondence. The Primitive Baptists were holding a big Assembly in Troutdale and we went to hear the preaching and dine outdoors with the Baptists. The preaching was a half wild song. There was a great crowd of mountain people.

—SHERWOOD ANDERSON (1940)

SEPTEMBER 16

A company of troops passed the church while we were reciting our bible lesson. It is strange that we can so soon become so accustomed to such sights that in a very short time we cease to feel any peculiar emotion when we see men marching on to slaughter their fellow men—or be slaughtered themselves. War has a deadening influence on every feeling of the heart.

—JOHN PALMER FINLEY (1861)

*T*he old bromide about the South "still fighting the Civil War" don't hold up so good. It was suggested to the Northern boys at their reunion the other day that they hold a joint reunion with the Southerners. Well, they just pulled out their whiskers and started firing 'em at the suggester. Said they would never meet 'em till the South admitted they was wrong. So that is one merger that is off indefinitely. The North got all the pensions and the postoffices. They don't need anything else.

—WILL ROGERS (1929)

$\mathcal{O}$n the way to the theatre a man, when we tooted our horn, asking him to move over so we could round the corner . . . swore at us so violently, calling us such filthy names, that even Julie, rougher and tougher than me, was shocked. . . . This sort of filthy abuse, this violence, this wrath lies so close under the surface in American life. Julie and I moved on . . . in shocked sober silence. . . . To consciously fix limitations of the self (accepting the boundaries of the self) is an act of locating the self (situating). Few Americans will do this, preferring instead to live in hopes of another or "better" self. Thus the self never grows, never functions or realizes itself.

—CLIFFORD ODETS (1940)

SEPTEMBER 17

$\mathcal{M}$et in Convention, when the Constitution received the unanimous assent of 11 States and Colo. Hamilton's from New York (the only delegate from thence in Convention), and was subscribed to by every Member present except Govr. Randolph and Colo. Mason from Virginia, and Mr. Gerry from Massachusetts. The business being thus closed, the Members adjourned to the City Tavern, dined together and took a cordial leave of each other; after which I returned to my lodgings, did some business with, and received the papers from the Secretary of the Convention, and retired to meditate on the momentous w[or]k which had been executed, after not less than five, for a large part of the time Six, and sometimes 7 hours sitting every day, [except] sundays and the ten days adjournment to give a comee. opportunity and time to arrange the business, for more than four months.

—GEORGE WASHINGTON (1787)

*F*red & sister Addie, and I went over to and thro' their Cotton-field, this afternoon; it is a fine one. . . . We are both very much in love with Oklahoma, but the red soil looks odd to us; and all the streams we crossed in coming looked like rivers of red ink and I could not help laughing at the sight; but there had just been heavy rains, was why; they tell us the streams are clear as any water, except after a rain. But even nature tells us, it is the Redmen's country, for the rich dark *green* of the Cotton-fields and prairies the brilliant *yellow* of the wild flowers and the flaming *scarlet* of the soil, are the colors of his War-paints.

—MARTHA FARNSWORTH (1908)

*W*ent to the house of Dolores del Rio in Bel Air . . . to have dinner with her and Orson Welles, her light of love. . . . He was very gracious and articulate. . . . But he has a peculiarly American audacity. Of other people he said just what he thought of them, with scorn and derision. . . . I liked best when he suddenly said of himself, "I have a touch of rhinestones in my blood," meaning he is part-charlatan. . . . I found that I disagreed with everything Welles said and like him in spite of that. He is a very octopus of ego, but for all of that there is a good side to him. . . . A communion of intelligence is possible with him; finally, too, he also is in opposition to the values around him, even though they may finally swallow him up.

—CLIFFORD ODETS (1940)

341

SEPTEMBER 18

$\mathcal{T}$o Paterson's and back, six miles. There I saw a young woman who had had the jerks two years and was very wicked (her parents were Baptists). I told her I believed the jerks would never leave her until she prayed in earnest to God. She said it would be time enough for her several years hence and said the jerks came from the devil and would go back to him again. I told her to pray; or I did not know but what the jerks would kill her and she would go to hell. She said she wished I might go to hell.

—JOHN EARLY (1807)

$\mathcal{O}$ne day a Puerto Rican friend of mine . . . came out here, and was pleased to see my various wisteria on the garage, up on one corner of the house, and in the wild acre. "Oh, my mother in Puerto Rico loves wisteria, she has many vines and bushes." "Alas, mine almost never blossoms. Does your mother know what to do about that?" "Yes, she does. . . . She has the Negro boys whip it!" Monroe has tried something like this in the past, I mean just conversationally, to no avail.

—GLENWAY WESCOTT (1955)

SEPTEMBER 19

$\mathcal{P}$revented by Rain (much of which fell in the Night) from setting off till about 8 oclock, when it ceased and promising to be fair, we departed, baited at Wilmington, dined at Christiana bridge and lodged at the head of Elk. At the bridge near to which (I narrowly escaped an ugly accidt. to my Chariot and horses) my horses (two of them) and Carriage had a very narrow escape. For the Rain which had fallen the preceding evening having swelled the water considerably, there was no

342

fording it safely, I was reduced to the necessity therefore of remaining on the other side or of attempting to cross on an old, rotten and long disused bridge. Being anxious to get on I preferred the latter, and in the attempt one of my horses fell 15 feet at least, the other very near following, which had (had it happened) would have taken the Carriage with baggage along with him and destroyed the whole effectually. However by prompt assistance of some people at a Mill just by and great exertion, the first horse was disengaged from his harness, the 2d. prevented from going quite through and drawn off and the Carriage rescued from hurt.

—GEORGE WASHINGTON (1787)

*W*hat is the final cause of mosquitoes? Why have they this power to torment the best men, the sweetest & loveliest women, & innocent children? These are the questions that will constantly arise to perplex & sadden thoughtful minds in things more important than mosquitoes.

—SIDNEY GEORGE FISHER (1869)

*T*here is an old well and well-house in our farmyard, and the old oaken bucket still hangs there. Nowadays we pump water from it and carry it under pressure to the house. When the pump goes wrong, and I have to carry water and heat it for a shave, I ain't fit to live with. But when I come in from the orchard after a morning's work, a drink still tastes sweeter when hauled up by hand.

—JAMES WEBB YOUNG (1942)

SEPTEMBER 20

*A*bout a mile from town I met a monstruous appearance. . . . It was a carter driving his cart along the road who

343

seemed to be half man, half woman. All above from the crown of his head to the girdle seemed quite masculine, the creature having a great, hideous, unshorn black beard and strong course features, a slouch hat, cloth jacket, and great brawny fists, but below the girdle there was nothing to be seen but petticoats, a white apron, and the exact shape of a woman with relation to broad, round buttocks. I would have given something to have seen this creature turned topsy turvy, to have known whether or not it was an hermaphrodite, having often heard of such animals but never having seen any to my knowledge; but I thought it most prudent to pass by peaceably, asking no questions lest it should prove the devil in disguise. Some miles farther I met two handsome country girls and enquired the road of them. One seemed fearfull, and the other was very forward and brisk. I liked the humour and vivacity of the latter and lighted from my horse as if I had been going to salute her, but they both set up a scream and run off like wild bucks into the woods.

—ALEXANDER HAMILTON (1744)

I walked in the burying-yard, and viewed the granite tombstones erected over the graves of my ancestors by my father. Henry Adams, the first of the family, who came from England; Joseph Adams, Sr., and Abigail Baxter, his wife; Joseph Adams, Jr., and Hannah Bass, his second wife; John Adams, Sr., my father's father, and Susannah Boylston, his wife. Four generations, of whom very little more is known than is recorded upon these stones. There are three succeeding generations of us now living. Pass another century, and we shall all be mouldering in the same dust, or resolved into the same elements. Who then of our posterity shall visit this yard? And what shall he read engraved upon the stones? This is known only to the Creator of all. The record may be longer. May it be of as blameless lives!

—JOHN QUINCY ADAMS (1824)

[In upstate New York] *C*all on Mr. Snyder County clerk. Inspect old treaties in Dutch & English with Indians tied by

344

Wampum belt—Records &c Kept in great . . . chest with curious, cumbersom old dutch steel lock. . . . Among the records
are accounts of trials &c in what concerned Hildyonda Van
Sleghenhorst. She once Kept a Store—was summoned to appear in court [and] asked if ready for trial. Yes if Judge would
swear & kiss the book that he would decide rightly between
all parties; said he had sworn so when he had entered upon
office—well she thot he could have no objection to swearing
again by way of refreshing his memory. . . . She sues a boy
for breaking her window with a pebble. [The] stone appears
to have been a Shrew.

—Washington Irving (1833)

*T*he fact detached is ugly. Replace it in its series of cause
and effect, and it is beautiful. Putrefaction is loathsome; but
putrefaction seen as a step in the circle of nature, pleases.

—Ralph Waldo Emerson (1838)

SEPTEMBER 21

*H*ad a very striking instance of the frailty of human nature; as I was passing by a tent door two men brought one
out to all appearance dead; however he breathed once more &
expired, this was the second breath, after they perceived any
alteration in him; he was sitting at the table, dining upon a
Beef stake, as well, as he had been for some days, thus from
a state of usual health, two breaths, landed him in the Eternal world. By instances of this kind, we learn the uncertainty
of Life.

—Lewis Beebe (1776)

345

[Immigrating to New York] *N*ine-thirty o'clock. Rockets in the air. Gun fired. Ten-twenty-five o'clock: anchored in the channel. Passengers checked until Wed. 22 at 8 o'clock by customs inspectors. Not until eleven-thirty o'clock by steamboat to Castel Garden, entered my name; then to the Sackspear [Shakespeare] Hotel. . . . I paid particular attention to the Hirschberg family: father, mother, three daughters, and a brother-in-law, who were to go to Milwoke. . . . But man proposes and God disposes, for I had hardly arrived in Castel Garden when I became separated from this family. In spite of my searching I could not find the family, for New York is altogether too big to find anyone. This noise, this tumult, rattling traffic, drove me out of my mind. Without thinking it over too much, I bought a ticket . . . in order to take the morning train on the Twenty-seventh to Chicago.

—JACOB SAUL LANZIT (1858)

*T*he weather has been very fine and warm for some weeks. I have been trying to improve this weather by pulling fodder and cutting hay. . . . My hogs are doing well. I am feeding well to fatten them. Bacon is high. I have sold some at 20 cents. I think bacon will be high this fall and I intend to make all I can. My pigs are beautiful.

—DAVID GOLIGHTLY HARRIS (1861)

SEPTEMBER 22

*A*t night we had a meeting at Mr. Thompson's. Christians shouted and jumped and jerked and rolled . . . for three or four hours. . . . The Lord of all mercies came to the deliverance of the above young woman who only the week before wished I might go to hell. She had the most powerful manifestation I ever saw. She leaped from the floor and jumped and shouted and jerked all night and until I left the next day at ten o'clock. I hardly think, besides many others, I ever saw the like before.

—JOHN EARLY (1807)

A special Cabinet-meeting. The subject was the Proclamation for emancipating the slaves after a certain date, in States that shall then be in rebellion. For several weeks the subject has been suspended, but the President says never lost sight of. When it was submitted, and now in taking up the Proclamation, the President stated that the question was finally decided, the act and the consequences were his, but that he felt it due to us to make us acquainted with the fact and to invite criticism on the paper which he had prepared. . . . He remarked that he had made a vow, a covenant, that if God gave us the victory in the approaching battle, he would consider it an indication of Divine will, and that it was his duty to move forward in the cause of emancipation. It might be thought strange, he said, that he had in this way submitted the disposal of matters when the way was not clear to his mind what he should do. God had decided this question in favor of the slaves.

—GIDEON WELLES (1862)

*W*as it ominous that I should find my pen split when I took it up to write tonight? In these troublous times how superstitious we become. Shall I dare hope that this new Journal which I am commencing will record Peace, an independent Southern Confederacy? Truly the skies are gloomy and the heavy storm appears ready to discharge its thunders in our very midst. Yet how calm, how indifferent we are—we laugh, we smile, we talk, we jest, just as tho no enemy were at our door. And yet the idea has several times suggested itself to me that someday I would have to aid in earning my own support. We have made no arrangement whatever for such a contingency.

—ELLA THOMAS (1864)

347

*S*unk deeply into the blues—the black dog constantly on my back, hating the summer's end, feeling my own inefficiency. It seems to me that I have done nothing. Still cold but the skies clear. Why do I always feel I must be accomplishing?

—SHERWOOD ANDERSON (1938)

SEPTEMBER 23

*A*n Awfull Providence yesterday at Mr. Checkleys meeting House in Boston. Three or Four Persons kill'd in the crowd, and many wounded—among the wounded sister Esther and her Dauter. Mr. Whitefield preaches Twice every Day to the astonishment of all.

—EBENEZER PARKMAN (1740)

*W*atertown Miller[ite] Meeting, which I went to with White. At a private house. A dozen or so of men and oldish women were seated silently about the room. We sat down, and for a long time the silence was interrupted only by sighs and groans. At length a big stout fellow struck up a hymn, which was fervently sung by all. Then they dropped on their knees, while another prayed aloud in a hasty and earnest manner, responded to by sighs, exclamations, and cries of "Amen." Several other prayers were made. . . . All rose from their knees. A moment after, the large man by the table rose slowly, and fixing his eyes on vacuity, exclaimed: "How bright the vision! Oh, how long shall this bright hour delay?". . . . He was speaking from the immediate impulse of the holy spirit within him, and his discourse was rambling and bungling enough. He said he once went out West; and described, a la Yankee, the difficulties he encountered, and drew a parallel between his journey and the Christian heavenly journey. . . . Several speakers followed him. One woman modestly remarked that it was easy to endure the cross and the stake,

348

and such like great evils, but it tried the Christian's soul when it came to parting with little ornaments and dresses. . . . With screams, ejaculations, and prayers, the meeting was going on when we left.

—FRANCIS PARKMAN (1844)

*C*harles, Caro and Lyman were down this P.M. to attend Tom Thumb's levee. . . . A large audience was in attendance. A case containing his presents was on the table. . . . A frame was at one end of the table, a small brass staircase, with side rails, two small chairs about 8 or 10 inches high, and a small sofa, red cushioned, 18 inches, I should judge, long. He made his appearance in the hands of Barnum, raised above the crowd, and shouting in a childish but clear voice, "How do you do, *lad*dies and gentle-men." My first emotion and which occurred to me several times after was of surprise that such a morsel, a mere crumb of humanity could be the resident of a soul! Two feet, three inches! Then I was bewildered in wonder in regard to his physiological formation. . . . His frame was elegantly proportioned and extremely agile and for his size graceful in his movements.

—BENJAMIN BROWNE FOSTER (1847)

SEPTEMBER 24

*I*n a closet of my mother's bed-chamber, there was . . . a small edition, in two volumes, of Milton's *Paradise Lost*, which, I attempted ten times to read, and never could get through half a book. I might as well have attempted to read Homer before I had learnt the Greek alphabet. I was mortified, even to the shedding of solitary tears, that I could not even conceive what it was that my father and mother admired so much in that book, and yet I was ashamed to ask them an explanation. I smoked tobacco and read Milton at the same time, and from the same motive—to find out what was the recondite charm in them which gave my father so much pleasure. After making myself four or five times sick with smoking, I mastered that accomplishment, and acquired a habit which, thirty years afterwards, I had much more difficulty in breaking off. But I did not master Milton. I was nearly thirty when I first read the *Paradise Lost* with delight and astonishment. But of late years I have lost the relish for fiction. I see nothing with sympathy but men, women, and children of flesh and blood.

—JOHN QUINCY ADAMS (1829)

*T*ook an ambulance and drove off over the Sharpsburg turnpike. . . . We soon entered an atmosphere pervaded by the scent of the battlefield—the bloody and memorable field of Antietam ("Antee'tum") Creek. Long lines of trenches marked the burial places; scores of dead horses, swollen, with their limbs protruding stiffly at strange angles, and the ground at their noses blackened with hemorrhage, lay all around. Sharpsburg, a commonplace little village, was scarified with shot. In one little brick house I counted more than a dozen shot-holes, cleanly made, probably by rifle projectiles. . . . Proceeded in the direction of Keedysville and French's Division Hospital. . . . Horrible congregation of wounded men there and at Porter's—our men and rebel prisoners both—on straw, in their bloody stiffened clothes mostly, some in barns and cowhouses, some in the open air. It was fearful to see; Gustave Dore's pictures embodied in shivering, agonizing, suppurating flesh and blood.

—GEORGE TEMPLETON STRONG (1862)

*C*old; and plains, plains, plainier than ever. The single track and the monotonous flat brown landscape depress Papa and make him nervous. We had occasional mirages today just like on the sea and for hours we saw no human habitation or any sign that man had ever been on this desolate stretch of prairie before, except the straight line of track behind us. . . .

Once or twice we caught a glimpse of a little shabby tent near the track with a woman or child peering through the canvas opening at the train coming through the driving snow. Near it might be a prairie wagon and huddled together the poor horses, so thin and cold. Or we might see a lonely cowboy— not at all picturesque—doubled over on his forlorn pony, fighting against the snow. . . . We got out at the tiny Log Station, and looked all around at the bold mountains on all sides. Three Indians were coming slowly down the road on their ponies and I pointed my Kodak at them. . . . My! they were mad, and I was quite afraid of them but I snapped them again. I thought they would shoot me but they contented themselves with sticking out their tongues and making faces.

—MARIAN LAWRENCE PEABODY (1901)

SEPTEMBER 25

This day, till twelve o'clock, the road was mighty quiet, when Hobson Jones came riding along. About that time he made a stop at our door, and said the British were at Skippack road; that we should soon see their light horse, and [that] a party of Hessians had actually turn'd into our lane. My Dadda and Mamma gave it the credit it deserv'd, for he does not keep strictly to the truth in all respects; but the delicate, chicken-hearted Liddy and I were wretchedly scar'd. We cou'd say nothing but "Oh! what shall we do? What will become of us?" These questions only augmented the terror we were in. Well, the fright went off. We saw no light horse or Hessians.

—SALLY WISTER (1777)

Hemmed my suit skirt in the dense fog and mended my red gown. My boy is out, renewing old acquaintances and telling them lies, no doubt, of the big world about which they

351

care nothing. Most of them have seen it anyway. But few of them know where they were, beyond remembering the docks and the waterfront ginmills. . . . Mother B. is bright and smart and jolly. She was the favorite of her father's ten children, the tom-boy who would help him launch vessels, and she can still row a boat so well that she made Fred give her the oars to the dory yesterday when he was setting her on the island to visit her brother Orrin. Still she wouldn't eat the famous strawberries in Rio in December, because at home they were out of season, and she still can't understand why sailing south from the equator isn't easier than sailing the other way because it's downhill all the way. I do believe, though, that she's joshing me, and I'd better be a bit less proud of my brilliance in the company of these people, who like to act ignorant when they really are quite adept, in their own way, at things that matter to them.

—Dorothea Moulton Balano (1911)

SEPTEMBER 26

I was standing in the kitchen about 12, when somebody came to me in a hurry, screaming, "Sally, Sally, here are the light horse!" This was by far the greatest fright I had endured; fear tack'd wings to my feet; I was at the house in a moment; at the porch I stopt, and it really was the light horse. . . . They rode up to the door and halted, and enquired if we had horses to sell. . . . The officer and men behav'd perfectly civil; the first drank two glasses of wine, rode away, bidding his men follow, which, after adieus in number, they did. . . . The men, to our great joy, were Americans, and but 4 in all. What made us imagine them British, they wore blue and red, which with us is not common.

—Sally Wister (1777)

The squaws are cheerful, fine-looking women, not handsome; high cheeks; dressed in skins; a petticoat and robe, which folds back over their shoulder, with long wool. Do all their laborious work, and, I may say, perfect slaves to the men. . . . After a smoke had taken place, and a short harangue to his people, we were requested to take the meal, and they put before us the dog which they had been cooking, and pemmican, and ground potato in several platters. Pemmican is buffalo meat dried or jerked, pounded, and mixed with grease, raw. Dog, Sioux think great dish, used on festivals. Ate little of dog—pemmican and potato good.

—WILLIAM CLARK (1804)

Rode down to French Church walk with my daughter & accompanied her to ye Swan Steam boat. Meet there Wash[ington] Irving & H. Brevoort. Irving professes himself convinced that Democracy is the only true system & expreses his astonishment after 17 years residence in various parts of Europe to see the superiority in our state of Society. . . . The contrast between the misery of some parts of Europe and the discontents & anxieties of all, with the general animation, cheerful pressing on to something better ahead & enjoyment of the present which appeared every where in this country was amazing to himself & kept him in a fever of excitement & exultation.

—WILLIAM DUNLAP (1833)

Called on Mr. Ripley, whom I found in the 4th story of a huge dirty building, attained by winding, narrow, dirty stairs, amid the whissing & clanking of steam machinery, sitting in his shirt sleeves, paragraphing & clipping for the Tribune. Nowhere is the contrast between circumstances & influence greater, than in the office of an editor in N. York. Wielding an influence wh. hardly has its superior in the Republic, the editors of the leading journals still write in their little closets, in fourth stories, on pine tables, amid noise, dirt & confusion.

—RICHARD HENRY DANA (1849)

$\mathscr{M}$r Fowler leaves this morning with the rest of the volunteers for the fort. He leaves an excellent wife and three small children the youngest not 4 weeks old. No wonder our breakfast is eaten in silence. Here is an intelligent and conscientious young husband and father about to sever at least for a long time and very likely for ever the dearest earthly ties. I wish I could go too.

—MITCHELL JACKSON (1861)

$\mathscr{I}$ was sick of the Asthma last night. I sat up for 4 successive hours, and Papa made me smoke a cigar.

—THEODORE ROOSEVELT (1869)

SEPTEMBER 27

$\mathscr{A}$n avenging God is surely witnessing the affairs of men. . . . A perfect storm has been raging today, so much so that it sometimes required our united exertions to keep our tent from being blown away. The large hospital tent of our Regt. was blown down while it was full of sick. They, however were immediately removed, but not until they were completely drenched. . . . So common has death become, that when a man dies, he is as soon forgotten. Yesterday I passed by the graveyard of our Regt., it being in a line of the timber which we were felling as a blockade. A few tall hemlock pines were left around them, in respect for the dead. They lie far from the road, in a secluded spot. This may possibly be our fighting ground. The din and clangor of battle may sweep over them, as opposing squadrons meet in terrible combat. But they will sleep on. In that bright sphere their pure souls shall forever stand unmoved during the wreck of time, and crush of worlds.

—JAMES E. HALL (1861)

The girls have had some amusing adventures. While boarding in Lynchburg with a party of refugees, they began to perceive that the people were not as kindly disposed to refugees as they were in other places, and even displayed their disapproval when the wanderers ventured to occupy their pews in church. One Sunday in the Rev. Mr. Kimble's church a party of these girls had seated themselves, when the pastor rose and said that the congregation were incommoded by having their seats occupied by strangers, and that for the future the refugees would find seats in the gallery. On this they all rose and went to the gallery. After they were seated the pastor gave out the hymn. His selection proved a very unfortunate one, being "Rise my soul and stretch thy wings," when the two last lines of the first stanza were read. "Haste my soul; Oh! haste away/To seats prepared above." There was a titter in the gallery, and the faces of pastor and congregation reddened perceptibly. The next Sunday a church warden met the refugees at the door and invited them into the pews, but the girls told them they preferred "The seats prepared above."

—CORNELIA PEAKE MCDONALD (1862)

A fine day at the races. I took a vacation and went early. It's nice in the morning, seeing the horses work. I sat in the betting shed. The races in the p.m. were all close and exciting. I bet a little and then quit. Came back here early. There was a fight, two young drunken country boys in the street under my window.

—SHERWOOD ANDERSON (1939)

SEPTEMBER 28

We march'd to Norwark thiss Day. The houses Being much Crouded we was obligd to teak Up our Quarters in an old shop amongst the Rubish & about mid Night I was Awaked By something Puling me & a Voice Crying turn out Dam you, Look here see and Behold. I Looked & saw five fat Geese. Some was fit for the Cook. The others was a Dressing By the fire side & Some Good Potatoes for sauce for Goos that Came to our Loging. I Eat a hearty meal, Asking no Questions with the Rest of my Brother Soldiers who Seamed Hearty in the Cause of Liberty. By the Rhoad in the morning we Eat the fragments & Rested in our hut or Rather Den of Th—fs.

—JOHN SMITH (1776)

*H*ad a conversation with [Rives?] about South Carolina. Amazed at his ignorance of statistical facts. Spoke of Vermont as having one hundred thousand souls!! And yet this description of men form the mass of the talkers in this world. If one did not know that the people were of use negatively, in governments, by preventing abuses, one might be tempted to distrust the advantage of popular forms, from such specimens!

—JAMES FENIMORE COOPER (1830)

*M*ud never seems to faze the Ford. Dad used to have a big touring car. Because the Model T is so much simpler to handle and repair, he traded for it when I started driving us to town to school. He intended to buy a new touring car for himself but hasn't been able to afford it. I just hope the Model T keeps running until good times come again. If it doesn't, we are out of luck. Even as it is, I have to drive the kids to school in the horse and buggy several days each fall.

—ANN MARIE LOW (1929)

SEPTEMBER 29

*T*oday came to the Executive Mansion an assembly of cold-water men & cold-water women to make a temperance speech at the Tycoon & receive a response. They filed into the East Room looking blue & thin in the keen autumnal air; Cooper, my coachman, who was about half tight, gazing at them with an air of complacent contempt and mild wonder. Three blue-skinned damsels did Love, Purity, & Fidelity in Red, White & Blue gowns. A few invalid soldiers stumped along in the dismal procession. They made a long speech at the Tycoon in which they called Intemperance the cause of our defeats. He could not see it, as the rebels drink more & worse whisky than we do. They filed off drearily to a collation of cold water & green apples, & then home to mulligrubs.

—JOHN HAY (1863)

*B*reakfasted with Dave in the new breakfast room and then we went to Harlem, where we got into a launch and went up the Hudson to see the floats of Victory and Peace. The streets and cars were crowded everywhere and there were pictures of Dewey in every shop window and wherever one looked. Staging and decorations were going up all around. The river we found very rough and Dave and the engineer tried to advise the launch owner how to steer it, and were a good deal worried I think. I was cowering in a corner in all the wraps I could find but in spite of this I was soaking wet. However, we saw the floats and very *few* did so, as that afternoon, even before the fleet got there, the wind smashed Victory and decapitated her down to the waist.

—MARIAN LAWRENCE PEABODY (1899)

[In Hollywood] *I*n the late afternoon, there was a cocktail party given by Dotty Parker. . . . In one silent empty room there was enough food—whole turkeys and hams—for a regiment. Among those present were . . . : Judith Anderson, looking as if she had just gotten out of bed, having slept on a crocheted pillow slip; the former Mrs. Jock Whitney yclept Liz, insolent . . . a red medal appearing on each handsome cheek when she is approaching the drunk stage; F. Scott Fitzgerald, pale, unhealthy, as if the tension of life had been

357

wrenched out of him . . . and many gabbling hens and gay cocks drinking up as quickly as they could be poured. . . . At the bitter end, Dotty Parker cornered me near the door and flatteringly said, "You are the first person I have talked to in three hours who doesn't make me want to vomit." I was too polite to say that I didn't believe her.

—CLIFFORD ODETS (1940)

SEPTEMBER 30

*E*very house along the line had been decorated somehow, and at 7 A.M. all their steps were filled with people, including our own, alas! Fortunately there was a small balcony on the second story and . . . from there . . . we saw them come around the corner from the Riverside Drive and then down the whole length of 72nd Street. After five hours of clapping and cheering and yelling until we were hoarse and dirty from chewing dust, I couldn't help thinking how must the soldiers feel who got up at 4:30 and were still marching at 7 P.M. . . . Then the sailors of the Olympia and the well-set-up Marines led by the one who drilled them this summer. They were followed by more sailors, marines and soldiers—an endless number and then the Rough Riders led by Teddy on horseback and grinning to beat the band. He got an ovation! The people in the next house to us threw a giant firecracker which landed right by his horse and made him jump wildly, entertaining the crowd immensely. . . . When a company of old Confederate veterans went by to the strains of Dixie, old Mrs. Morris nearly fell off the balcony in her excitement.

—MARIAN LAWRENCE PEABODY (1899)

*W*hy produce more poetry in New England, when the fields and the woods as well as the bookstores are saturated with it, when every chit of fifteen is pouring out verses as good as

Shakespeare's, to all intents and purposes? If you could get people to read it all, it would be something. But who does, except those that write it? Still, I make no complaint. I like to write poetry myself, and I especially like to sell it. Let others do the same, if they can.

—GAMALIEL BRADFORD (1921)

A Washington newspaper tried to do away with its society column; *Time* says the day of the socialite (a term it invented) is over; *The New Yorker* seems to agree; and a popular motion picture is built around the resentment of ordinary Englishmen to their upper crust. These are signs of the times which might seem to indicate a passing of the snob appeal, of society women testimonials, and such. But I have my doubts whether it is more than a spell of cloudy weather. Every society which the anthropologists have ever studied has had its *elite,* whose doings were a matter of great curiosity to the rest. Even in Russia today the engineers seem to be developing into such a class.

—JAMES WEBB YOUNG (1942)

~OCTOBER~

OCTOBER 1

*I*t seams we have troublesome times a Coming for there is great Disturbance a Broad in the earth & they say it is tea that caused it. So then if they will Quarel about such a trifling thing as that What must we expect But war & I think or at least fear it will be so.

—JEMIMA CONDICT (1774)

*J*ust put a fugitive slave, who has taken the name of Henry Williams, into the cars for Canada. He escaped from Stafford County, Virginia, to Boston last October; has been in Shadrach's place at the Cornhill Coffee-House; had been corresponding through an agent with his master, who is his father, about buying himself, his master asking six hundred dollars, but he having been able to raise only five hundred dollars. Heard that there were writs out for two Williamses, fugitives, and was informed by his fellow-servants and employer that Augerhole Burns and others of the police had called for him when he was out. Accordingly fled to Concord last night on foot, bringing a letter to our family from Mr. Lovejoy of Cambridge and another which Garrison had formerly given him on another occasion. He lodged with us, and waited in the house till funds were collected with which to forward him.

Intended to dispatch him at noon through to Burlington, but when I went to buy his ticket, saw one at the depot who looked and behaved so much like a Boston policeman that I did not venture that time. An intelligent and very well-behaved man, a mulatto.

—HENRY DAVID THOREAU (1851)

*H*ow shall we subsist this winter? There is not a supply of wood or coal in the city—and it is said that there are not adequate means of transporting it hither. Flour at sixteen dollars per barrel and bacon at seventy-five cents a pound threaten a famine. . . . The newspapers are printed on half sheets—and I think the publishers make money; the extras (published almost every day) are sold to the newsboys for ten cents and often sold by them for twenty-five cents. These are mere slips of paper, seldom containing more than a column . . . mostly made up from the Northern papers, brought hither by persons running the blockade. . . . We often get the first accounts of battles at a distance in this way, as our generals and our government are famed for a prudential reticence.

—JOHN BEAUCHAMP JONES (1862)

*W*hen [Theodore] Dreiser was warmed up, a bottle of Pommard drunk between us, he began to expound a theory of life that strangely enough sounded very fascistic. . . . : you are born with certain chemical elements in you which you can never change or condition. . . . What you are you have to be, he insisted. This made man very primal, I said. Dreiser's answer was that he is. Yet, he said, there are people of good heart and they must be good no matter what they do or say. It is they who fight the evil. In short, there is no free will, he said. . . . John Steinbeck came in and sat with us for ten minutes, shy, uneasy, off-balance. . . . After this Chaplin walked in, soft, feminine, saying "Sit down—you make me feel feminine," when Steinbeck stood up to shake hands. It was strange to see him move his arms and hands, handle his eyeglasses, lift his mouth as Chaplin does on the screen. I

361

know one thing: seldom meet an artist that you respect (whose work you admire) in real life—always a disappointing thing.

—CLIFFORD ODETS (1940)

OCTOBER 2

I have become a politician. I must immediately read the Constitution of the United States, also that of the State of New York, and make notes of those instruments respectively. . . . Find myself on several committees and quite likely to be a great statesman some day. . . . Governor Floyd [of Virginia] made a speech in front of the [New York] Exchange this afternoon. Large assemblage at first, but far from enthusiastic; reason good therefor—at least half were Fremonters or Fillmoreites. A few claquers did the cheering in a perfunctory way. Saw only one man whose applause seemed genuine, and that was a soap-lock, about a block and a half from the orator, who said, "That old feller is making a *big* speech, now I tell yer." People generally listened with sad civility, and I was glad of the example of good breeding and fair play shewn to a secessionist from Virginia, where a free-soil Cicero would be lynched. To my surprise the speech was read from manuscript.

—GEORGE TEMPLETON STRONG (1856)

[In the Sierra Nevadas] *F*ather decided he would not remain here so this morning the family left camp. . . . One and one half miles from camp crossed the summit. There was some difficulty in locating it, and at once we could see that all water ways led westward. The mountains are very heavily timbered and many of the trees come in so closely to the road that it takes a lot of dodging to miss all of them.

—HELEN CARPENTER (1857)

362

School is going well, and I enjoy life here, but there is nothing special to write about. This is one of those innumerable little towns along the Soo Railroad where nothing ever happens but morning, noon, and night. . . . The CCCs [Civilian Conservation Corps] are making a duck pond in the Big Pasture now. With Caterpillar tractors and about 100 men they are changing the course of the river a few feet in one place. There's nothing like improving on Nature. While they were about it they cut the pasture wires. I worked all day Sunday getting the cattle back in and fence fixed. . . . Dad is busy plowing firebreaks. There has been no rain this fall. He has not plowed firebreaks for many years, but is scared of the CCCs with their careless use of matches and cigarettes.

—ANN MARIE LOW (1935)

OCTOBER 3

About 8 in the morning, I with the post proceeded forward without observing anything remarkable; and about two, afternoon, arrived at the post's second stage, where the western post met him and exchanged letters. Here, having called for something to eat, the woman brought in a twisted thing like a cable, but something whiter; and laying it on the board, tugged for life to bring it into a capacity to spread; which having with great pains accomplished, she served in a dish of pork and cabbage, I suppose the remains of Dinner. The sauce was of a deep purple, which I thought was boiled in her dye kettle. . . . I, being hungry, got a little down; but my stomach was soon cloyed, and what cabbage I swallowed served me for a cud the whole day after.

—SARAH KEMBLE KNIGHT (1704)

The biggest nuisance, that seems so troublesome for me here [in America], are the so-called muskitos. That is a sort of fly, really gnats, that fly around buzzing at night and bite particularly the foreigner because he is new; he is more sensitive. My hands and face are full of bites.

—JACOB SAUL LANZIT (1858)

A fishing party to troll for Black Bass started about 9½ o.c. . . . The greatest excitement was occasioned by Governor [Salmon] Chase finding his line caught & held by what he at first supposed was a snag at the bottom—but which soon proved to be a very large 'Muscalunge.' The noble specimen of the Fish family in these waters on a tour of exploration rebelled stoutly against being brought before the Chief Justice of our nation. Perhaps he was a Canadian sympathizer with Southern rebels, & had a sense of guilt that made him fear to be thus summarily arraigned before one of such authority. . . . The Justice persisted in enforcing the 'Habeus Corpus' act, and the prisoner, caught but not captured—persisted in his resistance. Close up to the Boat he came. . . . But just then, Finance tampered with Justice and Muscalunge, availing of the interference, snapped asunder the line of Justice and . . . made the best speed he could for Canada by the under water rail road, carrying away with him as a trophy of his exploit, a most beautiful trolling hook.

—JAY COOKE (1865)

OCTOBER 4

The President of the United States and Cabinet passed through Utica and stopped for a half hour on their passage. Mr. Doolittle made the welcoming speech reading it from the manuscript. Mr. [Andrew] Johnson replied in a very forcible and expressive speech. He is a very thick set man, large bull head, broad, firm and decided mouth, but rather a dead eye. The reply was one of the best he made on the way. The street was crowded to see Grant and Farragut, whom they continually cheered. Mr. Johnson was decidedly snubbed. It is wonderful how he has lowered himself in the eyes of the people.

—JOHN WILLIAM STERLING (1866)

*P*ondering further on the place of the *elite,* it occurred to me that in all this talk about "freedoms," the one that nobody promises is the freedom to complete social equality with your neighbor. Both Democracy and Christianity originally implied that promise, but neither was able to fulfill it. Economic equality, political equality, and even equality in the sight of God are as nothing when they come up against that intangible but powerful thing called social status—as every woman knows.

—JAMES WEBB YOUNG (1942)

*M*arilyn Monroe appeared to me last night in a dream as a kind of fairy godmother. An occasion of "chatting" with audience much as the occasion with Eliot will turn out, I suppose. I spoke, almost in tears, of how much she and Arthur Miller meant to us, although they could, of course, not know us at all. She gave me an expert manicure. I had not washed my hair, and asked her about hairdressers, saying no matter where I went, they always imposed a horrid cut on me. She invited me to visit her during the Christmas holidays, promising a new, flowering life.

—SYLVIA PLATH (1959)

OCTOBER 5

*A*fter the fight on Thursday some of our men went over to the ground occupied by the Yankees. The ground was literally plowed up with our cannon shot. Much blood was seen. Several arms and bones were found along the edge of the field where they had drawn up their infantry. Many canteens and blankets were found. I have a spring socket bayonet. We found several dead. Among others was a young man who more particularly took attention. He was lying by the edge of the forest—having been struck by a cannon ball. His name was Abbott, from an Indiana Regt. In his portmanteau we found three twists of nicely braided hair, from his sisters. He had a furlough for several days. He had written a letter to his sisters saying he would not start home as soon as he expected, as the army was going down the mountain to whip the rebels, and he was going to accompany it so he could tell them about it when he came home. Poor fellow. His furlough was exchanged into a *fur-long*. I have the blues very badly today. Oh how I long to see my friends.

—JAMES E. HALL (1861)

*W*hat aroused me more than any political thing that I had read in many years was that Mr. Al Smith went up to Mr. Roosevelt and said, "Hello, you old potato!" Which seemed to me to be one of the most electrically inspired bits of wording ever I heard in politicks, and I think in itself will make more votes for Roosevelt than a thousand campaign speeches would.

—FRANKLIN PIERCE ADAMS (1932)

*L*unch at the Colony Club with Mrs. Gifford Pinchot. . . . She didn't know whether Franklin Roosevelt was quite right in his head—she and Gifford had gone to Hyde Park, and Roosevelt had talked very earnestly about the coal situation— Gifford said something about getting [Robert] Moses to sign. Roosevelt said, "But he *has* signed." Gifford made him call up Richberg at Washington to make sure. Roosevelt asked whether the Frick Company had signed and apparently got affirmative answers—then Gifford took the phone and asked whether he had agreed to the check-off, collective bargaining, etc., and got negative answers. (Were they trying to make Roosevelt sign under false pretenses?—getting it to him late at night? . . .). Roosevelt sat there without changing his expression or making any comment. "The house is burning down, the house is not burning down, don't you know?—If somebody says there's going to be rice pudding for dessert, and then they bring in baked apple, you expect them at least to say, 'Oh, I thought it was going to be rice pudding,' don't you know? like something in *Alice in Wonderland.*" The wages and hours were also bad and it had to be sent back as unacceptable.

—EDMUND WILSON (1933)

OCTOBER 6

*F*rom hence we went pretty briskly forward, and arrived at Saybrook ferry about two of the clock afternoon; and crossing it, we called at an inn to bait (foreseeing we should not have such another opportunity 'til we come to Killingsworth). Landlady come in, with her hair about her ears, and hands at full pay scratching. She told us she had some mutton which she would broil, which I was glad to hear; but I suppose forgot to wash her scratches; in a little time she brought it in; but it being pickled, and my guide said it smelled strong of head sauce, we left it, and paid sixpence a piece for our dinners, which was only smell.

—SARAH KEMBLE KNIGHT (1704)

*B*een flying, train-riding, automobiling, horseback and buggy riding over Texas for thirty-three years and I've never seen a tenth of it. If it had been in Europe, eighty wars would have been fought over it. There is single ranches here bigger than France. Counties bigger than England. Saddle horse pastures big as Alsace-Lorraine. The lakes of Switzerland would be buffalo wallows in Texas. . . . It's so far to town that the cowboys started in to vote for "Teddy" and arrived in time to register for "Franklin." Its "Vatican" is the town of Uvalde, its pope is John Nance Garner. Its sole industry is internal politics. It's so big that no one Governor can handle it; they have to have a man and his wife. . . . P.S. They would use California for a telephone booth down here.

—WILL ROGERS (1932)

A note from F. Scott Fitzgerald in answer to me. We must meet on a Sunday afternoon. A gay poof of a note, it seemed to me—an appearance, not a reality. [Fitzgerald died two months later in Hollywood.]

—CLIFFORD ODETS (1940)

OCTOBER 7

*M*ajr. Silly, who is rightly named is a very silly man: yet the fool, has learned to swear & damn by rule: to such a degree of perfection, that his equal is scarcely to be found in the Camp. . . . Our officers & soldiers in general, are remarkably expert in the swearing way. Nothing comes more handy, or gives such power and force to their words, as a Blasphemous oath. In general the Regt. is composed of Deists, Arminians, and a few who ridicule the Bible, and everything of a sacred nature. In short they Laugh at death, mock at Hell and damnation; & even challeng the Deity, to remove them out of this world by Thunder and Lightning.

—LEWIS BEEBE (1776)

$\mathcal{I}$ have just started for a long journey to the far South . . . to learn what among them is the life of a "Yankee teacher." . . . At one on Sunday morning heard the "all aboard for Washington" sounded. Another rush—jam, pell-mell confusion & in ten minutes we were off again. . . . Our next change was to a quiet slow boat—to go 50 miles on the Potomac. . . . We passed Mt. Vernon . . . little could be seen, but enough to recall the grateful recollections of him who was indeed a "Father of his country." . . . We were roused at two next morning to get ready for crossing the river. . . . We went slowly down to the bank of the Great Pedee—through deep sand. . . . Every-body rubbing eyes—shivering, stamping,—& so we crowded on a little flat boat—to wait until our baggage & a heavy mail were brought down—on the backs of negroes. . . . They carried torches of fat pine. . . . Their shiny black faces loomed up from the grey surroundings. We could but be reminded of Charon & the Styx, when we . . . were pushed off & pulled across by a stout man who drew the boat by ropes fastened on each side of the river—a specimen I suppose of Southern engineering. It was slow work . . . but, we were going to a new country of course to see new institutions—we knew there was at least one, a "peculiar institution."

—CAROLINE SEABURY (1854)

$\mathcal{A}$s we were coming along today in the piney woods we passed an old man who had been to mill. Sitting on his horse by the side of the road, waiting for us to pass. This was 1 OClock PM. and he said he had been there nearly all day. He said he didn't know that there were so many men in the whole world.

—SAMUEL T. FOSTER (1864)

OCTOBER 8

$\mathcal{W}$hen I woke up, the first thought I got was, "It's Mother's birthday: I must be very good." I ran and wished her a happy birthday, and gave her my kiss. After breakfast we gave her our presents. I had a moss cross and a piece of poetry for her. We did not have any school, and played in the woods and got red leaves. In the evening we danced and sung, and I read a story about "Contentment." I wish I was rich, I was good, and we were all a happy family this day.

—LOUISA MAY ALCOTT (1843)

Marmee's birthday; sixty-eight. After breakfast she found her gifts on a table in the study. Father escorted her to the big red chair, the boys prancing before blowing their trumpets, while we "girls" marched behind, glad to see the dear old Mother better and able to enjoy our little fete. The boys proudly handed her the little parcels, and she laughed and cried over our gifts and verses. I feel as if the decline had begun for her, and each year will add to the change which is going on, as time alters the energetic, enthusiastic home-mother into a gentle, feeble old woman, to be cherished and helped tenderly down the long hill she has climbed so bravely with her many burdens.

—LOUISA MAY ALCOTT (1868)

Dear Marmee's birthday. Never forgotten. Lovely day. Go to Sleepy Hollow with flowers. Her grave is green, black berry vines with red leaves trail over it. A little white stone with her initials is at the head, & among the tall grass over her breast a little bird had made a nest. Empty now, but a pretty symbol of the refuge that tender bosom always was for all feeble and sweet things. Her favorite asters bloomed all about, & the pines sang overhead.

—LOUISA MAY ALCOTT (1879)

This afternoon I went to my Bible Class at Y.W.C.A. and at 3:30 to the Auditorium to meet some of Good Gov. Club

ladies and distribute our Suffrage Campaign Literature to
the crowds of men gathered to see and hear Gov. Woodrow
Wilson of New Jersey, the Democratic nominee for President.
We found the majority of men for us, and almost every one
courteous: occasionally there was a "smart aleck." But Wilson's train was delayed and it was almost 6 o'clock when he
reached the Auditorium, so I took a look at the man and
hiked for home.

—MARTHA FARNSWORTH (1912)

OCTOBER 9

$\mathscr{A}$ windy, rainy night, and cold—so much so we could not
speak with the Indians today. . . . We gave them some tobacco, and informed them we would speak tomorrow. . . . Canoes of skins passed down from the two villages a short
distance above, and many came to view us all day.

—WILLIAM CLARK (1804)

$\mathscr{T}$he prosperity of the country, independent of all agency of
the Government, is so great that the people have nothing to
disturb them but their own waywardness and corruption.
They quarrel upon dissensions of a doit, and split up into
gangs of partisans of A, B, C, and D, without knowing why
they prefer one to another. Caucuses, County, State, and National Conventions, public dinners, and dinner-table
speeches two or three hours long, constitute the operating
power of electioneering; and the parties are working-
men, temperance reformers, Anti-Masons, Union and States-
Rights men, Nullifiers, and, above all, Jackson men,
Van Buren men, Clay men, Calhoun men, Webster men, and
MacLean men, Whigs and Tories, Republicans and Democrats, without one ounce of honest principle to choose between them. . . . There are five or six candidates for the

successsion to the Presidency, all of them demagogues, and not one of them having any consistency of system for the government of the Union.

—JOHN QUINCY ADAMS (1834)

*T*o the Rev. Brother Bellows's . . . where I spent two hours oddly enough. Some thirty people, generally notabilities, had been assembled to meet the illustrious Alcott, the father, I suppose, of Yankee-Platonism and hyperflutination, and to talk to Great Alcott and be talked to by him; the subject of tonight's discourse being announced in a sphinx of a printed card as "Descent," which left it uncertain whether we were to be enlightened about family history and pedigree from an aesthetic standpoint, the canons of art applicable to bathos, or the formulas expressing the law of gravitation. Bellows introduced Great Alcott in his usual pleasant conversation immediately, but everybody was afraid to begin. At last the Rev. Mr. Osgood plunged heroically into the dark profound of silence, and uttered certain dark sayings, and he and Alcott and Bellows had it all to themselves for an hour or so, belaboring each other with "representative men" and "cosmic men" and "whole men" (analogous, I suppose, to "entire horses"), "pre-existent souls," "ideal archetypes," "genial receptivity," and the "Handle of the Cosmos." The first ray of light I got came from the Rev. Mr. Osgood, who lifted up his voice after a pause that was becoming formidable, and affirmed the proposition: "A Cat is an Individual. A Cat is not a Person."

—GEORGE TEMPLETON STRONG (1856)

OCTOBER 10

*M*ade three chiefs, one for each village. Gave them presents. After the council was over, we shot the air gun, which astonished them much. They then departed, and we rested secure all night. Those Indians were much astonished at my servant. They never saw a black man before. All flocked around him and examined him from top to toe. He carried on the joke and made himself more terrible than we wished him to do. Those Indians are not fond of spirits—liquor of any kind.

—WILLIAM CLARK (1804)

Caught a head cold, leaning out the window, in pajamas, watching the crowd, standing about Joe Louis's car, at stage entrance to Hippodrome. Blacks and whites all cheering.

—SHERWOOD ANDERSON (1936)

Our quarrel with Japan seems to be that she is able strategically to cut off our supply of tin and rubber which we get from Dutch and French colonies in the Orient. This makes it possible for a few million men, white, yellow, and black, to say in the near future: "I was killed for some tin, for some ingots of rubber." . . . It struck me the other day that Hitler must die of contradictions soon. . . . Mr. Hitler is a skyrocket whose fuse has already been lighted. He is a one-chance rocket. Soon he must fall and come to earth, fulfilling the nature of the rocket by spluttering to death in the dark. This does not mean he will not do great damage before he dies, probably by his own hand.

—CLIFFORD ODETS (1940)

OCTOBER 11

A mother brought her four-weeks-old girl baby twenty-five miles in a carriage, so she might tell it, when grown, that

Susan B. Anthony had taken it in her arms. "And the trip has not hurt baby a particle," she said brightly.

—SUSAN B. ANTHONY (1886)

*M*y barber, who was originally a Missouri farm boy, has always been rabidly anti-English. Today I discovered the source of his feelings. As a doughboy in the last war he visited London, and called on a prosperous English business man to whom he had a letter of introduction from a brother back in Missouri. The Englishman's first remark on seeing him was: "Why would my brother give you, a common soldier, a letter of introduction to *me*?" My barber friend did not know that there is a type of Londoner who apes the gentleman without his education and gentleness.

—JAMES WEBB YOUNG (1943)

*T*he temperature on the roof outside my bathroom, when I arose this morning, was 45. Fallen leaves fill the backyard and the street before my office window. Darkness comes down soon after 6 p.m. and there is a sad, sickly feeling in the air. The year is drawing to its close, and I look forward to 1945 without too much hope. I am definitely aging, and throwing off a 700-page book is no longer the easy task it used to be. I plan to devote the next six months to some miscellaneous writing . . . and maybe a short book setting forth my conclusions about human life on this ball. In all probability it will be impossible to print it, if I do it, until after the war—and the uproars bound to follow the war. . . . The time has come to see to my shutters.

—H. L. MENCKEN (1944)

OCTOBER 12

*A*ttended Bugbee's book auction last evening. . . . Rather a trashy collection of books. . . . [A book auction] is an excel-

374

lent place to study human and individual nature. It is curious to observe how very avarice will inveigh a man into extravagance, and the idea of buying articles cheap induce him to purchase things useless to him. How they will be carried away by the gab and chatter of the auctioneer and pay prices they wouldn't listen to at private sale. The lion of the evening was old Durgin, who bought forty-five volumes. . . . Everybody was laughing and joking him . . . for bidding off so many works, but he persevered from obstinacy—nothing else.

—BENJAMIN BROWNE FOSTER (1848)

While on the route from Richmond, an incident occurred illustrative of the peculiar pride of the soldier. As the passenger coach was crowded, an old farmer found himself compelled to come into the soldier car and took possession of the only vacant seat, which happened to be alongside of a rough-looking Georgian. The farmer began to get restive as he noticed his neighbor rub or scratch certain portions of his body and limbs, and at last ventured the remark: "My friend, you seem to be troubled with fleas?" With a scathing glance, the veteran growled out: "Fleas? You son of a bitch, do you take me for a dog?" The pair were not very sociable after the above brief colloquy.

—EUGENE HENRY LEVY (1864)

At five o'clock I went to the White House for an interview with the President. It was the President's day for officially receiving the members of the Supreme Court. We waited in the parlor until this reception was over. On our way to the second floor the President remarked that whenever he saw a certain member of the Supreme Court he thought of that musical comedy—*Of Thee I Sing*. I told him I had the same feeling; that I didn't see why the member of the court in question hadn't shaved off his whiskers after that play.

—HAROLD L. ICKES (1933)

OCTOBER 13

*B*ee hunt. . . . See the bees about a hole high up—men go to work at foot with axes. By & bye down comes the tree with great crash and breaks to shivers—one man runs up with whisp of lighted hay to smoke off the bees. . . . Trunk spread open discovers stores of honey—cut open the part above & combs much broken—some white clean & new, others older. Take out flakes in a pail—every one with spoon & knife helps himself to the rich booty. . . . Some strange bees arrive and begin to banquet on the honey of their ruined neighbors. Men know them by their greediness & their clean jackets.

—WASHINGTON IRVING (1832)

A little soldier from the Maryland camp came this evening—a mere boy, but with his black eyes full of fire, eagerness to join the flag. He had just come from Paris, France, where his family are living, to join the Maryland line. He said his father wished him to come; did not think it honourable to remain in a foreign land while Maryland struggled for her freedom. His mother was not so anxious. He spoke gaily and enthusiastically of the life in the camp, and the battles he expected to take part in; and I did not like to be a prophet of evil, and tell him about the dark side of war that I had seen.

—CORNELIA PEAKE McDONALD (1862)

*C*urious that rank counts for so much more among Yanks, than with any of Allies. Newer at game, look more closely at insignia. Promotion very slow in French army. Chap may have functions of general, with one stripe on sleeve. In consequence, pay small attention to tunic. We pay a lot, and rather droll in deference to outward symbols of importance. Plenty of morons carrying silver hardware.

—HOWARD O'BRIEN (1918)

OCTOBER 14

I hear a man laughed at because he went to Europe twice in search of an imaginary wife who he thought was there, though he had never seen nor heard of her. But the majority have gone further while they stayed in America, have actually allied themselves to one whom they thought their wife, and found out their mistake too late to mend it. It would be cruel to laugh at them.

—HENRY DAVID THOREAU (1859)

*C*lear and warm. A charming day. . . . At 1:30 Mr. Ramsey calls up and wants to come down. . . . He is an intense admirer of mine, but a little dull. He is a botanist and ornithologist. Tells me of biologists in American colleges who can't teach truth for fear of losing their jobs. . . . Dinner at Luchow's. A dull affair. I see Germans singing *America!* At 9:30 we go to Sunshine Coffee House on East Side. I plan to get in with one of the pretty waitresses there. Walk along 2d Avenue and see Socialist parade demanding a free press and free speech. They are likely to get it—here!

—THEODORE DREISER (1917)

*T*here was a piece in the *Times* yesterday about a chap who teaches CEOs and others how to remember. He himself once purportedly remembered the names of all 644 people in a room (sounds more like a convention hall), and he can memorize *Time* or *Newsweek* in an hour. I would like to get hold of him, for a lesson or two, but the paper got thrown out and I can't remember his name.

—E. J. KAHN, JR. (1987)

OCTOBER 15

*S*ome would think to look at me almost helpless and a prisoner of war, that I hadn't much to feel glad about. Well, let them go through what I have and then see. . . . Shall appreciate life, health and enough to eat hereafter. Am anxious for only one thing, and that is to get news home to Michigan of my safety. Have no doubt but I am given up for dead, as I heard I was so reported. Drizzling rain has set in. Birds chipper from among the trees. Hear bells ring about the city of Savannah.

—JOHN RANSOM (1864)

*S*tate of my pants gives direct and personal interest in progress towards peace. Question—how long can we hold out? Wearing thin in many spots. Can hold out, maybe, till new year. After that, tremble for consequences. . . . Pet peeve—the swine in the rear, afraid war will end before we can "punish" Germany. Fellows in line all for a knockout and out of the ring as quickly as possible. Not much patience with blood-and-iron spirit of folk who've never seen war outside a cinema.

—HOWARD O'BRIEN (1918)

A few days ago I hired a boy of nineteen, who had been rejected by the Army on his eyesight. He is the son of a coal-miner, and since finishing the ninth grade in school has been working at the job of picking stone out of the coal. But I haven't seen a kid for a long time with as much ambition and git-up-and-go. Thank God there is still such yeast in the American dough.

—JAMES WEBB YOUNG (1943)

OCTOBER 16

[In Beaufort, South Carolina] *P*revious to the landing of our troops there were well kept yards and beautiful gardens, full of rare flowers—Mansions furnished with almost princely magnificense—whole libraries full of costly books—indeed, this little place contained everything which art could furnish and wealth procure . . . but our crazy solderly [soldiers] made sad havoc with its beauty and its wealth. Much of the rich furniture was stolen by officers and sent north to friends—more of it was wantonly destroyed by the soldiers. . . . The churches were robbed of all ornament—the keys torn from the organs to make letters for their caps—the fences and out buildings torn away to build fires or make tent floors—and even the brick wall enclosing the dead, torn away to build chimney—and after a few months of military occupation Beaufort's left only in name. If our soldiers had been content with destroying the rebel property—there might be found excuse for them—but every indignity which human ingenuity could devise was heaped upon the poor negroes, who had hailed their coming so joyfully—and during the first year of our soldiers coming the blacks probably suffered more from their tyranny and insults, than ever in their lives before.

—ESTHER HILL HAWKS (1862)

*C*old grey fall day and the street full of young men registering for the draft. It was like a return to World War days. They try to make a joke of it but do not succeed very well. Some 1300 registering from this town. Took a long ride, after work, to look at the lovely fall colors in the grey light.

—SHERWOOD ANDERSON (1940)

*T*he registration board was meeting in a little private home, an American flag hung in front of the porch. Two men rocked on the porch and we exchanged greetings. Inside, three middle-aged women were gossiping—not unpleasant women. A

379

dressmaker took down my answers to the form questions. . . .
I was overpolite, treated everything gingerly. I signed the
blank she had filled out; in turn she signed and filled out a
small card which all registrants must carry on their person.
Now is the time for all good men. . . . Do you ever get tired
of having to walk around in the world with a gun hidden in
your coat? I do. Everyone carries a gun in the world, it seems
to me.

—CLIFFORD ODETS (1940)

OCTOBER 17

$\mathscr{W}$hat I put into my pocket, whether berry or apple, generally has to keep company with an arrow-head or two. I hear
the latter chinking against a key as I walk. These are the
perennial crop of Concord fields. If they were sure it would
pay, we should see farmers raking the fields for them.

—HENRY DAVID THOREAU (1859)

$\mathscr{A}$ large multitude assembled [at an agricultural exhibi-
tion] . . . attracted not by the objects interesting to a farmer
of education, but by the race track. . . . On this occasion,
there were [also] several tents where humbugs & catchpen-
nies, dwarfs, deformed women, &c, were to be seen. Two or
three vendors of quack medicines were haranguing gaping
crowds about the grounds, and all the time scrub races, free
to all comers, were going on. At 1½ I went with some of the
members [of the agricultural society] to the platform [to give
an address on agriculture]. I saw at once that beyond a few
around me there were none present who cared a farthing
about . . . agriculture or any topic connected with it. . . . The
members were profuse in thanks & regrets, but I treated the
whole affair as a good joke. . . . I did not fail, however, to
point out to them how this was an illustration of the bad

policy they were pursuing by using means to attract a vulgar crowd for the sake of making money & thus degrading their Society and defeating its purposes.

—SIDNEY GEORGE FISHER (1860)

*chicago
fire*

$\mathcal{T}$he fire [in Chicago] began at twelveth street on Sunday night. It swept the two magnificent avenues, & every building on the South side from twelveth street to the river. The Court House, with the original copy of Father's will & no one knows how many invaluable papers, legal documents, records, the beautiful Crosbie Opera house, a perfect bijoux of a theatre, all the banks, insurance offices, railway depots, churches & block after block of stores, unequalled any where. And then, oh misery, the fire, the red, angry, unrelenting fire, lept across the river, & burnt & burnt, till Mr. Mahlon Ogden's house was the only one left standing up to Lincoln Park. Yes the whole north Side is in ashes, literally in ashes, & every memory connected with my home is gone. . . . No one ever loved their home more than I did mine; I loved every angle in the house, every carpet, every table, every picture on the walls, every book in the library, the stairs, the basement, the garret.

—JULIA NEWBERRY (1871)

OCTOBER 18

$\mathcal{T}$he Arikaras [Indians] are not fond of spirituous liquors, nor do they appear to be fond of receiving any or thankful for it. They say we are no friends or we would not give them what makes them fools.

—WILLIAM CLARK (1804)

381

[At a historical pageant commemorating the Revolutionary War] *I* was there before the militia had gone off. Some had the large skirted coats of revolutionary officers; some wore battered helmets; some three-cornered hats; some nothing. They had every variety of weapon, from blunderbuss to rusty saw; and were of all ages and sizes. A more ragamuffin assemblage I never saw. "Officers to the front," exclaimed the general on his horse. The long line of ragamuffins, who stood leaning on their rifles or muskets in every variety of outlandish costume, looked as if they had never an officer among them. But at the word a number of fellows straddled out from the line—with yellow breeches and red coats; or with false beards and dirty shirts; armed with axes, swords, or guns. These marched up to the front and faced gravely towards the general. "Gentleman officers," he began.

—FRANCIS PARKMAN (1844)

*A*lfred Knopf and I went to Garden City today to have lunch with the executives of Doubleday, Doran and Company. . . . The talk was almost wholly about the horrible state of the publishing business. Standing on the floor of one of the rooms, along one of the walls, was a series of bronze busts of authors . . . and the report is that they cost Doubleday, Doran and Company $5,000 a piece. They were ordered by Doran, and his imprudence, so I hear, was one of the main reasons for his expulsion from the firm. The rest of the executives obviously look upon them with an unfriendly eye, for they were not even decently displayed.

—H. L. MENCKEN (1932)

OCTOBER 19

*T*he British had left Germantown, and our Army was marching to take possession. . . . Sister Betsy and myself, and G. E. went about half a mile from home, where we cou'd see the army pass. . . . We made no great stay, but return'd with excellent appetites for our breakfast. Several officers call'd to get some refreshment, but none of consequence till the afternoon. . . . When we were alone our dress and lips were put in order for conquest.

—SALLY WISTER (1777)

$\mathscr{I}$t strikes me that this institution—slavery as it *exists* at the South with all its "safe-guards" and "necessary legisla- tion"—is the greatest crime on the largest scale known in modern history. . . . It is deliberate legislation intended to ex- tinguish and annihilate the moral being of men for profit; systematic murder, not of the physical, but of the moral and intellectual being; blasphemy, not in word, but in systematic action against the Spirit of God which dwells in the souls of men to elevate, purify, and ennoble them. So I feel now; per- haps it's partly the dominant election furor that colors my notions.

—GEORGE TEMPLETON STRONG (1856)

$\mathscr{W}$hat queer times we live in & how hardened we are to danger. Kate says Betsey [a house slave] brought her bed in to sleep in her room when she was left alone—& she thought, "Is this to protect me or to murder me?" . . . The same day at dinner Mrs. C rushed in urging the family not to taste the soup, it was so bitter. *Some thing* was in it! She meant *poison.* The family quietly eat on to keep the negroes from supposing it possible they should suspect such a thing. . . . A Dr. K that I knew full well was poisoned by his negroes. . . . Mr. Taylor . . . said to him, "Keitt, these negroes are poisoning you. Do not let them know you suspect them unless you take them up instantly, but I advise you to go away at once, say to day—& see if this extraordinary disease will not stop." He promised. Just after Mr. Taylor left the house a woman brought him a cup of coffee & as he stirred it—it was so evident some white powder was at the bottom of the cup—

383

that in a passion he dashed the cup in her face without drinking it. That night his throat was cut. Afterwards, by their confession it [was] proved they had been giving him calomel for months every morning in his coffee. Three were hung—but two suspected men escaped because a brother of his believed them honest & guiltless.

—MARY BOYKIN CHESNUT (1861)

OCTOBER 20

I had gone but little way on the old Carlisle road when I saw Brooks Clark, who is now about eighty, and bent like a bow. . . . When he got up to me, I saw that beside the axe in one hand, he had his shoes in the other, filled with knurly apples and a dead robin. . . . I asked if he had found the robin dead. No, he said, he found it with its wing broken, and killed it. He also added that he had found some apples in the woods, and as he had not anything to carry them in, he put them in his shoes. They were queer looking trays to carry fruit in. How many he got in along toward the toes, I don't know. . . . He was happy to be nature's pensioner still, and bird-like to pick up his living. Better his robin than your turkey, his shoes full of apples than your barrels full. They will be sweeter, and suggest a better tale. He can afford to tell how he got them, and I to listen.

—HENRY DAVID THOREAU (1857)

*E*llen Glasgow was here to lunch last Sunday. . . . The old girl is deaf and carried a loud speaker, but she uses it adroitly, and is pretty good company. She drank two stiff sherrys before lunch, got her full share of a bottle of claret, and then topped off with a big drink of brandy. These stimulants made her garrulous. . . . She pretended to loathe the literary teas and other such parties to which she has been going in New York, but it is well known in publishing circles that she really enjoys such things vastly, and is keenly alive to their advertising value to her books.

—H. L. Mencken (1932)

*M*acArthur & the Pres. of the Philippines landed and made a radio address at 1520. "I have returned," said Doug. How much better it would have been to say "we," particularly when at that moment men were dying that he could return. . . . Nothing better illustrates the need of a single command than the news summaries by the Army & Navy on this historic day. Pure claptrap & bombast by both sides with a personal angle. For posterity I can say, yes, I realize that today I stood on the very threshold of history and it is every bit as exciting as I could expect or imagine. The Blue Goose is hit pretty bad and they were about to beach her as we pulled out.

—Walter L. Rhinehart (1944)

OCTOBER 21

*T*he Female Anti Slavery Society announced a meeting for this afternoon, and 2 or 3000 persons assembled in front of 46 Washington St, expecting George Thompson would be present: the mayer assured the populace he was out of the City, when they cried for Garrison: the sign "Anti Slavery Society" was taken down, and torn into a thousand pieces: some persons who unfortunately resembled Garrison, were roughly handled: Garrison escaped by a back window, into a carpenter's shop in Widow's Lane, where for some time he lay concealed under a heap of shavings, till one of the apprentices gave the information where he was, when he was taken by the crowd into State Street, with the avowed purpose of applying a coat of tar & feathers: the mayer, assisted by a number of his friends, came to his rescue, and as he was opposite the south door of the City Hall, the mayer made a rush, and was fortunate enough to get him into City Hall: from one of the windows, he desired the multitude to disperse, and soon after Garrison was conducted to jail for safekeeping.

—BRADLEY N. CUMINGS (1835)

*G*rand day in Lewisburg. Curtin and Lincoln Jubilee & Ox roast. Evening Illumination and torchlight parade. Busy all morning getting apparatus ready to illume the house. At times Mattie, Father and Uncle Hewett Helped me. . . . Very busy to get my lights ready by 6½ o'c. . . . There was a whole "forum" of folks here to tea did not know them. Went with Tom S around town to see the Illumination procession, hear band, & etc & etc. A most beautiful day & evening, but I am awfully tired.

—SALLIE MEIXELL (1863)

*Y*ou know it just dont seem like we have any game in America where one man stands out so prominently and so far ahead of all the others in his line as Babe Ruth does in Baseball. . . . As he would go to his position out in the field why the St. Louis fans with their accustomed hospitality conferred on him a shower . . . of Pop Bottles. . . . Then in the very last of the ninth inning when St. Louis had two runners on bases and their heavy hitters up with two out, a long high foul was hit, and even though being crippled, he leaped from bottle to bottle, like Liza crossing the ice. He finally found two bottles standing on top of each other and that give him a little higher lift, so all he was able to do was make a sensational one-handed catch and come down among a case of what had been home brew containers. He is the only athlete that ever rose to heights with nothing but a foundation of Coca Cola under him.

—WILL ROGERS (1928)

386

OCTOBER 22

I do not wish to see another English Transl[ation of the Bible], till the English Dialect of the two last Ages shall have become obsolete & untilligible to posterity. But this will not be till English America is fully settled from the Atlantic to Mississippi, When the English of the present Idiom may be spoken by One hundred Million, all of whom may be able to read the Scriptures in Tyndall's Translation. Probably the English will become the vernacular Tongue of more people than anyone Tongue ever was on Earth, except the Chinese.

—EZRA STILES (1770)

*W*hen in town [Philadelphia] the other day, I met with a rather singular circumstance, considering the abject state in which the blacks are held in these United States. A Negro man named Fortune or Forton accosted me in the street by offering his hand to me, which (knowing his respectability) I accepted, when he told me that at my late election to Congress, he had taken 15 white men to vote for me. In my sail-loft (he is a sailmaker) I have 30 persons at work, said he, and among them are 22 journeymen—15 of whom are white, the rest coloured. It is very uncommon in America to see *coloured* men, as they are called, conducting business upon a large scale, and, notwithstanding the laws of Pennsylvania do not forbid it, no blacks vote at elections, at least in the eastern part of the state.

—SAMUEL BRECK (1822)

[In Richmond] *A* poor woman yesterday applied to a merchant in Carey Street to purchase a barrel of flour. The price he demanded was $70. "My God!" exclaimed she, "how can I pay such prices? I have seven children; what shall I do?" "I don't know, madam," said he coolly, "unless you eat your children." Such is the power of cupidity—it transforms men into demons.

—JOHN BEAUCHAMP JONES (1863)

OCTOBER 23

*P*assed nearly all the day very pleasantly in "the quiet and still air of delightful studies," that is, in writing my article, in which I am greatly interested. What a blessing is an absorbing occupation of which one never tires, which exercises the higher faculties of the mind and calls forth elevated sentiment, which gives wings to the hours and delightful excitement also. I do not wonder that poets & thinkers have always been poor. Business and moneymaking to one who has tasted this intoxicating pleasure are loathsome, and poverty with truth & beauty & thought a thousand times better than wealth without them.

—SIDNEY GEORGE FISHER (1856)

*W*e had an audience of Lincoln from nine to eleven A.M. . . . He is lank and hard-featured, among the ugliest white men I have seen. Decidedly plebeian. Superficially vulgar and a snob. But not essentially. He seems to be clearheaded and sound-hearted, though his laugh is the laugh of a yahoo, with a wrinkling of the nose that suggests affinity with the tapir and other pachyderms; and his grammar is weak. After we had presented our views about the Surgeon General, and after Lincoln had charged us with "wanting to run the machine" and had been confuted, Bishop Clark introduced the subject of exchange of prisoners. Of course, Lincoln replied that such exchange implied recognition of the rebel government as a legitimate belligerent power, and spoke of the flag of truce sent out to recover Colonel Cameron's body after the battle of Bull Run, and of General Scott's reluc-

388

tance to send it. The General said he had always held that if he fell in battle, he should be quite satisfied to rest on the battlefield with his soldiers.

—GEORGE TEMPLETON STRONG (1861)

$\mathscr{F}$or a long time, seeing the obvious hokum of most of the picture [*City for Conquest*], I could not understand why I was so moved. I wondered if I still believed all the bunk about the poor boy reaching the top, the usual success story. No, it was not that. What it was was that Jimmy [Cagney] made real the ASPIRATION of the leading character—the people in the picture aspired to development, to wealth and unfolding of their talents. . . . As one moves from impoverished obscurity to opulent success, one is trading not death for life but certain true values for other often more tawdry values. . . . Poverty has its beauties, its rich human values, and it seems for the most part to be the only soil in which aspiration flourishes. . . . Racking my memory does not make me remember one successful man who truly keeps his aspiration; very few American artists too.

—CLIFFORD ODETS (1940)

OCTOBER 24

$\mathscr{I}$n Congress, nibbling and quibbling as usual. There is no greater mortification than to sit with half a dozen wits, deliberating upon a petition, address, or memorial. These great wits, these subtle critics, these refined geniuses, these learned lawyers, these wise statesmen, are so fond of showing their parts and powers, as to make their consultations very tedious.

—JOHN ADAMS (1774)

So cometh a man to install our radio set, which I did bring with me last night and it worked very well, and I have ceased marveling at it, as I no longer at the telephone nor the electric light, neither of which I understand at all. And I heard some of the radio announcers, and could not believe that I was hearing aright, some of the advertising being pretentious and silly, as when one man spoke many times of the slogan of a company being "You might as well have the best," and I wondered how long it took that concern, and how many conferences were held, before they made that slogan up.

—FRANKLIN PIERCE ADAMS (1927)

OCTOBER 25

It is a queer sight now, to observe the straggling emigrants coming up and going in. Wagons of every kind, oxen, horses, mules, bulls, cows, and people,—men, women & children, all packed. A few weeks travel has wrought a great change in their circumstances.—Many of them I recognized as old acquaintances as far back as Pittsburgh, and all along our western waters, and over the long travel. Large companies, fine animals, a great amount of provisions & stores, and smiling faces; were now a scattered, broken, selfish stragglers, dusty in faces and dress, and many of them, thin with hunger, as well as anxiety.

—J. GOLDSBOROUGH BRUFF (1849)

What does the sensational collapse of Wall Street mean? Nothing. Why, if the cows of this country failed to come up and get milked one night it would be more of a panic than if Morgan and Lamont had never held a meeting. Why, an old sow and a litter of pigs make more people a living than all the steel and General Motors stock combined. Why, the whole 120,000,000 of us are more dependent on the cackling of a hen than if the Stock Exchange was turned into a night club. And New Yorkers call them rubes.

—WILL ROGERS (1929)

*O*utside, it is wet and penetratingly cold. My sugar maple perhaps intended to turn scarlet, then decided on yellow, the strangest yellow, as if it were strawberry gilded over . . . I have an almost theological belief in gardens and I think that trees should be cared for as if they stood in flower pots.

—GLENWAY WESCOTT (1945)

OCTOBER 26

*T*hrashing machine—Merill's—at house. Father dropped his pitchfork and the machine thrashed the handle till it got itself out of kilter. Sixteen bushels oats, seven bushels rye.

—BENJAMIN BROWNE FOSTER (1847)

*I*n this time of profound emotional tension it is natural that there should be a reaching for lofty themes in advertising. But I wonder whether we may not be overdoing it. I observe (1) that at the very time when cloth needs saving, women all the way from Vogue to Montgomery Ward develop a cape style of wearing coats which flaunts the uselessness of sleeves; (2) that even the boys on the bombing fronts still want to know the sports scores; and (3) that most of my middle-aged friends are still worrying about their waistlines. So maybe the homely things are still worth dealing with. As the beer people say, morale is a lot of little things.

—JAMES WEBB YOUNG (1942)

OCTOBER 27

It is rather humiliating to attend a public meeting such as this New York Caucus last evening, and see what words are best received, and what a low, animal hope and fear patriotism is. . . . Greatest care is taken instinctively on both sides to represent their own cause as the winning one. . . . This party-lie aims to secure the votes of that numerous class . . . of indifferent, effeminate, stupid persons, who in the absence of all internal strength, obey whatever seems the voice of their street, their ward, their town, or whatever domineering strength will be at the trouble of civilly dictating to them. But their votes count like real votes.

—RALPH WALDO EMERSON (1834)

Rambling talk with Henry Thoreau last night. . . . We disposed pretty fast of America and England, I maintaining that our people did not get ripened, but, like the peaches and grapes of this season, wanted a fortnight's more sun and remained green, whilst in England, because of the density, perhaps, of cultivated population, more caloric was generated and more completeness obtained.

—RALPH WALDO EMERSON (1850)

Silly U.S. editorials: "Talk war, not peace." Ought to talk peace and think peace, because making of peace soon to be chief occupation of world. Beside peace problem, war-making relatively simple. . . . Disgusted with cheap damnation of all things German at home. Hope children aren't already poisoned with it. Not possible to protect them against atmosphere of hate. But hope for counteracting reasonableness. Going to grow up in world tremendously different from one we have known. Have to grapple with new problems. Dreadful to think of them handicapped with useles rancors held over from past best forgotten. . . . Home folks seem to think more of trumpets, banners and fit of uniforms than of *why* of it all.

—HOWARD O'BRIEN (1918)

OCTOBER 28

For a year or two past, my publisher, falsely so called, has been writing from time to time, to ask what disposition should be made of the copies of "A Week on the Concord and Merrimack Rivers" still on hand, and at last suggesting that he had use for the room they occupied in his cellar. So I had them all sent to me here, and they have arrived to-day by express, filling the man's wagon, 706 copies out of an edition of 1000, which I bought of Munroe four years ago, and have been ever since paying for and have not quite paid for yet. The wares are sent to me at last, and I have an opportunity to examine my purchase. They are something more substantial than fame, as my back knows, which has borne them up two flights of stairs to a place similar to that to which they trace their origin. Of the remaining 290 and odd, 75 were given away, the rest sold. I have now a library of nearly 900 volumes, over 700 of which I wrote myself. Is it not well that the author should behold the fruits of his labor?

—HENRY DAVID THOREAU (1853)

A ward-meeting is no Witenagemot. Gas, bad grammar, bad manners, bad taste, bad temper, unnecessary rhetoric,

393

and excitement, and affected enthusiasm about "our" candidate for this or that twopenny office, agonizings and wrestlings over momentous points of order, conscientious misgivings whether we can "legally" take this question till we've taken that other question, dirty little substrata of intrigue and jealousy about chairmanships and the like. It doesn't raise one's estimate of humanity.

—GEORGE TEMPLETON STRONG (1856)

*T*elephoned by a mighty hunter to come and eat some pheasants which he had brought home from North Dakota; but had to take a train out of town instead. I never cease to be astounded at the relatively high percentage of his income this man will spend on his hunting trips and equipment. The worst nickel pinchers I know are the same when it comes to any hobby. If I wanted a business that would withstand the fall of empires I think I would pick one in the hobby field.

—JAMES WEBB YOUNG (1942)

OCTOBER 29

*S*aw an Indian submit to the barbarous operation of having his hair pulled out of his head, excepting the scalp on the crown, and likewise his ears cut. An Indian dipped his fingers in ashes, and violently jerked out by the roots, one lock after another, until his head around the scalp was bald. He then laid his patient on his back, and placing a piece of wood under his ear, he cut, with his jack nife, which was rather dull, the rim of each ear, from top to bottom, leaving the ends adhering to the source. On the bow made of the rim, he fixed pieces of thin lead, to prevent adhesion and to stretch it. He bore the operation with wonderful fortitude. Now and then he shouted *Hocki,* that is, I am a great man.

—DAVID MCCLURE (1772)

[Watching Benjamin Franklin's election as president of Pennsylvania] The Doctor sat with a black Cane in his hand, it had an Ivory top to it. He had Ruffles on his hands and supported one or sometimes both of them on his Cane and sometimes would hold the nob to his forehead. He wore a purple Velvet Coat and Waistcoat and tho rather corpulent they hung loose upon him & checked Silk Stockings. Age seems to have Lowered his Stature as by it he appears round shouldered. He wore a Neck Cloth. And the features of his face having past 79 years under the Joint hands of Care and time they have given sufficient Testimony by the Furrows they have made the Honourable Grey Locks they have produced of his Antiquity. . . . I felt myself rather in a gloom, much more so than might be expected on a occasion that gave all other pleasures. I supposd to myself that I saw an old man that with infinite Labour and Toil had just reared up a darling State Child that he must so soon be obliged to quit and for ever leave to the Care of an Unkind or Bad meaning Stepmother.

—JOHN HALL (1785)

*L*eft Boston at 7¾ A.M. via Cohassett, for Marshfield, to attend the funeral [of Daniel Webster]. . . . The day was a warm autumn hasy day, with a falling & fallen leaf, & a sere look of the grass. . . . At every cross road carriages joined us, & as we neared Marshfield it became a perfect funeral procession. As far as the eye could reach, before & behind, was a long file of carriages. . . . Under a tree in front of the house stood the coffin, uncovered, & in it lay stretched, at length, in the full dress that he wore at his last speech, "all that is mortal of Daniel Webster." He had on a blue coat with gilt buttons, & a white neck-cloth, . . . while the huge, massy forehead, the dome of thought, lay open, under the N. England sky, gased upon by the thousands of his own race & nation, in silent awe. . . . Daniel Webster was a true product of N. England, & . . . on her most sacred spot, the home of the Pilgrims, was he to return. . . . The body was borne to the tomb . . . & the great crowd began to disperse. . . . One of the most touching things in all that met the eye or ear at Marshfield, was the lowing of the cattle, shut up in their barns.

They seemed like real mourners for him whose large heart went out in affection to them.

—RICHARD HENRY DANA (1852)

*T*rial of [John] Brown and the other Harper's Ferry conspirators on indictments for treason and murder is pushed vigorously, and it will result in a speedy verdict of prompt execution. The conduct of the prosecution is rigorous, or seems so in these days of rose-water criminal practice. . . . The rigor of this Virginia court is right enough, but eminently inexpedient. The court should give Brown the maximum of indulgence and vigilantly shut out his claim to the honors of martyrdom. It should be astute in protecting him by subtlety of quibbling or by inventing pleas of insanity for his benefit. If the slaveholding interest were wise, it would exert itself to secure his conviction on some minor offense, inciting to a riot, or the like, and his punishment by flogging, imprisonment, and the pillory. I'm not sure the South can afford to hang him, though he plainly deserves it.

—GEORGE TEMPLETON STRONG (1859)

OCTOBER 30

A tall swaggering young man who came yesterday from Petersburg, drinking Cocktails at the Bar and talking & swearing very loud, was accosted by the black barber with "Will you have your beard taken off, Sir?" "Hay! Yes! By God! I'll have any thing taken off; Damn me! by God I dont care if I have my head taken off!" The negroe grinning & at the same time looking down with a kind of mock humility replied "very happy to serve you, Sir."

—WILLIAM DUNLAP (1819)

$\mathcal{S}$argent, the portrait painter, said John D. Rockefeller was the most interesting sitter he ever had. His brother, William Rockefeller, said the portrait was good, but he didn't like the look of John D.'s hand—it was still reaching.

—CLARENCE W. BARRON (1922)

$\mathcal{J}$im Tully says that the Hearst palace is of enormous extent, and that Hearst employs a woman architect by the year to build additions to it. Week in and week out it is filled with guests, some of them politicians . . . but most of them movie people from Hollywood. . . . Hearst does not show up for breakfast, and usually he is also invisible at lunch, but he is always present at dinner. The guests are informed that they are expected to be prompt at dinner, but sometimes Hearst keeps them waiting for an hour. They stand around somewhat uneasily, for most of them are afraid of him. . . . The whole atmosphere of the place is sinister and unpleasant. . . . It is not uncommon for the guests to fight. When this happens they are summoned to their rooms, their bags are packed. . . . It is considered disgraceful in Hollywood to suffer that experience. . . . It is common for forty guests to be present and Hearst, at a pinch, could entertain two hundred. Tully says that the house is hideous, but that some of the rooms are beautifully turned out. The library, in particular, is a lovely room. Tully says that he went into it half a dozen times, but never met any other guests there. The more valuable books are all under lock and key, for it would be folly to trust them to some of the movie guests.

—H. L. MENCKEN (1932)

$\mathcal{T}$oday I retired my old Bible, bought in 1904. During the writing of the two Treatise books I put it to very heavy use, and it is now in tatters, with the binding and many of the leaves loose and some of the leaves torn. It has served me for more than forty years, and I retire it with some regret. Its original cost, I believe, was 50c. Today I dropped into the Methodist bookstore in Charles street and bought another

397

Bible of substantially the same print and binding. The price was $1.50. Even God, it appears, begins to profiteer.

—H. L. MENCKEN (1946)

OCTOBER 31

*H*ow superficial are our fears and hopes! We meet with a single individual, or read a single newspaper expressing malignant sentiments, and we despond for the republic. By one declaimer of an opposite character our confidence is renewed that all will go well. In these times a ragged coat looks sinister and revolutionary. "Who injures one threatens all."

—RALPH WALDO EMERSON (1834)

*W*ent to church as usual. Walked uptown tonight after going to Murray Street and back. Looked in at St. Thomas's and heard some admirable music. Let the enemies of church music only mark the effect it has in soothing and quieting one when he's in a black rage at matters and things in general and feels disposed to be ugly and vicious and savage and selfish, and to bite his own nose off, and cut all his friends and acquaintances, and abandon everything, do nothing, say nothing to nobody and just vegetate venomously. Let them note how soon it will bring one who's in such a beastly temper back to healthy and natural feelings and I think they'll abandon their opposition.

—GEORGE TEMPLETON STRONG (1841)

*E*llie doesn't think I got the eyes right on my pumpkin, but otherwise this year it passes muster. I thought I had given them just the right blend of idiosyncracy and insouciance.

—E. J. KAHN, JR. (1987)

⇜ NOVEMBER ⇝

NOVEMBER 1

*L*iddy, Betsy, and a T. L., prisoner of this State, went to the Mill. We made very free with some Continental flour. We powder'd mighty white, to be sure. Home we came. Col. Wood was standing at a window with a young officer. He gave him a push forward, as much as to say, "Observe what fine girls we have here." . . . Liddy and I had a kind of an adventure with him this morn. We were in his chamber, chatting about our little affairs, . . . standing up, each an arm on a chest of drawers; the door bang'd open!—Col. Wood was in the room. . . . We ran by him like two partridges, into mamma's room, threw ourselves into chairs, and reproach'd each other for being so foolish as to blush and look so silly. . . . The Col. laugh'd at us, and it blew over. The Army had orders to march today; the regulars accordingly did. Gen'l Smallwood had the command of Militia at that time, and they being in the rear, were not to leave their encampment until Second-day. Observe how militaryish I talk. No wonder, when I am surrounded by people of that order.

—SALLY WISTER (1777)

*I*n this country it is looked upon as unmanly not to vote. I suppose, if we could go into houses and family circles we

399

should find that each of the independent electors and each of the high candidates, too, is not original in his vote, or his platform, but is under personal influences. He is very free and unembarrassed in his discourse with you, a man of the people, making up his mind on general grounds of public good. But, at last, he disappoints you, and, still talking plausibly, votes and acts with the enemy. It is that he has a tyrant in his acquaintance who takes care to visit him at proper moments, has acquired an influence by manners, and, belonging to a more accomplished circle, flatters his ambition, and poisons his ear against his natural allies and plain duties, and controls his vote. This is an affair of degrees. That mischievous person who poisons his ear is himself reached and used by another or by others. Everything is in series. But the whole interweaving of the social canvas betrays an absence of original perception and will, in any quarter, as if God had left himself out of the world.

—RALPH WALDO EMERSON (1862)

*B*egan the second part of "Little Women." I can do a chapter a day, and in a month I mean to be done. A little success is so inspiring that I now find my "Marches" sober, nice people, and as I can launch into the future, my fancy has more play. Girls write to ask who the little women marry, as if that was the only end and aim of a woman's life. I won't marry Jo to Laurie to please any one.

—LOUISA MAY ALCOTT (1868)

NOVEMBER 2

I rose at 6 o'clock and read a chapter in Hebrew and some Greek in Lucian. I said my prayers and ate milk for breakfast, and settled some accounts, and then went to court where we made an end of the business. We went to dinner about 4 o'clock and I ate boiled beef again. In the evening I went to Dr. (Barret's) where my wife came this afternoon. Here I found Mrs. Chiswell, my sister Custis, and other ladies. We sat and talked till about 11 o'clock and then retired to our chambers. I played at (r-m) with Mrs. Chiswell and kissed her on the bed till she was angry and my wife also was uneasy about it, and cried as soon as the company was gone. I neglected to say my prayers, which I should not have done, because I ought to beg pardon for the lust I had for another man's wife. However I had good health, good thoughts, and good humor, thanks be to God Almighty.

—WILLIAM BYRD (1709)

Last weekend a bad blizzard struck and it snowed so much all week we couldn't get to school at all. Dad and Bud and I had a real struggle getting the cattle in from the hills in that blinding snow. Dad said it reminded him of the winter of 1896–97 when rain on the 28th of October turned into a blizzard. Dad killed the best horse he ever rode getting his cattle home. Coal had not yet been shipped into the state. There was some at Pingree, but it took men days to get it. John Roach was gone a week. Meanwhile his wife burned furniture and grain to keep from freezing and walked the floor in anxiety lest John be lying frozen along the road somewhere. Some men had to haul coal home on handsleds. The snow kept coming; winter lasted until May. Fences and houses were buried under deep drifts and the coulees were level with the hills.

—ANN MARIE LOW (1929)

It is astonishing how little the war impinges upon me. I am, of course, rooked like everyone else by excessive taxes, and now and then some eatable that I like is unprocurable (or procurable only by giving up an enormous number of ration points); but in general I am hardly affected by the great effort to save humanity and ruin the United States. So far, no one that I know has been killed in the war, or even injured, and

401

I find it hard to pump up any interest in the tall talk in the newspapers every day. . . . Their correspondence from the various fronts seldom undertakes to tell precisely what is going on: it is simply rooting for the home team. . . . If any effort were made to report the war objectively and truthfully there would be a public sensation. . . . The American people are now wholly at the mercy of demagogues, and it would take a revolution to liberate and disillusion them. . . . When the soldiers come home it will become infamous to doubt— and dangerous to life and limb.

—H. L. MENCKEN (1944)

NOVEMBER 3

The family of _____. He himself is a generous, open, hospitable, kind-tempered man of vulgar birth and education who has got an enormous fortune. His delight is in liberality, and he scatters money like water. His lady—a very dull and vulgar personage—is chiefly solicitous to make a display of the "tasty" and "genteel." They have a score of half-gentleman hangers-on around them. . . . His children, who play at whist with the aforesaid hangers-on all evening, are much petted, and provided with lapdogs. . . . Where in America is to be found that spirit of sport and bluff hearty enjoyment, that is seen in English country gentlemen and others. Business here absorbs everything, and renders people incapable of every other *pleasure*.

—FRANCIS PARKMAN (1844)

In the artificial nitre beds in Richmond & elsewhere, the carcases of brute animals are used . . . as a necessary material for the formation of nitre. The horses, mules & other animals dying naturally, & dogs killed under city ordinances, serve but insufficiently to supply the necessary material. It would be an economical & a very proper application of a portion of the carcases of the slain Yankees that Gen. Grant has so abundantly supplied by his attacks on our fortification, & left within our lines, near Richmond & Petersburg, to use them for the animal matter needed for the government nitre beds. Then, the gunpowder to be manufactured from nitre produced from the bodies of dead invaders of our soil would be used hereafter to kill more of those yet living.

—EDMUND RUFFIN (1864)

We rode across town to Lindy's and ate a heavy dinner. More discussion of politics. . . . On top of this, in came Lyons and wife, Irving Berlin and wife (I thought her very charming, liked her face), back from a Roosevelt preelection night rally at Carnegie Hall. They had with them a portable radio which they put on the table, and through it we listened to late-minute pro-R. speeches by Wallace, Hull, finally FDR himself, a quiet calm country-squire speech from his Hyde Park home, ending with a prayer for the welfare of the country. . . . Later. . . . I was looking out the window while playing the bagatelles, finishing up with the *Caprice* Rondo in G. The river traffic is amazing, the boats going by in the dark, tugging or pushing or dragging immense barges loaded with freight trains. The tugboats breathe in a low hoarse way, ever so busy, concentrated on their tasks, seeming not to look left or right but only ahead with a certain touch of glumness added. It does not take them long to disappear down the river.

—CLIFFORD ODETS (1940)

NOVEMBER 4

Tonight an excellent supper was set by the ladies of our village, which was designed to raise funds to light up the Methodist Church with lamps. Besides the supper, there were

403

many little plans for depriving one of his surplus change. Two post-offices showered the letters out upon you, for the enormous postage of twenty-five cents a piece. Then you must have your fortune told, by a young lady and her magic wheel. Several cakes were to be cut, and at every cut, your purse bleeds. I consider that I escaped well, at paying for the whole affair only two dollars and a half.

—THOMAS HUBBARD HOBBS (1847)

*A*s it is a "legal holiday," my office did not open. I voted. Looked in at the great Barnum show. Infinite claptrap, but many of the animals are fine specimens, and the menagerie is worth visiting. Barnum's shewbills, by the by, present a life-sized portrait of him as Phoenix T. Barnum, with a pair of wings appended to his shoulders.

—GEORGE TEMPLETON STRONG (1873)

I went tonight to my favorite bar ("Ann's Kitchen") and again watched the television . . . a program called "This Is Your Life." A retired schoolteacher . . . comes up from the audience . . . Her beauty, dignity, sweetness, and her composure under astonishing surprises are a large element in what follows. Photographs of her parents; of herself a baby, young girl, young woman; of the schools where she successively taught. Then people suddenly appear from behind a curtain: a beau whom she had not seen for thirty-five years; her sister; a sergeant from World War I who had known her when she ran a canteen in France; a member of the first class she had taught. . . . This ended up with the view of the audience, which contained one hundred former pupils . . . out of the ten thousand who had been her pupils. Why was I so strongly confirmed in my sense that this is the greatest country in the world?

—THORNTON WILDER (1953)

NOVEMBER 5

*N*oisy election; flags, boy processions, placards, badges, medals, bannered coaches, everything to get the hurrah on our side. That is the main end. Great anxiety, pale faces are become florid. They count that 1600 minutes are all the time allowed in all three days. Indisposition to business, and great promptness to spend.

—RALPH WALDO EMERSON (1834)

*O*ld [John] Brown convicted. He made a brief speech that was worthy of the best of the early reformers. To-day I was told that his wife was in Boston, and I went . . . to see her. She appears well. She is a large, strong woman, good-looking, and when young she must have been handsome. . . . She says that it is a matter of religious conviction with her husband; that he would make the same attempt again if set free. I admire the old man; but considering that three persons were killed by his party, I do not see how he can escape death, even had the occurrence been in a free State. He will be lauded by the abolitionists as a martyred hero, and he does resemble that. His death will hasten the removal of slaves from Virginia.

—AMOS A. LAWRENCE (1859)

*F*red Essary was at the office telling about Hoover's adventures on the stump. As everyone knows, Hoover was disinclined to make any active campaign. His original plan was to sit in Washington and maintain a magnificent silence. But when it became apparent that things were going against him, he had to take to the road . . . in mortal terror of assassination. During his first two trips he refused absolutely to take part in any street parades. At Cleveland the town was thick with police and militia, and guards were actually posted in the sewers under the streets that Hoover had to traverse. He was booed everywhere he went. At Detroit the police threat-

405

ened to beat up any one who booed him, so the crowd compromised by thumbing its noses at him as he passed. . . . As the campaign progressed and no bombs were set off Hoover began to recover his courage.

—H. L. MENCKEN (1932)

NOVEMBER 6

*J*oseph threw a knop of Brass and hit his Sister Betty on the forhead so as to make it bleed and swell; upon which, and for his playing at Prayer-time, and eating when Return Thanks, I whipd him pretty smartly. When I first went in (call'd by his Grandmother) he sought to shadow and hide himself from me behind the head of the Cradle: which gave me the sorrowfull remembrance of Adam's carriage.

—SAMUEL SEWALL (1692)

I rose at 8 o'clock after I had given my wife a flourish. I read two chapters in Hebrew and some Greek in Lucian. I said my prayers and ate boiled milk for breakfast. I danced my dance. I cleaned my head and was shaved. I ate cold roast beef for dinner. In the afternoon the wind was northeast and in the evening it began to rain. I danced my dance again and said my prayers. I sent for the tailor to cut my coat shorter. At night my wife and I played at piquet and had a small quarrel about [our count]. We ate some pears and milk for supper. I wrote a letter to Mr. Will Eppes and sent him some [sage] to cure his looseness. I prepared for my journey to Williamsburg. I had good health, good thoughts, and good humor, thank God Almighty. The negro woman ran away again.

—WILLIAM BYRD (1710)

*A*ssafoedita was burned on our stove this morning, which made a most execrable stench and some commotion in tutor and class. Sherman and Hunter did it. P.M. The mathematical recitation room was fastened by Jones and Eaton. Adams kicked it in. Evening, Commons were fastened against the freshmen who were last out of the chapel. We smashed in two panels and then battered the door open. Without these incidents of foolish mischief, how dull and lifeless would college be.

—BENJAMIN BROWNE FOSTER (1851)

*D*ad never wanted to be a farmer, but now, in his 50's, is still caught up in the everlasting struggle. . . . Actually, he was quite prosperous for many years until recently. Now times are hard, prices low, and this year we are hailed out. I guess he will manage. He always has. Come to think of it, Dad never plays his violin any more. Before Grandpa's violin burned up, he taught Dad a little about playing it. Years later Dad bought one, though he never could read a note of music. If he could whistle a tune, he could play it. Winter evenings he used to get out his violin and play a long time. But not these last few years. I guess a man gets old and tired.

—ANN MARIE LOW (1928)

NOVEMBER 7

*E*very man by God's arrangements whilst he ministers and receives influence from all others is absolutely, imperially free. When I look at the rainbow I find myself the centre of its arch. But so are you; and so is the man that sees it, a mile from both of us. So also the globe is round, and every man therefore stands on the top. King George and the chimney-sweep no less.

—RALPH WALDO EMERSON (1829)

407

$\mathcal{M}$elting-pot process going on under high pressure. In making this heterogeneous mass into army, also making Americans. Separatist politicians going to have rude shocks when they try old tricks on these lads.

—HOWARD O'BRIEN (1918)

$\mathcal{O}$ur people are very honest; we have less evil impulse in us than any other people in the world. This is true, too, of idealism as a raw impulse. But we are not a very deep people, so what does the honesty and the idealism avail? . . . By typical Americans I mean the sort of people . . . who emigrate to big towns like New York, who live alone, who eat with one another, read *Esquire* and *The New Yorker*, who beat one another on the heads, who begin to sag at forty, honest, never evil, essentially mediocre, hanging on to respectability, trying to be fashionable, trying to be "in the know" and "in the swim," not moral and not immoral, aspiring dimly, proud to be "regular," little fishes in the brook!

—CLIFFORD ODETS (1940)

NOVEMBER 8

$\mathcal{S}$et off at ½ past 7 in high spirits for the ford of the Arkansas. . . . Get on tracks of Indians—at length to our joy come in sight of habitations of men—Creek Indians log houses among trees—push on. Horse fagged—arrive at log house owned by White man with black fat wife—delightful sight of hogs, poultry—crowing of cocks &c. horse pricks his ears— Stop at the door, Capt & others eating at a table—huge Iron pot with beef & turnips—put in for a share—fat negress gives a plate heaping with beef & turnips. Corn bread & butter— apologizes for giving it in such poor style!

—WASHINGTON IRVING (1832)

$\mathcal{I}$ came home after an absence of about six months on & near James Island in the confederate service. . . . I am quite tired. There is no pleasure in being from home so long & at the same time being half fed doing hard duty getting but little grain and no thanks. . . . I have not yet been in a hard battle, but several small ones. . . . The batteries in & about the City of Charleston are constantly shelling each other with not a days interruption. I have heard the whizzing of shell until I am tired of the sound. I am on a furlough of 15 days & will soon return again. I left home before the crop was planted & returned to find it being gathered. My wife, children and negroes have done well in my absence & have made enough to live upon if they are permitted to use it. . . . The war has been in progress nearly four years, & as far as I can see, we are as far from the end as we were at the beginning.

—DAVID GOLIGHTLY HARRIS (1864)

$\mathcal{M}$ rs. Pennard stopped in today to ask me if I would give a talk to the Women's Institute of Yeobridge next May. . . . "What do you want me to talk about?" I asked in a manner the reverse of eager. "America," said Mrs. Pennard dolefully. "Well," I replied dubiously, "it's rather a large subject." Mrs. Pennard looked as if she did not believe me. "Hadn't I better take some single aspect of it?" I went on. Mrs. Pennard pressed her lips together and the corners of her mouth went down like express elevators. "Just America," she said in a mutinous quaver.

—MARGARET HALSEY (1937)

NOVEMBER 9

$\mathcal{A}$ fter many difficulties in boisterous storms, at length by God's providence, by break of the day we espied land which we deemed to be Cape Cod, and so afterward it proved. And the appearance of it much comforted us, especially, seeing so goodly a land, and wooded to the brink of the sea, it caused us to rejoice together and praise God.

—WILLIAM BRADFORD AND EDWARD WINSLOW (1620)

The court also sent for Mrs. Hutchinson, and charged her with divers matters . . . which were clearly proved against her, though she sought to shift it off. And, after many speeches to and fro, at last she was so full as she could not contain, but vented her revelations; amongst which this was one, that she had it revealed to her, that she should come into New England, and should here be persecuted, and that God would ruin us and our posterity, and the whole state, for the same. So the court proceeded and banished her; but, because it was winter, they committed her to a private house, where she was well provided, and her own friends and the elders permitted to go to her, but none else.

—JOHN WINTHROP (1637)

The Ministers of this town Come to the Court and complain against a Dancing Master who seeks to set up here and hath mixt Dances, and his time of Meeting is Lecture-Day; and 'tis reported he should say that by one Play he could teach more Divinity than Mr. Willard or the Old Testament. Mr. Moodey said 'twas not a time for N. E. to dance.

—SAMUEL SEWALL (1685)

Leave my horse at the agency & set off after breakfast, for the garrison [Fort Gibson, Arkansas]. . . . At night serenade of the widow by the quartermaster & one or two other old Bachelors. In the fort is the widow Nix; a plump buxom dame, whose husband was 50 years of age when he married her, amassed 20 000 $ as Sutler to the Garrison, which functions he discharged from the first establishment of the fort. The

410

widow came to the fort a short time since & is the object of desires of all the men. The ghastly Qr Master—Capt Clark. The old Col himself—all aspire to her favor. A Lawyer with the Militia title of Major Lewis has just made his appearance at the fortress as aspirant, & occasions some jealousy among the military men who all unite agst. the intrusion of the black coat. The Serenade of the widow was a horrible chorse voice that broke the sleep of man, woman & dog throughout the fortress.

—WASHINGTON IRVING (1832)

NOVEMBER 10

*L*ast night a rumour reached us that the Federalists were within 10 miles of Savannah, and that several car loads of women and children had left that place anticipating an attack. . . . There is one feature I particularly dislike. In their company they have it is reported 1000 Negroes whom they have stolen or who have run away from their owners in Virginia. These they might scatter through our state and do us some harm. They openly boast they have red Zouave uniforms for the Negroes whom they intend forming into regiments when they commence their inland attack. Oh for a whirlwind of destruction to drive from our land the footsteps of the hated foe.

—ELLA THOMAS (1861)

*I*n Rome, and felt as if I had been there before and knew all about it. Always oppressed with a sense of sin, dirt, and general decay of all things. Not well, so saw things through blue glasses. . . . The artists were the best company; counts and princes very dull, what we saw of them. May and I went off on the Campagna, and criticised all the world like two audacious Yankees.

—LOUISA MAY ALCOTT (1870)

$\mathcal{W}$orked on a short story for Reader's Digest. . . . We all went to dine and then to the horse show. I thought the animals very beautiful but the whole effect rather too snobbish and soon grew tired of it. It was a shock to see the parade of big death dealing war machines on display.

—SHERWOOD ANDERSON (1940)

$\mathcal{T}$he CBS evening news echoes my own dark fears that knowledge of geography is rapidly and inexcusably eroding. Thirty-nine percent of Boston high-school students couldn't name all the New England states. A not inconsiderable proportion of them, given a blank map of the earth, couldn't fill in the United States. One kid said this sort of ignorance was irrelevant and on being asked why, answered, "Because I am here." Shades of prewar isolationism!

—E. J. KAHN, JR. (1987)

NOVEMBER 11

$\mathcal{W}$e came to an anchor in the bay, which is a good harbor. And every day we saw whales playing hard by us. . . . This day before we came to harbor, observing some not well affected to unity and concord, but gave some appearance of faction, it was thought good there should be an association and agreement, that we should combine together in one body, and to submit to such government and governors as we should by common consent agree to make and choose, and set our hands to this that follows. . . . Having undertaken for the glory of God, and advancement of the Christian faith and honor of our King and country, a voyage to plant the first colony in the northern parts of Virginia, do by these presents solemnly and mutually in the presence of God and one of another, covenant, and combine our selves together into a civil body politic, for our better ordering and preservation,

412

and furtherance of the end aforesaid; and by virtue hereof to enact, constitute, and frame such just and equal laws, ordinances, acts, constitutions and offices from time to time as shall be thought most meet and convenient for the general good of the colony.

—WILLIAM BRADFORD AND EDWARD WINSLOW (1620)

A grand day, an *ideal* day, and *World Peace* at last—Germany has signed the "Peace" terms. At three o'clock this morning, or to be exact, 3:15, I was awakened by the blowing of whistles. . . . And almost immediately, guns were being fired, bells rung, people shouting and a tremendous din everywhere. . . . When we got up I hung out "Old Glory." . . . Noise pounded out of everything that noise *could* be pounded out of: every kind of whistle and bells, strings of old tin cans, whoops and howls and yells, big and little and old and young, every color and nationality—and the streets jammed, going in every direction everyone hilariously happy because *we licked the kaiser—we helped* with America's best young men—flags, flags, flags, everywhere.

—MARTHA FARNSWORTH (1918)

In the days before Hitler came to power . . . there were rumors that Hitler's iron cross was bogus, and [H. R.] Knickerbocker [foreign correspondent for Hearst] one day ventured to ask him about it. Hitler said that . . . during the war he was a dispatch rider, and one day he was sent across a part of the front that was a kind of No Man's Land. The Germans assumed that there were no Frenchmen in it, but when he had got half way across Hitler heard French voices and on investigation found that there were a number of Frenchmen in a dugout. Hitler approached the only entrance and barked several loud orders, hoping to convince the men within that a considerable German party was above. The trick worked, and in a few minutes Hitler had the Frenchmen coming out one by one, their hands in the air. He was armed only with a pistol, but inasmuch as they came out wholly unarmed, he

413

was able to line them up and march them back to the German lines. It was for this exploit that he received the iron cross. . . . Hitler said politely: "If these Frenchmen had been either Englishmen or Americans the chances are that I'd not be here." Knickerbocker said that Hitler in his private relations is a very amiable fellow, and has a considerable sense of humor. But whenever he gets on public matters he begins to orate. . . . He'll start in an ordinary tone and . . . in a few minutes he'll be howling like a stump speaker, with his arms sawing the air.

—H. L. MENCKEN (1938)

[While fighting in Europe] *A*rmistice Day! It doesn't make much difference to us. No doubt someone forgot to inform us to stop for a few minutes around eleven o'clock. When going to school, we would pause for a while on this day. Now that is only a memory to us. Will the world ever learn? What a price to pay.

—DONALD J. WILLIS (1944)

NOVEMBER 12

*H*ow many attractions for us have our passing fellows in the streets, both male and female, which our ethics forbid us to express, which yet infuse so much pleasure into life. A lovely child, a handsome youth, a beautiful girl, a heroic man, a maternal woman, a venerable old man, charm us, though strangers, and we cannot say so, or look at them but for a moment.

—RALPH WALDO EMERSON (1836)

414

I went to the road for JC but met Minnie Frierson. Her news is bad—hanging negroes for fear of insurrection in Louisiana & Mississippi like black birds. East Tennessee with fifteen thousand against us—ready to resist—who have already torn up rail roads & burnt bridges. Five hundred negroes on James Island refused to be moved out of the reach of the enemy & they sent for a troop of Cavalry to force them! . . . . Aunt Betsey & Mrs. Reynolds both are horror stricken by the evident exultation they perceive in their servants at the approach of the Yankees. Two people who have been so kind to their servants.

—MARY BOYKIN CHESNUT (1861)

S unday and yesterday there were great earthquakes in Rumania and great windstorms in America: that is a neat combination for Nostradamus to put into one of his illiterate quatrains. . . . I have an idea Hitler will die of nothing spectacular, like a bomb, but will succumb to some children's disease, like chicken pox or the mumps. It is a very violent and dangerous world, even around here. . . . One of my students was beating up a freshman when he fell into a hedge and got a thorn so deep in his hand the doctor had to cut it out. . . . The football coach has been bitten by Father H.'s black spaniel. . . . Somebody told me that a pig, when it attacks a human being, gores out the entrails and eats them but will touch positively nothing else. I saw what I thought was a photograph of the Three Ritz Brothers dressed up as women, but it turned out to be the Three Andrews Sisters in their ordinary clothes.

—THOMAS MERTON (1940)

NOVEMBER 13

T he *Regard*, a ship of Barnstable, of about two hundred tons, arrived with twenty passengers and about fifty cattle. . . . There came in this ship one Mansfield, a poor godly man of Exeter, being very desirous to come to us, but not able to transport his family. There was in the city a rich merchant, one Marshall, who being troubled in his dreams about the said poor man, could not be quiet till he had sent for him, and given him £50, and lent him £100, willing him withal, that, if he wanted, he should send to him for more. This Mansfield grew suddenly rich, and then lost his godliness, and his wealth soon after.

—JOHN WINTHROP (1634)

*H*ow convenient an overcoat is. I have just had one made from olive broadcloth at a cost of about 15$ (the most expensive garment I ever owned) and it covers my seedy, black frock and pants and my coarse lasting vest nicely, and I wear a "goodly outside seeming" as I pass the streets. A young man's pride might be shocked on my usual walk to meals by meeting, if shabby, the troop of high school girls who throng Pleasant Street.

—BENJAMIN BROWNE FOSTER (1849)

*W*ell at last, our journey has commenced and tonight after only a few miles of travel, I am *very* tired and the jolting of the wagon, caused me to *suffer much.* We were late in getting away from Topeka, leaving about 3 o'clock; the weather fine and a lovely evening. From our camp tonight at Mulhollen Hill, or a little West, we can see the lights of my beloved Topeka, and it makes my heart ache; when shall I see them again, if ever: my husband in poor health and at the end of a *long hard* journey, my little one to be born, without the help of Doctor or Nurse. But *for an ever present* God, I would be in *utter despair.*

—MARTHA FARNSWORTH (1891)

NOVEMBER 14

[At Fort Clark in the Dakotas] *C*aught two foxes and one wolf last night. Went to the Village to see the Old Woman, that was abandoned by the Mandans, at their departure for above, found the Old Lady Dead, and half eat up by the Wolves. Killed a Wolf to day With a Beaver trap fast to his leg, and has been in that situation since 14 days.

—FRANCIS CHARDON (1838)

'*T*is the coldest November I have ever known. This morning the mercury is at 26. Yesterday afternoon cold, fine ride with Ellery to Sudbury Inn. . . . Finest picture through wintry air of the russet Massachusetts. The landscape is democratic, not gathered into one city or baronial castle, but equally scattered into these white steeples, round which a town clusters in every place where six roads meet, or where a river branches or falls, or where the pan of soil is a little deeper. The horizon line marched by hills tossing like waves in a storm: firm indigo line. T is a pretty revolution which is effected in the landscape by simply turning your head upside down, or, looking through your legs: an infinite softness and loveliness is added to the picture. It changes the landscape at once from November to June, or, as Ellery declared, makes *Campagna* of it at once; so, he said, Massachusetts is Italy upside down.

—RALPH WALDO EMERSON (1848)

*I*n the evening I went to a party. It is a bad place to go to, thirty or forty persons, mostly young women, in a small room, warm and noisy. . . . I could imagine better places for conversation, where there should be a certain degree of silence surrounding you, and less than forty talking at once. Why, this afternoon even I did better. Old Mr. Joseph Hosmer and I ate luncheon of cracker and cheese together in the woods. I heard all he said, though it was not much, to be sure, and he could hear me; and then he talked out of such a glorious repose, taking a leisurely bite at the cracker and cheese between his words, and so some of him was communicated to me, and some of me to him, I trust. These parties, I think, are a part of the machinery of modern society that young people may be brought together to form marriage connections. What is the use in going to see people whom yet you never see, and who never see you?

—HENRY DAVID THOREAU (1851)

I rode down to the Depot yesterday afternoon to bring up Maria, who arrived from Charleston. She tells us of the state of panic in which the people of Charleston have been since the appearance of the Yankee fleet. . . . Large gangs of negroes on the islands have refused to leave the plantations & on Edisto there are still about 6 000 that have remained. They are unwilling to leave their homes, & moreover have been told that no harm would come to them if they stayed. The planters of the islands have generally burned their cotton, but not their corn or other provision crops. Many who were wealthy men a week ago, are now reduced to poverty, leaving home with only their clothes. . . . The shipment or transportation of all groceries & provisions from the city is now interdicted by military authority, these being wanted for the troops.

—HENRY RAVENEL (1861)

NOVEMBER 15

This day has been appointed by proclamation of Presdt. Davis to be observed through the Confederate States as a day of Fasting, Humiliation & Prayer,—when we are all exhorted to humble ourselves before our Heavenly Father & confessing our individual as well as our national sins . . . Our soil is invaded, vast numbers of our people have been reduced to poverty & destitution, have been driven from their homes,—& terror & alarm have driven even the people of Charleston from their homes there to seek an asylum in the upper country. . . . By the paper we learn that the Yankees have landed at Pinckney island in large numbers.

—HENRY RAVENEL (1861)

*W*e passed what was once the town of Hamburg, two years ago a bustling village—a large cluster of miners' cabins, three hotels, three stores, two billiard salons, and all the other accompaniments of a mining town—now all is gone. . . . A cluster of graves of the miners who had died . . . remained. Boards had once been set up at their graves, but most had rotted off and fallen—the rest will soon follow. Bushes have grown over the graves, and soon they, as well as the old town, will be forgotten. Friends in distant lands, mothers in far off homes, may still be wondering, often with a sign, what has become of loved sons who years ago thought their fortunes in the land of gold, but who laid their bones on the banks of the Klamath and left no tidings behind. Alas, how many a sad history is hidden in the neglected and forgotten graves that are scattered among the wild mountains that face the Pacific!

—WILLIAM HENRY BREWER (1863)

*C*old and rainy but I got in a long morning of work and then went off to lunch at Cafe Royal with Dr. Joe. We went then to see Chaplin's The Great Dictator and were both made very sad to find it dull. It seemed patched together—did not say anything—the old Chaplin gift seemingly quite gone. I wanted to weep.

—SHERWOOD ANDERSON (1940)

419

NOVEMBER 16

*A*bout ten o'clock we came into a deep valley, full of brush and long grass, through which we found little paths or tracts, and there we saw a deer and found springs of fresh water, of which we were heartily glad, and sat us down and drunk our first New England water with as much delight as ever we drunk drink in all our lives. We went on further and found where a house had been, and four or five old planks laid together. Also we found a great kettle which had been some ship's kettle and brought out of Europe. There was also a heap of sand, which we digged up, and in it we found a little old basket full of very fair corn of this year, with some thirty-six goodly ears of corn, some yellow, and some red, and others mixed wth blue, which was a very goodly sight. . . . We returned that night to the fresh water pond and there we made our rendezvous, making a great fire, and a barricado to windward of us, and kept good watch with three sentinels all night.

—WILLIAM BRADFORD AND EDWARD WINSLOW (1620)

[General Ulysses S. Grant] *I*s deeply impressed with the vast importance and significance of the late Presidential election. The point which impressed him most powerfully was that which I regarded as the critical one—the pivotal centre of our history—the quiet and orderly character of the whole affair. No bloodshed or riot—few frauds, and those detected and punished in an exemplary manner. It proves our worthiness of free institutions, and our capability of preserving them without running into anarchy or despotism.

—JOHN HAY (1864)

NOVEMBER 17

*F*ine pleasant day. A Bull Made his appearance on the hill. Caught one wolf last night. Gave a good Whipping to my young Wife, the first since our union, as I am united to one, that I stole from my friend, J. Halsey, on my visit to Fort Pierre last summer.

—FRANCIS CHARDON (1838)

I hired a man to rustle for some chickens and he found three after a two days' hunt. He paid $24 for them and with his horse hire and time they cost me $50, but I don't begrudge it for I made chicken broth and Pard said it went right to the spot. . . . The grass is coming up, the hill sides are all green and it looks like spring instead of fall. While it is mighty pretty, it isn't like autumn back in old Litchfield where the sumachs and the maples are all ablaze at this time of the year. . . . Pard says I would do better to buy land in California, but that's foolishness. The gold will all be dug out after a while, and after that I don't see what there is to stay in this country for.

—ALFRED T. JACKSON (1850)

*L*ast night Boris Aronson and Sid Benson came here for a pot roast dinner. We drank some good American wine about which I am inordinately delighted. Boris is always despairing within. Life, he says again and again, is not intimate enough for him. He protests that he would not work on Broadway were it not for his money needs. He is horrified that everything lacks character, strongly condemns the business of the theatre, almost weeps that a man cannot exist as an artist, that he is "typed" once he has made a success in a particular field, that everything is *accidental* here, including success; all is confusion and waste. Well, it's an old story. But we talked for two hours about these things and finally agreed that the Americans do not know life but live instead a nervous abstraction.

—CLIFFORD ODETS (1940)

NOVEMBER 18

*D*ONE PICKING COTTON. I went to town today and drove our new horse, Roland. I am pleased with him. I paid $6.00 for a pound of soda and $5.00 for a paper of pins. Every body seems to be distressed about the war. The dark days have surely come. The Confederacy! I almost hate the word. May the Lord have mercy and incline our hearts to do his will.

—EMILY HARRIS (1864)

*I*t is lucky I bought the typewriter. The rest of my money is gone. The bank failed last Friday, so the whole community is pretty blue. Since the July 1 hailstorm farmers have drawn out more than $50,000 and had nothing to put in. Now the money, some of it borrowed, they counted on for living expenses this winter and for seed grain in the spring is gone. . . . I asked Dad what we will do now that the bank has failed. "Never mind, Doodler (his nickname for me) we'll pull out of this, but you better buy your shoes before I run out of money." I won't use Dad's money for shoes and other things I need. The surplus chickens aren't sold yet. The Superintendent will pay me to do school typing and his personal typing after school and weekends. Typewriters are as scarce in this town as people who can type.

—ANN MARIE LOW (1928)

*I*t occurred to me today, as I sat stirring my third cup of tea, that this relaxed, late-afternoon atmosphere extends over a good deal of English life. An American living in England is constantly fetching up with a whang against the caste system; against a corrosive envy of the United States; against the worn-outness of an old country; and against that death-in-life which the Britons, with characteristic understatement, like to call English reserve. In the irritation resulting from these collisions, the American tends to overlook the fact that he can read his English newspapers in the relative peace en-

422

gendered by an absence of race riots, lynchings, Vigilantes, rackets, wholesale murders, police brutalities and Roman holidays like the Hauptmann execution. . . . A good deal in England makes the blood boil, but there is not nearly so much occasion as there is in America for blood to run cold.

—MARGARET HALSEY (1937)

[Joe Hergesheimer] *T*old me that the most violent of all the Nazis in Washington is an old woman named Lee, the widow of a grandson of the General. She has a fine house and plenty of money, and has now reached such an age that she can safely speak her mind freely. Joe said that she insists at dinner parties on arguing that the greatest man living in the world today is Hitler.

—H. L. MENCKEN (1944)

NOVEMBER 19

*N*ear this Town [of Mount Holly] in a Wood, a Hermit has dwelt these 27 years, living on Bread and water. His bed is a hole dug in the ground about one foot and a half below the surface, and cover'd at pleasure with a board. . . . When he goes to bed he crawls into his hut and at the further end slips into his hole which he calls his grave, drawing over the Board and goes to sleep. He crawls night and morning on his hands and knees about two rods to a particular tree to pray. He says he was warned of God in a remarkable Dream when he first came to America to take this course of Life. He has many Latin and other Books in his lonely Cell, and is said to write considerably. He kisses every man's hand that visits him and thankfully accepts of what is gave him, except Money, which he refuses. His Beard is done up in a loose club under his chin. . . . He says he shall come out purified & live like other folks if he continues in this State till he is eighty. He says he often wishes for Death, being frequently afflicted with pains of Body by this method of life. He never goes near a fire in the coldest time.

—ALBIGENCE WALDO (1777)

A man dies every now and then in our Regiment. I felt extremely sorry for one poor fellow who was lying in a tent without any fire. He had the fever, but was suffering greatly from the extreme cold. Sickness is more to be dreaded by far in the army, than the bullets. No bravery can achieve anything against it. The soldier may sicken and die, without receiving any attenton, but from the rough hands of his fellow soldiers. When buried he is soon forgotten.

—JAMES E. HALL (1861)

*S*lept in my clothes last night, as I heard that the Yankees went to neighbor Montgomery's on Thursday night at one o'clock, searched his house, drank his wine and took his money and valuables. As we were not disturbed, I walked after breakfast, with Sadai, up to Mr. Joe Perry's, my nearest neighbor, where the Yankees were yesterday. . . . Happening to turn and look behind, as we stood there, I saw some blue-coats coming down the hill. . . . I hastened back to my frightened servants and told them they had better hide, and then went back to the gate to claim protection and a guard. But like demons they rush in! My yards are full. To my smoke-house, my dairy, pantry, kitchen and cellar, like famished wolves they come, breaking locks and whatever is in their way.

—DOLLY LUNT BURGE (1864)

*T*ook out the last extra blankets this morning as the paper predicted "Fair and much colder tonight." Every once in a while the weather man is right. "Such a remark is simply

424

childish," says Jim. "So is the weather," says I. Whereupon I slip another section of apple pie onto his plate and we both feel better. We agree on practically nothing—except the essentials. . . . Nice to stand together at night as we cover up the children the last thing before we go to bed. Blankets he has worked hard to buy, and I have worked hard to care for, keep them warm and well.

—Dorothy Robinson (1937)

NOVEMBER 20

*H*ere I have been these forty years learning the language of these fields that I may the better express myself. If I should travel to the prairies, I should much less understand them, and my past life would serve me but ill to describe them. Many a weed stands for more of life to me than the big trees of California would if I should go there. We need only travel enough to give our intellects an airing. In spite of Malthus and the rest, there will be plenty of room in this world, if every man will mind his own business. I have not heard of any planet running against another yet.

—Henry David Thoreau (1857)

*T*he public is kept in ignorance at present of the disposition of our large army now concentrating between Charleston & Beaufort. As fast as troops arrive they are hurried off to the scene of operations. . . . Every thing shows the military ascendency. The grey uniforms & military caps are met every where about the streets, more of them than citizens dress. The deserted streets & closed stores tell how many have left their peaceful avocations to take their places in the army of defence.

—Henry Ravenel (1861)

$\mathcal{I}$ had a protracted and interesting interview to-day with a gaudily dressed and rather diminutive lieutenant, who applied for a passport to the Mississippi River. . . . It appeared that he was not going under special orders of the adjutant-general . . . and my curiosity was excited. . . . Finally he escaped further interrogatories by snatching up the passport I had signed and departing hastily. But instead of the usual military salute at parting, he *courtesied*. This, when I reflected on the fineness of his speech, the fullnes of his breast, his attitudes and his short steps, led me to believe the person was a woman instead of a lieutenant.

—JOHN BEAUCHAMP JONES (1861)

NOVEMBER 21

$\mathcal{I}$t has rained all day and rains on. . . . I have not been well today. The children have been confined to the house. Their noise and confusion and the trials that I see in the future have made me a miserable day. I have felt crazy. I could almost feel the wrinkles coming on my face and the hair turn gray on my head. . . . I feel old and miserable and ugly. . . . The wants of the family are never satisfied and their wants weigh heavily on me. I have often heard my old mother in law say that they who raised the most children had the most trouble. . . . I suppose that when I am no longer of use here I shall be called hence.

—EMILY HARRIS (1861)

$\mathcal{T}$his week is Thanksgiving Week. . . . There are many things that farm folks can be thankful for. There are supposed to be so many thousands of unemployed, mostly in the cities, and many of them are the folks that a few years ago left the farms because they thot they were smart enough that they did not need to work the long hours . . . for the small pay that the farmer got. . . . They traded the security of the land for what has it turned out to be. I dressed turkeys for the Thanksgiving trade. Bill husked corn all day. The weather was quite warm and Bill says the fields are in fair shape again. Rumor says a prominent banker shot himself this morning. Supposedly too many complications to attempt to find a way out.

—ELMER G. POWERS (1932)

I went to a party of a lot of middle-aged youngish men, all of the rather successful type, no threat to each other's peace of mind or reputation or pocketbook or anything. All wore pullovers, etc., but elegant Italian imports for the most part; and work trousers, but beautifully tailored. There were some "exceptional" persons . . . but as the midnight hour passed I'm afraid we all got to looking alike—the terrible pull of American collectivity.

—GLENWAY WESCOTT (1955)

*W*hen the news of the seven-year persecution of Martin Luther King by the FBI came out yesterday and the day before, I felt rather *sick*. We live in such a dirty world, and as individuals seem more and more helpless to change it. . . . Franco's death the other day had reminded me of the idealism, the lifting up of so much courage thirty-six years ago in the rallying of youth from all over the world to help the Republic—long, long ago. . . . Then, before the Nazi camps, we could still believe in the goodness of man. Now man looks more and more like the murderer of all life, animals too—he is the killer of whales and of his own species—the death bringer. Under everything I do there is this sense that there is no foundation anymore. In what do we believe? can we believe? On what to stand firm? There has to be something greater than each individual . . . that gives him the sense that his life is vital to the whole.

—MAY SARTON (1975)

NOVEMBER 22

*S*till chugging along in convoy—a seasick homesick rather blue bunch of troops. . . . The conversation with a man in the dark—a pitch black moonless rainy night—and the terror of submarines and loneliness and strange unaccustomed things . . . The feeling of the frightfulness of the unknown—sea cold, sea dark—the little comfortable soul born out of its groove and shivering in the great shaggy world. In a dream in Verdun as I looked the sun was filmed over like a bloodshot eye and began to sway and wabble in the sky as a spent top sways and wabbles and whirling rolled into the seas vermillion ways so that pitblackness covered me.

—JOHN DOS PASSOS (1918)

I was sitting in government class, sixth period. Two social science teachers came in, one taking Mr. Huizenga out in the hall, and the other rushing to the back of the room and grabbing a radio. We laughed. Mr. Huizenga came back in and continued talking. Then he couldn't talk any longer. . . . Mr. Huizenga walked over to the blackboard and leaned against it. He didn't say anything for a minute. Then . . . "President Kennedy was shot through the head and killed." . . . Seventh period was homeroom guidance. In homeroom the radio was turned on. Nothing was said by anyone. "The President is still alive. We repeat, the President is still alive . . . We have an unconfirmed report from Dallas that the President is dead. We repeat, there is an unconfirmed report from Dallas that the President is now dead . . . President Kennedy is dead." Oh no—gasps, sobs, cries—oh, no, oh, no. . . . Down the hallway the phones rang and echoed one by one—the only sound heard was the eerie peal of the phone. It sliced the silence; wailing, it reechoed its cry. The Star Spangled Banner began playing over the radio. . . . At the end of the period we all rose and faced the windows of 330. Outside, silhouetted against the gray sky, the flag of our United States flew at half-mast. The thin metal strip dividing the glass of the window cut across the red and white stripes. The wind and rain clutched at the cloth, pulled at it, beat against it. It clung to the rope, its grip ever sure. The rope pulled away from the pole, but the banner held tightly. I held my hand over my beating heart. As one we said the pledge to the flag.

—LINDA RAE PATTERSON (1963)

NOVEMBER 23

Vital day at A. F. of L. Session until midnight. . . . Impression, at A. F. of L. of everyone lying. Green, in final speech, queerly suggestive of angry impotence. Force got by shouting and violent swinging of arms. Labor in a mess. Could not sleep. Had again night of faces. In semi-conscious state they kept coming—all women, all sad, all hurt. The faces, one after another, seemed to draw very slowly nearer and nearer. Soft lips met mine. There was a feeling of aroused sex. There was something very sad, very gentle, very beautiful felt.

—SHERWOOD ANDERSON (1936)

I do not like those little American boys who come rushing in to the room when I am visiting their parents and interrupt an otherwise enjoyable conversation by snatching the ice from my highball and putting it down my neck. I like it still less when (after the ice has been retrieved and the little boy has waggishly dropped it back into the glass) I arrange my face and mind to accept an apology as gracefully as may be, and the boy's mother gives me a fond and secret glance and murmurs reverently, "Isn't it marvelous? He isn't the least bit shy." Not to mention the little boy's father supplementing her with a hearty, "I'm really not a partial parent. That kid's got poise." Some day, I suppose, I am going to be pushed down an elevator shaft by one of these pocket-edition Calibans— and his father and mother will smile with a tender pride as they explain to my mourning relatives that it was part of a project in gravitation. . . . Nobody agrees with you more completely when you deplore the bad manners of modern children, than a set of modern parents. They never think you mean their children.

—MARGARET HALSEY (1937)

My brother August and I, sitting by the fire in the evening, often congratulate ourselves on the fact that we have no children. . . . I can imagine nothing more distressing today than the thoughts of a man with a family growing up. The boys stand a good chance of being butchered in their young manhood, and boys and girls together face a world that will be enormously more uncomforable than the one my generation has known. There will be wars off and on for years to come, and in the intervals of peace every American will be burdened and afflicted by the national debt. I read yesterday that it amounts even now to $6,800 a family—far more than the average American family accumulates as capital by a lifetime of work. By the time Roosevelt is got rid of at last it may be two or three times as much.

—H. L. MENCKEN (1944)

NOVEMBER 24

There was a large mail came to-day in which I received a couple of Gazetts which gave me all the news from Lewistown. We received some hard tack, and the boys walked into them like mince pies. The troops are still coming in in this direction. Everything is dull around camp, and nothing can be heard but the monotonous tap of the drum.

—HOWARD HELMAN (1862)

*T*hanksgiving. . . . After dinner I took Lawrence down to see the newsboys take theirs in Eighteenth St. It was a fearful scene of stuffing and I called his attention to how "piggy" they ate. . . . I am having so much dining out this winter that I am forced to put myself on strict *regimen*. I have stopped smoking and coffee; I suppose I shall always have to be patching myself up in order to be equal to the ordinary duties of life, till the day comes when I shall be pronounced not worth further repairs.

—E. L. GODKIN (1870)

*I*n from the farm came His Majesty the Gobbler, fattened to a full twenty pounds of double breasted perfection. The butcher who undertook to dress him for the basting pan nearly cried when he parted with him, and made several sly suggestions of a black market character. But I lugged him home like any Pilgrim Father, and tucked him away in the cooler along with the bottle of *Berncastler Doktor* designed to wash him down.

—JAMES WEBB YOUNG (1943)

NOVEMBER 25

*Y*esterday I read Dickens's *American Notes*. . . . Truth is not his object for a single instant, but merely to make good points in a lively sequence, and he proceeds very well. . . . Monstrous exaggeration is an easy secret of romance. But Americans who, like some of us Massachusetts people, are not fond of spitting, will go from Maine to New Orleans, and meet no more annoyance than we should in Britain or France. So with "yes," so with "fixings," so with soap and towels; and all the other trivialities which this trifler detected in travelling over half the world.

—RALPH WALDO EMERSON (1842)

[Gertrude Stein] *Spent* the years from 1897 to 1902 in the Johns Hopkins Medical School. She never got her degree. Dr. J. Whitridge Williams, head of the department of obstetrics, plucked her in that subject. He detested women doctors and, in addition, had a violent prejudice against all women who were fat. La Stein, even in those days, weighed nearly 200 pounds. . . . She was known to the other students as the Battle-ax. Women medical students were then something of a novelty and the men held aloof from them. The girls accordingly decided to give some parties. . . . Stein showed up smoking a pipe. This was a dreadful shock in those innocent days. If it had been done by a woman of normal attractiveness all the male students present would have invited her to bed at once. But inasmuch as the revolutionist was Stein, no such suggestion was made.

—H. L. MENCKEN (1938)

On the 21st I fasted to be in communion with the 250,000 who did so, especially students in New England. I have felt so strongly that we could not sit passively while so many starve in Africa and I have been miserable for weeks that Ford does nothing and Butz and the others more or less wrecked the food conference in Rome, when some positive action on our part might have lit the fire. It is not enough to send money all the time as we all do. Somehow one has to give part of oneself. . . . I have nightmares about us Americans, weighed down as we are by "things" and by excessive eating. I read yesterday that Americans eat fifty times the meat the British do. . . . Many of us are literally weighed down.

—MAY SARTON (1974)

NOVEMBER 26

Set a mouse trap last night in case Bess and I might want to get his skeleton. Caught him but he wasn't dead. Neither

432

Julie nor Netty would kill him so I heroicly dropped the trap in a pail of water and rushed out of the room. . . . The poor fellow being drowned by this time we took our victim out in yard, bared our glittering knives and commenced operations. But the horrid mouse's fur was so soft that we couldn't make a hole and besides it made us sick and our hands trembled so we couldn't do a thing. But concluding it was *feminine* nonsense we made a hole and squeezed his insides out. It was the most disgusting thing I ever did. We then took off his skin. It came off elegantly just like a glove. . . . Finally put it on the fire to boil. . . . Picked all the meat off it and saved its tongue and eyes to look through the microscope and then the mouse looked like a real skeleton. We then put it out the window to bleach and then as Bess had to go I walked with her. . . . When I got home I found that Netty had thrown away our tongue and eyes, and worst of all woe woe is me that our skeleton that had taken us 3 mortal hours to get, had fallen out of the window and smashed. Oh Science! Why will thou not protect thy votaries! . . . Bess said when she told her father about our getting the mouse he looked grave and said, Bessie Bessie thee is loosing all thy *feminine* traits. I'm afraid I haven't got any to loose for I greatly prefer cutting up mice to sewing worsted.

—M. Carey Thomas (1870)

$\mathcal{W}$e are the first nation to starve to death in a storehouse that's overfilled with everything we want.

—Will Rogers (1930)

[Heading home for Thanksgiving during World War II]
$\mathcal{S}$ighted turkey. Sank same.

—James Webb Young (1942)

NOVEMBER 27

*A*bout 5 M. Boston's greatest Fire brake forth at Mr. Moors, through the default of a Taylour Boy, who rising alone and early to work, fell asleep and let his Light fire the House, which gave fire to the next, so that about fifty Landlords were despoyled of their Housing. N. B. The House of the Man of God, Mr. Mather, and Gods House were burnt with fire. Yet God mingled mercy, and sent a considerable rain, which gave check in great measure to the (otherwise) masterless flames: lasted all the time of the fire, though fair before and after. Mr. Mather saved his Books and other Goods.

—SAMUEL SEWALL (1676)

*L*iving in New York is exorbitantly dear, and it falls pretty hard upon persons like me, who live upon their income, and harder still upon that large and respectable class consisting of the officers and clerks in public institutions whose support is derived from fixed salaries. . . . I paid . . . for my winter butter, 400 to 500 lbs., $2.14 per pound. In the long course of thirty-four years' housekeeping I never buttered my bread at so extravagant a rate. Good butter is almost an indispensable article in the family; but there are many persons in New York as good as myself who must be content to eat dry bread this winter, or at least to spread the children's slices confoundedly thin.

—PHILIP HONE (1835)

*T*oday I think: should I be going to Harlem, or to the Trappists? . . . I would have to renounce more in entering the Trappists. That would be one place where I would have to give up *everything*. . . . Harlem will be full of confusions. I don't particularly like the idea of working with a lot of girls. Going to live in Harlem does not seem to me to be anything special. It is a good and reasonable way to follow Christ. But going to the Trappists is exciting, it fills me with awe and

434

with desire. I return to the idea again and again: "Give up *everything*, give up *everything*!" I shall speak to one of the Friars.

—THOMAS MERTON (1941)

In Cincinnati found the first day of Christmas shopping going full blast. The merchants had given the downtown streets a festive air, and the public had responded. Traffic seemed to be on a pre-rationing spree; sidewalks were crowded; stores packed; and the hotels full of pretty girls and uniforms. At a newsstand I heard a woman ask: "Have you any magazines that are not full of war stories?"

—JAMES WEBB YOUNG (1942)

NOVEMBER 28

Saturday, I forgot to mention Gen. Hill's division passed through town. They were very destitute, many without shoes, and all without overcoats or gloves, although the weather is freezing. Their poor hands looked so red and cold holding their muskets in the biting wind. Such delicate, small hands and feet some of them had. One South Carolina regiment I especially noticed, had hands and feet that looked as if they belonged to women, and so cold and red and dirty they were. That last must have been the hardest to bear, the dirt, for gentlemen, as most of them were. They did not, however, look dejected, but went on their way right joyously.

—CORNELIA PEAKE MCDONALD (1862)

We decide to go uptown to see Lincoln Square Vaudeville show. . . . We go to the theatre. A poor show. Audience rises

435

at some ham actor singing the Marseillaise in an act! And because Bert and I refuse to rise, we are glared at! More American patriotism—and heavy thought! Home at 12. We have tea, and to bed.

—THEODORE DREISER (1917)

J.P.'s gave Thanksgiving banquet. . . . Strange gathering. Harvard graduate in chevrons listening to Polish miner. California newspaper owner discussing Romain Rolland's "Life of Beethoven" with ex-waiter. College professor being bawled out for bad language by Armenian sheep-herder. The new America. U.S. no longer mere geographic term. Nation at last. Caste and origin forgotten. Too bad rough, frank fraternity of *la vie militaire* can't last. Hat off to Yank. Independent, freer than any man world yet seen, but with respect for self and purpose that makes one glad to salute him as *man* in response to his salute to *insignia*. Great fellow!

—HOWARD O'BRIEN (1918)

NOVEMBER 29

[A] *F*riend drove me over to Warm Springs, where I was the personal guest of the President. He has a small cottage beautifully located on the edge of a well-wooded ravine. . . . He has only three bedrooms but Mrs. Roosevelt was not there and I occupied her room. A common bathroom connected the President's room and mine. Miss Le Hand, his personal secretary, had the other bedroom. Meals are served in the living room and the President works there. The President is always charming but he was delightful at Warm Springs. Everyone there loves him, and crowds hang outside the gate, especially on Sundays, just to see him and cheer him as he drives in and out occassionally . . . [in] an open Plymouth, so arranged with some contraption on the steering wheel that he can operate it without having to use his feet which are helpless.

—HAROLD L. ICKES (1933)

*A*l Capone . . . is a patient . . . at the Union Memorial Hospital. He is suffering from paresis, the end result of a syphilitic infection. . . . His mental disturbance takes the form of delusions of grandeur. He believes that he is the owner of a factory somewhere in Florida employing 25,000 men, and he predicts freely that he'll soon be employing 75,000. . . . He is occupying two rooms and a bath at a cost of $30 a day. He sleeps in one room himself, and the other is a sort of meeting place for his old mother, his three brothers, and his wife. The brothers spend all day playing checkers. . . . The mother is an ancient Italian woman of the peasant type, and can barely speak English. . . . The wife, who is ignorant but apparently not unintelligent, moves a cot into Capone's room every night and sleeps there. He is naturally very popular with the hospital staff . . . for he is not only a good patient, he is also likely to leave large tips. . . . The Federal Bureau of Investigation has notified [Dr. Joseph E.] Moore that so far as it knows there is no project on foot to kill Capone. Thus no guard upon him is maintained, and any visitor to the hospital is free to barge into his room.

—H. L. MENCKEN (1939)

*T*he psychiatrist makes this mistake. One should say to the neurotic person, "Your self—it is material. So start using it, for it is as good as any other you will get. In fact the so-called normal will be less interesting." But in America particularly, the psychiatrist reaps a rich harvest—every American wants another personality which, once acquired, he would sterilize and render as useless as the old one.

—CLIFFORD ODETS (1940)

437

NOVEMBER 30

*H*aving discovered this place, it was controversial amongst us, what to do touching our abode and settling there. Some thought it best for many reasons to abide there. Robert Coppin, our pilot, made relation of a great navigable river and good harbor in the other headland of this bay, almost right over against Cape Cod, not much above eight leagues distant, in which he had been once; and because that one of the wild men with whom they had some trucking stole a harping iron from them, they called it Thievish Harbor [Plymouth, Massachusetts] and beyond that place they were enjoined not to go, whereupon, a company was chosen to go out upon a third discovery. Whilst some were employed in this discovery, it pleased God that Mistress White was brought to bed of a son, which was called Peregrine.

—WILLIAM BRADFORD AND EDWARD WINSLOW (1620)

*B*usiness having deserted K Street, where we were, we rented a house on J Street . . . to continue the hotel business. . . . Mr. Frink bought three cows for $275.00. The milk was worth $2.00 per gallon, but instead of selling it, we used it all in the hotel, placing most of it on the table for our customers. . . . People would come from distant parts of the city to get meals on account of the fresh milk. Business now increased rapidly. . . . Our customers began leaving their gold-dust with us for safe keeping, until sometimes there would be as much as eight or ten thousand dollars worth at one time. . . . We had come here as gold-seekers only, not as settlers. But after a year's residence in the delightful valley of the Sacramento, we had satisfied ourselves that no pleasanter land for a home could be found, though we should roam the wide world over. . . . The future of California seemed to us full of promise, and here we resolved to rest from our pilgrimage.

—MARGARET A. FRINK (1850)

438

$\mathcal{I}$n Elizabeth City one Addison White proposed to join a band of Guerrillas & arming himslf went at night to a rendezvous where he expected to meet them. The Yankee's had, however, been before him and he found a band of them there who arrested him. After keeping him prisoner for some weeks, threatening daily to shoot him if he did not take the oath, one night about sundown without trial or orders of any kind, a squad of them took him down to the wharf & putting him up as a target, one by one they shot at him until they killed him & refusing to allow his body to be moved, would let no one come near it. . . . Mr James Skinner was also arrested & that night a party of negroes headed by his foreman, who sometime before had gone to the Yankees, came to his dwelling & suddenly burst open the doors & the first thing Mrs Skinner knew of their presence was their firing pistols through the house. . . . Mrs S, on hearing the firing, opened her door & thinking they were Yankees called out to them to behave themselves, that there was no one to make resistance to them, & that such conduct was as useless as it was improper," when one of the negroes answered, "if she did not take her d____ head in that door they would blow her d____ brains out!" They afterwards learned that Mr S was arrested at the instance of the negro foreman, who feared & wanted him out of the way.

—CATHERINE EDMONDSTON (1863)

$\mathcal{A}$fter supper. The family are all sitting in the piazza. Today I have heard of robbery of various kinds. A party of deserters have robbed Dr Mills who lives about thirty miles from us. Several negroes belonging to our neighbors have been stealing on [a] small scale to the great annoyance of their owners and others. Times are getting more desperate everyday. Some say the war will continue four years more. If it does we will be nowhere and nobody.

—EMILY HARRIS (1864)

⟨ DECEMBER ⟩

DECEMBER 1

𝒯here was a Nigger boy at the College this morning making his way to Wilmington [Delaware] and the North and asking for shelter until night but Rev. Graham would not let him stay and said the college must not break the law even when the law seems wrong and after he had said that to the boys he went away and did not ask what was done with him. So we put him in the second floor lumber room until night and when he got cold Savin took him in and the boys in his room gave him a coat and went out collecting. I gave the boots that came to me for mine and Turner calls me "Nigger lover" but would have given too I think if he had had anything to give. He left during study hour. There is a strange suppressed excitement and it is a kind of sober quiet too.

—JOSEPH CLEAVER, JR. (1853)

𝒯 understand it now. Keeping journals is for those who cannot, or dare not, speak out. So I shall set up a journal, being only a rather lonely young girl in a very small and hated minority. . . . Surely no native-born woman loves her country better than I love America. The blood of one of its Revolutionary patriots flows in my veins, and it is the Union for which he pledged his "life, fortune, and sacred honor" that I love, not any

440

divided, or special section of it. . . . Living from birth in slave countries, both foreign and American, and passing through one slave insurrection in early childhood, the saddest and also the pleasantest features of slavery have been familiar. If the South goes to war for slavery, slavery is doomed in this country. To say so is like opposing one drop to a roaring torrent.

—ANONYMOUS WOMAN (1860)

$\mathcal{G}$od speed the day of peace! Our patriotism is mainly in the army and among the ladies of the South. The avarice and cupidity of the men at home could only be excelled by the ravenous wolves; and most of our sufferings are fully deserved. Where a people will not have mercy on one another, how can they expect mercy? . . . A portion of the people look like vagabonds. We see men and women and children in the streets in dingy and dilapidated clothes; and some seem gaunt and pale with hunger—the speculators, and thieving quartermasters and commissaries only, looking sleek and comfortable.

—JOHN BEAUCHAMP JONES (1862)

$\mathcal{V}$ery cold. In the evening snow that turned to rain and then froze. Icy pavements. Dreamed at night of taking part in a long and ugly strike. It was a day of gloom. Began Green Grass from a new angle. In sharp reaction to ugliness of labor meeting at Tampa. Went for a walk in icy streets. The streets [of Durham, N.C.] full of negro cigarette factory workers.

—SHERWOOD ANDERSON (1936)

DECEMBER 2

$\mathcal{R}$ead the trial of Sullivan & others, engaged in the prise fight betwen Lilly & McCoy, in N. York, in wh. the latter was killed. . . . Poor McCoy fought 124 rounds, several of wh. he fought with both his eyes blinded. . . . The most affecting thing was when his poor half witted brother came to the place with a basket containing fruit, spirit, spunges &c. for his brother, & the managers refused to let him in. In half an hour his brother was dead. I cd. not help crying over this touch. . . . The picture of this poor, anxious, half-witted brother, with his basket of provisions wh. he had carefuly prepared, denied admission, & then hearing of the death,— has been before me ever & anon for days. We ought to have such things in our knowledge that we may be reminded of the depravity of human nature.

—RICHARD HENRY DANA (1842)

$\mathscr{T}$he history of Kansas already knows *John Brown* of Osawatomie. . . . In this struggle John Brown lost two *noble boys*—one was murdered unarmed and another taken prisoner and driven with heavy chains before these merciless slavery extensionists for 30 miles through the blistering sunshine and choking dust which cruel treatment ended in his death. Not the strangest thing in history will be the fact that John Brown after this merciless destruction of his sons to make room for slavery should become a Mono Maniac and conscientiously battle against it wherever found. . . . He crossed the Missouri line and actually liberated about a dozen Slaves. . . . Led them Moses like through Iowa and several other states to Canada. And now for attempting to repeat this daring deed in the state of Virginia on a much larger scale he is overpowered . . . and surrenders. . . . He is to be hung to day charged by the grand jury of Charlestown with Murder, Treason and causing an insurrection.

—MITCHELL JACKSON (1859)

$\mathscr{A}$ dark day for our country. *John Brown* is to be hung. . . . When I reflect upon his devoted Christian character, his love of freedom drawn from God's Word, and from his Puritan ancestors, his sufferings in Kansas, his bold and dar-

442

ing courage, mixed with mercy, the humane purpose of his heart in going to Virginia, his gallant treatment of those he had in his power, his neglect of his own safety, his frankness on the trial, his coolness and undisturbed serenity when the terrible sentence was pronounced, his terse, manly and eloquent speech, so full of soul and heroism . . . a gray-haired veteran standing on the fatal scaffold surrounded as he is at this moment by 2,000 American soldiers. . . . When I remember all this, it seems as though God's warning angel would sound through that infatuated assembly the words of a patriot of other and better days, the words "I tremble for my country when I reflect that God is just, and his Justice will not always slumber." Brave man, Old Hero, Farewell. Your death shall be the dawn of a better day.

—JAMES A. GARFIELD (1859)

*O*ld John Brown was hanged this morning; justly, say I, but his name may be a word of power for the next half-century. It was unwise to give fanaticism a martyr.

—GEORGE TEMPLETON STRONG (1859)

DECEMBER 3

*W*as called to debate the justice of taking America from the Indians but the Nigger boy [trying to escape from slavery] has upset my thoughts about justice.

—JOSEPH CLEAVER, JR. (1853)

*M*izzles and rains all day, making sloshy walking, which sends us all to the shoemaker's. Bought me a pair of cowhide boots to be prepared for winter walks. The shoemaker praised them, because they were made a year ago. I feel like an armed man now. The man who has bought his boots feels like him who has got in his winter's wood. There they stand beside me in the chamber, expectant, dreaming of far woods and wood paths, or frost-bound or sloshy roads, or of being bound with skate-straps and clogged with ice-dust. For years my appetite [for walking] was so strong that I browsed on the pine forest's edge seen against the winter horizon. . . . I ranged about like a gray moose looking at the spiring tops of the trees, and fed my imagination on them,—far away, ideal trees, not disturbed by the axe of the wood-cutter. . . . How I love the simple, reserved countrymen, my neighbors, who mind their own business and let me alone, who never waylaid nor shot at me, to my knowledge, when I crossed their fields, though each one has a gun in his house.

—HENRY DAVID THOREAU (1856)

DECEMBER 4

*I*n bad order; tooth and jaws, but the lip which was bitten by a venomous animal [a woman] on Friday last has swollen, and is very painful. . . . The bite was given in a paroxysm of great good humour. . . . My tooth still growling. At length made up my mind to have it [drawn]. . . . Went off to the dentist's full of resolution. He was out, and would not be home till morning. So that I shall have again to make all this effort to get myself in a tooth-drawing humour. . . . Brought home my tooth and my lip, both in bad condition.

—AARON BURR (1809)

*G*eorge Anthon looked in just before tea in great excitement. The corpus of old John Brown is in the city at No. something in the Bowery. . . . George Anthon . . . wanted me to go, which I didn't. . . . Old Brown's demeanor has undoubtedly made a

444

great impression. Many heroes of the Newgate Calendar have died game, as he did; but his simplicity and consistency, the absence of fuss, parade and bravado, the strength and clearness of his letters, all indicate a depth of conviction that one does not expect in an Abolitionist (who is apt to be a mere talker and sophist). . . . Slavery has received no such blow in my time as his strangulation. . . . One's faith in anything is terribly shaken by anybody who is ready to go to the gallows condemning and denouncing it.

—GEORGE TEMPLETON STRONG (1859)

*T*his morning just after breakfast we were startled at the announcement of a fire in the negro yard. Old Nanny's (the Dairy woman) house was burned, & all her clothing, bedding & other possessions. She seems much distressed at the loss, & as it is her whole wordly goods, she must feel it no less than those who have more to lose. I have given her two dollars to replace some of her things.

—HENRY RAVENAL (1861)

DECEMBER 5

*A*fter we had all Eat our Brakfasts, Paked up our things, it Began to Rain, & after we had Paraded our men, all the Lame & Lasey & the Faint Hearted & all that had no shoes nor Clothes to Keep them warm was Drafted out to Be Left Be hind. We marched in the Rain to Kings ferey & Crosed over & march'd thro mud & water as far as haverstraw, about 3 miles from the ferey & halted where we Drew fresh Beef & flower & had no salt to Season it. We was obligd to Lie on the Cold wet Ground all night. It Being a Verey Blustring night & our tents not Being Come, we was Obligd to meak Us huts with Rails & Coverd with Straw for Us to Sleep Under this Night.

—JOHN SMITH (1776)

445

$\mathscr{D}$uHamel heard in Wilmington [Delaware] of a niger boy being taken which sounds like our boy but not certain and did not dare ask details. Most of our boys are very sorry to hear of it and we hoped it is not the boy we helped which seems to me not to be the matter but that a black boy had been taken back from freedom to live all his life a slave. I am uncertain what I shall compose for Society. I may write about a black boy.

—JOSEPH CLEAVER, JR. (1853)

$\mathscr{N}$ight has at last put an end to a very troublesome day. I have had company last night and to day. It has rained all day, the children have been cross and ungovernable. Old Judah and Edom are both sick. Ann is trying to weave, and a poor weave it is. . . . Laura is coughing a rough ominous cough, has scarcely any shoes on her feet, and no hope of getting any this week, West has the croup. I am trying to wean the baby and the cows laid out last night, and last and worst of all I know my husband is somewhere miserably cold, wet, and comfortless. "The soldier in his tent."

—EMILY HARRIS (1862)

$\mathscr{G}$hostliness, dreariness, of night of Repeal. Not enough liquor, soon gave out—ghostliness of the Astor [hotel], police and locked doors, people locked inside, lobby and corridors deserted. Reubens [restaurant]: couldn't get in after I had checked my coat and hat, crowded with German Jews in opera hats. . . . I ended up at Childs on 59th Street, which was now serving wine—uninviting rather crass-looking people. Algonquin dining rooms had been dark and closed—late, 3 or 4 a.m.—Difficulty of getting drinks for several days.

—EDMUND WILSON (1933)

446

DECEMBER 6

$\mathscr{T}$alked with Zab about Newton, Bacon, Locke, Martin and Chambers, Rowning, Desaguliers, S'Gravesande, &c. I told him I had a low opinion of the compilers, abridgers, and abstract makers; we had better draw science from its fountain in original authors. These writers, the hirelings of the booksellers, only vend us the discoveries of other philosophers, in another form and under another title, in order to get bread to eat and raiment to put on.

—JOHN ADAMS (1760)

$\mathscr{I}$ did not do much writing or desk work today. I spent quite a little time looking over old farm records. In one filing cabinet I found some material I had put away during the epidemic of Hoof and Mouth disease some years ago. Time gives value to almost any sort of records.

—ELMER G. POWERS (1931)

$\mathscr{H}$ickey tells about a visit to Europe to consult with branch managers of the [Gillette Razor] company. . . . The company's business was talked of at every dinner party, and in the end Mrs. Hickey was moved to protest. Finally, she and Hickey went to Rome, and being Catholics, sought an audience with the Pope. Mrs. Hickey approached His Holiness with great reverence, and was almost shocked out of her wits by what the Pope said. . . . "I am glad to welcome you both to Rome, first because we are all children of the same Holy Mother, but also because I understand, Mr. Hickey, that you are the General Manager of the Gillette Razor Company, and, you know, I have used a Gillette razor for many, many years and I think it is a wonderful invention. But tell me, what *is* the matter with the blades?"

—H. L. MENCKEN (1934)

DECEMBER 7

About five o'clock in the morning we began to be stirring. Anon, all upon a sudden, we heard a great and strange cry, which we knew to be the same voices, though they varied their notes. One of our company being abroad came running in and cried, *They are men! Indians! Indians!* And withal, their arrows came flying amongst us. . . . The cry of our enemies was dreadful, especially when our men ran out to recover their arms. . . . A lusty man, and no wit less valiant, who was thought to be their captain, stood behind a tree within half a musket shot of us, and there let his arrows fly at us. . . . He stood three shots of a musket. At length one took full aim at him, after which he gave an extraordinary cry, and away they went all. . . . By the especial providence of God none of them either hit or hurt us, though many came close by us, and on every side of us, and some coats which hung up in our barricado were shot through and through.

—WILLIAM BRADFORD AND EDWARD WINSLOW (1620)

Pearl Harbor. We are at war! Jesus Christ, the Japs bombed Hawaii and the entire fleet has been sunk. . . . The radio says there are riots in Los Angeles, and they think it is sabotage. . . . I don't know what is going to happen to us, but I just can't think of it. I think of the Japs coming to bomb us, but I will go and fight even if I think I am a coward and I don't believe in wars but this time it has to be. I am selfish about it. I think not of California and America, but I wonder what is going to happen to the Nisei and to our parents. They may lock up the aliens. . . . If we are ever going to prove our Americanism, this is the time. The Anti-Jap feeling is bound to rise to hysterical heights. . . . I don't know what to think or do. Everybody is in a daze.

—CHARLES KIKUCHI (1941)

DECEMBER 8

*A*ll at our Several Posts. Provisions & Whiskey very scarce. Were Soldiers to have plenty of Food & Rum, I believe they would Storm Tophet. . . . At 12 o'clock at Night our Regt, with Sixteen more were Ordered to parade immediately before his Excellencies [Washington's] Quarters under Command of Sullivan & Wayne. We were there by One, when Intelligence came that the Enemy had made a precipitate retreat and was safely got into the City. We were all Chagrin'd at this, as we were more willing to Chase them in Rear, than meet such Sulkey Dogs in Front. We were now remanded back with several draughts of Rum in our frozen bellies, which made us so glad we all fell asleep in our open huts, nor experienced the Coldness of the Night 'till we found ourselves much stiffened by it in the Morning.

—ALBIGENCE WALDO (1777)

*H*ave driven *all* day, today, without a *sight* of a *living* thing; *not a bird*, bush or tree; the Plain as level as a floor, with only Buffalo grass growing; not the *slightest hollow* or *raise* of ground—just a *monotony* of *"distance."*

—MARTHA FARNSWORTH (1891)

DECEMBER 9

I rose about 8 o'clock and read a chapter in Hebrew and some Greek. I said my prayers, and had milk for breakfast. The weather was cloudy and cold, the wind northwest. I danced my dance. About 10 o'clock I went to Mr. Southwell's where I drank tea and stayed till eleven. Then I went to the Cockpit where I talked with Mr. B-m-f-l. Then I went home and danced again. Then about 2 o'clock I returned again to

Mr. Southwell's where I ate some boiled beef. After dinner we sat and drank a bottle till 5 o'clock and then I took a coach and called on my milliner. My daughter had the chariot to go to the ball. About 6 o'clock I went to Mrs. Lindsay's where I drank tea and chocolate and then took a walk and picked up a woman and put her in the coach and committed uncleanness. Then I went to Will's and had some cake and milk and read the news. Then I went home in a chair because it rained and said my prayers.

—WILLIAM BYRD (1718)

*T*here has been a long gap in my diary, my last entry being on the 31st of December of last year, when I finished a volume. I wish to resume a habit which has been a source of much pleasure & some mental improvement and which has accumulated many records of my life to which I often recur with interest & gratification. The gratification, however, is not unmixed with regret & mortification at meeting too often the expression of crude & hasty opinions, overwrought feelings, extravagant sentiments, exaggerated statements.

—SIDNEY GEORGE FISHER (1852)

DECEMBER 10

I confess I am a little cynical on some topics, and when a whole nation is roaring Patriotism at the top of its voice, I am fain to explore the cleanness of its hands and purity of its heart. I have generally found the gravest and most useful citizens are not the easiest provoked to swell the noise, though they may be punctual at the polls.

—RALPH WALDO EMERSON (1824)

*Y*esterday I walked under the murderous Lincoln bridge, where at least ten men have been swept dead from the cars within as many years. I looked to see if their heads had indented the bridge, if there were sturdy blows given as well as received, and if their brains lay about. The place looks as innocent as "a bank whereon the wild thyme grows." The bridge does its work in an artistic manner. We have another of exactly the same character in another part of the town, which has killed one, at least, to my knowledge. Surely the approaches to our town are well guarded. These are our modern dragons of Wantley. Buccaneers of the Fitchburg Railroad, they lie in wait at the narrow passes, and decimate the employees. The Company has signed a bond to give up one employee at this pass annually. The Vermont mother commits her son to their charge, and when she asks for him again, the directors say, "I am not your son's keeper; go look beneath the ribs of the Lincoln bridge."

—HENRY DAVID THOREAU (1856)

[Following the invasion of Finland by the Soviet Union on November 30] *I* went to Washington yesterday for the Gridiron Club dinner. . . . Three Ambassadors were present, and as usual they were introduced, each with a spotlight on him. The Dane got a perfunctory round of applause. The British Ambassador, Lord Lothian, got a little more, but not much more. But when the Finn arose . . . the whole audience got to its feet and the applause lasted half a minute at least. The Finn was apparently much affected. He stood as stiff as a ramrod, but tears rolled down his cheeks. He sat four or five places from Roosevelt, who called him over and shook hands with him. . . . This was the one really dramatic feature of an extremely dull dinner.

—H. L. MENCKEN (1939)

DECEMBER 11

A fortunate thing it is for us in this Confederacy that it is not 'de rigueur' to testify grief on the receipt of bad news by rending one's clothes! Did that ancient custom prevail the frequency with which one misfortune follows another would tell sadly upon our slender wardrobes! Perhaps, however, the ancients mingled economy in their sorrow and rent their clothes at the seams only.

—CATHERINE EDMONDSTON (1863)

*B*usy day. Oh! how we are enjoying the Venison Pa sent us tho' Antelope is not nearly so good as Buffalo-meat, which we *lived on* away back in the '70's, when I was a little girl and Kansas was all Buffalo and Indians.

—MARTHA FARNSWORTH (1895)

*T*he buildings gray, varnished and arid as the winter walls and pavements of the town, among which one would soon be making one's colorless way.

—EDMUND WILSON (1929)

DECEMBER 12

*O*ne day when my shawls were falling off to the left, my cushions falling out to the right, and the duvet off my knees,—one of those crises of misery, in short, which are all in the day's work for an invalid, K. exclaimed "What an awful pity it is that you can't say damn." I agreed with her from my heart; . . . at such moments of trial refinement is a feeble reed to lean upon.

—ALICE JAMES (1889)

$\mathcal{T}$oday I have been thinking of [Baronesse H. P. J. Van Till] . . . [whose] husband, a naval officer, had been aide-de-camp of the governor of Java in World War II. . . . They were taken prisoners by the Japanese—Hans interned in a rather comfortable prison for men and Hannie in a concentration camp for ten thousand women and children. . . . Hannie's job was to make the coffins so she was taken to measure the dying every morning. . . . Hannie made the coffins but neither she nor any of the prisoners had ever seen where the coffins went. When she managed to bring the commandant the door he had wanted, he asked her what she wanted as a reward and she answered "to go with a coffin to the cemetery." He granted her request. It happened that the coffin that day contained the body of a child whom Hannie had heard feverishly begging for an orange. The child never got his orange; in fact, prisoners never saw fresh fruit. There, in the cemetery, however, a bowl of fruit was laid in the Japanese mores on top of the earth. Hannie, for once, lost her control, and screamed and shouted at the guards and tore the Japanese flag down. Of course she was taken at once to the commandant who struck her across the face and pushed her into a corner. She felt sure she would be shot. Instead when they were alone he asked her to explain her rage—and she told him about the child and the oranges. The next day . . . a train load of oranges was delivered to the camp.

—MAY SARTON (1986)

DECEMBER 13

$\mathcal{I}$ have none but negroes to tend my children nor can I get anyone and they use their own children to such loads of

Gross food that they are not Judges when a child not so used to be exposed to different weathers and not so inured to exercise Comes to eat. They let them press their appetites as their own children did and thus they are constantly sick. Judy Carter, who has been as well for many weeks as ever child was, by being suffered after her dinner to some of her sister's barley broth yesterday took in such a load as could not be contained in her stomach and this day she was seized with a natural vomiting. I . . . ordered a small dose of Ipecacuana to help to clear the over burthened Stomach . . . but it had too powerfull an effect . . . for she vomited 6 times yellow bile, . . . lost her pulse for two hours and quite dead coldness and hardly alive with nervous Catchings in her hands and Jaws so that I fancyed her death near. However I gave her Pulvis Cantian 5 grains, Salt tartar 5 grains, Pulvis Castor 2 grains in a weak Julep of Rum, water and mint and in about 2½ hours her pulse beat and after a good sleep Nature seemed to recover and a Small fever ensued which wore away by night gradually and the Child mended, grew cheerful and had an appetite to eat which I sparingly indulged but she lost all her bloom off her face this morning.

—Landon Carter (1757)

I observe it is a general custom on Sundays here, with Gentlemen to invite one another home to dine, after Church; and to consult about, determine their common business, either before or after Service—It is not the Custom for Gentlemen to go into Church til Service is beginning, when they enter in a Body, in the same manner as they come out; I have known the Clerk to come out and call them in to prayers.— They stay also after the Service is over, usually as long, sometimes longer, than the Parson was preaching—Almost every Lady wears a red Cloak; and when they ride out they tye a white handkerchief over their Head and face, so that when I first came into Virginia, I was distress'd whenever I saw a Lady, for I thought She had the Tooth-Ach!

—Philip Vickers Fithian (1773)

DECEMBER 14

*S*eth Shove was brought to our House to dwell, i. e. Father Hull's. N. B. In the evening, seeing a shagged dogg in the Kitchin, I spake to John Alcock, *I am fraid we shall be troubled with the ugly dogg:* whereupon John asked which way he went. I said out at the Street door. He presently went that way, and meeting Seth (who went out a little before) took him for the dogg, and smote him so hard upon the bare head with a pipe staff, or something like it, that it grieved me that he had strook the dogg so hard. There arose a considerable wheal in the childs head, but it seems the weapon smote him plain, for the Rising was almost from the forehead to the Crown, grew well quickly, wearing a Cap that night. 'Twas God's mercy the stick and manner of the blow was not such as to have spilled his Brains on the ground. The Devil, (I think) seemed to be angry at the childs coming to dwell here.

—SAMUEL SEWALL (1676)

[At Valley Forge] *T*he Army which has been surprisingly healthy hitherto, now begins to grow sickly. . . . I am Sick—discontented—and out of humour. Poor food—hard lodging—Cold Weather—fatigue—Nasty Cloaths—nasty Cookery—Vomit half my time—smoak'd out of my senses—the Devil's in't—I can't Endure it—Why are we sent here to starve and Freeze—What sweet Felicitie have I left at home; A charming Wife—pretty Children—Good Beds—good food—good Cookery—all agreeable—all harmonious. Here all Confusion—smoke & Cold—hunger & filthyness—A pox on my bad luck. . . . People who live at home in Luxury and Ease, quietly possessing their habitations, Enjoying their Wives & families in peace, have but a very faint Idea of the unpleasing sensations, and continual Anxiety the Man endures who is in a Camp. . . . These same People are willing we should suffer every thing for their Benefit & advantage, and yet are the first to Condemn us for not doing more!!

—ALBIGENCE WALDO (1777)

DECEMBER 15

*R*ode to a settlement of Virginians, near Yohiogoeni. Preached on the last Judgment.

—DAVID MCCLURE (1772)

[On a Mississippi riverboat] *I* like this sort of life. Table equal to our best hotels. . . . Two ladies and two gentlemen generally play cards in the after cabin (ladies'). Next, towards the bow [is] another table of social card-players, consisting of a loud-talking, boastful youngster (a Jew, Moses, of Cincinnati), whose garb and gab alike proclaim a volunteer officer; a good-natured, laughing Hoosier; a third only remarkable for his height and the prodigious length of his arms. I noticed him today at dinner; he reaches like a well-sweep to all parts of the table, gathering and storing away an unheard of quantity of provisions. Next forward, a table of chess or chequer players, with a few gaping lookers-on. Next is a group of nondescripts, quite at a loss how to bestow themselves; some dozing listlessly in their armchairs, waiting patiently for the next meal, others reading cheap tales of pirates, "love and murder," etc., etc. Last group forward, four professional gentlemen busy at poker for money.

—RUTHERFORD B. HAYES (1848)

*W*ith Paul Patterson I went to Washington yesterday afternoon for the dinner of the Gridiron Club. . . . My place was at the elevated guest-table two places from Truman on the one side and three from the Duke of Windsor on the other. . . . At my left was the British ambassador and at my right the Philippine ambassador. . . . There is a sort of seventh-inning stretch at about 10 o'clock, and the guests all rush for the pissoirs. When I got to the nearest I found dignitaries lined up before each stall, with the Duke at the end of one line. Patterson, who was with me . . . whooped it up as a proof of the Duke's democratic spirit. . . . When he departed

456

the [British] ambassador . . . told me he had been warned that I was anti-English. I replied that this was a gross calumny, circulated by Japs. We got on very well, and I invited him to come to Baltimore some day for lunch at the Maryland Club.

—H. L. MENCKEN (1946)

DECEMBER 16

*A*bout Day Break the Adgutent Came & ordred our tents Struck, Saying that the Enemy was a Coming after us & were Almost Round us. We were oblig'd to thro away our Broth that we had made for our breakfasts & Loud our Kittles into the waggons and march without Breakfast. This Day I was sent forward to Get Something Hot for Breakfast for three Officers for it was a Verey Cold Day. I went to Every house in my way for 10 or 11 miles But Got none till noon. Then we Came to Bethlehem to Mr Delers who gave Vitules to Near 70 men, Officers & Soldiers, saying they had Rather we should have it then the Enemy who was Expected their as soon as we had Crosed over Deleware. They gave us Cyder & Aples as Long as they had any Left. Tho they Appeard to Be But Poor people, they refus'd to teak any Pay for what we had. I crosed over the ferey to Easton in the Evening & went to Several houses to Get Liberty to Lay By the fire But Could not & So was Oblig'd to Lay my self Down on the frozen Grownd & snow for we Could not Pitch our tent. The Ground was frose so hard we made a Little fire with Some Railes that we took, for their was no other wood here about to Be had. The ferey men was Oblig'd to work all night to Get our Baggage over the Deleware & all the Next Day, But Did not Get it all over untill the Day after.

—JOHN SMITH (1776)

[Departing Camp Carson to go overseas] *U*ntil you have risen at 5:30 a.m., folded your tent like an Arab and taken it and the mattress and all the linen, quilts and blankets next door, stood in line for breakfast at 6:30 a.m., packed a suitcase, a duffel bag and a musette bag before 7 a.m., climbed aboard an open truck where you stood in the cold, wintry wind of a Colorado morning, holding on with both hands as you go around corners, and riding a few miles to board a troop train, with helmets falling off on the average of twice a mile so that the driver has to stop the truck with a terrific jolt that sends everybody flying to the forward part of the truck . . . you haven't lived. . . . Behind us . . . lay the great peaks of the Rocky Mountains, representing America, fine and big and clean, room and place for everyone. Ahead of us lay new experiences, untried talents for great challenges. . . . It was good to climb off the truck as we reached the troop train and march along in our slacks and uniform coats with the heavy musette bag hitting the right hip and the light musette bag hitting the left hip. We Red Crossers were at the end of the line of nurses and as we passed the lines of enlisted men one of them said, "Look, something new has been added—the Red Cross."

—Anne McCaughey (1943)

*W*illiam Faulkner . . . who has been visiting New York for six or eight weeks past, has gone home at last. . . . Among those who entertained him was Alfred Knopf. . . . Knopf took along a couple of copies of Faulkner's books and asked him to autograph them. Faulkner replied about as follows: . . . "Too many people are asking me for autographs. Yesterday a bell-boy at my hotel wanted one. I believe that it is a mistake for an author to make his signature too common. However, inasmuch as it is you, I think I might very well autograph one of the books." This extraordinary boorishness . . . struck the whole assemblage dumb. Knopf himself made no reply, and did not mention the books again. . . . The town is full of tales about his incessant boozing. He had a roaring time while he was here, and will go back to Prohibition Mississippi with enough alcohol in his veins to last him a year.

—H. L. Mencken (1931)

DECEMBER 17

*A*ttended a marriage, where the guests were all Virginians. It was a scene of wild and confused merriment. The log house which was large, was filled. They were dancing to the music of a fiddle. They took little or no notice of me, on my entrance. After setting a while at the fire, I arose and desired the music and dancing to cease, & requested the Bride and Bridegroom to come forward. They came snickering and very merry. I desired the company who still appeared to be mirthful & noisy, to attend with becoming seriousness, the solemnity. . . . The manners of the people of Virginia, who have removed into these parts, are different from those of the presbyterians and germans. They are much addicted to drinking parties, gambling, horse race & fighting. They are hospitable & prodigal. Several of them, have run through their property in the old settlements, & have sought an asylum in this wilderness.

—DAVID McCLURE (1772)

*L*ast night, three cargoes of Bohea tea were emptied into the sea. This morning a man-of-war sails. This is the most magnificent movement of all. There is a dignity, a majesty, a sublimity, in this last effort of the patriots, that I greatly admire. The people should never rise without doing something to be remembered, something notable and striking. This destruction of the tea is so bold, so daring, so firm, intrepid and inflexible, and it must have so important consequences, and so lasting, that I cannot but consider it as an epocha in history.

—JOHN ADAMS (1773)

*E*arly turn'd out But Eat no Breakfast, having not thing But Bread & fresh beaf & no salt to season it, nor Could we Get any here. The inhabitents were all Dutch & not the Kindest in the world. . . . We went to seek for Quarters amongst the houses But had some Dificulty, their Being no Room for Us. Some Companies was Oblig'd to Lie out again on the Ground. I had a fine warm Room with a Stove in it where our Company all Stoed in this night. . . . After the Dutchman & his frow had gone to sleep, went Down in the Selor & got some Cyder & Aples and Potatoes & held a feast this nit. In the morning the old woman, heaving Ocasion to Draw Cyder, missing the Aples & Cyder, made a Great Gabber about it But got no satisfaction for it, & some other of her Neighbours Lost their Bees that made the Honey, But Could not tell where to find them for the Swarm in the night And flew from their Quarters to ours where they had Care teaken of them.

—JOHN SMITH (1776)

DECEMBER 18

Universal Thanksgiving—a Roasted pig at Night. . . . Rank & Precedence make a good deal of disturbance & confusion in the American Army. The Army are poorly supplied with Provision, occasioned it is said by the Neglect of the Commissary of Purchases. Much talk among Officers about discharges. Money has become of too little consequence. The Congress have not made their Commissions valuable Enough. Heaven avert the bad consequences of these things. . . . Our brethren who are unfortunately Prisoners in Philadelphia meet with the most savage and inhumane treatments. . . . Our Enemies do not knock them in the head or burn them with torches to death, or flee them alive, or gradually dismember them till they die, which is customary among Savages & Barbarians. No, they are worse by far. They suffer them to starve. . . . One of these poor unhappy men, drove to the last extreem by the rage of hunger, eat his own fingers up to the first joint from the hand, before he died. Others eat the Clay, the Lime, the Stones of the Prison Walls. Several who died in the Yard had pieces of Bark, Wood, Clay & Stones in their mouths, which the ravings of hunger had caused them to take in for food in the last Agonies of Life! "These are thy *mercies*, O Britain!"

—ALBIGENCE WALDO (1777)

*Y*esterday after the gale of two days, high wind . . . the sun came out and there was that washed blue sky that so often follows a storm. But the seas were still running high and . . . it was glorious to watch one great comber after another sweep in and break on the rocks. Earlier I set out to get the tree. . . . Raymond helped me cut it so the star won't hit the ceiling and we left it in the cool of the garage, upright in its stand. I'll bring it in tomorrow. . . . So Christmas is really on the way.

—MAY SARTON (1974)

DECEMBER 19

*I*n all the woods is heard now, far and near, the sound of the woodchopper's axe; a twilight sound now in the night of the year, as if men had stolen forth in the arctic night to get fuel to keep their fires a-going. The sound of the axes far in the horizon is like the dropping of the eaves.

—HENRY DAVID THOREAU (1851)

*A*bout one hundred ornaments of our liberal and enlightened profession—one hundred "gentlemen of the bar"—were congregated in the Special Term room this morning. I scrutinized the crowd, to determine how many there were whom I would be willing to receive as visitors at this house, or rather whom I would not be annoyed and disgusted to receive. There were really not more than *three* who were not stamped by

461

appearance, diction, or manner as belonging to a low social station, and as having no claims to the conventional title of "gentlemen." It was manifestly a mob of low-bred, illiterate, tenth-rate attorneys, though it included many successful and conspicuous practitioners.

—GEORGE TEMPLETON STRONG (1859)

I feel . . . like a clock that is run down and the key lost.

—GAMALIEL BRADFORD (1917)

*T*here have been houses stoned in Placer County, [California,] and some of the newspapers are raising hell and making all kinds of wild statements about even the Nisei. Kenny showed me a lot of clippings, and it is very dangerous. Yet, I feel that we are so helpless. Who in the hell is going to worry about the Nisei when we are at war? Maybe the thing to do is to get into the Army. . . . We must wave the old flag like the very first patriot. I think the Nisei are loyal, but we may be too short for the Army, and I refuse to be a messboy.

—CHARLES KIKUCHI (1941)

DECEMBER 20

*M*y habits now are to rise at 7. I go to my dressing room which is in the back building & is very comfortable, having a bath with hot & cold water & a water closet adjoining, also a sink to carry off waste water & slops, all which are among the modern improvements which add so much to the comfort of life & which are now contained in houses of moderate cost. . . . I am in debt, I must work, I am not free to follow the bent of my mind, to gratify my taste for undisturbed, secluded study, apart from the business & contact of the world. Then again, it is in town & not in the country. In this barren, brick wilderness, with its hateful crowds & bustle & noise, I sigh for nature, its serenity, quiet & beauty, for the woods & fields, their loved companionship, their varied charms & sweet voices, their inspiring & holy influences. But it is as it is; we must take our lot in life as it is given us & seek such enjoyments in it as it can afford.

—SIDNEY GEORGE FISHER (1852)

The Knopf board meeting in the afternoon was a long one. . . . Lesser was in favor of giving the run-of-mine employees large Christmas bonuses, but the rest of us voted him down. They belong to a C.I.O. union and the union goons make frequent demands, many of them extravagant and not a few preposterous. I am in favor of giving such enemies of the house as much as they can get, but not a cent more. But what of the employees who do not belong to the union? They are the best workers in the office, and do not come and go like the unionists. I argued for giving them larger bonuses than the latter, on the plain ground that they are worth more. Lesser protested that this would give the union leaders something to complain of. I then suggested that one or two union members of unusual diligence and usefulness be chosen for larger bonuses also. This plan was adopted. It will not shut off the union leaders altogether, but it will at least weaken their argument.

—H. L. MENCKEN (1945)

DECEMBER 21

Began my visits among the Camp Hospitals in the Army of the Potomac. Spent a good part of the day in a large brick mansion, on the banks of the Rappahannock, used as a Hospital since the battle—Seems to have receiv'd only the worst cases. Out doors, at the foot of a tree, within ten yards of the front of the house, I notice a heap of amputated feet, legs, arms, hands, &c. . . . Several dead bodies lie near, each cover'd with its brown woollen blanket. In the door-yard, towards the river, are fresh graves, mostly of officers, their names on pieces of barrel-staves or broken board, stuck in the dirt. . . . Everything is quiet now . . . but there was noise enough a week or so ago . . . when Gen. Burnside order'd all the batteries of the army to combine for the bombardment of Fredericksburgh. . . . The perfect hush of the just-ending night was suddenly broken by the first gun, and in an instant all the thunderers, big and little, were in full chorus, which they kept up without intermission for several hours.

—Walt Whitman (1862)

*M*r. Sweetser presented me with a ticket to Dickens reading . . . Dombey & Son and the Pickwick trial. He is an exceedingly foppish man, exquisitely dressed, with a triple gold chain, which takes a great deal of his attention. Diamonds, swallow tail, immense bosom, etc. etc. He has quite a husky voice and . . . is a great mimic, screws his face and turns his body into all conceivable shapes. . . . The rush for seats continues unabated and the speculators are making great fortunes. Men have stood from 12 A.M. to 12 Noon in line about the ticket office. . . . Our office boy reached there about 6 A.M. and there were then 350 ahead of him, and thus discouraged he left.

—John William Sterling (1867)

DECEMBER 22

[At Valley Forge] *L*ay excessive Cold & uncomfortable last Night—my eyes are started out from their Orbits like a Rabbit's eyes, occasion'd by a great Cold & Smoke. . . . This evening a Party with two field pieces were order'd out. At 12 of the Clock at Night, Providence sent us a little mutton, with which we immediately had some Broth made, & a fine Stomach for same. Ye who Eat Pumkin Pie and Roast Turkies, and yet Curse fortune for using you ill, Curse her no more, least she reduce your Allowance of her favours to a bit of Fire Cake, & a draught of Cold Water, & in Cold Weather too.

—ALBIGENCE WALDO (1777)

*A*t night went to Presbyterian Church and heard a speech from the Rev Mr Holmes of St Louis in commemoration of the landing of the Pilgrims. It was only a common place production. I did not attend the supper although invited, as I doubt the propriety of observing such celebrations. They are understood to be exclusively by the descendents of the pilgrims, and tend to keep up mere sectional distinctions and divisions. National days should be observed, for instance 4th July, 22nd. Feby, thanksgiving &c. In these all can participate and each feel that he has an equal share with every other, and they contribute to the growth and development of a healthy sentiment of patriotism.

—ORVILLE BROWNING (1852)

*F*orefathers' Day. A procession of all the regiments which have been to the war, with all their flags. . . . Most of the regiments were represented by a score or two of men, with their colonel in most cases at their head. . . . Some had one old, tattered, faded flag. Some had several. The men had but little uniform. Being disbanded, they had gone to their old pursuits. . . . Some were wounded, one poor fellow had lost both arms. There were over sixty regiments in all, and when all the flags had been taken by the Governor they were displayed in front of the state house. . . . Many a poor wounded and dying soldier had looked on one or another of these flags, now displayed to an admiring throng of his fellow countrymen who enjoy what he gave his life to obtain, a good, stable government.

—AMOS A. LAWRENCE (1865)

*C*oming back to New York . . . as if you were going down into the whole great big city or into a subway. . . . the *Herald Tribune* had to arrange extensions in order to make the drops on the chart go low enough—only thing Amalgamated was buying were short-term government bonds—no bonds at all, not even government bonds, otherwise—$3 million cash in bank—just trying to stay fluid. . . . People looked whiter, more emaciated than ever—dyed brass waves on girls' foreheads like too-pale eggshells. . . . We heard shouts and saw out the window at the edge of the park what we took to be a hunger march of the park bums being organized by Communists, but when I went down to investigate, it turned out to be NYU freshmen starting a snake dance—ominous and dreary like everything else.

—EDMUND WILSON (1931)

DECEMBER 23

[Journey to the French Commandent] *O*ur Horses were now so weak & feeble, & the Baggage heavy . . . ; therefore my Self & others . . . gave up our Horses for Packs . . . & put my Self into an Indian walking Dress, & continue'd with them three Day's. . . . Just after we had pass'd a Place call'd the Murdering Town . . . we fell in with a Party of French Indians, which had laid in wait for us, one of them fired at Mr. Gist or me, not 15 Steps, but fortunately missed. . . . The next Day we continued traveling 'till it was quite Dark, & got to the River. . . . There was no way for us to get over but upon a Raft, which we set about with but one poor Hatchet. . . . We got it launch'd, & on board of it, & sett off; but before we

466

got half over, we were jamed in the Ice. . . . I put out my seting Pole . . . that the Ice might pass by, when the Rapidity of the Stream through it with so much Violence against the Pole, that it Jirk'd me into 10 Feet Water, but I fortunately saved my Self by catching hold of one of the Raft Logs. . . . [We] were oblig'd, as we were pretty near an Island, to quit our Raft & wade to it. The Cold was so extream severe . . . & the Water was shut up so hard, that We found no Difficulty in getting off the Island on the Ice in the Morning, & went to Mr. Frazers.

—GEORGE WASHINGTON (1753)

The Party that went out last evening not Return'd to Day. This evening an excellent Player on the Violin in that soft Musick, which is so finely adapted to stirr up the tender Passions, while he was playing in the next Tent to mine, these kind of soft Airs it immediately called up in remembrance all the endearing expressions, the Tender Sentiments, the sympathetic friendship that has given so much satisfaction and sensible pleasure to me from the first time I gained the heart & affections of the tenderest of the Fair. . . . I wish'd to have the Musick Cease, and yet dreaded its ceasing, least I should loose sight of these dear Ideas, which gave me pain and pleasure at the same instant.

—ALBIGENCE WALDO (1777)

DECEMBER 24

Cuscalah, the Indian who had treated me so politely when I was at the Clatsops' village, came up in a canoe with his young brother and two squaws. He laid before Captain Lewis and myself each a mat and a parcel of roots. Some time in the evening, two files were demanded for the presents of mats and roots. As we had no files to part with, we each returned the present which we had received, which displeased Cuscalah a little. He then offered a woman to each of us, which we also declined accepting of, which displeased the whole party very much. The female part appeared to be highly disgusted at our refusing to accept of their favors.

—WILLIAM CLARK (1805)

*C*alled on the President [Lincoln] to commute the punishment of a person condemned to be hung. He at once assented. Is always disposed to mitigate punishment, and to grant favors. Sometimes this is a weakness. As a matter of duty and friendship I mentioned to him the case of Laura Jones, a young lady who was residing in Richmond and there engaged to be married but came up three years ago to attend her sick mother and had been unable to pass through the lines and return. I briefly stated her case and handed a letter from her to Mrs. Welles that he might read. It was a touching appeal from the poor girl, who says truly the years of her youth are passing away. I knew if the President read the letter, Laura would get the pass. . . . I told him her sympathies were with the Secessionists, and it would be better he should read her own statement. But he declined and said he would let her go; the war had depopulated the country and prevented marriages enough.

—GIDEON WELLES (1864)

[At the Battle of the Bulge] *C*hristmas Eve is a beautiful, clear, crispy cold night. Snow is falling slowly upon the pine forest, adding to the cover already on the ground. There is no spirit of Christmas among our troops as wave after wave of frenzied enemy soldiers attempt to overwhelm us. Every available soldier is on the line this night with a weapon. Still, our defending strength is small. The Germans are trying assaults with large Tiger tanks. They loom awesome in the moonlight. . . . Our heavy guns sound like thunder as exploding shells turn night into day. . . . Mounds of dead are left on the ground as the fresh white snow is turned to red.

—DONALD J. WILLIS (1944)

DECEMBER 25

Carts come to Town and Shops open as is usual. Some somehow observe the day; but are vexed I believe that the Body of People profane it, and blessed be God no Authority yet to compell them to keep it. A great Snow fell last night so this day and night very cold.

—SAMUEL SEWALL (1685)

Genl. St. Clare's brigade formed & marcht out of town about sunset, on their way to Trenton, they stopt & took Ammunition & flints at Wm. Heath's, proceeded to Yarley's Ferry, about 9 miles above Trenton—we made an halt—struck up fires, left our packs, & all got across the Delaware by 3 oC. in the morning, when we proceeded to Trenton, & arrived just before the action was over. Genls. Washington, Green & Sullivan with several brigadiers, & about 3000 men crost the river before us.

—DAVID AVERY (1776)

At daylight this morning, we were awakened by the discharge of the firearms of all our party and a salute, shouts, and a song which the whole party joined in under our windows. . . . Were cheerful all the morning. . . . The Indians left us in the evening. All the party snugly fixed in their huts. I received a present of Captain Lewis of a fleece hosiery shirt, drawers and socks, a pair of moccasins of Whitehouse, a small Indian basket of Goodrich, two dozen white weasels' tails of the Indian woman, and some black root of the Indians before their departure. . . . We would have spent this day, the nativity of Christ, in feasting, had we had anything either to raise our spirits or even gratify our appetites. Our dinner consisted of poor elk, so much spoiled that we ate it through mere necessity, some spoiled pounded fish, and a few roots.

—WILLIAM CLARK (1805)

*C*hristmas dinner at Shaws with fresh asparagus soup, meats, and vegetables for beginners followed by *lechon asado* for fillers and topped off with Christmas pudding served all aflame in glowing brandy, which also made me glow. Drank a secret toast to my mother's efforts in the W.C.T.U. [Women's Christian Temperance Union].

—DOROTHEA MOULTON BALANO (1911)

*T*he usual Christmas disorder. . . . Big turkey dinner with cocktails and wine. . . . Afterwards to the top of Walker Mountain—the roads very greasy. The view strange and misty—the world of hills like a woman's skirt, thrown on the floor. Something out there very far away from all we were feeling to each other.

—SHERWOOD ANDERSON (1936)

*W*e find that one of our task forces is surrounded by enemy armor. Unable to break out and hopelessly outnumbered, these troops are at last ordered to destroy all their vehicles and other equipment. . . . The enemy is continuing the attack all along the front. Many truckloads of frozen uniforms are observed on the roads after last night's battle. It is impossible to keep warm in this frigid weather, as we cannot build fires. The rolling fields are covered with snow, and every road is a sheet of ice. This adds to our problems as a cold wind blows across the Ardennes this gloomy Christmas Day.

—Donald J. Willis (1944)

*I*t has been a dismal Christmas. The temperature is about 35 degrees, and rain has been falling intermittently all day. There was snow four or five days ago, but it was light and the rain has washed it away. On the long trip to Gertie's house in Gwynn Oak avenue I saw but two Christmas trees in houses. There were no tree ornaments in the stores this year, and the effects of the war are beginning to be felt in a thousand ways. The Christmas news from the front must be extraordinarily depressing to persons who have relatives in Eisenhower's army. The Army press-agents are making desperate efforts to turn the German break-through into a German rout, but I suspect that even the generality of Americans, as stupid as they are, are beginning to doubt this official optimism.

—H. L. Mencken (1944)

DECEMBER 26

*G*enl. Washington began his attack on the Hessians about sun-rise, by first taking & driving in their out-guards—in about 20 minutes the fire on & from the town became general when the fieldpieces & musquetry played briskly on both sides—which continued about 25 minutes, & then the Enemy left the town, & soon surrendered Prisoners of war. We took 6 excellent brass field pieces, about 1400 stands of small arms, a waggon load of ammunition &c &c about 1180 prisoners. . . . The lower divisions not being able to cross the river by reason of ice, the Genl. ordered us to return immediately. We were greatly distrest with a very cold storm of rain, hail & snow, which blew with great Violence from N. East from four oC. till night. . . . I was extremely chilled, & came near perishing before I could get to a fire.

—David Avery (1776)

*O*ur Mt. Misery friends inundated us tonight. Certain of them are very nice people, i.e., they are simple country girls and they pretend to be nothing more than what they are—but certain others—If there's anything that has a strong tendency to set one's teeth on edge it's to see womankind from the country whom nature and their habits of life tend to make so much more unaffected and every way respectable than the denizens of a city like this—to see them aping the frivolity and trying successfully to acquire the follies that by habit and education they're free from.

—George Templeton Strong (1841)

*W*orked, went to the mountains, with Mazie and Channing, for leaves—played cards. A dull and stupid day inside me. There is a brotherhood that seemingly can't exist. Everyone seems to live on a false basis, including myself, with myself. People both help and hurt too much, and yet I cannot draw away from people. I hate it when E and I go to bed in comparative silence, each drawn away from the other. She remains the best one, of all living people I have known.

—Sherwood Anderson (1936)

DECEMBER 27

*A*ttended the funeral of Mr. Burrill . . . After the ceremony was over, Mr. Calhoun rode with me, and I left him at the War Office. We were remarking upon the number of members

472

of Congress already mingling with the dust of this region. . . .
There are plain, modest, and tasteless marble monuments
over their remains, which the lapse of a few short years will
demolish. We were remarking how exclusively by the nature
and genius of our institutions we confine all our thoughts
and cares to present time. We have neither forefathers nor
posterity. This burying-ground is remote from any church.
The funeral is a mere commitment of earth to earth.

—JOHN QUINCY ADAMS (1820)

[Off the coast of California] *M*orning calm & foggy. . . .
Shortly after breakfast, we were standing at the shop door of
Mr. Spear conversing, when a crow lighting on a post in front
of us, Mr. [Robert Davis] requested me to take a shot at it
with my rifle which was standing behind the door. I took the
rifle and wiped it out, and felt sure of there being no charge
in it. . . . Mr. D. took the gun in his hand to examine it and
I turned the muzzle towards my own head to feel if any wind
came out, and desired him to pull the trigger. Had he done
so, I should have been killed instantly. As it was, he placed
the rifle in my hands saying that he was unacquainted with
guns and would hold his hand at the muzzle in order to feel
if any wind came out. The first cap broke without any effect,
but at the second trial the result was that a bullet passed
through the middle of his right hand. . . . Much as I regretted
the accident, I was truely thankful that it was my friend's
hand instead of my own head. But still more serious would
have been the results had Mrs. Spear occupied her usual
seat at the breakfast table this morning, as the ball passed
through the room where 5 or 6 persons were breakfasting
and in a direct line over Mrs. S's vacant chair, and would no
doubt have killed her.

—WILLIAM DANE PHELPS (1841)

*A*t the late battle at Sand Creek Col Shivington destroyed
a village of 1000 Cheyennes. The next day while the soldiers
were burning the wigwams three little Indian children were

473

found hidden under some Buffalo robes. They were nearly frightened to death. The soldiers brought them here and are getting clothes made for them. Bell has made a dress for the little girl and I have made her an apron. She is very shy and afraid of white people but seems much pleased with her new clothes. The man who took her intends sending her to the states to be educated.

—HARRIET HITCHCOCK (1864)

DECEMBER 28

The snow and frost continued very severe. I here experienced how much habit adds to our necessities. I had five blankets (Indian ones I mean) of which I gave one to my servant, who complained of having nothing to cover him. With this one he slept perfectly contented, while I could hardly keep myself warm with the other four. He had laid down in his clothes, rolling himself up in a blanket, while I stript myself according to custom, and the room being accessible to the four winds of heaven, it was no easy matter to recover the warmth which was lost in uncasing.

—ARTHUR LEE (1784)

I gave out this morning pans, spoons & fish to all the negroes here for Christmas present—all happy & delighted. A pleasant gratification purchased at little cost.

—HENRY RAVENAL (1859)

An old punchy prizefighter, inspired to tell the story of his life to one of John Huston's wives, began with this sentence: "You see how it was, I was a change-of-life baby."

—GLENWAY WESCOTT (1945)

DECEMBER 29

*H*ad myself Daguerreotyped this morning. I tried it yesterday, but for some reason or other they failed signally at every attempt. It's a great bore—one doesn't know till he has tried how hard it is to sit without moving a muscle for two minutes. . . . As it is, the portrait of a man staring intently into vacancy and striving desperately to keep still must be unlike his usual appearance.

—GEORGE TEMPLETON STRONG (1842)

*S*herman has effected a brilliant "coup," to march through the whole State of Geo, take its principal city & seaport in spite of our utmost endeavour, nay in our very teeth, to effect a communication with the fleet, with an army too which we proclaimed jaded and foot sore (but of whom he gives a very different account). It does indeed entitle him to pride and exultation. Well may we hang our heads & say "The King does not dine today." Would that we had boasted less!

—CATHERINE EDMONDSTON (1864)

[Delayed in a snowdrift while crossing the Rockies on a train] *S*tarting and backing, then starting and backing again. Prospect very discouraging. Mr. Sargent makes the tea, unpacks the hampers and serves as general steward, but draws the line at washing the dishes. We women-folks take that as our part.

—SUSAN B. ANTHONY (1871)

DECEMBER 30

*I*n the Afternoon our Brigade was sent for into the feild where we Paraded Befor the General who was present with all the feild Officers & after meaking many fair promises to them he Begged them to tarey one month Longer in the Scervice & Almost Every man Consented to stay Longer who Received 10 Doler Bounty as soon as Signd their names. Then the Genll with the soldiers gave three Huzzas, with Claping of hands for Joy amongst the Specttators, & as soon as that was over the Genell ordered us to heave a gill of Rum pr man & set out to trenton to acquaint Genll Washington with his Good success as he termd it to Meak his heart Glad Once more. We was Dismisd to Goe to our Quarters with great Applause, the inhabitents & others saying we had Done honour to our Country.

—JOHN SMITH (1776)

[Sunday] *B*ob Titcomb was at church for the first time for several weeks. He says all the inmates of the house (Stickney's) except himself are victims to the revival. He compares it to the dress goods business. Fashion rules, and when the fashion changes, the goods and the religion are sold at half price or thrown away. Evening. I went down to the South End to hear Gallaher on the Deluge. There was a perfect jam and I was lucky in getting a chance to stand in an aisle, occasionally relieved by a seat on a settee relinquished alternately to Jake Brown and self by one or two pretty girls. . . . If I believed that doctrine true which I have heard this evening, I think I should immediately put in practice what they term the "means of grace." . . . It seems not, then, strange to me the course of revivals. I cannot sneer at it as a maniac fanaticism which has thus set Newburyport all agog.

—BENJAMIN BROWNE FOSTER (1849)

*O*ur old cook has left me to go home to rest for the winter, and the new one makes housekeeping rather onerous. But the necessary exercise is just what I need. . . . I have written a speech on "The Disabilities and the Limitations of Sex."

—ELIZABETH CADY STANTON (1884)

*W*ell the old year is leaving us flat, plenty flat. But in reality it's been our most beneficial year. It's took some of the conceit out of us. We have enjoyed special blessings over other nations. And we couldn't see why they shouldn't be permanent. We was a mighty cocky nation. We originated mass production. And mass produced everybody out of a job with our boasted labor saving machinery. It saved labor, the very thing we are now appropriating money to get a job for. They forgot that machinery don't eat, rent houses, or buy clothes. We had begun to believe that the height of civilization was a good road, bath tub, radio and automobile. I don't think Hoover, the Republicans, or even Russia is responsible for this. I think the Lord just looked us over and decided to set us back where we belonged.

—WILL ROGERS (1930)

DECEMBER 31

*T*he year ends, and how much the years teach which the days never know!

—RALPH WALDO EMERSON (1843)

*D*enuded pines stand in the clearings with no old cloak to wrap about them, only the apexes of their cones entire, telling a pathetic story of the companions that clothed them. So stands a man. His clearing around him, he has no companions on the hills. The lonely traveler, looking up, wonders why he was left when his companions were taken.

—HENRY DAVID THOREAU (1851)

[With General Sherman in Savannah] *R*ead the Testament through for the fifth time. Considerable firing in Evening. Cool night. All['s] well that ends well.

—VALENTINE REIMANN (1864)

478

DRAMATIS PERSONAE

Franklin Pierce Adams (1881–1960), journalist, poet, and humorist, whose popular Saturday diary columns in various Chicago and New York papers, written in a style reminiscent of Samuel Pepys, reinvigorated the public diary form in America.

John Adams (1735–1826), lawyer, patriot, and president, whose sometimes testy journals, filled with Puritan-like probings of his and others' faults and foibles, say much about his private and American public life.

John Quincy Adams (1767–1848), son of John Adams, public servant, and president, whose journal, maintained religiously throughout his life, reveals an honest self-awareness within a young republic coming of age and says much about American public affairs.

Louisa May Alcott (1832–1888), novelist, who for over forty years recorded in her diary personal, social, and literary concerns about her life in and near Boston and Concord and in reform circles.

Sherwood Anderson (1876–1941), novelist, whose epigramatic daily jottings run from the most mundane matters to reflections on America.

Eliza Frances Andrews (b. 1840), a planter's daughter in Georgia, who in her diary from December 1864 through August 1865 charted the last days of the Confederacy and regretted the end of slavery.

Anonymous (?), pro-Union woman living mostly in Mississippi and Louisiana, whose secret diary from 1860 to 1863 counted the costs of war in repressed thought, bloodshed, and boredom.

Susan B. Anthony (1820-1906), women's rights activist, whose sporadic diary documents Anthony on the road and at work for suffrage and other causes.

David Avery (1746–1818), chaplain, whose Revolutionary War diary includes his eyewitness accounts of such famous American moments as standing with the patriots at Bunker Hill and the siege of Boston and crossing the Delaware River with George Washington's troops to surprise the Hessians at Trenton.

Dorothea Moulton Balano (b. 1882), mariner, whose salty logs of her voyages aboard a windjammer, captained by her Maine-born husband, show a Minnesota-born, college-educated woman taking to sea and understanding America.

Martha Ballard (1735–1812), midwife to the births of almost 1,000 children in Maine, who catalogues a host of domestic concerns in her matter-of-fact journal entries.

Clarence Barron (1855–1928), financier, whose diaries from 1891–1928 provide an insider's view of the personalities, politics, and power of Wall Street and big business.

John Bartram (1699–1777), Quaker naturalist, whose travel diaries from botanical and exploratory expeditions as far south as Florida limn the land and wildlife, including people, he observed along the way.

Lewis Beebe (1749–1816), surgeon, who in his journal agonized over the miserable conditions, diseases, and sufferings of the Continental Army during the American Revolutionary War.

John Boit (1774–1829), naval officer, who logged his experience sailing with Captain Robert Gray on the *Columbia*, from Boston, around the Horn, to the Pacific Northwest, and then around the world.

John Wilkes Booth (1838–1865), actor and assassin, who turned to his diary of April 1865 to give his side of the story in his murder of Lincoln and flight from Ford's Theater.

Gamaliel Bradford (1863–1932), reclusive man of letters, whose large diary recounts a man of many interests crippled by self-doubt and illness.

William Bradford (1589/90-1657), Pilgrim father and governor of Plymouth Plantation, whose early accounts of the Pilgrim adventure saved the colony from obscurity and defined the Pilgrims' errand into the wilderness (*see also* entry on Edward Winslow).

Samuel Breck (1771–1862), Philadelphia gentleman, whose active public and social life, as related in his diary, gave him an eye on America's one-time premier city and early republican society.

Lucy Gilmer Breckinridge (1834–1865), Virginia planter's daughter, whose wartime diary records Union insults and Confederate concerns and the vagaries of domestic life during the Civil War.

William Henry Brewer (1828–1910), botanist and geologist, whose journal describes people, plants, and placer mining in California after the gold rush.

Orville Hickman Browning (1806–1881), politician from Illinois, whose massive diary catalogues his and other public servants' careers and especially the economic and social development of the Midwest at mid-century.

Joseph Goldsborough Bruff (1804–1889), mining executive, who closely observed the rigors and rewards of California gold rush days.

Dolly Sumner Lunt Lewis Burge (1817–1891), Methodist schoolteacher, who after her move from Maine to Georgia, filled her diary with a mixture of personal, religious, and war news and sometimes self-pity.

Aaron Burr (1756–1836), politician, political exile, and bon vivant, whose diary, which he kept while in London and Paris, comments on American habits and his active social life.

William Byrd (1674–1744), wealthy Virginia gentleman, surveyor, and land-grabber, whose secret diaries recount Byrd's daily regimen of diet, exercise, sexual activity, and socializing while he moved in "genteel" circles.

Helen McCowen Carpenter (?), overland emigrant, whose diary relates her wagon trek from Kansas to California as a bride in 1857.

Landon Carter (1710-1778), Virginia planter, whose detailed diary entries on plantation management, slavery, social life, and failed ambition from 1752–1778 provide revealing commentary on the colonial Chesapeake world.

Francis Auguste Chardon (d. 1848), fur trader, who in his journal recounts life among traders, the Mandans, and others at Fort Clark in the upper Missouri River area.

Mary Boykin Miller Chesnut (1823–1886), South Carolina aristocrat, who in the privacy of her diaries recognized the chimera of the Confederacy even as she endorsed and supported it and who looked deep inside her and her people's mind and soul during victory and defeat.

Charles W. Chesnutt (1858–1932), novelist, whose diaries (1874–1882) reveal an emerging African-American artist struggling to win recognition and respect in the post-Civil War South.

William Clark (1770-1838), explorer, whose field notes and journals from the Lewis and Clark expedition, which he co-captained, opened the West to the American mind and mapped the routes of overland trade, scientific collecting, and potential settlement for a young America (*see also* entry on Meriwether Lewis).

Samuel A. Clear (b. 1836), Pennsylvania-born sergeant in the famous Irish brigade, whose diary, transcribed and edited by fellow soldier Daniel Chisholm, details camp life and campaigns.

Joseph Cleaver, Jr. (1833–1909), college student in Delaware, whose diary of college days shows a young man facing difficult moral choices, even while planning pranks and reveling in campus male camaraderie.

Samuel Langhorne Clemens (*see* entry on Mark Twain).

Miriam Davis Colt (b. 1817), pioneer, whose diary reveals the pains and disappointments of relocating from Potsdam, New York, to Kansas territory, where her ambitions died with the loss of husband and child on the hard sod prairie.

Jemima Condict (1754–1779), daughter of a New Jersey farmer, whose diary reveals a young woman's struggles with religion and family concerns during the American Revolution.

Jay Cooke (1821–1905), banker, who kept a journal of fishing, friends, and faith during his stays at his Lake Erie island retreat.

James Fenimore Cooper (1789–1851), novelist, whose jottings in his journals as he traveled about often provided material for his Leatherstocking and other tales.

Davy Crockett (1786–1836), frontiersman and teller of tall tales, whose diary from his last days at the Alamo embellished his legend, though some scholars now doubt the document's authenticity.

Bradley N. Cumings (1811–1876), self-educated workingman and dry goods storeowner, whose candid diary described business, politics, reform, and society in and around Boston.

Richard Henry Dana (1815–1882), Boston lawyer, whose detailed diary of legal, political, cultural, and social affairs in his beloved New England provide as copious an examination of natural and human-made habitats and habits as found in Dana's famous account of a trip to California, *Two Years Before the Mast.*

Charles E. Davis (c. 1843–1915), soldier, whose Civil War diary dotes on camp life and military duties while serving with a Massachusetts regiment.

Dorothy Day (1897–1980), Catholic reformer, whose diary combines Day's philosophy with the joys of visits to rural America and the simple life.

John Dos Passos (1896–1970), novelist and socialist visionary, whose diary carries him from his New England school days to World War I battlefields in France and Italy, where his experiences informed his early writing.

Theodore Dreiser (1871–1945), novelist, whose self-conscious journal tracks Dreiser's travels to Florida, Savannah, Hollywood, and elsewhere and his unrewarding literary and romantic life in Philadelphia and New York.

Alice Moore Dunbar-Nelson (1875–1935), poet and clubwoman, whose diary follows her work for a variety of African-American organizations and women's groups in the mid-Atlantic area and the fate of African-American publishing.

William Dunlap (1766–1839), playwright and painter, who comments on literary figures in his circle and the natural history of the America he saw and depicted in his art.

Sophie Madeleine du Pont (1810-1888), aristocrat, whose diary, kept while a young woman growing up in the famous du Pont family, describes and caricatures society in the young republic.

John Early (1786–1873), Methodist minister, who recorded the sins and salvations he witnessed in the early republic, especially in the Chesapeake region where he traveled.

Thomas Alva Edison (1847–1931), inventor, whose brief diary from his home in Menlo Park, New Jersey, and his holiday retreat in Massachusetts reveals Edison's humor and love of ironic circumstance.

Catherine Ann Devereaux Edmondston (1823–1875), North Carolina plantation mistress, whose thick wartime diary accents an ardent southern nationalism amid an unraveling world of refractory slaves and advancing Union armies.

Myra Fairbanks Eells (1805–1878), missionary, whose 1838 travel diary traces her overland journey to Walla Walla, Washington.

Edward Robb Ellis (b. 1911), journalist, whose diary from Okinawa, where he was stationed as a navy corpsman in 1945, reports on the destructiveness and demands of war.

Alfred Ely (1815–1892), Republican congressman, whose diary, kept while a prisoner of war in Richmond, relates prison life and reflections on civil war.

Ralph Waldo Emerson (1803–1882), essayist and Romantic, who in his many journals and notebooks communed with Nature and the American soul as he discovered his own American voice and self-reliance.

Martha Farnsworth (1867–1924), teacher and suffragist, whose diary running from the 1880s through World War I chronicles life on the Kansas plains and Farnsworth's interests in temperance, voting, and family.

John Palmer Finley (1822–1889), Presbyterian minister, whose diary stretching from 1848 to 1887 depicts church, social, and cultural life.

Joseph Fish (1706–1781), Congregational minister, whose diary relates his often frustrating ministry among the Narragansetts in Rhode Island and other concerns of colonial America.

Sidney George Fisher (1809–1871), Philadelphia gentleman and Maryland landholder, who, in his journal, poured out his vexations with Jacksonian America, his own blighted ambitions, and his bemused look at social life in a democratizing America that little tolerated aristocratic airs.

Philip Vickers Fithian (1747–1776), New Jersey-born tutor, whose diary records his adaptation to Virginia culture and society while teaching and living on the Carter family plantation (*see also* entry on Landon Carter).

Mary Wilder Foote (1810-1857), middle-class woman, who in a diary filled with reflections on her faith and devotion to

485

family recorded her impressions of society and culture in and around Salem, Massachusetts.

James Vincent Forrestal (1892–1949), Secretary of the Navy, whose private diaries from 1944 to 1949 give an insider's view of decision-making and personalities such as Roosevelt, Truman, and Eisenhower.

Charlotte L. Forten (1838–1914), teacher and reformer, whose diaries relate her growth from a young intellectual born to a prominent Philadelphia African-American family to a teacher among the ex-slaves in South Carolina.

Benjamin Browne Foster (1831–1903), lawyer and journalist, whose diary of life as a shop-clerk and college student in Maine describes small-town New England society, manners, and politics and the various amusements and fads of his day.

Samuel T. Foster (1829–1919), lawyer and judge, whose diary, kept while an officer with a Texas cavalry unit during the Civil War, describes life in and out of the saddle and in battle in the western theater of the war.

John C. Frémont (1813–1890), pathfinder and military officer, whose journals of western expeditions from St. Louis, to Fort Laramie, to Salt Lake, and beyond further mapped the trans-Mississippi West and extended American scientific, commercial, and political interest there.

Margaret Ann Alsip Frink (?), overland emigrant, whose 1850 journal of her family's trek from Indiana to the California gold fields comments on the many wonders and hardships along the way.

Wanda Gag (1893–1940), author and illustrator of children's books, whose diary of growing up in Minnesota, amid poverty and social proscriptions, reveals the daughter of immigrants finding her own way in America.

James A. Garfield (1831–1881), politician and president, whose diary runs from his youthful days full of tent meetings and church doings in Ohio, through his military service in the Civil War, to his national political career.

Allen Ginsberg (1926–), poet, whose diaries during the 1950s and 1960s as a member of the "Beat Generation" throb with fantasies and fascinations experienced in New York, California, and overseas.

Edwin L. Godkin (1831–1902), immigrant journalist and editor, whose brief diary kept during his wife's absence showed the man who took on corrupt politicoes in his editorials trying to manage a household.

Andrew Gordon (?), miner Forty-niner, who kept a gold rush diary assaying the physical and psychological costs of seeking gold in California.

Lorenzo J. Greene (1899–1988), historian, whose diary comments, often despairingly, on religion, intellectual life, and the arts, among several subjects, from the perspective of a young African-American historian.

Josephine Clay Habersham (1821–1893), Georgia aristocrat, whose 1863 diary portrays life among the plantation elite during a time of marked social change.

James Edmond Hall (1841–1915), Confederate soldier, whose wartime diary complains about the miseries of a soldier's life and the ignobility of death on the battlefield.

John Hall (?), English immigrant and farmer, whose diary from 1785 to 1812 reveals a man fascinated by republican government and manners and American science and technology.

Margaret Halsey (b. 1910), iconoclast and writer, whose diary while in England in 1936–1937, and elsewhere, made her conscious of her Americanness.

Alexander Hamilton (1712–1756), physician, who chronicled the rough-hewn American culture and "open" society he encountered while traveling from Annapolis to New Hampshire and back in 1744.

James Henry Hammond (1807–1864), South Carolina planter and politician, whose diaries show a man who while unsuccessful in seeking mastery over self, slaves, and society had much to report on politics, plantations, and public improvements around him.

David Golightly Harris (1824–1875), South Carolina farmer, whose pithy diary focuses on running a farm with seven slaves and coming to grips with war and the demands of ex-slaves for land and respect.

Emily Jane Lyles Harris (1827–1899), wife of David Golightly Harris, who resumed her husband's diary after he joined the Confederate army.

Esther Hill Hawks (1833–1906), physician, whose diary relates her experiences working with Union troops and the freedmen in South Carolina and Florida during and after the Civil War.

Nathaniel Hawthorne (1804–1864), novelist, whose sometimes bleak but satirical diaries and notebooks follow Hawthorne in his walks around Salem and sow the seeds of his stories.

John Hay (1838–1905), assistant to Lincoln's secretary John Nicolay, diplomat, and secretary of state, whose diaries (1861–1868) go deep inside the Lincoln administration, the society of wartime Washington, and the politics of Reconstruction.

Rutherford B. Hayes (1822–1893), president, whose diaries mark Hayes's path from college and lawyerly days in Ohio, through the Civil War, to the presidency, with much on American public affairs and personalities.

Howard Helman (1844–1886), printer, whose Civil War diary reveals the maturing process of war on a young Union recruit from Pennsylvania.

Sallie Hester (b. 1835), overland emigrant, whose journal of her trip from Indiana to California in 1849–1850 sees the westward march from a teenager's perspective.

Thomas Wentworth Higginson (1823–1911), minister, reformer, and essayist, whose account of army life in a black regiment in South Carolina during the Civil War measured Higginson's own and his black soldiers' adjustment to freedom.

Harriet Hitchcock (?), overland emigrant, whose 1864 diary of a covered wagon train rumbling in well-rutted routes across plains and over mountains captures a developing yet still wild West.

Thomas Hubbard Hobbs (1826–1862), lawyer, whose diary (1840-1862) relates the educational, domestic, religious, and social affairs in rural and small-town Alabama.

Oliver Wendell Holmes, Jr. (1841–1935), jurist, whose Civil War diary from the eastern theater reflects on war and his own mortality.

Philip Hone (1780-1851), wealthy New York gentleman, whose extensive diary applauds American technological progress and literary aspiration while it also laments the decline of American manners and morals in a democratic age.

Franklin Horner (c. 1836–1904), Union army sergeant from the Pennsylvania coal fields, whose Civil War diary gives impressions of the countryside and combat, especially the Battle of Gettysburg.

Harold L. Ickes (1874–1952), Secretary of the Interior and New Dealer, whose secret diaries ring up the costs and conflicts of the New Deal programs, rate a variety of personalities, and reveal much about Franklin D. Roosevelt and his age.

Washington Irving (1783–1859), novelist, whose travel diaries, which provided notes for his tales, illustrate his keen sense for local landscape and lore.

Alfred T. Jackson (?), Connecticut-born Forty-niner, whose diary recounts the loneliness and labors of prospecting in California and in San Francisco.

Mitchell Young Jackson (1816–1900), farmer, whose diaries from 1852–1863 muse on farming, church, Republican politics, and society in Minnesota and on slavery and the Civil War.

Alice James (1848–1892), literary salon doyenne, whose astute and sometimes acerbic diary, kept while away in Europe, remarks on a host of literary figures and affairs.

John Beauchamp Jones (1810-1866), author and editor, whose diary, written from the perspective of a clerk serving in the Confederate government, provides a full accounting of life and death in Richmond during the Civil War.

Ely J. Kahn, Jr. (1916–1994), journalist and author, whose anecdotal diary comments on life and leisure in the New York city area and inside *The New Yorker*, where he worked for many years.

James Lawson Kemper (1823–1895), lawyer, whose Mexican War diary covers the war years in Washington, D.C., and with the troops.

James Kenny (?), Quaker trader, whose diaries describe frontier life in colonial Pennsylvania and Maryland during trips to Pittsburgh and the Ohio country.

Charles Kikuchi (b. 1915), Nisei student, whose diary from Tanforan Assembly Center in California and elsewhere observes the effects of internment on Japanese Americans during World War II and his own loyalties to America.

Sarah Kemble Knight (1666–1727), New York lady, whose travel diary from Boston to New York and back comments on the characters, communities, and conversations along the way.

David S. Kogan (1929–1951), student, whose diary reflects on Jewish-American identity as Kogan records his life growing up in a Jewish family in Yonkers, New York, and school days at Cornell.

Jacob Saul Lanzit (c. 1830-1912), shirtmaker and printer, whose diary documents the struggles of a Jewish immigrant adapting to low wages and a new language in America.

Amos A. Lawrence (1814–1886), merchant, textile manufacturer, and philanthropist, whose diary affirms the success

490

of American enterprise and recounts commercial and social activity in and around Boston.

John Lawson (d. 1712), surveyor, whose journal describes the Indians and backcountry of early Carolina.

Arthur Lee (1740-1792), planter and patriot, whose journal relates the customs and conditions of the Indian and settler communities he met traveling across Pennsylvania.

Lewis Leon (1841–1919), clerk and storeowner, whose wartime diary gives a North Carolina Jewish Confederate private's view of southern society and service with Robert E. Lee's army.

Eugene Henry Levy (1840-1921), planter, broker, and later New York bookstore owner, whose wartime diary offers a cultured Jewish southerner's views on war and the South.

Meriwether Lewis (1774–1809), explorer, whose field notes and journals from the Lewis and Clark expedition, which he co-captained with William Clark, likewise opened the West to the American mind (*see also* entry on William Clark).

Charles A. Lindbergh (1902–1974), aviator, whose journal records his full public life during and surrounding World War II and the fame that trapped him.

John Davis Long (1838–1915), politician and Secretary of the Navy, whose diary carries Long from his boyhood days in New England through his public career with Theodore Roosevelt and others.

Ann Marie Riebe Low (b. 1912), teacher, whose diary from 1928 to 1937 reveals the hard life of a North Dakota farming community during the dust bowl years and the Depression.

Joseph Lyons (1813–1837), lawyer, who in his journal struggles with self-identity as a young man studying law in Georgia.

William Maclay (1734–1804), politician, whose diary, kept while a senator from Pennsylvania, gives an antifederalist view of politics, people, and protocol in the early republic.

Susan Shelby Magoffin (1827–1855), overland emigrant, whose diary, which she kept as a bride accompanying her trader husband to Santa Fe and beyond, contrasts American customs and culture with those of Indians, Mexicans, and others she met along the way.

Christopher Marshall (1709–1797), patriot, whose diary follows the course of the American Revolutionary War effort at home and in the army.

Anne McCaughey (b. 1915), nurse, whose diary from World War II gives candid views of training in Colorado to meeting the realities of war while serving with the Red Cross in Great Britain and France.

David McClure (1748–1820), Presbyterian missionary, whose diary records ministries to the Indians and others in the mid-Atlantic and New England regions.

Cornelia Peake McDonald (1822–1909), southern householder and slaveowner, whose Civil War diary tallies the trials of refugee life and efforts to sustain family and fortune in the war-torn Shenandoah.

Judith White Brockenbrough McGuire (1812–1896), minister's wife, whose Civil War diary depicts refugee life, from an ardent Virginia Confederate's perspective, as armies ravaged the land, disrupted society, and changed southern life forever.

Sallie [Sarah Rebecca] Meixell [Shorkley] (b. 1844), homemaker and clubwoman, whose diary (1863–1869) comments on politics, war, church, and family in an upstate Pennsylvania town.

Henry Louis Mencken (1880-1956), journalist, editor, and critic, whose copious diary provides candid and sometimes caustic comments on American literary, cultural, and social life and the development of the American language between the world wars.

Thomas Merton (1915–1968), thinker and monk, whose secular journal chronicles Catholic social concerns and work in

492

Harlem and elsewhere, World War II, and the meaning of Catholic devotion and vocation.

Thearl Mesecher (b. 1914), soldier, whose diary relates the World War II coming of age of an Iowa-born private exposed to suffering and brutality while a prisoner of war in Germany.

Isaac Mickle (1822–1855), lawyer and editor, who in his diary, kept while a young man in Camden, New Jersey, observes political, social, and cultural events around him and the loss of his own Quaker identity.

Emma Mordecai (c. 1812–1906), daughter of a prominent Richmond, Virginia, Jewish family, whose wartime diary describes the effects of the Civil War on soldiers, civilians, and slaves.

Gouverneur Morris (1752–1816), patriot and statesman, whose diary reports on political and social life in the early republic and the character of the French Revolution.

Peter [John Peter Gabriel] Muhlenberg (1746–1807), patriot, land speculator, and Lutheran minister, whose journal of travel to the Kentucky country records impressions of natural and human phenomena seen along the way.

Julia Rosa Newberry (1853–1876), Chicago aristocrat, whose diary, kept while a teenager, relates the interests and liaisons of high society, travel abroad, and the effects of the great Chicago fire.

Timothy Newell (1718–1799), deacon, whose diary catalogues the sufferings Americans experienced, especially in Massachusetts, during the early Revolutionary War period.

Howard Vincent O'Brien (1888–1947), author and newspaper columnist, whose irreverent diary of World War I, which likely was edited by O'Brien after the war, observes Americans abroad and comments on American habits and values from the perspective of an officer serving in France.

Clifford Odets (1906–1963), playwright and actor, whose 1940 journal draws highly personal portraits of American

493

places, people, and pastimes, especially in New York and California, as he contemplates what it means to be an American.

Ebenezer Parkman (1703–1782), Congregational minister, whose copious diary, which Parkman kept most of his life, details the beliefs and superstitions, behavior, and social rhythms of rural and small-town New England.

Francis Parkman (1823–1893), Romantic historian, whose journals recorded Parkman's often unflattering impressions of people and places, especially in his western trips, that he would write about later.

Linda Rae Patterson [Miller] (1946–), college professor, whose journal reflects on growing up in an affluent Chicago suburb from the perspective of a minister's daughter.

Marian Lawrence Peabody (b. 1875), genteel woman, whose diary relates growing up in Protestant Episcopal clerical circles, New England school days, travel abroad, and charity work.

Elizabeth Robins Pennell (1855–1936) and **Joseph Pennell** (1857–1926), artists, whose joint diary from 1898 to 1903, kept while living abroad in close association with the artist James Whistler, notes the comings and goings of American artists and literary expatriates.

Frances Dallam Peter (1843–1864), staunch Unionist, whose diary denounces Confederate occupation of her native Lexington, Kentucky, and scores the effects of war on family, community, and economy.

William Dane Phelps (1802–1875), ship captain, whose journals log impressions of American manners and marine commerce, the Pacific Northwest, and western lands and waters he visited.

Zebulon Montgomery Pike (1779–1813), explorer, whose journals of expeditions to find the sources of great western rivers and through Colorado and the Southwest marked the boundaries and promise of the Louisiana Purchase and further staked claims to the continent in the American mind.

Sylvia Plath (1932–1963), poet, whose introspective diaries mark her student, teaching, and writing career, with much attention to the concerns of being a woman writer set against the landscape of 1950s America, and chart her descent into depression.

Elmer G. Powers (1886–1942), farmer, whose diary from 1931 to 1936 records an Iowa farm community's struggles with drought and economic depression and efforts to hold onto the agricultural land and life they love.

William Hickling Prescott (1796–1859), nationalist historian, whose notebooks from 1823 to 1858 record his literary habits and observations.

Elizabeth Waties Allston Pringle (1845–1921), rice planter, whose diaries (1903–1905) relate the hard life of managing plantations and her interactions with family and black workers during the last days of rice culture in the South Carolina low country.

[Charles] Merrill Proudfoot (1923–), college professor and civil rights activist, whose diary of sit-ins in Knoxville in 1960, from the perspective of a white Presbyterian minister, reveals the makings of the "holy community" among civil rights supporters in the face of physical and psychological attacks.

John L. Ransom (1843–1919), Michigan-born printer and Union cavalryman, whose diary records his and other prisoners' efforts to survive the miserable conditions, disease, and social and moral breakdowns at the infamous Andersonville prison in 1863–1864.

Henry William Ravenel (1814–1887), South Carolina planter and botanist, whose journal records scientific investigations of plant life, plantation management, and politics during a time of rising sectional animosity, civil war, and Reconstruction.

Bernard J. Reid (1823–1904), trader and gold-seeker, whose diary details the exhaustion, disease, and disappointments of an ill-fated journey from Pennsylvania to California during gold rush days (*see also* entry on Niles Searls).

Valentine Reimann (1828–1903), German immigrant, whose diary sketches life as a soldier in the Union army during the Civil War and Sherman's march to the sea.

Walter Rhinehart (b. 1909), naval officer, whose diary remarks on life aboard a destroyer in the Pacific during World War II.

Caroline Cowles Richards [Clarke] (1842–1913), longtime resident of Canandaigua, New York, whose diary from 1852 to 1872 details village life, religion, Civil War news, and family concerns in upstate New York.

Dorothy Atkinson Robinson (b. 1892), editor, whose diaries (published under the pseudonym Dorothy Blake) of 1935 and 1941–1942 reflect on household duties, family, and community life from the perspective of a Long Island suburban housewife.

Thomas Rodney (1744–1811), patriot and lawyer, whose diary from the Revolutionary War describes service with Washington's army.

Will Rogers (1879–1935), homespun humorist, whose "diary" consists of stories he heard and told and his observations on politics and the American personality, including his own.

Edith Kermit Roosevelt (1861–1948), First Lady, whose diary relates life among the patrician class in America and personalities and interests associated with her husband (Theodore Roosevelt) and family.

Theodore Roosevelt (1858–1919), author and president, whose diary, principally from his boyhood through early adult years, relates life among the patrician class in America and his musings about and muscular demonstrations of Victorian masculinity.

Edmund Ruffin (1794–1865), planter and secessionist, whose detailed diaries, especially of the Civil War years, comment on scientific agriculture, plantation management, relations with slaves, family matters, military affairs, and, as southern fortunes flagged, God's judgment on the Confederacy.

May Sarton (1912–), poet, whose journals reflect on solitude, aging, her physical and spiritual recovery from surgery, the loss of loved ones, and the regenerative power of Nature.

Caroline Seabury (1827–1893), teacher, whose diary (1854–1863) tracks her movement from Brooklyn, New York, to her work in and adaptation to antebellum and wartime Mississippi.

Niles Searls (1825–1907), lawyer and judge, whose 1849 diary, kept while traveling to California on the Pioneer Line (*see also* entry on Bernard J. Reid), records the demoralizing effects of disease, drink, and disappointments on the trek westward.

Samuel Sewall (1652–1730), merchant and magistrate, whose diaries record local and personal affairs and lore, natural phenomena, court cases, and society in colonial Massachusetts.

James B. Sheeran (1819–1881), Irish immigrant priest, whose Civil War journal, kept while serving as a Catholic chaplain to Louisiana troops, comments on the morality and manners of camp life, morale, and military action with Robert E. Lee's army.

Jedediah Smith (1798–1831), explorer, trader, and mountain man, whose journals describe the fur trade, Indians, wilderness, and the western advance he observed during his travels across the Rockies into Utah, California, and Oregon.

John Smith (?), Rhode Island Continental soldier, whose diary of 1776 remarks on campaigning with Washington's army.

Sarah Gilbert White Smith (c. 1813–1855), missionary, whose 1838 diary records the difficulties of the overland journey to the mission at Walla Walla.

Elizabeth Cady Stanton (1815–1902), women's rights activist, whose journal documents her women's rights interests and actions and her personal affairs and associations with other reformers and family.

John Steinbeck (1902–1968), novelist, whose journal entries, kept while preparing for a cruise off Mexico, comment on life in southern California.

John William Sterling (1844–1918), lawyer and philanthropist, whose diary records his education and career as a prominent New York lawyer, including some interactions with the so-called robber barons.

Sarah Christie Stevens (1844–1919), Irish immigrant teacher, farmer, and Populist, whose diary describes running a farm in Minnesota, fighting for women's rights and temperance, and seeking office as a Populist.

Ezra Stiles (1727–1795), Congregational minister and college president, who filled his "literary diary" with gossip and news and observations on science and superstition, religion, politics, the American Revolution, and the development of American culture and identity.

Amos Stouffer (1842–1924), farmer, whose 1863 diary gives a Pennsylvania German view of the Civil War when Lee's army invaded his state.

George Templeton Strong (1820-1875), lawyer, whose thick, lifelong (1835–1875) diary spans America at mid-century and discusses education, literature and the arts, society, politics and civic life, war, technology, and a host of other subjects from the perspective of an upper-class New Yorker uneasy with democracy.

Cyrus Leo Sulzberger (1912–1993), journalist, whose diaries record his observations on post-World War II United States and foreign politicians and policies and the Americans he met abroad.

Ella Gertrude Clanton Thomas (1834–1907), Georgia plantation mistress, whose diaries (1848–1889) detail church and home affairs, plantation management, relations with slaves and freedmen, and war and its aftermath in and around Augusta.

M[artha] Carey Thomas (1857–1935), college president, who in her diary relates growing up in a Quaker family, women's education, women's rights, and her own efforts to realize herself beyond Victorian conventions.

Henry David Thoreau (1817–1862), transcendental thinker and writer, whose diaries, which formed his life's work, reflect on the natural world around him, his Concord neighbors, and his musings on such varied subjects as civil disobedience, work, philosophy, local lore, and human nature.

Richard W. Tregaskis (1916–1973), journalist, whose diaries, kept while a war correspondent in World War II, capture combat from the soldiers' perspective, especially in his account of the Marines' invasion of Guadalcanal in 1942.

Mark Twain [Samuel Langhorne Clemens] (1835–1910), writer and storyteller, whose journals and notebooks, which provided much material for his stories, recorded his observations on the mundane, local lore, characters, and places he observed during his time on the Mississippi, his stay in California, and his travels across America and abroad.

Albigence Waldo (1750-1794), surgeon, whose diary, kept while wintering with Washington's army at Valley Forge, details the sufferings, homesickness, and hardships of that fateful stay.

Elkanah Walker (1805–1877), missionary, whose diaries (1838–1848) describe the overland journey to Oregon and missionary work among the Spokane Indians.

Henry A. Wallace (1888–1965), Secretary of Agriculture and New Dealer, whose diaries reveal the internal politics of New Deal planning, personalities, and concern for farmers' interests in modernizing America.

Robert A. Ware (?), Confederate soldier, who resumed his brother Thomas Ware's diary (*see* following entry) after Thomas was killed at Gettysburg.

Thomas L. Ware (1838–1863), Confederate soldier, whose Civil War diary describes camp life and military action with Robert E. Lee's army.

George Washington (1732–1799), planter, patriot, and president, whose diaries briefly record his dog and horse breeding interests, plantation management, social life, and more fully, his surveying and land speculating trips into the backcountry, as well as his military roles in the French and Indian and American Revolutionary wars.

Gideon Welles (1802–1878), Secretary of the Navy, whose diaries (1862–1869) detail personalities and politics inside the Abraham Lincoln and Andrew Johnson administrations, with poignant and full descriptions of Lincoln's death and the nation's mourning.

Glenway Wescott (1901–1987), novelist and poet, whose journal (1937–1955) celebrates work, landscape, sex, money, health, and more within the New York area artistic milieu.

Alphonso Wetmore (1793–1849), military officer and explorer, whose 1828 journal of a trip to Santa Fe comments on the places, people, and prospects seen along the way.

Narcissa Prentiss Whitman (1808–1847), missionary and pioneer, whose diaries describe the rigors of overland travel to the Oregon territory and settling a mission among the Indians.

Walt Whitman (1819–1892), poet, whose daybooks and notebooks of travel and especially his lyrical journal, kept while he comforted soldiers in hospitals during the Civil War, reveal his soul and love for mankind, his reverence for Lincoln and his memory, and his reflections on the American spirit.

Thornton Wilder (1897–1975), playwright, whose journals (1939–1961), which he intended as a means of self-discipline to help formulate ideas for lectures and writing, comment on

American literature and literary figures, the social landscape, and his work in progress.

Donald J. Willis (b. 1919), World War II soldier, whose 1944 diary views the American GIs' experiences in the European war from D-Day onward, from the perspective of an Iowa-born draftee serving with an armored division.

Edmund Wilson (1895–1972), author and critic, whose self-indulgent diaries and notebooks, which he maintained religiously from 1919 through the 1950s, detail American literary, political, social, and cultural life, observed both in the United States and abroad, describe a host of American personalities, and record his many and varied liaisons, predilections, and passions.

Edward Winslow (1595–1655), Pilgrim father, who in 1622 sent back to England four narratives of exploration, settlement, and Pilgrims' progress, including the journal of the migration to Plymouth Plantation he and William Bradford wrote (*see also* entry on William Bradford), that cast the colony in a favorable light.

John Winthrop (1587/88–1649), Puritan and first governor of Massachusetts Bay colony, whose introspective journal became the first "history of New England" in its record of the settlement of Massachusetts Bay, of the colony's divine purpose, of struggles with dissenters and others, and of natural wonders.

Sally [Sarah] Wister (1761–1804), Quaker woman, whose journal, kept during the American Revolutionary War, describes society, family, and relations with soldiers, from the perspective of a teenager living on a farm near Valley Forge.

James Webb Young (b. 1886), advertising executive, whose diary (1942–1943), which he began with an eye to writing a history of American business, consists of daily observations on civilian adjustments during wartime, American heroism and character, business, gardening and farming, and tips on advertising and marketing.

⤳ SOURCES AND PERMISSIONS ⤳

The following bibliography lists the sources from which the diary entries came. It also includes any formal credit lines and statements granting permission to publish material, wherever appropriate and necessary. In several instances where the original diaries in manuscript were used, published versions of those diaries also are listed for the convenience of readers who might want to sample such works. When more than one edition of a diary was used for diary entries, every edition consulted will be cited. The citations and permissions are arranged alphabetically by name of the diarist. If the diarist's name is not evident from the citation, it will be noted within brackets at the head of the citation.

For more general information on American diaries, Laura Arksey, Nancy Pries, and Marcia Reed, *American Diaries: An Annotated Bibliography of Published American Diaries and Journals* (2 vols., Detroit: Gale Research Company, 1983–1987), is indispensable. Also useful are William Matthews, *American Diaries in Manuscript, 1580–1954: A Descriptive Bibliography* (Athens: University of Georgia Press, 1974); Joyce D. Goodfriend, *The Published Diaries and Letters of American Women: An Annotated Bibliography* (Boston: G. K. Hall & Company, 1987); and Michael Barton, "Selected Bibliography of Civil War Soldiers' Diaries," *Bulletin of Bibliography & Magazine Notes* 35 (January–March 1978): 19–29. In the large literature on diaries, probably the best introduction is Thomas Mallon, *A Book of One's Own: People and Their Diaries* (New York: Ticknor & Fields, 1984). Also useful for understanding the American diary tradition is Steven E.

502

Kagle, *American Diary Literature 1620–1799* (Boston: Twayne Publishers, 1979).

Franklin Pierce Adams, *Diary of Our Own Samuel Pepys* (New York: Simon & Schuster, 1935).

Charles Francis Adams, ed., *The Works of John Adams, Second President of the United States; With a Life of the Author* (10 vols., Boston: Little, Brown & Company, 1850–1856).

Charles Francis Adams, ed., *Memoirs of John Quincy Adams, Comprising Portions of His Diary from 1798 to 1848* (12 vols., Philadelphia: J. B. Lippincott, 1874–1877); and Allan Nevins, ed., *The Diary of John Quincy Adams, 1794–1845: American Political, Social, and Intellectual Life from Washington to Polk* (New York: Longman's, 1929).

Journals of Louisa May Alcott, Alcott Family Papers (Manuscript Department, Houghton Library, Harvard University). Printed by permission of The Houghton Library, Harvard University. And Ednah D. Cheney, ed., *Louisa May Alcott, Her Life, Letters, and Journals* (Boston: Roberts Brothers, 1889). *See also* Joel Myerson and Daniel Shealy, eds., *The Journals of Louisa May Alcott* (Boston: Little, Brown & Company, 1989).

Hilbert H. Campbell, ed., *The Sherwood Anderson Diaries, 1936–1941* (Athens: University of Georgia Press, 1987). Reprinted by permission of Harold Ober Associates Incorporated. Copyright © 1987 by the Trustees of the Sherwood Anderson Literary Estate.

Eliza Frances Andrews, *The War-Time Journal of a Georgia Girl, 1864–1865* (New York: D. Appleton & Company, 1908).

[Anonymous], G. W. Cable, ed., "War Diary of a Union Woman in the South," in *Famous Adventures & Prison Escapes of the Civil War* (New York: Century Company, 1893), pp. 1–82.

Ida Husted Harper, *Life and Work of Susan B. Anthony* (3 vols., Indianapolis: Hollenbeck Press, 1898–1908), diary extracts throughout.

Diaries of David Avery, David Avery Papers (Connecticut Historical Society). Printed by permission of The Connecticut Historical Society. Typescript of the Diaries of David Avery (Speed Library, Princeton Theological Seminary). Also available in the microfilm edition, John M. Mulder, ed., *The Papers of David Avery, 1746–1818*. Used by permission of John M. Mulder.

[Dorothea Moulton Balano] James W. Balano, ed., *The Log of the Skipper's Wife* (Camden, ME: Down East Books, 1979). Reprinted by permission of Elsie Gage Balano.

The Diary of Martha Moore Ballard, 2 vols. (1785–1812) (Maine State Library, Augusta). Printed by permission of The Maine State Library. *See also* Charles E. Nash, ed., *The History of Augusta, Maine* (Augusta: Charles Nash & Sons, 1904), pp. 229–464; and Laurel Thatcher Ulrich, *A Midwife's Tale: The Life of Martha Ballard, Based on Her Diary, 1785–1812* (New York: Alfred A. Knopf, 1990), diary entries throughout.

[Clarence W. Barron], Arthur Pound and Samuel T. Moore, eds., *They Told Barron* (New York: Harper, 1930); and Arthur Pound and Samuel T. Moore, eds., *More They Told Barron: Conversations and Revelations of an American Pepys in Wall Street* (New York: Harper, 1931).

John Bartram, *Observations on the Inhabitants, Climate, Soil, Rivers, Productions, Animals, and Other Matters Worthy of Notice. Made by Mr. John Bartram in his Travels from Pensilvania . . .* (London: Printed for J. Whiston and B. White, 1751).

[Lewis Beebe] Frederic R. Kirkland, ed., "Journal of a Physician on the Expedition Against Canada, 1776," *Pennsylvania Magazine of History and Biography* 59 (1935): 321–61.

[John Boit], "Boit's Log of the *Columbia,* 1790–1792," *Proceedings of the Massachusetts Historical Society* 53 (1920): 217–75; Frederic W. Howay and T. C. Elliott, eds., "The John Boit and Captain Gray's Log of the Ship *Columbia,*" *Oregon Historical Quarterly* 22 (1921): 257–356; and Edmond S. Meany, ed., "New Log of the *Columbia,*" *Washington Historical Quarterly* 12 (1921): 2–50.

John Wilkes Booth Diary (Ford's Theatre National Historic Site, Washington); Alfred H. Guernsey and Henry M. Alden, *Harper's Pictorial History of the Civil War* (2 parts, New York: Harper & Brothers, 1868), part 2, pp. 784–85 wording used herein. With slightly different wording, *see also* "From the Diary of John Wilkes Booth," *Confederate Veteran* 18 (1910): 403.

Van Wyck Brooks, ed., *The Journal of Gamaliel Bradford, 1883–1932* (Boston: Houghton Mifflin Company, 1933).

[William Bradford and Edward Winslow], *A Relation or Journall of the Beginning and Proceedings of the English Plantation Settled at Plimoth in New England, by Certaine English Adven-*

504

turers both Merchants and Others. . . . (London: Printed for John Bellamie, 1622).

Nicholas Wainwright, ed., "The Diary of Samuel Breck, 1814–1822," *Pennsylvania Magazine of History and Biography* 102 (1978): 469–508; 103 (1979): 85–113, 222–51, 356–82; 497–527. Reprinted by permission of *The Pennsylvania Magazine of History and Biography.*

Mary D. Robertson, ed., *Lucy Breckinridge of Grove Hill: The Journal of a Virginia Girl, 1862–1864* (Kent: Kent State University Press, 1979). Reprinted by permission of Mary D. Robertson.

[William Henry Brewer] Francis Farquhar, ed., *Up and Down California in 1860–64* (New Haven: Yale University Press, 1930).

Theodore C. Pease and James G. Randall, eds., *The Diary of Orville Hickman Browning* (2 vols., Springfield: Illinois State Historical Society, 1925–1927).

George W. Read and Ruth Gaines, eds., *Gold Rush: The Journals, Drawings and Other Papers of J. Goldsborough Bruff, Captain, Washington City and California Mining Association* (2 vols., New York: Columbia University Press, 1944).

[Dolly Sumner Lunt Burge] Julian Street, ed., *A Woman's Wartime Journal: An Account of the Passage over a Georgia Plantation of Sherman's Army on the March to the Sea* (New York: Century Company, 1918).

Matthew L. Davis, ed., *The Private Journal of Aaron Burr, During His Residence of Four Years in Europe* (2 vols., New York: Harper & Brothers, 1888).

Louis B. Wright and Marion Tinling, eds., *The Secret Diary of William Byrd of Westover, 1709–1712* (Richmond: Dietz Press, 1941); Louis B. Wright and Marion Tinling, eds., *The London Diary (1717–1721) and Other Writings* (New York: Oxford University Press, 1958); and Maude H. Woodfin, ed., *Another Secret Diary of William Byrd of Westover* (Richmond: Dietz Press, 1942).

Diary of Helen Carpenter, 1857 (#HM 16994) (Huntington Library). Printed by permission of The Huntington Library, San Marino, California. *See also* Sandra L. Myres, ed., *Ho for California!: Women's Overland Diaries from the Huntington Library* (San Marino: Huntington Library, 1980), pp. 93–188.

Jack P. Greene, ed., *The Diary of Colonel Landon Carter of Sabine Hall, 1752–1778* (2 vols., Charlottesville: University

Press of Virginia, 1965). Used by permission of the University Press of Virginia.

[Francis A. Chardon] Annie Heloise Abel, ed., *Chardon's Journal at Fort Clark, 1834–1839: Descriptive of Life on the Upper Missouri; of a Fur Trader's Experiences Among the Mandans . . .* (Pierre, SD: n.p., 1932).

C. Vann Woodward and Elisabeth Muhlenfeld, eds., *The Private Mary Chesnut: The Unpublished Civil War Diaries* (New York: Oxford University Press, 1984). Reprinted by permission of Harold Ober Associates Incorporated. Copyright © 1984 by C. Vann Woodward, Elisabeth Muhlenfeld, McCoy Metts Hill, Barbara G. Carpenter, Sally Bland Johnson, and Katherine W. Herbert.

Richard Brodhead, ed., *The Journals of Charles W. Chesnutt* (Durham: Duke University Press, 1993). Reprinted with permission.

[William Clark] Reuben G. Thwaites, ed., *The Original Journals of the Lewis and Clark Expedition, 1804–1806* (8 vols., New York: Dodd, Mead & Company, 1904–1905).

[Samuel A. Clear] W. Springer Menge and J. August Shimrak, eds., *The Civil War Notebook of Daniel Chisholm: A Chronicle of Daily Life in the Union Army, 1864–1865* (New York: Orion Books, 1989). From *The Civil War Notebook of Daniel Chisholm* edited by Bill Menge and Gus Shimrak, Copyright © 1989 by Bill Menge and Gus Shimrak. Reprinted by permission of Orion Books, a division of Crown Publishers, Inc.

[Joseph Cleaver, Jr.] William D. Lewis, ed., "Diary of a Student at Delaware College," *Delaware Notes,* 24th series (1951): 1–87.

Miriam Davis Colt, *Went to Kansas: Being a Thrilling Account of an Ill-Fated Expedition to That Fairy Land and Its Sad Results* (Watertown: printed by L. Ingalls & Company, 1862).

Jemima Condict, Her Book: Being a Transcript of the Diary of an Essex County Maid during the Revolutionary War (Newark: Carteret Book Club, 1930).

James E. Pollard, ed., *The Journal of Jay Cooke; or, the Gibraltor Records* (Columbus: Ohio State University Press, 1935).

[James Fenimore Cooper] (diary extracts) *Putnam's Magazine,* new series, 1 (1868): 167–72, 730–37. *See also* James F. Beard, ed., *The Letters and Journals of James Fenimore Cooper* (6 vols., Cambridge: Harvard University Press, 1960–1968).

Life of David Crockett, The Original Humorist and Irresponsible Backwoodsman . . . to Which Is Added on Account of His Glorious Death at the Alamo While Fighting in Defence of Teton Independence (Philadelphia: John E. Patterson & Company, [1865]), pp. 378–94 (diary).

Journal of Bradley Newcomb Cumings (Massachusetts Historical Society). Excerpts in the *M.H.S. Miscellany*, no. 52 (Autumn 1992): 5–7. Printed by permission of the Massachusetts Historical Society.

Robert F. Lucid, ed., *The Journal of Richard Henry Dana, Jr.* (3 vols., Cambridge: Harvard University Press, 1968). Reprinted by permission of the publishers from *The Journal of Richard Henry Dana, Jr., 3 Volumes*, edited by Robert F. Lucid, Cambridge, Mass.: The Belknap Press of Harvard University Press, Copyright © 1968 by the Massachusetts Historical Society, copyright © 1968 by the President and Fellows of Harvard College.

Charles E. Davis, Jr., *Three Years in the Army: The Story of the Thirteenth Massachusetts Volunteers from July 16, 1861, to August 1, 1864* (Boston: Estes & Lauriat, 1894).

William Miller, ed., *All is Grace: The Spirituality of Dorothy Day* (Garden City: Doubleday & Company, 1987). Reprinted by permission of William D. Miller.

Townsend Ludington, ed., *The Fourteenth Chronicle: Letters and Diaries of John Dos Passos* (Boston: Gambit, 1973). Reprinted by permission of Elizabeth (Mrs. John) Dos Passos, Estate of John Dos Passos.

Thomas P. Riggio, ed., *Theodore Dreiser: American Diaries 1902–1926* (Philadelphia: University of Pennsylvania Press, 1982). Reprinted by permission of The University of Pennsylvania Press.

Gloria T. Hull, ed., *Give Us Each Day: The Diary of Alice Dunbar-Nelson* (New York: W. W. Norton & Company, 1984). Reprinted by permission of Akasha (Gloria) Hull.

The Diary of William Dunlap (1766–1839): The Memoirs of a Dramatist, Theatrical Manager, Painter, Critic, Novelist, and Historian, in *New-York Historical Society Collections*, numbers 62–64 (3 vols., New York: New-York Historical Society, 1930).

Sophie M. du Pont Diaries, Sophie M. (du Pont) Du Pont Papers (Hagley Museum and Library). Printed by courtesy of Hagley Museum and Library, Wilmington, Delaware. *See also* Betty Bright Low and Jacqueline Hinsley, *Sophie du Point: A*

Young Lady in America, Sketches, Diaries & Letters (New York: Harry N. Abrams, 1987), diary excerpts throughout.

Collins Denny, ed., "The Diary of John Early, Bishop of the Methodist Episcopal Church, South," *Virginia Magazine of History and Biography* 33 (1925): 166–74, 283–87; 34 (1926): 130–37, 237–51, 299–312; 35 (1927): 7–12, 280–86; 36 (1928): 175–79, 239–48, 328–32; 37 (1929): 130–38, 256–60; 38 (1930): 251–58; 39 (1931): 41–45, 146–51; 40 (1932): 70–74, 147–54.

Dagobert D. Runes, ed., *The Diary and Sundry Observations of Thomas Alva Edison* (New York: Philosophical Library, 1948).

Beth G. Crabtree and James W. Patton, eds., *"Journal of a Secesh Lady": The Diary of Catherine Ann Devereux Edmondston 1860–1866* (Raleigh: North Carolina Division of Archives and History, 1979). Reprinted by permission of the North Carolina Division of Archives and History.

"Journal of Myra F. Eells," *Transactions of the Oregon Pioneer Association,* 17th annual reunion (1889): 54–88.

[Edward Robb Ellis] Donald Vining, ed., *American Diaries of World War II* (New York: Pepys Press, 1982). Reprinted by permission of Donald Vining and The Pepys Press.

Charles Lanman, ed., *Journal of Alfred Ely, A Prisoner of War in Richmond* (New York: D. Appleton & Company, 1862).

Edward Aldo Emerson and Waldo Emerson Forbes, eds., *Journals of Ralph Waldo Emerson, With Annotations* (10 vols., Boston: Houghton Mifflin Company, 1909–1914).

Marlene Springer and Haskell Springer, eds., *Plains Woman: The Diary of Martha Farnsworth, 1882–1922* (Bloomington: Indiana University Press, 1986). Reprinted by permission of Haskell Springer and Indiana University Press.

John Palmer Finley Diaries, Record Group 219, John Palmer Finley Papers (Presbyterian Historical Society). Printed by permission of The Department of History, Presbyterian Church (U.S.A.), Philadelphia, Pennsylvania.

William S. Simmons and Cheryl L. Simmons, eds., *Old Light on Separate Ways: The Narragansett Diary of Joseph Fish, 1765–1776* (Hanover: University Press of New England, 1982). Reprinted by permission from William S. Simmons and Cheryl L. Simmons, entries for June 20, 1768, May 9, 1774, from *Old Light on Separate Ways: The Narragansett Diary of Joseph Fish.* Copyright © 1982 by the University Press of New England.

Nicholas B. Wainwright, ed., *A Philadelphia Perspective: The Diary of Sidney George Fisher Covering the Years 1834–1871* (Philadelphia: Historical Society of Pennsylvania, 1967). Reprinted by permission of The Historical Society of Pennsylvania.

John R. Williams, ed., *Philip Vickers Fithian, Journal and Letters, 1767–1774, Student at Princeton College, 1770–72, Tutor at Nomini Hall in Virginia, 1773–74* (2 vols., Princeton: Princeton University Library, 1900–1934); and Hunter D. Farish, ed., *Journal & Letters of Philip Vickers Fithian, 1773–1774: A Plantation Tutor of the Old Dominion* (Williamsburg: Colonial Williamsburg, 1943).

Mary Wilder Tileston, ed., *Caleb and Mary Wilder Foote: Reminiscences and Letters* (Boston: Houghton Mifflin Company, 1918), diary entries throughout.

James V. Forrestal Diaries, James Forrestal Papers (Seeley G. Mudd Manuscript Library, Princeton University). Printed with permission of Princeton University Libraries from Volume 2, Box 1 of the James V. Forrestal Diaries, James Forrestal Papers, Seeley G. Mudd Manuscript Library, Princeton University. *See also* Walter Millis, ed., *The Forrestal Diaries* (New York: Viking Press, 1951).

Charlotte Forten Diaries, Francis Grimke Papers (Moorland-Spingarn Research Center, Howard University). Printed by permission of the Moorland-Spingarn Research Center from the Francis Grimke Papers, Charlotte Forten Diaries, Box 40–45, Folders 1814, 1815, Moorland-Spingarn Research Center, Howard University. *See also* Ray Allen Billington, ed., *The Journal of Charlotte Forten* (New York: Dryden Press, 1953).

[Benjamin Browne Foster] Charles H. Foster, ed., *Down East Diary* (Orono: University of Maine Press, 1975). Reprinted by permission of The University of Maine Press at Orono.

Norman D. Brown, ed., *One of Cleburne's Command: The Civil War Reminiscences and Diary of Capt. Samuel T. Foster, Granbury's Texas Brigade, CSA* (Austin: University of Texas Press, 1980). Reprinted by permission of the University of Texas Press, copyright © 1980.

John C. Frémont, *Report of the Exploring Expedition to the Rocky Mountains in the Year 1842 and to Oregon and North California in the Years 1843–'44*, in *U. S. Senate, 28th Congress, 2nd Session, Executive Document 174* (Washington: Gales & Seaton, Printers, 1845); and John C. Frémont, *Memoirs of My Life, Including the Narrative Five Journeys of West-*

ern *Exploration, During the Years 1842, 1843–4, 1845–6–7, 1853–4* (Chicago: Belford, Clarke, 1887).

Margaret A. Frink, *Journal of the Adventures of a Party of California Gold-Seekers Under the Guidance of Mr. Ledyard Frink . . . 1850* ([Oakland]: n.p., 1897).

Wanda Gag, *Growing Pains: Diaries and Drawings for the Years 1908–1917* (New York: Coward-McCann, Publishers, 1940).

Harry James Brown and Frederick D. Williams, eds. *The Diary of James A. Garfield* (4 vols., East Lansing: Michigan State University Press, 1967–1981). Reprinted by permission of The Michigan State University Press.

[Allen Ginsberg] Gordon Ball, ed., *Journals: Early Fifties Early Sixties* (New York: Grove Press, 1977). Reprinted by permission of Allen Ginsberg.

Rollo Ogden, ed., *Life and Letters of Edwin Lawrence Godkin* (2 vols, New York: Macmillan, 1907), II, 100–105 (diary).

[Andrew Gordon] William E. Woodward, ed., *The Way Our People Lived: An Intimate American History* (New York: E. P. Dutton & Company, 1944), pp. 244–77 (diary excerpts).

Arvarh E. Strickland, ed., *Working with Carter G. Woodson, the Father of Black History: A Diary, 1928–1930 [by] Lorenzo J. Greene* (Baton Rouge: Louisiana State University Press, 1989). Reprinted by permission of The Louisiana State University Press.

Spencer Bidwell King, Jr., ed., *Ebb Tide, As Seen Through the Diary of Josephine Clay Habersham 1863* (Athens: University of Georgia Press, 1958). Reprinted by permission of Caroline P. (Mrs. Spencer) King.

Ruth Woods Dayton, ed., *The Diary of a Confederate Soldier: James E. Hall* (Lewisburg, WV: privately printed, 1961). Reprinted by permission of Sylvia H. Markley.

John Hall Diary (Library Company of Philadelphia). Printed by permission of the Library Company of Philadelphia.

Margaret Halsey, *With Malice Toward Some* (New York: Simon & Schuster, 1938).

[Alexander Hamilton] Albert Bushnell Hart, ed., *Hamilton's Itinerarium: Being a Narrative of a Journey from Annapolis, Maryland, through Delaware, Pennsylvania, New York, New Jersey, Connecticut, Rhode Island, Massachusetts and New Hampshire, from May to September 1744* (St. Louis: W. K. Bixby, 1907). *See also* Carl Bridenbaugh, ed., *Gentleman's*

Progress: The Itinerarium of Dr. Alexander Hamilton (Chapel Hill: University of North Carolina Press, 1948).

James Henry Hammond Diaries, James Henry Hammond Papers (South Caroliniana Library, University of South Carolina). Printed by permission of the South Caroliniana Library, University of South Carolina. *See also* Carol Bleser, ed., *Secret and Sacred: The Diaries of James Henry Hammond, A Southern Slaveholder* (New York: Oxford University Press, 1988).

[David Golightly Harris and Emily Harris] Philip N. Racine, *Piedmont Farmer: The Journals of David Golightly Harris, 1855–1870* (Knoxville: University of Tennessee Press, 1990). Reprinted by permission of The University of Tennessee Press. From *Piedmont Farmer: The Journals of David Golightly Harris, 1855–1870,* edited by Philip N. Racine. Copyright © 1990 by The University of Tennessee Press.

Gerald Schwartz, ed., *A Woman Doctor's Civil War: Esther Hill Hawks' Diary* (Columbia: University of South Carolina Press, 1984). Reprinted by permission of The University of South Carolina Press.

George P. Lathrop, ed., *The Complete Works of Nathaniel Hawthorne* (10 vols., Boston: Houghton Mifflin Company, 1914); and Randall Stewart, ed., *The American Notebooks* (New Haven: Yale University Press, 1932).

Tyler Dennett, ed., *Lincoln and the Civil War in the Diaries and Letters of John Hay* (New York: Dodd, Mead & Company, 1939).

Charles Richard Williams, ed., *Diary and Letters of Rutherford Birchard Hayes, Nineteenth President of the United States* (5 vols., Columbus: Ohio State Archaeological and Historical Society, 1922–1926).

Arthur W. Thurner, "A Young Soldier in the Army of the Potomac: Diary of Howard Helman, 1862," *Pennsylvania Magazine of History and Biography* 87 (1963): 139–55. Reprinted by permission of *The Pennsylvania Magazine of History and Biography.*

"The Diary of a Pioneer Girl: The Adventures of Sallie Hester, Aged Twelve in a Trip Overland in 1849," *The Argonaut,* September 1, 1925–October 24, 1925. *See also* Kenneth Holmes, ed., *Covered Wagon Women: Diaries & Letters from the Western Trails, 1840–1890* (8 vols., Glendale, CA, and Spokane, WA: Arthur H. Clark Company, 1984–1989), I, 231–46.

Thomas Wentworth Higginson, *Army Life in a Black Regiment* (Boston: Fields, Osgood, 1870). *See also* Howard Mumford Jones, ed., *Army Life in a Black Regiment* (East Lansing: Michigan State University Press, 1960), pp. 5–47, 83–84, 88–90, and 182–88.

[Harriet Hitchcock] Kenneth Holmes, ed., *Covered Wagon Women: Diaries & Letters from the Western Trails, 1840–1890* (8 vols., Glendale, CA, and Spokane, WA: Arthur H. Clark Company, 1984–1989), VIII, 233–64. Reprinted by permission of The Arthur H. Clark Company.

Faye Action Axford, ed., *The Journals of Thomas Hubbard Hobbs: A Contemporary Record of an Aristocrat from Athens, Alabama, Written between 1840, When the Diarist Was Fourteen Years Old and 1862 When He Died Serving the Confederate States of America* (University: University of Alabama Press, 1976). Reprinted by permission of Faye A. Axford.

Mark De Wolfe Howe, ed., *Touched With Fire: Civil War Letters and Diary of Oliver Wendell Holmes, Jr., 1861–1864* (Cambridge: Harvard University Press, 1946).

Bayard Tuckerman, ed., *The Diary of Philip Hone* (2 vols., New York: Dodd, Mead & Company, 1889); and Allan Nevins, ed., *The Diary of Philip Hone, 1825–1851* (2 vols., New York: Dodd, Mead & Company, 1927).

[Franklin Horner] Mark Nesbitt, *25 Days to Gettysburg: The Campaign Diaries of Two American Enemies* (Harrisburg: Stackpole Books, 1992). Reprinted by permission of Stackpole Books.

Harold L. Ickes, *The Secret Diary of Harold L. Ickes* (3 vols., New York: Simon & Schuster, 1953). Excerpts from The *Secret Diary of Harold L. Ickes*, vol. I: *The First Thousand Days 1933–1936*. Copyright 1953 by Simon & Schuster, Inc. Copyright renewed © 1981 by Harold M. Ickes and Elizabeth Ickes. Reprinted by permission of Simon & Schuster, Inc.

Washington Irving Journals, Seligman Collection of Irvingiana, Washington Irving Papers (Rare Books and Manuscripts Division, The New York Public Library, Astor, Lenox and Tilden Foundations). Printed by permission of The New York Public Library. *See also* William P. Trent and George S. Hellman, eds., *The Journals of Washington Irving (Hitherto Unpublished)* (3 vols., Boston: Bibliophile Society, 1919); and Nathalia Wright, et al., eds., *Journals and Notebooks*, vols. 1–5 of *The Complete Works of Washington Irving* (Madison:

University of Wisconsin Press; and Boston: Twayne Publishers, 1969–1986).

[Alfred T. Jackson] Chauncey de Leon Canfield, ed., *Diary of a Forty-Niner* (New York: M. Shepard Company, 1906).

Rodney C. Loehr, ed., *Minnesota Farmers' Diaries: William R. Brown, 1845–46, Mitchell Y. Jackson, 1852–63* (St. Paul: Minnesota Historical Society, 1939), pp. 85–220.

Anna R. Burr, ed., *Alice James, Her Brother—Her Journal* (New York: Dodd, Mead & Company, 1934).

[John Beauchamp Jones] *A Rebel War Clerk's Diary at the Confederate States Capital* (2 vols., Philadelphia: J. B. Lippincott, 1866); and Howard Swiggert, ed., *A Rebel War Clerk's Diary at the Confederate States Capital* (2 vols., New York: Old Hickory Bookshop, 1935).

E. J. Kahn, Jr., *Year of Change: More about The New Yorker & Me* (New York: Viking Press, 1988). Reprinted by permission of E. J. Kahn, Jr.

Robert R. Jones, ed., "The Mexican War Diary of James Lawson Kemper," *Virginia Magazine of History and Biography* 74 (1966): 387–428. Reprinted by permission of *The Virginia Magazine of History and Biography*.

John W. Jordan, ed., "Journal of James Kenny, 1761–63," *Pennsylvania Magazine of History and Biography* 23 (1913): 1–47, 152–201; and John W. Jordan, ed., "John Kenny's 'Journal to Ye Westward,' 1758–59," ibid., 23 (1913): 395–449.

John Modell, ed., *The Kikuchi Diary: Chronicle from an American Concentration Camp—The Tanforan Journals of Charles Kikuchi* (Urbana: University of Illinois Press, 1973). Reprinted by permission of The University of Illinois Press.

[Sarah Kemble Knight] *The Journals of Madam Knight, and Rev. Mr. Buckingham from the Original Manuscripts in 1704 & 1710* (New York: Wilder & Campbell, 1825), pp. 1–70.

Meyer Levin, ed., *Diary of David S. Kogan* (New York: Beechhurst Press, 1955).

[Jacob Saul Lanzit] Jacob R. Marcus, ed., *Memoirs of American Jews, 1765–1865* (3 vols., Philadelphia: Jewish Publication Society, 1956), III, 33–37. Reprinted by permission of The Jewish Publication Society.

William Lawrence, *Life of Amos A. Lawrence, with Extracts from His Diary and Correspondence* (Boston: Houghton Mifflin Company, 1888).

John Lawson, *A New Voyage to Carolina; Containing the*

Exact Description and Natural History of that Country: Together with the Present State Thereof. And a Journal of a Thousand Miles, Travel'd Thro' Several Nations of Indians. Giving a Particular Account of their Customs, Manners, &. (London, n. p., 1709).

Richard Henry Lee, *The Life of Arthur Lee, LL.D., Joint Commissioner of the United States to the Court of France* (2 vols., Boston: Wells & Lilly, 1829), II, 377–99 (diary).

Lewis Leon, *Diary of a Tar Heel Confederate Soldier* (Charlotte: Stone Publishing Company, 1913).

[Eugene Henry Levy] Jacob R. Marcus, ed., *Memoirs of American Jews, 1765–1865* (3 vols., Jewish Publication Society, 1956), III, 299–323. Reprinted by permission of The Jewish Publication Society.

[Meriwether Lewis] Reuben G. Thwaites, ed., *The Original Journals of the Lewis and Clark Expedition, 1804–1806* (8 vols., New York: Dodd, Mead & Company, 1904–1905).

Charles A. Lindbergh, *The Wartime Journals of Charles A. Lindbergh* (New York: Harcourt Brace Jovanovich, Inc., 1970). Excerpt from *The Wartime Journals of Charles A. Lindbergh*, copyright © 1970 by Charles A. Lindbergh, reprinted by permission of Harcourt Brace & Company.

John Davis Long Journal, John Davis Long Papers (Massachusetts Historical Society); and Stefan Lorant, *The Life and Times of Theodore Roosevelt* (Garden City: Doubleday & Company, 1959, several extracts throughout, including the April 25, 1898, entry (p. 293) used herein. *See also* Margaret Long, ed., *Journal of John Davis Long* (Rindge, NH: R. R. Smith, 1956).

Ann Marie Low, *Dust Bowl Diary* (Lincoln: University of Nebraska Press, 1984). Reprinted from *Dust Bowl Diary*, by Ann Marie Low, by permission of the University of Nebraska Press. Copyright © 1984 by the University of Nebraska Press.

[Joseph Lyons] Jacob R. Marcus, ed., *Memoirs of American Jews, 1765–1865* (3 vols., Philadelphia: Jewish Publication Society, 1956), I, 239–60. Reprinted by permission of The Jewish Publication Society.

Edgar S. Maclay, ed., *The Journal of William Maclay, United States Senator from Pennsylvania, 1789–1791* (New York: D. Appleton & Company, 1890).

Stella M. Drumm, ed., *Down the Sante Fe Trail and into Mexico: The Diary of Susan Shelby Magoffin, 1846–1847* (New Haven: Yale University Press, 1926).

514

William Duane, ed., *Extracts from the Diary of Christopher Marshall, Kept in Philadelphia and Lancaster, During the American Revolution, 1774–1781* (Albany, NY: Joel Munsell, 1877).

[Anne McCaughey] Donald Vining, ed., *American Diaries of World War II* (New York: Pepys Press, 1982), pp. 82–106. Reprinted by permission of Donald Vining and The Pepys Press.

Franklin B. Dexter, ed., *The Diary of David McClure, Doctor of Divinity* (New York: Knickerbocker Press, 1899).

[Cornelia Peake McDonald], *A Diary with Reminiscences of the War and Refugee Life in the Shenandoah Valley, 1860–1865* (Nashville: Cullom & Ghertner Company, 1935). *See also* Minrose C. Gwin, ed., *A Woman's Civil War: A Diary, with Reminiscences of the War, from March 1862* (Madison: University of Wisconsin Press, 1992).

[Judith White Brockenbrough McGuire], *Diary of a Southern Refugee During the War* (New York: E. J. Hale & Son, 1867).

Sallie [Sarah Rebecca] Meixell Diary (Special Collections, Bertrand Library, Bucknell University). Printed by courtesy of the Ellen Clarke Bertrand Library, Bucknell University.

Charles A. Fecher, ed., *The Diary of H. L. Mencken* (New York: Alfred A. Knopf, 1989). Reprinted by permission of the Enoch Pratt Free Library in accordance with the terms of the will of H. L. Mencken.

Thomas Merton, *The Secular Journal of Thomas Merton* (Combermere, Canada: Madonna House, 1959). Reprinted by permission of the Merton Legacy Trust.

[Thearl Mesecher], Donald Vining, ed., *American Diaries of World War II* (New York: Pepys Press, 1982), pp. 343–73. Reprinted by permission of Donald Vining and The Pepys Press.

Philip E. Mackey, ed., *A Gentleman of Much Promise: The Diary of Isaac Mickle, 1837–1845* (2 vols., Philadelphia: University of Pennsylvania Press, 1977). Reprinted by permission of the Camden County Historical Society, Camden, New Jersey.

[Emma Mordecai] Jacob R. Marcus, ed., *Memoirs of American Jews, 1765–1865* (3 vols., Philadelphia: Jewish Publication Society, 1956), III, 324–48. Reprinted by permission of The Jewish Publication Society.

Anne Cary Morris, ed., *The Diary and Letters of Gouverneur Morris, Minister of the United States to France* (2 vols., New York: Charles Scribner's Sons, 1888).

Henry A. Muhlenberg, *The Life of Major-General Peter Muh-*

lenberg, of the Revolutionary Army (Philadelphia: Carey & Hart, 1849), pp. 425–53 (diary).

Margaret A. Barnes and Janet A. Fairbank, eds., *Julia Newberry's Diary* (New York: W. W. Norton & Company, 1933).

[Timothy Newell] "A Journal Kept During the Time that Boston was Shut Up in 1775–6," *Collections of the Massachusetts Historical Society,* 4th series, 1 (1852): 261–76.

[Howard O'Brien], *Wine, Women and War: A Diary of Disillusionment* (New York: J. H. Sears & Company, 1926).

[Clifford Odets], *The Time Is Ripe: The 1940 Journal of Clifford Odets* (New York: Grove Press, 1988). Used by permission of Grove/Atlantic, Inc. Copyright © 1988 by Walt Whitman Odets and Nora Odets.

Francis G. Walett, ed., *The Diary of Ebenezer Parkman, 1703–1782* (Worcester: American Antiquarian Society, 1974). Reprinted by permission of The American Antiquarian Society, Worcester, Massachusetts.

Mason Wade, ed., *The Journals of Francis Parkman* (2 vols., New York: Harper & Row, 1947).

Linda Rae Patterson Journals, in private possession. Printed by permission of Linda Patterson Miller.

Marian Lawrence Peabody, *To Be Young Was Very Heaven* (Boston: Houghton Mifflin Company, 1967). Excerpts from *To Be Young Was Very Heaven* by Marian Lawrence Peabody. Copyright © 1967 by Marian Lawrence Peabody. Reprinted by permission of Houghton Mifflin Company. All rights reserved.

E[lizabeth Robins] Pennell and J[oseph] Pennell, *The Whistler Journal* (Philadelphia: J. B. Lippincott, 1921).

John David Smith and William Cooper, eds., *Window on the War: Frances Dallam Peter's Lexington Civil War Diary* (Lexington: Lexington-Fayette County Historic Commission, 1976). Reprinted by permission of The Lexington Historical Publishing Corporation.

William Dane Phelps Journal, William Dane Phelps Papers (Manuscript Department, Houghton Library, Harvard University). Printed by permission of the Houghton Library, Harvard University. *See also* Briton Cooper Busch, ed., *Alta California 1840–1842: The Journal and Observations of William Dane Phelps, Master of the Ship "Alert"* (Glendale: Arthur H. Clark Company, 1983).

Zebulon Pike, *An Account of Expeditions to the Sources of the Mississippi and Through the Western Parts of Louisiana*

. . . (Philadelphia: C. Conrad, 1810); Elliott Coues, ed., *The Expeditions of Zebulon Montgomery Pike, to Headwaters of the Mississippi River* (3 vols., New York: F. P. Harper, 1895); and Milo M. Quaife, ed., *The Southwestern Expedition of Zebulon M. Pike* (Chicago: R. R. Donnelley & Sons, 1925).

Ted Hughes and Frances McCullough, eds., *The Journals of Sylvia Plath* (New York: Dial Press, 1982). Reprinted from *The Journals of Sylvia Plath* by Ted Hughes (ed.). Copyright © 1982 by Ted Hughes as Executor of the Estate of Sylvia Plath. Used by permission of Doubleday, a division of Bantam Doubleday Dell Publishing Group, Inc.

H. Roger Grant and L. Edward Purcell, eds., *Years of Struggle: The Farm Diary of Elmer G. Powers, 1931–1936* (Ames: Iowa State University Press, 1976). Reprinted by permission from *Years of Struggle: The Farm Diary of Elmer G. Powers, 1931–1936* edited by H. R. Grant and L. E. Purcell, copyright © 1987 by Iowa State University Press, Ames 50010.

Rollo Ogden, *William Hickling Prescott* (Boston: Houghton Mifflin Company, 1904), diary entries throughout.

[Elizabeth Pringle] Patience Pennington (pseud.), *A Woman Rice Planter* (New York: Macmillan, 1913).

Merrill Proudfoot, *Diary of a Sit-In* (Chapel Hill: University of North Carolina Press, 1962). Reprinted from *Diary of a Sit-In,* by C. Merrill Proudfoot. Copyright © 1962. Renewed 1990 by The University of North Carolina Press. Used by permission of the author and publisher.

John L. Ransom, *Andersonville Diary* (Cincinnati: Douglass Brothers & Payne, 1883). *See also John Ransom's Diary* (New York: Dell Publishing, 1964).

Arney R. Childs, ed., *The Private Journal of Henry William Ravenel 1859–1887* (Columbia: University of South Carolina Press, 1947).

Diary of Bernard J. Reid, Reid Papers (Santa Clara University Archives, Santa Clara, CA). Printed by permission of the Santa Clara University Archives. *See also* Mary McDougall Gordon, ed., *Overland to California with the Pioneer Line: The Gold Rush Diary of Bernard J. Reid* (Stanford: Stanford University Press, 1983).

Valentine Reimann Diary, Valentine Reimann Papers, SC 19 (Balch Institute for Ethnic Studies, Philadelphia, PA). Printed by permission of the Balch Institute for Ethnic Studies.

[Walter L. Rhinehart] Donald Vining, ed., *American Diaries of World War II* (New York: Pepys Press, 1982), pp. 244–50. Reprinted by permission of Donald Vining and The Pepys Press.

Caroline Cowles Richards, *Village Life in America 1852–1872, Including the Period of the American Civil War, As Told in the Diary of a School-Girl* (New York: Henry Holt & Company, 1912).

[Dorothy Atkinson Robinson] Dorothy Blake (pseud.), *Diary of a Suburban Housewife* (New York: William Morrow & Company, 1936).

"The Diary of Captain Thomas Rodney, 1776–1777," *Papers of the Historical Society of Delaware* 8 (1888): 11–50.

Donald Day, ed., *The Autobiography of Will Rogers* (Boston: Houghton Mifflin, 1949), "diary" entries throughout. From *The Autobiography of Will Rogers*, edited by Donald Day. Copyright © 1949 by Rogers Company, renewed 1977 by Donald and Beth Day. Reprinted by permission of Houghton Mifflin Company. All rights reserved.

Edith Kermit Roosevelt Diary, 1904, Roosevelt-Derby Papers, Theodore Roosevelt Collection (Houghton Library, Harvard University). Printed by permission of the Houghton Library, Harvard University.

Theodore Roosevelt Diaries, Theodore Roosevelt Collection (Houghton Library, Harvard University). Printed by permission of The Theodore Roosevelt Association. *See also* Mrs. Douglas Robinson, ed., *Theodore Roosevelt's Diaries of Boyhood and Youth* (New York: Charles Scribner's Sons, 1928); and "Theodore Roosevelt's Diaries," *Personality: A Magazine of Biography* 1, no. 6 (1928): 3–33; 2, no. 1 (1929): 69–82; no. 2, 54–62; and no. 3, 65–72.

William Kauffman Scarborough, ed., *The Diary of Edmund Ruffin* (3 vols., Baton Rouge: Louisiana State University Press, 1972–1989). Reprinted by permission of Louisiana State University Press from *The Diary of Edmund Ruffin, Volume I, Toward Independence: October, 1856–April, 1861*, edited by William Kauffman Scarborough. Copyright © 1972 by Louisiana State University Press. *Volume II, The Years of Hope: April, 1861–June, 1863*. Copyright © 1976 by Louisiana State University Press. *Volume III, A Dream Shattered: June, 1863–June, 1865*. Copyright © 1989 by Louisiana State University Press.

May Sarton, *After the Stroke: A Journal* (New York: W. W. Norton, 1988). Entries reprinted from *After the Stroke* by May

Jr. Used by permission of Viking Penguin, a division of Penguin Books USA, Inc.

John A. Garver, *John William Sterling: A Biographical Sketch* (New Haven: Yale University Press, 1929), diary entries throughout.

Diary of Sarah Christie Stevens, James C. Christie and Family Papers (Minnesota Historical Society). Printed by permission of the Minnesota Historical Society, St. Paul, Minnesota.

Franklin B. Dexter, ed., *The Literary Diary of Ezra Stiles . . . President of Yale College* (3 vols., New York: Charles Scribner's Sons, 1901).

William Garrett Piston, ed., " 'The Rebs Are Yet Thick About Us': The Civil War Diary of Amos Stouffer of Chambersburg," *Civil War History* 38 (1992): 210–31. Reprinted with permission of The Kent State University Press.

Allan Nevins and M. Halsey Thomas, eds., *The Diary of George Templeton Strong* (4 vols., New York: Macmillan Company, 1952). Reprinted with the permission of Macmillan Publishing Company from *The Diary of George Templeton Strong* by Allan Nevins and Milton Halsey Thomas. Copyright © 1952 by Macmillan Publishing Company, renewed 1980 by Milton Halsey Thomas.

C. L. Sulzberger, *A Long Row of Candles: Memoirs & Diaries (1934–1954)* (New York: Macmillan Company, 1969). Reprinted by permission of Marina Berry.

Journal of Ella Gertrude Clanton Thomas, 1848–1889, 13 vols. (Manuscript Department, Perkins Library, Duke University). Printed by permission of the Special Collections Library, Duke University, and Virginia I. Burr. *See also* Virginia Ingraham Burr, ed., *The Secret Eye: The Journal of Ella Gertrude Clanton Thomas, 1848–1889* (Chapel Hill: University of North Carolina Press, 1990). Used by permission of Virginia I. Burr.

Marjorie Housepian Dobkin, ed., *The Making of a Feminist: Early Journals and Letters of M. Carey Thomas* (Kent: Kent State University Press, 1979). Reprinted by permission of Marjorie Housepian Dobkin

Bradford Torrey and Franklin B. Sanborn, eds., *The Writings of Henry David Thoreau* (20 vols., Boston: Houghton, Mifflin and Company, 1906) (journals in volumes 7–20).

Richard Tregaskis, *Guadalcanal Diary* (New York: Random House, 1943).

Frederick Anderson, et al., eds., *Mark Twain's Notebooks &*

Journals (3 vols., Berkeley: University of California Press, 1975–1979). Reprinted by permission of The University of California Press from Mark Twain, *Notebooks and Journals. 3 Volumes.* Edited/translated by Robert Browning. Copyright © 1975–1979 Mark Twain Company.

"Valley Forge, 1777–1778: Diary of Surgeon Albigence Waldo, of the Connecticut Line," *Pennsylvania Magazine of History and Biography* 21 (1897), 299–323.

Elkanah Walker Diary, 1838 (#WA 56) (Huntington Library). Printed by permission of The Huntington Library, San Marino, California. *See also* Clifford M. Drury, ed., *The First White Women Over the Rockies: Diaries, Letters and Biographical Sketches of the Six Women of the Oregon Mission* (3 vols., Glendale: Arthur H. Clark Company, 1963–1966), I, 254–65.

Henry A. Wallace Diary, Henry Agard Wallace Papers (Archives, University Libraries, University of Iowa). Entry for August 7, 1945, printed by permission of The University Libraries, University of Iowa. *See also* John M. Blum, ed., *The Price of Vision: The Diary of Henry A. Wallace, 1942–1946* (Boston: Houghton Mifflin, 1973).

[Robert Ware and Thomas Ware] Mark Nesbitt, *35 Days to Gettysburg: The Campaign Diaries of Two American Enemies* (Harrisburg: Stackpole Books, 1992). Reprinted by permission of Stackpole Books.

John C. Fitzpatrick, ed., *The Diaries of George Washington 1748–1799* (4 vols., Boston: Houghton Mifflin Company for the Mount Vernon Ladies Association of the Union, 1925).

John T. Morse, Jr., ed., *The Diary of Gideon Welles, Secretary of the Navy under Lincoln and Johnson* (3 vols., Boston: Houghton Mifflin Company, 1911).

Robert Phelps and Jerry Rosco, eds., *Continual Lessons: The Journals of Glenway Wescott, 1937–1955* (New York: Farrar, Straus, and Giroux, 1990). Excerpts from *Continental Lessons: The Journals of Glenway Wescott 1937–1955*, edited by Robert Phelps with Jerry Rosco. Copyright © 1990 by Anatole Pohorilenko. Reprinted by permission of Farrar, Strous & Giroux, Inc.

F. F. Stephens, ed., "Major Alphonso Wetmore's Diary of a Journey to Santa Fe," *Missouri Historical Review* 8 (1913–1914): 177–97.

[Narcissa Prentiss Whitman] "A Journey Across the Plains in 1836," *Transactions of the Oregon Pioneer Association,* 19th annual reunion (1891): 40–68. *See also* Mary Osborn

Douthit, ed., *The Souvenir of Western Women* (Portland: Anderson & Duniway, 1905); and Clifford M. Drury, ed., *The First White Women Over the Rockies: Diaries, Letters and Biographical Sketches of the Six Women of the Oregon Mission* (3 vols., Glendale: Arthur H. Clark Company, 1963–1966), I, 71–127.

Walt Whitman, *Memoranda During the War* (Camden: New Republic Print for the author, 1875–1876).

Donald Gallup, ed., *The Journals of Thornton Wilder 1939–1961* (New Haven: Yale University Press, 1985). Reprinted by permission of Yale University Press. Copyright © 1985 by Union Trust Company, New Haven, Connecticut.

Donald J. Willis, *The Incredible Year* (Ames: Iowa State University Press, 1988). Reprinted by permission from *The Incredible Year* by D. J. Willis, copyright © 1988 by Iowa State University Press, Ames 50010.

Leon Edel, ed., *Edmund Wilson: The Twenties from Notebooks and Diaries of the Period* (New York: Farrar, Straus, and Giroux, 1975); Leon Edel, ed., *Edmund Wilson: The Thirties from Notebooks and Diaries of the Period* (New York: Farrar, Straus, and Giroux, 1980); Leon Edel, ed., *Edmund Wilson: The Forties from Notebooks and Diaries of the Period* (New York: Farrar, Straus, and Giroux, 1983); and Leon Edel, ed., *Edmund Wilson: The Fifties from Notebooks and Diaries of the Period* (New York: Farrar, Straus, and Giroux, 1986). Excerpts from *The Twenties* by Edmund Wilson and edited by Leon Edel. Copyright © 1975 by Elena Wilson. Excerpts from *The Thirties* by Emund Wilson and edited by Leon Edel. Copyright © 1980 by Helen Miranda Wilson. Excerpts from *The Forties* by Edmund Wilson and edited by Leon Edel. Copyright © 1983 by Helen Miranda Wilson. Excerpts from *The Fifties* by Edmund Wilson and edited by Leon Edel. Copyright © 1986 by Helen Miranda Wilson. Reprinted by permission of Farrar, Straus & Giroux.

[John Winthrop] James K. Hosmer, ed., *Winthrop's Journal: "History of New England" 1630–1649* (2 vols., New York: Charles Scribner's Sons, 1908).

Albert Cooke Myers, ed., *Sally Wister's Journal: A True Narrative, Being a Quaker Maiden's Account of Her Experiences with Officers of the Continental Army, 1777–1778* (Philadelphia: Ferris & Leach, 1902).

James Webb Young, *The Diary of an Ad Man: The War Years, June 1, 1942–December 31, 1943* (Chicago: Advertising Publications, 1944).